❑ Parliaments and Legislatures Series ❑

Samuel Patterson
General Advisory Editor

CHEAP SEATS

□□□□□□□□□□□□□□□□□□□□□□□□□□□□□□□

The Democratic Party's Advantage in U.S. House Elections

James E. Campbell

OHIO STATE UNIVERSITY PRESS

COLUMBUS

ALBRIGHT COLLEGE LIBRARY

Library of Congress Cataloging-in-Publication Data

Campbell, James E., 1952–
    Cheap seats : the Democratic Party's advantage in U.S. House
elections / James E. Campbell.
        p.   cm. — (Parliaments and legislatures series)
    Includes bibliographical references (p.   ) and index.
    ISBN 0-8142-0708-1 (cloth : alk. paper). — ISBN 0-8142-0709-X
(pbk. : alk paper).
    1. United States. Congress. House—Elections.   2. Elections—
United States. 3. Democratic Party (U.S.)   4. United States—
Politics and government—1945–1989.   5. United States—Politics and
government—1989–   I. Title.   II. Series.
JK1967.C23   1996
324.973—dc20   96-36122
                                                                              CIP

Text and cover design by Cynthia Brunk.
Cover illustration: National Graphic Center, Falls Church, Virginia.
Type set in Baskerville by Graphic Composition, Athens, Georgia.
Printed by Braun-Brumfield, Inc., Ann Arbor, Michigan.

For Susan

Contents

□□

List of Figures		ix
List of Tables		x
Foreword		xv
Preface		xvii
Acknowledgments		xxiii

1.	A Democratic Dynasty	1
2.	The Democratic Record	20
3.	Voters, Parties, and Candidates	45
4.	Bias in the Electoral System	69
5.	The Price of a Seat	95
6.	The Changing Price of a Seat	121
7.	The Historical Perspective	146
8.	The Collapse of the Democratic Dynasty	157
9.	Representation and Cheap Seats	189

Appendix A
The Effects of Candidate Advantages on the Vote — 225
Appendix B
The Unwasted-Vote Measure, Wasted Votes, and Alternative
Estimates of Bias — 232
Appendix C
The Carryover Effect of Partisan Bias through Incumbency — 242

Notes	247
Bibliography	309
Index	323

Figures

□ □

1.1 Suspected Effects of the Democratic Dynasty in the U.S.
House of Representatives on the Political System   8

1.2 Suspected Factors Maintaining the Democratic Dynasty in
the U.S. House of Representatives   11

2.1 The Relationship between Seats and Votes in Plurality and
Proportional Representation Electoral Systems   37

3.1 The Democratic Congressional Vote, 1954–1992   48

3.2 The Democratic Congressional Vote in Contested Districts,
1954–1992   51

4.1 The Mean District Vote and the National Congressional
Vote for Democrats, 1954–1992   84

4.2 A Causal Model of Responsiveness in Electoral Systems   90

4.3 A Causal Model of Partisan Bias in Electoral Systems   91

6.1 Trend in Partisan Bias, 1954–1992   125

6.2 Partisan Bias and Congressional Turnout, 1954–1992   132

6.3 Partisan Bias and the Democratic House Vote, 1954–1992   133

8.1 The National Estimate of Electoral System Bias,
1990–1994   174

Tables

囗囗

2.1 Longest Consecutive Partisan Majorities in the U.S. House of Representatives, 1855–1995   21

2.2 Democratic Representatives in the U.S. House of Representatives, 1954–1992   22

2.3 The Democratic Party's Success in Presidential Elections, 1956–1992   26

2.4 The History of Divided Government, 1868–1994   27

2.5 The Democratic Party's Electoral Success in Major Statewide Offices, 1954–1992   29

2.6 The Democratic Party's Electoral Success in State Legislatures, 1954–1992   31

2.7 Democratic Control of Various Offices, 1954–1992   33

2.8 The Overrepresentation of the Democratic House Vote, 1954–1992   35

3.1 The Expected Democratic Seat Percentages and the Necessary Swing Ratio to Obtain the Observed Democratic Seat Percentages in Five Elections   53

3.2 The Incumbency Advantage as a Democratic Party Advantage, 1954–1992   57

3.3 Uncontested Congressional Districts, by Political Party, 1954–1992   59

3.4 The Democratic Candidate Advantage, 1954–1992   61

3.5 The Democratic House Vote and the Simulated Vote, Removing the Incumbency and Uncontested Seat Advantages, 1954–1992   64

3.6 Four Elections in Which Democrats Won a Majority of Seats with a Minority of the Vote in Contested Districts   67

4.1 Hypothetical Examples of Electoral Systems with and without Partisan Bias   70

4.2 Tufte's Estimates of Partisan Bias, 1942–1988   75

4.3 Jacobson's Estimates of Partisan Bias, 1946–1988   76

4.4 Brady and Grofman's Estimates of Partisan Bias, 1946–1980   78

4.5 King and Gelman's Estimates of Partisan Bias, 1946–1984   79

4.6 The Relationship between Two Measures of the Democratic Party's House Vote and Its Share of House Seats, 1954–1992   81

4.7 Comparison of Turnout Effects on Nationally Aggregated and Mean District Congressional Votes, Using Two Hypothetical Districts   82

4.8 A Hypothetical Electoral System   87

4.9 The Mechanisms of Responsiveness and Partisan Bias in Electoral Systems   88

4.10 How the Minority Party Wastes More of Its Votes in Losing Causes   88

5.1 Variation of Total District Turnout in Contested Seats, 1954–1992   97

5.2 Turnout in Seven Congressional Districts in New York and the Two Congressional Districts in Maine, 1990   98

5.3 The Relationship between the Party of the Winning Congressional Candidate and District Turnout in Total Votes, 1954–1992   103

5.4 Contested Congressional Districts with Highest Total Congressional Voter Turnout, 1990   104

5.5 Contested Congressional Districts with Lowest Total Congressional Voter Turnout, 1990   105

5.6 The Relationship between the Party of the Winning Congressional Candidate and the Total Votes Cast for the Winning Candidate, 1954–1992   107

5.7 Mean Number of Votes for Winning Democratic and Republican Congressional Candidates in Contested Elections, 1954–1992   110

5.8 Number of Contested Seats Democrats Would Have Won Based on an Even Division of the Vote and the Mean Number of Unwasted Democratic Votes Per Victory, 1954–1992   112

5.9 Extent of Partisan Bias Resulting from the Different Expenditure of Votes Per Seat for Democratic and Republican Congressional Candidates, 1954–1992   113

5.10 Actual Party Distribution of Seats in the House of Representatives and the Distribution of Seats without Partisan Bias in the Electoral System, 1954–1992   115

6.1 The Effects of Redistricting on Partisan Bias, 1952–1992   128

6.2 The Democratic Congressional Vote and Success in Districts, by District Turnout and Number of Unwasted Votes, 1954–1992   135

6.3 Influences on Democratic Electoral Bias, 1954–1992   137

6.4 The Swing Ratio with and without an Adjustment for Unwasted-Vote Bias, 1954–1992   139

7.1 The Association between the Party of the Winning Congressional Candidate, District Turnout, and Unwasted Votes, 1936–1952   148

7.2 Unwasted Vote Bias in Contested Elections, 1936–1952   149

7.3 The Consistently Cheap Seats of the 1940s   153

8.1 Midterm Seat Losses for the President's Party, 1946–1990   159

8.2 The Gender Gap and the Republican Realignment, 1968–1994   167

8.3 Votes and Seats for the Party Receiving the Majority of the House Vote in the 1990, 1992, and 1994 Elections   172

8.4 Three District Analyses of Partisan Bias in the 1990s   177

8.5 The Proportionate-Vote-Swing Analysis of the 1992 and 1994 Elections to the U.S. House of Representatives   179

8.6   The Relationship of the Party of the Winning Candidate
to District Turnout and Unwasted Votes, 1994   180

8.7   Winning House Candidates in Contested Districts Who
Received Fewer than 70,000 Votes in 1994   181

8.8   Winning House Candidates in Contested Districts Who
Received More than 140,000 Votes in 1994   182

8.9   Partisan Bias and Unwasted Votes in Contested Districts,
1994   185

8.10 Partisan Bias and Unwasted Votes in All Districts, 1994   186

9.1   Ideological Bias of the Electoral System, 1984 and 1990   193

9.2   Effective Malapportionment in Congressional Districts in
the States, 1992   213

A.1   Votes Attributable to Democratic Incumbency and
Uncontested Seat Advantages, 1954–1992   227

A.2   Votes Attributable to Republican Incumbency and
Uncontested Seat Advantages, 1954–1992   228

A.3   Expected Democratic Vote without Incumbency
Advantage and Uncontested Seats, 1954–1992   229

A.4   Expected Republican Vote without Incumbency
Advantage and Uncontested Seats, 1954–1992   230

A.5   Democratic Congressional Vote Adjusted for Incumbency
and Uncontested Seat Advantages, 1954–1992   231

B.1   Votes in Contested Districts by Political Party, 1954–1992   235

B.2   Wasted Votes by Political Party, 1954–1992   236

B.3   The Effect of the National Vote on the Percentage of the
Vote Wasted on Losing Candidates in Contested Districts,
1954–1992   237

B.4   Three Estimates of Partisan Bias in Contested Seats,
1954–1992   239

Foreword

This book initiates the Parliaments and Legislatures Series published by Ohio State University Press. This series provides for the publication of studies of parliamentary or legislative institutions in democratic societies. The Inter-Parliamentary Union, an international organization of the parliaments of the world, headquartered in Geneva, Switzerland, counts 178 national parliaments in existence today. In addition to these national parliamentary bodies, there exist a substantial number of important subnational legislatures, particularly the state or provincial legislatures in federal systems.

A parliament may operate primarily as a sounding board and listening post for citizens in a democratic society who need a representative institution that can give them a voice in governing their country. Or, alternatively, a legislature may have a deep and penetrating role in formulating and enacting the laws of the land. Although parliaments and legislatures play a variety of roles in democratic societies, they are central and essential institutions for democracy. Free people govern themselves in large-scale societies only through elected representative assemblies empowered to speak and act for them. In short, parliaments and legislatures are at the heart of democracy.

That these institutions come in many sizes and shapes, and play different political and governing roles, makes them important and interesting to study. Yet assemblies, parliaments, and congresses are not particularly well-understood institutions. In the new democracies of eastern and central Europe, or in the renewed or developing democracies in Third World countries, there is an urgency about understanding parliamentary assemblies and how they work. In the well-established democracies of North America and western Europe, legislative bodies may seldom be the subjects of extensive research and study, and often they are excoriated (as Americans engage in "Congress bashing") because these institutions do not live up to citizens' expectations.

The United States Congress has been studied fairly extensively, and yet there is much left to be better understood. James E. Campbell illuminates one important curiosity about Congress, asking why the Democratic Party was able to maintain majority party status in the House of Representatives for fully four decades. His cogent argument and extensive data analysis enrich his claim that Democratic hegemony in the House stemmed from that party's enjoyment of a relatively large number of "cheap seats," winning disproportionately in congressional districts with markedly low electoral turnout.

Campbell anatomizes the congressional election system in detail in order to demonstrate how the system so systematically advantaged the Democratic Party. His analysis provides a convincing explanation for the era of Democratic House majorities. And it contributes importantly to the growing debate about the fairness and efficacy of the electoral system through which members of the House of Representatives are chosen. His discussion of the proposals and prospects for electoral reform so as to diminish the impact of "cheap seats" will provide valuable resource material for policy debate at home, and indicate potential sources of disputation about parliamentary electoral laws abroad.

Samuel C. Patterson
General Advisory Editor

Preface

□ □

In the 1950s and 1960s, every major sport had a dominant team. Baseball had Casey Stengel's New York Yankees. Pro football had Vince Lombardi's Green Bay Packers. Hockey had the Montreal Canadiens. In college basketball, it was John Wooden's UCLA teams. In the NBA, it was Red Auerbach's Boston Celtics. All were perennial winners. Everyone expected them to win, and year after year they did. They were the teams to beat. They were dynasties.

Though it did not seem so clear at the time, there was another dynasty in America's greatest sport, politics. It was the Democratic Party in the House of Representatives. It was a dynasty that outlasted all of the others. It survived until its surprising collapse in the 1994 midterm election. For better or worse, Democrats held a majority of seats in the House of Representatives, and therefore controlled the business of the House, for most of the last 60 years and for 40 consecutive years between the 1954 and 1994 elections. This longevity of a partisan majority is unprecedented in American history. No other party at any point in our history continuously controlled the House, the Senate, or the Presidency over such a prolonged period. As Norman Ornstein (1990: 24) put it, "One of the most enduring, puzzling, and contentious phenomena of modern American political life is the persistence of the Democratic majorities in Congress even as the Republicans tighten their stranglehold on the White House." But, while Republicans from time to time lost their grip or "stranglehold on the White House," the Democrats' hold on the House was impressively constant.

A political dynasty, unlike a sports dynasty, has real consequences, and a dynasty in American politics in the later half of the twentieth century has tremendous and far-reaching consequences. The Democratic dynasty in the House shaped policy, both in the specifics and in the government's approach to problems. It also shaped our politics—how well the government functions and how well elections serve as an institution of popular control of the government. Although the Democratic dynasty came to a startling close with the 1994 midterm, it has left an indelible imprint on American politics. Because of its pervasive effects, the Democratic Party's control of the House of Representatives may be the most important single feature of American politics in the second half of this century and, thus, should be thoroughly understood. How did Democrats achieve their lock on the House and how did they lose it? This book is about the many reasons for this dominance, particularly the structural reasons. An important and generally overlooked reason, I argue, is *the electoral system and, more specifically, that aspect of the system that allocates congressional representatives within states to single-member congressional districts. This system played a crucial role in preserving and augmenting the Democratic majority in the House.*

How were Democrats able to do what no other party was able to do at any other point of our history? Did a majority of American voters over the last 40 years freely choose the Democratic Party in fair and competitive elections to rule the House? Or, was the seemingly permanent Democratic majority a consequence of a breakdown in the political system, a breakdown in the fairness and competitiveness of elections that failed to offer voters a real choice? Cynics argued that Democrats rigged the system to keep themselves in power, suggesting that Democrats were actually less popular than Republicans with the public—a twist on the Republicans' "silent majority" theme of the late 1960s. Alternatively, I find a more fundamental basis for an institutional Democratic advantage. I contend that the electoral system, the single-member equal-population congressional district system, works to the benefit of the Democrats in House elections. It does so primarily because the system allows huge differences in the numbers of voters casting ballots from one congressional district to the next, notwithstanding "one-person, one-vote" judicial rulings. Democrats benefit from turnout disparities among districts because they consistently win many districts with very low turnouts. They win a large majority of the "cheap seats." This allows them to carry more districts. They get a "bigger bang for the buck" or "more seats for the vote." The analysis further finds that the benefit Democrats derive from this turnout disparity is considerable, that it has been greatest when they were most in need of seats, and that, therefore, the electoral system helped to maintain the four-decade-long Democratic majority.

Although the tilt to the electoral system had helped to buffer the Democratic majority against the shifting political winds of four decades, it was not enough to prevent the collapse of the Democratic dynasty in 1994. In the 1994 midterm election, the Democratic electoral system advantage was no match for the political tide of a Republican realignment. The realignment had begun in the late 1960s, with Nixon's Southern strategy, the racial polarization of the electorate (Carmines and Stimson, 1989), and "the gender-gap" movement of white males toward the GOP. Although set back by Watergate and sidetracked by a drifting Bush administration, the realignment was reinvigorated in the 1980s under the Reagan administration and eventually deepened to congressional contests in the 1990s. The shift was so great that by 1994 Democrats no longer enjoyed their usual advantage of having more uncontested congressional candidates than Republicans. With this sea change in public partisanship and a sitting Democratic president held in low esteem by much of the public, even a pro-Democratic electoral system could not retain the House for the Democrats. Nevertheless, beneath it all, the electoral system still made a difference. As in past years, Democrats carried a large majority of the cheap seats in 1994 and, as in past years, because of this more Democrats sat in the House than would have under a neutral electoral system.

While the underpinnings of the Democratic dynasty and its collapse are important to understand in order to understand American political history through much of the twentieth century, they are important to understand for broader purposes as well. This analysis sheds light more generally on a broad range of political subjects: elections, electoral systems, political geography, political parties, voter turnout, class politics, and representation. The consistent bias of the American electoral system for the House of Representatives has many very important consequences. It strikes at the very root of the democratic process. If the deck is stacked for one party in the electoral deal, it raises very real concerns about who plays the game, how the game is played, and who wins and who loses in policy disputes as well as in elections.

The argument that the electoral system has been significantly tilted in favor of Democrats is based on an examination of congressional election returns since 1936. To the extent possible, I have tried to keep this data analysis simple. Regression analysis is used at several points, but the book's central point is based on simple arithmetic. The findings do not rest on elaborate estimation techniques, with their sometimes nonobvious assumptions. The analysis asks how bias from all possible sources (gerrymandering, etc.) is created and then, on the basis of the answer to that question, directly computes an estimate of system bias. The approach necessarily makes some assumptions of its own, but these are examined in detail (appendix B), and, to provide further confidence in the findings, several different methods of estimating bias are also examined (also presented in appendix B). While there are a few points of disagreement, the analyses converged in support of the cheap-seats thesis. Democrats dominate the low-turnout districts, the cheap seats. The single-member district electoral system worked consistently to the advantage of the Democratic Party, up to and including the dramatic 1994 election, and this advantage augmented the party's control of the House. Just as the tilt of the electoral system helped to enlarge Democratic majorities in the past, it enlarged the Democratic House minority in 1994 and increases the prospects of Democrats regaining control of the House in the future.

❏ The Questions ❏

This research addresses two related questions: (1) why did the Democrats enjoy the longest continuous House majority in U.S. history, and (2) did electoral system bias significantly favor Democrats? My research into these questions began in 1991 when Democratic control of the House looked permanent and was completed in the fall of 1995 several months after Republicans, who had been 40 years in the minority, took control of the House following the stunning 1994 midterm election.

Three aspects of this project sustained my interest and, I hope, will sustain yours. They were the three P's: politics, puzzles, and precision. First, though the methods of this research are as coldly objective as I could make them, the subject is intensely political and very politically important. The reasons behind a party's control of the House and the possible existence of bias in the electoral system are both important political and very partisan issues. It is difficult to imagine a question of greater importance to a representative democracy than whether the will of citizens participating in the electoral process is fairly represented. Second, both subjects of this book present interesting puzzles. How did Democrats hold huge House majorities for four decades? Political scientists were late in addressing this important question. They only began asking the question in the 1990s and even then were indirect about it, asking why divided government had become common rather than why Democrats had a "lock" on the House. The question of electoral system bias was more heavily researched, as part of more general evaluations of electoral systems (usually focusing on the swing ratio rather than bias), yet almost no attention had been paid to the conflicting estimates of bias. Why had some found a pro-Democratic bias and others a pro-Republican bias? Finally, the electoral system bias question required a precise answer. Much research conducted under the rubric of social science is not remotely scientific. But even research that takes the "science" in social science seriously often aspires to little more than beating randomness, achieving statistical significance. To say that some effect probably exists, that it may not be due to dumb luck, may be to say something but usually is not to say much. While recognizing uncertainty and remaining sensitive to assumptions (even in the use of hard election return data), I wanted to answer not just whether electoral system bias existed but to gauge as precisely as possible and with several different measures (to add further certainty to the answer) the extent of bias and its basis. Each measure zeroed in on the same estimate of bias. The election returns of 1994 used in the analysis in chapter 8 proved to be especially fortuitous in this regard. With the majority party changing hands for the first time in 40 years, we could now make very certain and precise estimates of electoral system bias.

Acknowledgments

□ □

There are many people whom I thank for their help over the course of this project. First, I thank Gary King for many thought-provoking debates regarding electoral system bias and the appropriate vote measure for gauging bias. Gary was also very generous in sharing his data. I also thank the many researchers who have done excellent work on the subject of electoral systems effects. Among the many, the work of Edward Tufte stands out as particularly persuasive and insightful and influenced my research greatly.

Several institutions also deserve thanks. Congressional Quarterly, through its weekly publication, its *Guide to U.S. Elections,* and its biennial volumes of *Politics in America* is a valued source for all congressional scholars, as are Michael Barone's and his colleagues' volumes of *The Almanac of American Politics.* Some of the data for this study were obtained through the Inter-University Consortium for Political and Social Research (ICPSR). In addition to its support of the ICPSR, the National Science Foundation (NSF) deserves thanks. I served as a Political Science Program Director at NSF while conducting much of this research.

Many colleagues also helped in different ways. Frank Scioli and Allan Kornberg, as well as my other NSF colleagues, made my work there enjoyable and productive. Much of this research was also done while on the faculty at LSU, and I thank colleagues Jim Garand, Kit Kenny, and Gene Wittkopf for their help and advice. Several graduate students at LSU, particularly Steve Procopio, Ken Wink, Mike Barr, Mark Baldwin, Phil Ardoin, and Bill Blair, also helped at different stages of this project. Conversations with Bill Frenzel, Newt Gingrich, Gary Jacobson, Tom Mann, Bruce Oppenheimer, Ron Weber, Matthew Shuggart, David

Rohde, John Alford, Chuck Bullock, Ric Uslaner, Robert Boucher, Bob Grafstein, Mac Jewell, Morris Fiorina, and Michael Weber also shaped my thinking. Pat Patterson, John Hibbing, Jack Pitney, Richard Niemi, Simon Jackman, and several anonymous reviewers read and commented upon earlier versions of the manuscript. The manuscript is much improved because of their suggestions. I thank my wife Susan for her patience and support during the many hours spent on the analysis that follows. The manuscript is also much the better for her support. Finally, I thank Ralph, Annie, and Iggy for their companionship.

1

□ □

A Democratic Dynasty

On Tuesday, November 6, 1994, the politically unthinkable happened. The Republican Party won a majority of seats in the U.S. House of Representatives, taking control of the House away from the Democrats for the first time in 40 years. Republicans gained 52 seats, the greatest midterm seat change in nearly half a century. Some called it a political earthquake. Others declared it a revolution. The 231 Republican representatives were 13 more than necessary to end, dramatically and unexpectedly, what most had come to consider a permanent Democratic majority in the House. Everywhere, Republicans were jubilant, and Democrats stunned. It was little consolation to Democrats that the new Democratic minority was larger than any Republican minority in the prior four decades. The hard, cold fact remained: for the first time in 40 years, Democrats in the House were now in the minority.

When Republicans had last held a majority in the House, Winston Churchill was prime minister of Great Britain, Nikita Khrushchev was still years away from becoming premier of the Soviet Union, the French had recently suffered defeat in Vietnam, there were only 48 states, the U.S. Senate was deciding whether to censure communist-hunting Senator Joe McCarthy, Tom Dewey was governor of the state of New York, Rocky Marciano was heavyweight boxing champion, Studebaker made automobiles, television was in black and white, Ronald Reagan was the new host of the *General Electric Theater,* and the Dodgers were in Brooklyn.[1] It all seems like part of ancient history now.

The last Republican majority in the House ended with the 1954 election, Eisenhower's first midterm election. For the next four decades the Democratic Party's control of the House was uninterrupted. Election in and election out, Democrats won a majority of House seats. To put the

1

record on more human dimensions, not a single member of either party elected in 1994 had served in Congress when the Republicans were last in the majority.[2] Outside of Congress, a majority of Americans voting in 1994 had either not been born or had not yet entered elementary school when Republicans last held the House.[3] Even for elderly Americans the last Republican majority was a distant and fading memory. While political observers regularly speculated before elections about which party would win the White House or which party would control the Senate, for most of the last 40 years, no one seriously questioned who would control the House. A Democratic majority was taken for granted. In more regal terms, from 1954 to 1994, the House of Representatives was dominated by a Democratic dynasty. And though, like all dynasties, this one eventually came to an end, it was nonetheless impressive.

Actually, the Democratic dynasty in the House was established well before 1954. Democrats dominated the House for more than six decades. In all but four of the last 62 years, between 1932 and 1994, Democrats controlled a majority of the House. Republicans won fleeting majorities in the 1946 midterm and again in the 1952 elections (riding Eisenhower's coattails), but, otherwise, Democrats had a solid lock on the House. This book explores the reasons for this unusual success, the basis of the Democratic dynasty, and how the dynasty finally collapsed in the 1994 midterm election. More particularly, the book is about several structural advantages that Democrats have enjoyed in House elections, especially the electoral system advantage that Democrats have enjoyed in the way in which votes are translated into seats.

❑ The Effects of a Congressional Dynasty ❑

The lengthy tenure of the Democratic majority in the House had important consequences. To no small extent, Democratic dominance of the House shaped most aspects of political life for generations of Americans. It affected political leadership, the relationship between and the behavior of the political parties, the public's relationship to the government, the extent of political competition in the system, and the kinds of public policies adopted by the government. It would be difficult to exaggerate the effects of the Democratic dynasty.

The Power of Political Parties

Despite the common cynical view that parties do not matter and that partisans of either stripe are all the same, there is much to say otherwise.

Political parties matter. The parties differ in their policies and philosophies, and this makes a difference in the way they govern. Democrats and Republicans are not at the extremes of the political spectrum, but neither are they tweedledum and tweedledee. Democrats as a group are more liberal than Republicans on a variety of issues, and there is even greater divergence between Democratic and Republican lawmakers. Parties have, admittedly, weakened a bit both in the electorate and among leaders from the 1950s to the 1980s. Crises, assassinations, unrest, scandals, and the simple passage of time since the New Deal (with the natural succession of new generations of voters) took their toll on the stability of partisan preferences. But the decline of partisanship is often exaggerated (Keith et al., 1992). Most voters and, with rare exceptions, all elected leaders are affiliated with the Democratic or Republican Parties. Most of these partisans continue to be loyal to their party, whether in the voting booth or in the legislative chamber. Moreover, there is evidence that partisanship has been reinvigorated in the 1980s and 1990s (Miller, 1991; Rohde, 1991, 1992). Thus, the dynasty of a political party is not just a curiosity. It has real consequences.

The party that controls the House makes a difference in a number of ways. It determines House party and committee leadership, who in turn determine which legislation is considered. It determines how legislation is formed, what coalitions are built, what rules govern debate, and what amendments are permitted. As Schattschneider (1942) wrote some time ago, democratic politics is about numbers. If you have the numbers in the electorate or in the legislative chamber, you can wield power. The majority party controls the legislative process and thus shapes public policies that affect the day-to-day lives of Americans and people around the world.[4] A party that controls the levers of legislative power election after election for decades at a stretch and presumes that it will have that power indefinitely is in an especially powerful position.

Divided Government and Gridlock

The powers of the House, however, even when in the hands of a single party for decades at a time, are not without limits. The system of checks and balances in general and the prerogatives of the presidency in particular are impediments to an aggressive House majority, at least when the opposition party sits at the other end of Pennsylvania Avenue. Even with the restraint that a vigilant president can sometimes impose on the House majority, there is also a downside—divided government. With one party fixed as a majority in the House and with significant competition in presidential elections, divided government has become a more frequent occurrence.

While some debate its consequences, divided government is commonly thought to produce a whole host of institutional pathologies, summarized variously as "gridlock," "stalemate," or "deadlock." Governance is more difficult under divided government. Rather than bridging the separation of powers to foster cooperation, the political parties deepen differences and heighten conflict in a divided government. Compromise becomes both more necessary and less possible because of partisan differences. Moreover, when compromise is reached, neither party gets what it considers good policy. With coherent partisan policy a political impossibility, the process too often produces "lowest-common-denominator" policy and pandering to assemble a winning coalition. When compromise is not achieved because of partisan conflict, government grinds to a halt and crucial issues go to the back burner until they boil over into a crisis. Both the gargantuan budget deficits of the 1980s and early 1990s and the savings and loan debacle of the 1980s are prime examples of problems both precipitated and neglected by gridlocked, divided government.[5]

Political Competition

The importance of the permanent Democratic majority went beyond its policy consequences. The Democratic dynasty also both revealed and exacerbated an important weakness in our political system—a serious deficiency in political competition. The proper functioning of modern republican governments depends on political competition. Without it, there is little to check the abuse of power, to spur the adoption of sound policies, and to interest citizens in participating in the electoral process. The longevity of the Democratic majority in the House indicated that, in this most critical of American political institutions, competition was sorely lacking for a considerable stretch of recent history.

For several decades, serious competition was absent in most individual congressional elections.[6] In a significant number of districts, there was no competition whatsoever. While the number of uncontested districts varies a good deal from one election to the next, typically voters in 60 to 70 districts have lacked a choice between major party House candidates. Even in contested districts, competition is often more apparent than real (Jacobson, 1990). Most incumbents win reelection, and most win by sizable vote margins. In elections since the 1950s, typically more than 90 percent of incumbents seek reelection, and more than 90 percent of these are successful. Generally, incumbents win reelection with about 65 percent of the vote. Nationally, district-level competition has deteriorated since the 1960s. Indeed, from the 1950s to 1990, both the reelection rates of incumbents and their vote margins have increased, leading David Mayhew (1974) to write of "the vanishing marginals." In 1990, for example, 96 percent of incumbents seeking reelection were reelected, and three out of four who were returned to office won by a comfortably safe margin, receiving in excess of 60 percent of the vote. Even in 1992, in what appeared to be the worst of times for incumbents, with the House check-bouncing scandal, broadscale redistricting, and a public holding the Congress in very low regard, 93 percent of incumbents running in the general election were reelected. Again, in 1994, in one of the most tumultuous midterm elections in this century, with Congress sinking to new depths in public esteem, with term-limit propositions passing in one state after another, and with what political commentators viewed as general voter anger at "government as usual," 91 percent of incumbents running in the general election were still reelected.[7]

The uncompetitiveness of individual congressional elections undermines the electoral process. The purpose of elections is to exert popular control of government. Competitive elections are supposed to keep elected officials "on their toes." Fearing electoral reprisal in the next election, representatives have a strong incentive to respond to constituents and to support policies that constituents would approve of by the next election (even if they might not favor these policies immediately).[8] If elections are uncompetitive, the electoral incentive for good representation is missing, at least in the short run. While the anticipation of possible competition in future elections might induce attentive representation, the uncertainty of serious opposition in some future election may provide less of an inducement for good representation than the certain confrontation of a serious challenger in the next election. In addition, uncompetitive elections affect the relation of citizens to their government. The ability of citizens to shape government through the electoral process depends on their having a real choice between viable candidates. Without a real choice, democratic elections fail as instruments of popular control, and the public's sense of control over the course of government withers, and their willingness to participate in the democratic process wanes.

As regrettable as the lack of competition in individual congressional elections is, the larger absence of competition for control of the House was even more so. The fact that the same party held a majority in the

House for four decades led both leaders and citizens to believe that control of the House was not only unchanging but unchangeable. The Democratic House majority was a routine outcome, a fixture on the political scene. The consequences of a one-party political system in the House are easily predictable. If Democratic control of the House is a foregone conclusion in each election, citizens must feel less efficacious and more frustrated. However they vote locally and whomever they elect locally, the national result was, until 1994, never in doubt.[9] No matter how good times were for the Republicans or how bad they were for the Democrats, the results were the same: a Democratic majority.[10]

Political Leadership

The absence of competition for control of the House was also felt among political leaders. On the Republican side, for most of the last four decades, there was little real hope of being in the majority. Even well into the 1994 campaign itself, few thought a Republican majority was really possible. With serious doubts about ever serving in the majority, many Republicans sensed the futility of party building and worked instead for their personal goals. On the Democratic side, there was little fear of losing their majority. Taking for granted their party's power, Democratic candidates had less of an incentive to work in behalf of their party (since whatever they did, the Democratic majority survived) and less of a reason to restrain their use of institutional power. Presumably, weakened party discipline and loyalties among leaders ultimately weaken partisanship in the public, as policy differences between the parties (the foundation of reasoned partisanship) become less distinct.

The lack of competition certainly affected relations between the parties and the possibility of bipartisanship and collegiality in working together for the public interest. Lord Acton long ago observed that, "Power corrupts and absolute power corrupts absolutely." As far as the politics of the House were concerned, the uninterrupted 40-year rule by a single party was, in practice, too close to absolute power. Democrats ruled the House and many Republicans felt that they were second-class citizens. Near the end of the Democratic dynasty, three House Republicans (Dick Armey, Jennifer Dunn, and Christopher Shays) and their staffs (Koopman et al., 1994) produced a thorough review of the various political pathologies that they attributed to prolonged one-party rule. It was their judgment that the Democratic dynasty had been a corrupting influence on the political system.

Among other things, Armey and his colleagues suggested that the permanent Democratic House majority supported a system of special interest politics in which the broader public's concerns were neglected in favor of those of interest groups contributing heavily to Democratic campaign coffers. It built itself a bloated and irresponsible congressional bureaucracy and committee system. They also argued that the arrogance of the Democratic dynasty created a climate that too often led to outright corruption—including the Koreagate scandal of 1976, the Abscam scandal of 1980, former-speaker Jim Wright's book royalty scandal, former-representative Dan Rostenkowski's House post office scandal in 1992, and the House banking scandal. However, it is the institutional abuses of the system, the undemocratic manipulation of the rules and procedures of the House to squelch debate and to prevent Republican influence in the process, that most frustrated Republicans. As Armey and his colleagues saw it, Democratic leadership in the House, not satisfied with the natural powers of a majority, attempted to suppress the minority by frequently resorting to rules restricting or preventing floor amendments and by employing highly partisan leadership strategies designed to exclude Republicans from the process. Frustrated with their indefinite exclusion from a meaningful role in governing, many Republicans adopted more extreme and combative positions regarding the policies of the majority and more skeptical (or even cynical) views about government in general. Even if the report of Armey and his colleagues is not accepted as an unbiased assessment of the impact of the permanent Democratic House majority on American politics, it is indicative of how Republicans thought they had been treated, what they thought about the consequences of the Democratic dynasty, and how badly relations between the parties had deteriorated.

An Overview

Figure 1.1 takes an overview of the suspected consequences of the one-party House. This causal model links the various suspected effects of this dominance. The diagram suggests the far-ranging consequences of the Democratic dynasty. Five effects (indicated by bold causal paths in the figure) are likely.

First, the seemingly permanent Democratic House majority may have, both directly and indirectly, weakened the internal cohesion of the political parties. Serious competition rallies partisans, and, in its absence, they may feel less compelled to come to the aid of their party.[11]

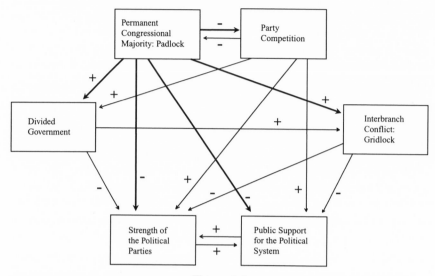

Figure 1.1

Suspected Effects of the Democratic Dynasty in the U.S. House of Representatives on the Political System

Note: Possible interaction effects of the strength of parties and party competition on divided government's impact on gridlock have been omitted for the sake of clarity. Also for clarity, a number of additional causal factors have been excluded. See figure 1.2 for other factors that might affect the permanence of the House majority.

Second, while the Democratic dynasty, in part, reflected an absence of political competition in the system, it also probably dampened competition. With the control of the House an apparently settled matter, there was less at stake in elections. Running for election or reelection to Congress is a tremendous emotional and financial commitment. The prospect of spending a career in the minority, effectively isolated from real policy making, must have discouraged some potentially strong Republican candidates (including Republican incumbents) from running for office. The end result: even less-competitive politics.

Third, the permanence of the Democratic majority, which was seemingly immune to what happened at the polls, may have had serious consequences for the public's attitudes about the political process and government in general. The fact that the Democratic majority survived, almost regardless of what voters did, would seem to have undermined public support for the political system, reduced the public's sense of political efficacy, fostered political cynicism, and reduced turnout.

Fourth, the Democratic dynasty, combined with competitive presidential elections, increased the likelihood of divided government. In the past, the party that won the White House would almost always win control of the House. When it occurred, divided government was usually the product of presidential party losses in the midterm election. This is no longer so. Democrats maintained their control of the House, even when Republican presidential candidates won in landslide elections. The result: more frequently divided government.

Finally, the permanence of the Democratic majority in the House accentuated conflict between presidents of either party and the Congress—producing institutional gridlock. An entrenched majority is an emboldened (perhaps arrogant) majority, less disposed to work cordially even with presidents of their own party. While great attention has been paid by scholars, journalists, and politicians to the problems of divided government and institutional gridlock, these problems and many of the pathologies associated with them may have deeper roots in the apparent permanence of the Democratic majority in the House. As Representative Jim Leach (R-IA) put it, the fundamental problem of American government may not have been "gridlock" but "padlock."[12] That is, Democratic control was so secure for 40 years, it was like having a padlock on the House.

As the causal model also suggests, the five suspected direct effects of padlock are often mutually reinforced by its indirect effects.[13] The entrenched majority in the House increases gridlock, which in turn strains public support for the political system. It also increases the likelihood of divided government, which in turn heightens institutional conflict (gridlock), and so on. In short, a long-standing congressional majority for one party, whether that one party is the Democratic Party or the Republican Party, is in many ways very unhealthy for the political system.

❑ Understanding the Democratic Dynasty ❑

The longevity of the Democratic House majority has been an important feature of the modern American political landscape and is important to understand. How did the Democratic majority become so firmly entrenched for so many years? What finally dislodged it? The following chapters examine a number of plausible answers.

Chapter 2 reviews the record of Democratic dominance in the House over the last four decades. It places the Democratic House record in historical perspective and compares it to the party's record in seeking other political offices. While Democrats were successful in winning other offices, and while parties have been successful in other times, the duration and extent of the Democratic majority in the House from 1954 to 1994 is unique. The analysis also discovers a pattern in the Democrats' success. The party had greater success in elections for offices with smaller electoral districts. Democrats have been more successful in running for state legislative and House seats than in statewide (Senate and gubernatorial) or national (presidential) races. This pattern suggests that the single-member-district electoral system may have something to do with Democratic success in House elections. (Some background on the House electoral system is provided in an appendix at the end of this chapter.) After establishing the pattern of greater Democratic success in House elections, a potential explanation for the permanent Democratic majority is proposed—the cheap-seats thesis. The thesis proposes that *to a significant extent, the Democratic dynasty was preserved and expanded as a result of the electoral system. As configured, the single-member-district electoral system required Republicans to receive more votes than Democrats in order to win the same number of seats. This systematic overrepresentation favoring the Democratic Party resulted from Democrats winning a disproportionate number of very-low-turnout districts— the cheap seats.*

The cheap-seats explanation is not the only explanation for the Democratic dynasty. Chapter 3 explores a number of alternatives, sources of the recently departed Democratic majority other than the electoral system. The fundamental causes that might have maintained the Democratic majority are presented in figure 1.2. As the causal diagram depicts it, there are two possible direct influences on Democratic padlock beyond the possible effects of partisan bias in the electoral system. One set of alternative explanations finds the basis of the Democratic dynasty in the intentional decisions of the voters. While such an explanation is seemingly straightforward, suggesting that the Democrats have controlled the House because voters want it that way, there are actually a variety of causes for these Democratic congressional votes. Some trace Democratic votes to the free choice of voters, while others suggest institutional reasons that might induce those votes. That is, some votes are cast for Democrats because more Democratic candidates enjoy the various advantages of incumbency, and Democrats receive some votes by default, since a number of Democratic congressional candidates run unopposed. Another explanation suggests that Democratic dominance can be traced directly to this lack of opposition: Democrats are set well on their way to a majority, since Republicans traditionally conceded some number of seats

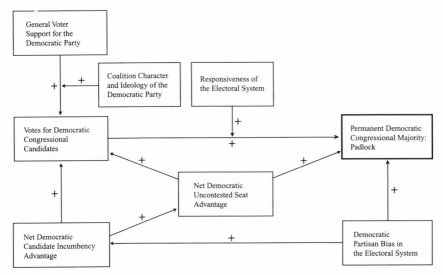

Figure 1.2

Suspected Factors Maintaining the Democratic Dynasty in the U.S. House of Representatives

Note: An arrow pointing at another arrow indicates an interaction effect. For instance, the responsiveness of the electoral system is suspected to magnify the effect of voter support for Democrats on the Democratic dynasty.

to the Democrats before any ballots are cast, giving the Democratic Party an uncontested-seat advantage.

There are two general explanations of the Democratic dynasty that find that voters wanted to fill a majority of House seats with Democrats. There is the simple explanation that more voters generally preferred Democrats in government and a more complex set of explanations claiming that voters have been particularly likely to prefer Democrats in Congress.

Most obviously, the Democratic majority may have simply reflected Democratic strength in the electorate. From the New Deal through at least the late 1970s, Democrats outnumbered Republicans in the electorate. Moreover, throughout the 40-year reign of the Democrats in the House, voters nationally cast a majority of votes for Democrats in congressional elections. This vote majority was then amplified into a larger seat majority by the responsiveness of the House electoral system. Thus, it is hardly surprising that more Democrats than Republicans were elected to the House.

While voters over the last 40 years may have generally favored Democratic government over Republican government, this does not explain why Democrats have been more successful in running for the House rather than for other offices. Although this differential success of Democrats, especially noticeable in contrasting their record in presidential elections to their record in House contests, may mean that features of the electoral systems distort the intentions of voters for or against Democrats, it may also mean that some critical number of voters, for any number of reasons, are especially inclined to want Democrats to serve in the House.

Several theories claim that voters deliberately chose a Democratic Congress as a vote for divided rather than unified party government. According to these theories, we have often had Democratic Congresses and usually had Republican presidents because that is what voters wanted. There are several possible reasons for wanting divided government. Some split-ticket voters may have believed that Republicans were better suited to executive duties and the representation of broader national interests while Democrats were better suited to legislative responsibilities and the representation of narrower local interests (though the results of the 1994 midterm seem to conflict with this view). Others may have wanted a moderate government. Either party governing alone would tilt away from the center. However, divided government would force compromise or a blending of the policy positions of the two parties. Still others may have felt alienated from both parties, opposed to the rule of either party on its own, and voted for divided government so that each party would have enough power to check and to frustrate the other. These theories are assessed in chapter 3.

The character of the parties may also account for the greater Democratic success in running for the House. There are two party-based explanations. They trace the Democratic strength in the House to the difference between the parties in their ideologies regarding government and the nature of the party coalitions. First, the Democratic Party's success in the House may have resulted from its progovernment or big-government philosophy. This perspective may have been particularly helpful in congressional races. As proponents of expansion of a variety of government programs, the Democrats were more willing and adept at serving diverse local interests. Democrats were more likely to "bring home the bacon" for their constituents. This constituency service may have been rewarded by the electorate, especially by the quarter of the electorate that was willing to split its ticket between candidates of different parties.[14]

Second, from the ideological tilt of the parties favoring legislative Democrats, the diversity of the two parties' coalitions may account for Democratic success in congressional elections. The Democratic coalition has been larger and more diverse than the Republican coalition (Axelrod, 1972; Stanley et al., 1986; and Erikson et al., 1989). Its diversity has presented problems for Democrats in national elections in which one candidate must appeal to the varied interests of the coalition in order to hold the pieces of the coalition together. Invariably some parts of the coalition—white southerners, blacks, labor, Catholics, or liberals—have felt shortchanged, and some members have sat out elections or even defected to vote for the Republican. Because congressional districts seldom contain the full range of these Democratic constituent groups, Democratic congressional candidates need not perform the same juggling act required of Democratic presidential candidates.[15] Congressional Democrats could win in southern white districts, urban black districts, and northeastern Catholic districts at the same time because their appeals could be tailored to the "political requirements" of each type of district.

Beyond considering the free will of the voters as a basis for Democratic rule, chapter 3 also considers another possible basis, the candidates. Two partisan advantages regarding congressional candidates—incumbency and uncontested seats—may have preserved the Democratic House.[16] Many speculated that incumbency was the foundation of the Democratic majority. Since a majority of incumbents were Democrats (until 1996), the Democratic Party has benefited more from the considerable advantages that candidates have who are incumbents. In addition, as a party, Democrats long enjoyed a candidate advantage in uncontested seats. Democrats have been much more likely than Republicans to win elections without a major-party opponent. By failing to offer a Republican candidate to voters, Republicans essentially conceded a significant number of seats (and votes) before the election was even held. This gave Democrats an automatic "leg up" toward a majority. As chapter 3 demonstrates, while the incumbency advantage and the uncontested-seat advantage for Democrats varied from one election to the next, these candidate advantages contributed significantly to sustaining the Democratic majority.

Chapter 4 begins the assessment of the electoral system as an explanation for the size and durability of the Democratic majority: Democrats

dominated the House for such a long period because of the extra seats
that they won as a result of winning districts in which relatively few votes
were cast. The chapter begins with an examination of the idea and the
measurement of partisan bias in the electoral system. *Partisan bias in an
electoral system is the difference between the parties in the number (or proportion)
of seats that each would win if they had received the same number of votes.* There
are good democratic reasons why a party should win more seats if it wins
more votes; but, in an unbiased electoral system, two parties winning an
equal number of votes should also win an equal number of seats. The
chapter reviews the existing research about partisan bias in the American
electoral system and assesses the appropriate way to measure bias. The
principal point of chapter 4 is that partisan bias has been incorrectly estimated in a number of previous studies and that it can be measured directly by comparing the average number of *unwasted votes* (that is, votes
cast for winning candidates) that each party receives.[17] Bias is revealed if
one party expends more unwasted votes per victory than the other party.

Chapter 5 presents the core of the case that the Democratic Party's
success in the cheap seats bolstered their long-standing majority in the
House. The chapter begins with an examination of turnout differences
across contested districts in elections from 1954 to 1992. Turnout is measured by the actual number of citizens voting for congressional candidates in the district. The extent of variation is surprisingly large. The
American system requires equal political representation in the sense of
"one person, one vote," but in practice voters living in some districts get
a lot more say about who gets to be a member of Congress than voters
who happen to live in other districts. The chapter introduces the idea of
the "unwasted vote," the number of votes cast for a winning candidate.[18]
An unbiased electoral system ought to require, on average, the same
number of unwasted votes from each party—to win one seat ought to
require the same number of votes from one party as it does from the
other. If the average winning Democrat receives 90,000 votes while the
average winning Republican receives 110,000 votes, the Democratic
Party has a distinct advantage.[19] In market terminology, the Republicans
are paying a higher price in terms of votes for their victories than Democrats are spending. This is what the evidence will demonstrate. It will also
demonstrate that although the electoral system has regularly favored the
Democrats, the extent of this bias has varied a good deal. In some election
years, the electoral system is nearly neutral. In others, it is strongly tilted
toward the Democrats.

Chapter 6 explains why partisan bias has varied from election to election. A variety of reasons, from legal changes regarding apportionment to a weakening of class politics, may have caused a long-term trend in partisan bias since 1954. Possible shorter-term trends involving the effects of partisan gerrymandering at the beginning of decades, following redistricting, and the gradual erosion of these effects in subsequent elections are also examined. Turnout may also have affected bias, if the nonvoters in some elections are Democratic voters when turnout surges in other elections. The factor most influential in affecting the extent of partisan bias is the congressional vote itself. The analysis shows that the Democrats' cheap-seat advantage was greatest when they needed it most, when their national congressional vote was at its lowest levels. While the alternative explanations of Democratic House strength explored in chapter 3 have merit, Democratic victories in the cheap seats provided an important foundation for their majority. Chapter 6 also reexamines the swing ratio, or the electoral system's responsiveness in light of the variability of partisan bias. Because partisan bias has varied with the congressional vote and prior estimates of the swing ratio have assumed that bias was a constant or stable feature of the electoral system, the responsiveness of the system has been underestimated.

Chapter 7 places the partisan bias of the electoral system in historical perspective. It compares the bias of the electoral system in the period since 1954 with that of earlier elections. The analysis indicates that the electoral system since at least 1936 has been biased in favor of the Democrats and that this bias also was greatest when Democrats were less popular.

Chapter 8 explores why the seemingly invincible Democratic majority came to its unexpected and dramatic end in the 1994 midterm. How did the unthinkable actually happen? How did partisan control of the House, that had for so long appeared unchangeable, finally change? The Democratic dynasty had been supported by the voters, candidate factors (incumbency and uncontested seats), the nature of the parties, and the electoral system. How did Republicans in 1994 surmount these factors to win a majority of seats? Was there a revolt against incumbents? Were congressional Democrats swept away by the electorate's anti-Clinton sentiment? Did Democrats lose their uncontested seat advantage? Did the cheap seats vanish, or did Democrats lose their hold on this advantage? Or was 1994 the long-postponed deepening of the gradual partisan realignment that had helped Republican presidential candidates in the 1980s?

The analysis in chapter 8 indicates that several of the factors that had sustained the Democratic dynasty remained potent in 1994. Democrats in 1994 maintained their incumbency advantage over Republicans, and the electoral system remained tilted in favor of the Democrats. However, these advantages were not enough to protect the Democratic majority against the loss of the party's advantage in uncontested seats and a deepening Republican realignment of voter allegiances. For the first time in 40 years, a majority of voters in 1994 voted for Republican congressional candidates, and, for the first time in more than 40 years, there were more uncontested Republican candidates than uncontested Democrats. Things, however, would have been much worse for Democrats if the electoral system had been neutral. As in previous elections, Democrats in 1994 won a large number of low-turnout districts. This extended their impact of Democratic votes and restrained the impact of Republican votes. Five different estimates of electoral system bias in 1994 indicate that the system was tilted in favor of the Democrats by about 4 percent of House seats. As a result, though the party with the largest share of votes in a plurality-rule electoral system normally wins a much larger share of seats, this was not true in 1994. The Republicans' share of seats about equalled their share of votes. By contrast, in the previous 20 elections, when Democrats won vote majorities, their share of seats consistently and significantly exceeded their share of votes.

The book concludes in chapter 9 with a discussion of the consequences of the cheap-seats phenomenon. The Democratic stronghold in low-turnout districts has had profound consequences for political representation. How do cheap seats, won disproportionately by one party, affect the representation of the general public, of those who turn out to vote, of congressional districts, of minority groups, and of individual citizens? Do cheap seats overrepresent liberal perspectives in the policy-making process? Do the cheap-seats phenomenon and the bias it creates in the electoral system help to explain why many Americans have become frustrated with the political system in general and with Congress in particular? Are the residents of low-turnout, cheap-seat districts represented well by the electoral system? What would happen if turnout in these cheap-seat districts rose? How would the results change? To push matters to the extreme of "what ifs," what would the electoral system produce and what bias would remain if everyone voted? At the group level, what is the relationship of the cheap-seats phenomenon to racial politics and efforts to redress social and political discrimination against African Americans? At the individual level, what are the implications of cheap seats for the principle of equal political representation? Finally, if one concludes that cheap seats are dysfunctional for the political system, that they undermine the representativeness of the government because they unfairly eliminate political competition or because they violate basic principles of political equality, can anything be done to reduce their impact or to eliminate them entirely?

First, however, we should survey the record. Setting aside for the moment the spectacular Democratic crash of 1994, how successful were Democrats in winning elections and controlling different parts of the government from 1954 to 1992? Were Democratic candidates particularly successful in seeking some offices rather than others?

❑ Appendix ❑

The House Electoral System

An electoral system encompasses everything that affects how votes are used to determine who wins elections and serves in office. The structure of an electoral system is derived from constitutional provisions and electoral laws. Among other things, they define who is eligible to vote and who is eligible to seek office, when and where elections are held, and, most important, how many votes are required to win an election. The major distinctions among electoral systems are between multimember-district proportional-representation systems, in which several representatives are selected from a district in proportion to the votes cast for the various political parties, and single-member-district, plurality-rule systems, in which the party receiving the most votes in a district elects a single representative. It is important to keep in mind that the consequences of these electoral laws, principles, and structures are determined by their interaction with the distribution of the vote. For instance, a plurality-rule, single-member-district system may greatly overreward the majority party if the vote is evenly distributed across the country. If the vote is more varied in parts of the country, the majority party would not be as greatly overrewarded in winning seats.

The House electoral system is based on constitutional provisions, federal and state laws, and judicial interpretations of both. The system has evolved over time into a single-member-district system in which representatives are elected by a plurality of the district vote. The U.S. Constitution defined only the most general features of the House electoral system. In Article 1, Section 2, and as amended by the Fourteenth

Amendment, the Constitution provides for the term of office for the House, voter eligibility standards, qualifications for service in the House, the standards and timing of apportionment of representatives to the states (by population reallocated every 10 years, with each state receiving a minimum of one seat), and provisions for filling vacancies in seats.[20] Section 4 of Article 1 leaves the designation of "the times, places, and manner of holding elections" to the U.S. House to the states, and Section 5 gives the power to judge election disputes to the House. Judicial interpretations of the "equal protection" clause of the Fourteenth Amendment have also affected the House electoral system. Arguably the two most important features of the House electoral system, single-member districts and the plurality-vote rule for deciding election winners, are not even mentioned in the U.S. Constitution.

The Constitution did provide for periodic reapportionment. Every 10 years the Congress redistributes House seats among the states on the basis of state populations, as measured by the census. Until 1911, Congress expanded the number of seats in the House and awarded seats to the states on the basis of the ratio of population to seats. After 1911, the House size was set by statute at 435 (with some temporary exceptions for the admission of new states between decennial reapportionments). Several methods have been used to apportion or allocate the 435 seats to the states at the beginning of every decade on the basis of state populations (see Congressional Quarterly, 1985, 683–90, and Butler and Cain, 1992, 19).

Once a state has received its allocation of seats, it may determine how they will be elected within the state. In the 1800s, most state legislatures designated areas of the state as single-member congressional districts. However, some chose to elect representatives to the House in at-large or statewide elections without districts, and still others provided for a combination of single-member districts and a single at-large statewide representative. Several states conducted at-large elections well into the twentieth century.[21] By 1970, however, all states had adopted the single-member-district system.

The redistricting process of drawing district boundaries within the states is primarily the responsibility of state legislatures, although others are often involved as well. As in the general legislative process, governors play a role in redistricting, through the threat of a veto. Some states, in an effort to reduce the impact of partisan politics, use commissions to draw district lines. The federal government is involved in the process both through court rulings mandating equally populated districts and federal laws (most notably the Voting Rights Act) prohibiting redistrictings that would dilute the influence of the votes of racial minorities. Federal laws not only bring the courts into the redistricting process but provide for an active role for the U.S. Department of Justice.

The prevailing decision rule for determining the winner of a congressional election is plurality rule. That is, the winning candidate is the one with more votes than any other candidate. Most states adopted plurality-rule from the outset. However, a few southern states use a majority-rule and runoff system. Under this system, a candidate is elected if he or she receives a majority of the vote (a likely occurrence, unless there are more than two candidates in the field). If no candidate receives a majority of the vote, the top two vote getters compete in a second, or runoff, election. The candidate receiving a majority of the vote in the runoff election is elected to serve a term in the House.

Finally, it is important to note that the evaluation of the electoral system depends only on the political reality of votes actually cast and seats actually awarded. To evaluate the system, analysts sometimes attempt to determine how voters might vote if the political climate were more or less favorable to a party; however, the starting point is always the actual votes cast and seats awarded. Electoral system analysis does not attempt to anticipate what would happen if new voters turned out to vote, if more districts were contested, if better candidates ran, if district boundaries were changed, or if the parties altered their appeals. Such analyses may be useful, but they entail the strong assumption that political changes can be made in isolation. For instance, if turnout rose from current levels to 100 percent of all eligible voters, undoubtedly a great many other changes would also take place. Electoral system analyses largely avoid this quagmire by examining only what would happen if vote shares for the parties shifted among those who actually voted, with all other conditions (e.g., district boundaries) unchanged.

2

□ □

The Democratic Record

Democrats dominated congressional politics from the 1930s to the 1990s. As impressive as this was, their uninterrupted control of the House from 1954 to 1994 was even more so. This chapter puts the four-decade-long Democratic dynasty in perspective—comparing it to prior congressional majorities, evaluating its durability in confronting forces hostile to such longevity, and contrasting the Democrats' success in the House to their success in other offices. The record shows that the recent Democratic majority was unprecedented and that Democrats had greater success in House elections than in elections for higher offices. This later fact suggests that there may be something about the House electoral system that provided Democrats with an edge. The principal thesis of this book explains the nature of this edge: the single-member-district electoral system, in combination with a steady constellation of socioeconomic, geographic, and political factors, allowed Democrats to win a significant number of congressional districts with relatively few votes, and this helped the Democratic Party maintain its substantial congressional majority.

❑ The Longevity of the Democratic Majority ❑

In the history of Congress, other consecutive majorities did not even come close to matching the duration of the Democratic majority from 1954 to 1994. Table 2.1 ranks the five longest party majorities in the House from 1855 to 1995. As the rankings indicate and as Ornstein (1990) observes, the Democratic Party's control of the House from the

Table 2.1
Longest Consecutive Partisan Majorites in the
U.S. House of Representatives, 1855–1995

Majority Party	First Election in Series	Period of Continuous Control	Number of Consecutive Congresses
1. Democrats	1954	1955–1995	20
2. Republicans	1894	1895–1911	8
2. Republicans	1858	1859–1875	8
4. Democrats*	1932	1933–1947	7
4. Republicans*	1918	1919–1933	7

Source: Ornstein et al. (1992: table 1-18). Since new Congresses are sworn in after the start of a new year, the years of control overlap. The 103rd Congress elected in November 1992 took office in January 1993 and will serve until January of 1995.

Note: The table includes all instances in which a party controlled the House for more than four consecutive terms since 1854.

*The 72nd Congress (1931–33) is counted as a Republican House. Republicans had won a bare majority of seats in the 1930 election, although Democrats gained a majority and organized the chamber after the death of several Republican members.

1950s into the 1990s was two-and-a-half times as long as any previous majority. Before the recent era of Democratic dominance, no party sustained its majority beyond eight consecutive congresses. The Democratic House majority installed in the 1954 election lasted 20 terms.[1]

From the mid-1950s to the 1994 midterm elections, Republicans were not even especially close to taking control of the House. Table 2.2 presents the magnitude of Democratic majorities over this period. Although the Democratic Party's majorities were modest following the 1954 and 1956 elections, their subsequent majorities were large (in excess of 55 percent). Democrats usually had a cushion of more than 40 seats. On three occasions they achieved "veto-proof majorities" of over 290 seats (or, more than 73 seats above a bare majority). Even at their low points, Democrats maintained substantial majorities. Republicans closed within 30 seats of a majority on only three occasions since the mid-1950s (1968, 1972, and 1980), and, from the mid-1950s to 1994, Republicans were never closer than a full 25 seats short of a bare majority. The Democratic dynasty was not only sustained over an unprecedented number of elections but was not seriously threatened for several decades.

Table 2.2
Democratic Representatives in the U.S. House of Representatives, 1954–1992

Resulting from Election	Number of Democratic Representatives	Democratic Seat Percentage	Size (in Seats) of Democratic Majority
1954	232	53.3	+15
1956	234	53.8	+17
1958	283	64.9	+65
1960	262	60.0	+44
1962	258	59.4	+41
1964	295	67.8	+78
1966	248	57.0	+31
1968	243	55.9	+26
1970	255	58.6	+38
1972	242	55.8	+25
1974	291	66.9	+74
1976	292	67.1	+75
1978	277	63.7	+60
1980	243	55.9	+26
1982	268	61.8	+51
1984	253	58.2	+36
1986	258	59.3	+41
1988	260	59.8	+43
1990	267	61.5	+50
1992	258	59.4	+41
Mean	261	60.0	+44
Nonmajorities		0 (0%)	
55% or Less		2 (10%)	

Note: The size of the Democratic majority is the number of seats in excess of a bare majority. This is generally the number of Democratic representatives less 217 seats, since a majority of a body of 435 would require 218 seats. The House expanded for the 1958 and 1960 elections to accommodate the entrance of Alaska and Hawaii as states. The minimum majority in 1958 and 1960 was thus 219 seats.

❑ The Durability of the Democratic Majority ❑

The Democratic majority in the House was remarkable for its durability as well as its longevity. It endured through a period that should have been very inhospitable to its survival. A number of developments should have made it very difficult for Democrats to sustain their majority. Partisan dealignment, political turbulence, Republican presidential landslides, and partisan realignments presented challenges to the Democratic dynasty. Despite these challenges, it survived.

First, through much of the past four decades, political parties were in decline. While of continuing importance to the political system, by several measures parties became less important than they had been (Wattenberg, 1990, 1991).[2] The persistence of a party's majority in a period of weakened partisanship is impressive. The weakening of partisanship should have worked against the majority party, which clearly was the Democratic Party until at least the 1980s. If a party holds an advantage in partisanship, it benefits to the extent that voters' decisions are based on that partisanship. At the extreme, the majority party would win every election if partisanship were the only thing that affected voters' decisions. The weakening of partisanship should have opened elections up to influences (candidates, issues, etc.) that on occasion might tilt in favor of the minority party. With more personalized politics, one would have expected less continuity in party majorities. With congressional elections more dependent on local factors and less dependent on partisanship, one might have expected less stable partisan results in the aggregate and more swings of majorities from one party to the other. In short, with partisan dealignment, a Democratic majority should have been less certain. Instead, it became a long-term political fixture.

Second, the great social and economic turbulence and change of the past 40 years of American history should have made it particularly difficult to reelect a House majority for either party. At different times and in different ways, foreign-policy issues, a variety of social issues, and the perennial economic issues divided the nation. The Vietnam War created especially deep divisions, and the scars from it remained long after the last American troops came home. Battles over civil rights were bitterly fought, and the racial divisions continue. Abortion policies activated deeply held convictions and created intense arguments. And then there were the ever-present economic issues. The period had stretches of sustained economic growth (under both Democratic and Republican administrations) and deep and long recessions and stagflation. There were times of runaway inflation and sky-high interest rates as well as times of high unemployment. Throughout all the tumult, the Democratic majority in the House was undisturbed.

Beyond the waxing and waning of various issues, the political landscape has changed in many other ways. These changes also should have hampered the preservation of a majority. Through the civil rights movement and the enactment of civil rights laws, the participation of African Americans in the electoral process steadily rose from the 1950s to the 1970s and beyond. New ethnic groups, particularly Hispanic Americans and Asian Americans, emerged as significant political interests. One might expect the emergence of new groups to create intraparty divisions for the Democrats' majority coalition and provide opportunities for growth in the Republicans' minority coalition. The methods of financing campaigns changed in this period, as did the general methods of conducting congressional campaigns. Congressional campaigns became more media intensive and far more costly. All of these changes might have disturbed "politics as usual," the politics in which the Democratic majority was first formed. But it did not. Through it all, House Democrats remained in the majority.

Third, the Democratic majority survived repeated Republican presidential victories, several of landslide proportions. Historically, the party winning the White House usually wins a majority in the House. Victorious presidential candidates throughout history have had coattails on which congressional candidates of their party have ridden into office. Although presidential coattails in recent years have been a bit shorter than they once were, they are still substantial (Campbell, 1986, 1991, 1992, 1993). It is, thus, especially impressive that House Democrats consistently won despite presidential coattails often helping their Republican opponents. Democrats held a majority through six of Eisenhower's eight years in the White House, the eight years of the Nixon-Ford administrations, the eight years of the Reagan administration, and the four years of the Bush administration. Republican presidents were in the White House for 26 of the 40 years (1954–94) that the Democrats held their House majority. Moreover, Democrats retained their majority even in the face of Nixon's 1972 landslide victory over McGovern and Reagan's 1984 landslide defeat of Mondale. Regardless of which party occupied the White House and regardless of which party was helped or hurt by the top of the ticket, Democrats won a majority of House seats election after election.

Fourth, the dealignment of the party system forged in the New Deal era set the stage for the emergence of a new party system, one much more favorably inclined toward Republicans. Until 1994, Democrats in the House had successfully weathered a partisan realignment favoring Republicans. From the 1930s through the 1950s and into the 1960s, a solid majority of the electorate thought of themselves as Democrats. In the 1950s and 1960s, Democrats in the electorate outnumbered Republicans by nearly two to one. With this advantage, a Democratic House majority was hardly surprising, though (as already noted) previous majority parties had been unable to maintain continuous control of the House for such a long period. This partisan balance in the public began to shift in the late 1960s and evidence of significant party identification shifts appeared in the 1980s. The nation became less Democratic (Petrocik, 1987; Bullock, 1988; Carmines and Stimson, 1989). By the mid-1980s, the parties were near parity (Miller, 1991, 561; Keene and Ladd, 1991, 92–93). Yet again, despite this trend against them, Democrats retained their House majority.

❑ The National, Statewide, and Local Records ❑

The fact that the Democratic House majority survived through partisan dealignment, social and economic turmoil, Republican presidential victories, and a pro-Republican partisan realignment is impressive. The Democratic domination of the House is even more intriguing in that it was not equally evident for other elective offices. Democrats did not dominate the Presidency or statewide offices to the same extent or with the same consistency that they dominated the House.

Within the framework of competitive two-party politics, a dominant or majority party is common. Party competition is rarely balanced perfectly. The majority party in the electorate usually is more successful than the minority party in races up and down the ticket. It is reasonable to expect that a majority party successful in seeking House seats should have about the same measure of success in running for the White House, the Senate, governorships, and state legislative seats. However, this was not the case over the past 40 years. Democrats were not equally successful in getting elected to all offices. To be sure, the Democrats over the past four decades were quite successful in seeking all offices other than the presidency, but they had no greater nor any more consistent success than in the House. The question is why? Why were Democrats particularly successful in electing a majority of the House? We should first review the record.

Competition for the Presidency

Democrats were not nearly as successful in presidential elections as they were in House elections. In fact, they occupied the White House for only 14 of the 40 years in which they continuously controlled the House. From one perspective, presidential elections have been quite competitive. The

Table 2.3
The Democratic Party's Success in Presidential Elections, 1956–1992

Year	Percentage of the Two-Party Presidential Popular Vote for the Democratic Candidate
1956	**42.25**
1960	50.09
1964	61.34
1968	**49.59**
1972	**38.21**
1976	51.07
1980	**44.71**
1984	**40.83**
1988	**46.06**
1992	53.40
Mean	47.76
Nonmajorities	6 (60%)
55% or Less	9 (90%)

Source: Computed from Congressional Quarterly's *Guide to U.S. Elections,* 2d ed. (1985).

Note: Democratic vote minorities are indicated in bold.

popular vote record is displayed in table 2.3. As the table shows, the 1960, 1968, and 1976 elections were all narrowly decided in the popular vote. Moreover, while there have been landslide victories, neither party had a monopoly of lopsided victories. On the Republican side, Eisenhower won a solid victory over Stevenson in 1956 and Nixon won in a landslide over McGovern in 1972. On the Democratic side, Johnson defeated Goldwater by a wide margin in 1964.

From another perspective, the parties have not been quite so competitive in recent presidential elections. Over the past 25 years, Republicans have had much more success than the Democrats in winning the White House. Beginning with the 1968 election, Republicans won five of seven presidential elections. Moreover, the two Republican presidential losses during that period were under unusual circumstances. In the post-Watergate election of 1976, unelected Republican incumbent Gerald Ford only won the Republican nomination after a bitterly fought contest with Ronald Reagan and then very narrowly lost to Jimmy Carter, who as a southerner managed to carry most of the southern states crucial to a

Table 2.4
The History of Divided Government, 1868–1994

Following Type of Election	1868–1950		1952–1994	
	Divided	Unified	Divided	Unified
All Elections	26%	**74%**	**64%**	36%
	(11)	(31)	(14)	(8)
Presidential Elections	10%	**90%**	**55%**	45%
	(2)	(19)	(6)	(5)
Midterm Elections	43%	**57%**	**73%**	27%
	(9)	(12)	(8)	(3)

Note: The most prevalent result among a type of election in the historical period is indicated in boldface. Percentages are of elections (all, presidential year, or midterm) yielding, respectively, either divided or unified government in the specified period of history. The number below the percentage is the actual number of elections in a given period resulting in divided or unified governments.

Democratic victory. In 1992, Bill Clinton, another southern Democratic governor, defeated Republican incumbent George Bush. Bush was especially vulnerable, having presided over a sluggish economy, having reneged on his 1988 (read-my-lips) campaign pledge not to raise taxes, and having billionaire third-party populist candidate Ross Perot campaigning against him as well.

Even with their 1976 and 1992 losses, the recent Republican record in presidential elections has been enviable. Indeed, prior to the 1992 election, commentators often referred to the Republican "lock on the Electoral College." However, the Republican record in presidential elections was not even close to equaling the Democratic Party's record in House elections. Republican presidential victories are much less certain. Unlike Democratic victories in the House, Republican presidential victories were never taken for granted. Nonetheless, the fact that Republicans have been so successful in presidential elections makes the Democratic record in House elections even more of a curiosity.

The disparity of Democratic success in House and presidential elections has greatly increased the incidence of divided government. The frequency of divided and unified governments resulting from elections between 1868 and 1950 and from 1952 to 1994 are presented in table 2.4 for all elections, on-year or presidential elections, and midterm elections. As the table indicates, once the exception, divided government is now the rule. From the end of the Civil War until the early 1950s, the party winning the presidency usually also won a majority of seats in both houses of Congress. Only about a quarter of the elections between 1868 and 1950 resulted in divided government. Moreover, presidential elections rarely produced divided government. Only 1 in 10 on-year elections during this period yielded divided results.[3] The results of elections since 1950 stand in stark contrast. Nearly two-thirds of elections from 1952 to 1994 produced divided government. The pattern is even stronger in the most recent elections. Since 1968, 11 of the last 14 elections (79 percent) resulted in divided government.[4] Although the consequences of this change are still not clear (Mayhew, 1991; Thurber, 1991; Fiorina, 1992a; Cox and Kernell, 1991), the ramifications of divided government are generally thought to be both substantial and detrimental to the proper functioning of the government (Burns, 1967; Cutler, 1986, 1987; Sundquist, 1987, 1988; Mezey, 1989).

Democratic Strength in Statewide Offices

Democrats have been much more successful in elections below the presidential level. In elections to both Senate seats and governorships, the two major elected statewide offices, Democrats were quite successful over the past four decades. However, despite this strong record, Democrats did not have quite the same degree and consistency of success in Senate and gubernatorial races that they had in House elections. The Democratic record in the Senate and in governorships is presented in table 2.5.

The Democratic record in Senate and House elections can be compared in two ways. One is to examine how often the party has held a majority of seats during the past 40 years. House Democrats held solid majorities for 40 consecutive years. In the Senate, Democrats held a majority from 1954 to 1978, an impressive tenure. In 1980 Democrats lost control of the Senate and did not regain it until the 1986 election. Although six years of Republican control in 40 years may not seem like a great deal of time, it is six more than enjoyed by House Republicans, who did not come even close to gaining a majority in this period.

Democratic success in House and Senate elections may also be compared using the percentage of election victories in Senate seats at stake in each election year. Again, while Democrats were successful in Senate elections, they were less successful in Senate elections than in House races. In the House, Democrats carried a majority of seats in 20 consecutive election years. In the Senate, Democrats carried a majority of seats

Table 2.5
The Democratic Party's Electoral Success in
Major Statewide Offices, 1954–1992

	Percentage of Seats Won or Held by Democrats			
	U.S. Senate		Governorships	
Year	Held	Won	Held	Won
1954	51	64	56	58
1956	51	51	58	58
1958	65	79	71	78
1960	64	63	68	58
1962	67	64	68	62
1964	68	80	66	70
1966	64	**49**	**50**	**38**
1968	58	53	**38**	**42**
1970	55	66	58	59
1972	57	**49**	62	65
1974	62	71	73	78
1976	62	67	76	71
1978	59	**43**	64	58
1980	**46**	**35**	54	**50**
1982	**46**	61	68	74
1984	**47**	**49**	68	**50**
1986	55	59	52	53
1988	55	58	56	53
1990	56	53	58	56
1992	57	50	60	67
Mean	57.3	58.2	61.2	59.9
Nonmajorities	3 (15%)	5 (25%)	2 (10%)	4 (20%)
55% or Less	8 (40%)	9 (45%)	4 (20%)	6 (30%)

Sources: Computed from Ornstein et al. (1992), ABC News' *The '88 Vote* (1989), and Congressional Quarterly's *Guide to U.S. Elections,* 2d ed. (1985), and the *Statistical Abstract of the United States* (1991).

Note: Democratic minorities are indicated in bold. The percentage of seats "Held" by Democrats is the two-party proportion of all seats occupied by Democrats after the election, whether or not those seats had been up for election in that year. The percentage of seats "Won" is the two-party percentage of all seats up for election in that year that were won by Democrats. The few odd-year gubernatorial elections were included in the subsequent even-year percentages.

in 15 of the 20 years, losing a majority of seats at stake on five occasions (1966, 1972, 1978, 1980, and 1984). In another two election years, Democrats just barely won a majority of seats that were at stake (1968 and 1990). In these two years, Democrats carried a smaller share of Senate seats than in their poorest performance in House elections over this period. The bottom line is this: although the Democratic Party's recent record in Senate elections is strong, it did not dominate the Senate to the same extent or with the same consistency that it dominated the House. In most elections, it was "thinkable" that the Republicans could win a majority of Senate contests and assemble a majority of seats to obtain control of the Senate.

The Democratic electoral record for governorships is similar to the Senate record. As in Senate elections, Democrats were quite successful in gubernatorial elections. Likewise, Democratic success in gubernatorial elections, though impressive, did not quite match their success in House elections. Because governorships are of varying terms and since different states schedule gubernatorial elections in different years, the Democrats' record in governorships can be examined in terms of the numbers they held at any point in time or the number that they won of those up for election in an election year. As table 2.5 shows, from 1954 to 1992, Democrats only failed to occupy a majority of governorships for a single two-year period (1968–69) and equaled Republican numbers in a second two-year period (1966–67). In 36 of the 40 years from 1954 to 1994, Democrats occupied a clear majority of statehouses.

The Democratic success rate in gubernatorial elections is also impressive. They won a clear majority of statehouses up for election in 16 of the past 20 election years. Moreover, in two of the four elections in which they did not win a clear majority of gubernatorial elections (1980 and 1984), Democrats and Republicans tied in their number of victories. Republicans were able to win a clear majority of gubernatorial elections in only 1966 and 1968. As in the Senate, Democrats were quite successful in governorships. Republican majorities were infrequent. Nevertheless, even this limited success surpassed the abysmal Republican record in House elections.

Democratic Dominance of State Legislatures

The Democratic record in state legislatures comes closest to equaling their House record. Table 2.6 presents the percentages of states with Democratic majorities in the lower and upper chambers of state legisla-

Table 2.6

The Democratic Party's Electoral Success in State Legislatures, 1954–1992

Year	Partisan Majorities in State Legislative Chambers					
	Upper Chambers			Lower Chambers		
	Dem.	Rep.	Percent Democratic	Dem.	Rep.	Percent Democratic
1954	20	25	**44**	25	21	54
1956	23	21	52	26	20	57
1958	31	17	65	39	8	83
1960	29	18	62	31	17	65
1962	28	19	60	28	19	60
1964	35	11	76	39	9	82
1966	30	17	64	25	23	52
1968	25	23	52	23	24	**49**
1970	27	19	59	28	20	58
1972	29	19	60	31	17	65
1974	39	8	83	41	8	84
1976	38	9	81	40	8	83
1978	34	14	71	34	13	72
1980	31	18	63	32	17	65
1982	34	15	69	39	10	80
1984	32	16	67	32	16	67
1986	31	16	66	35	13	73
1988	32	17	65	36	12	75
1990	34	12	74	39	10	80
1992	31	16	66	36	12	75
Mean	30.7	16.5	65	33.0	14.9	69
Nonmajorities			1 (5%)			1 (5%)
55% or Less			3 (15%)			3 (15%)

Sources: Computed from various volumes of *The Book of the States, Congressional Quarterly Weekly Reports,* and the *Statistical Abstract of the United States.*

Note: Democratic minorities are indicated in bold. The number of legislatures do not total to 50 in each year, since Alaska and Hawaii elected their first legislatures as states in 1958, Nebraska has a nonpartisan unicameral legislature, Minnesota also had a nonpartisan state legislature until the 1972 election, and, in several years, one or more legislatures were evenly divided between the parties.

tures. Democrats held control in a majority of upper houses of state legislatures following 19 of the 20 elections from 1954 to 1992. Prior to 1994, the last time that Republicans held a majority of upper chambers followed the 1954 election. In 1954, Republicans controlled 25 of the 45 upper houses in partisan state legislatures. In light of the fact that this election was before the one-person, one-vote court ruling requiring equally populated districts and that a number of these chambers had been elected in 1952 and were elected to four-year terms, one could easily conclude that since 1954, Democratic success in upper chambers of state legislatures was every bit as consistent as their success in the House of Representatives.

Democrats dominated the lower chamber of state legislatures with almost the same consistency that they dominated the House. They controlled a clear majority of lower chambers of state legislatures following 19 of the 20 elections in which Democrats controlled the House. Republicans came close to controlling a majority of state legislatures in 1966 and controlled a bare majority of chambers following the 1968 elections. If Democrats had won control of one additional lower chamber in 1968, their record of success at this level would have been as perfectly consistent as it was in the House of Representatives.[5]

The Records Compared

The record of the Democratic Party across the range of major offices reveals both interesting similarities and differences with their record of consistent and substantial victories in the House. In comparing the record of consecutive Democratic majorities in the House from 1954 to 1992 to the party's record in other offices (see table 2.7), there is some order. Democrats were least successful in running for the sole national office, the presidency.[6] For offices that require statewide votes (the U.S. Senate and governorships), they were more successful, though not as successful as they were in the House. Democrats were most successful in running for offices in which votes are cast within districts within the states—for the House of Representatives and for both the upper and lower chambers of state legislatures. This pattern has also been noted by Fiorina, who observes that "a large element in the increased incidence of divided government—both nationally and in the states—is the decline in Republican legislative strength" (1992a, 58).[7]

The similarities and differences in the consistency with which Democrats have dominated different offices suggests why they were successful

Table 2.7
Democratic Control of Various Offices, 1954–1992

Level of Voting	Office	Degree of Democratic Party Success
National	The Presidency	Moderate
Statewide	U.S. Senate, Governorships	Great
District	U.S. House of Representatives, Upper Chamber and Lower Chamber of State Legislature	Perfect or Near Perfect

Note: Voting for the presidency might also be interpreted as occuring at the state level, because of the Electoral College. However, since each state as an electoral unit is not counted equally (as are states in senate and gubernatorial contests) and the candidates are common to all states, it may be more appropriate to treat presidential elections as a quasi-national election.

in general and why they dominated the House in particular. In view of the similarity of Democratic records for the two statewide offices (the Senate and governorships), the similarity of the records for districted offices (the House and state legislative offices), and the order of differences among the three levels, it is clear that Democrats have had an advantage in running for offices from smaller electoral districts. They have been more consistently successful in seeking districted offices.

Why have Democrats been more successful in running for these more localized or districted offices? Several reasons are possible.[8] Democrats may be better at delivering government benefits to local areas. Their philosophy of government and their longtime control of the levers of governmental power may have helped them "bring home the bacon." Their more progovernment philosophy may have made it easier to coax competent potential candidates into running (Ehrenhalt, 1991), and this may have been especially important at lower levels of office, where the rewards for running are smaller and the pool of potential candidates not so well established.

The thesis proposed here is that Democrats do particularly well in districted offices because the organization of votes into districts helps Democrats running for the House and state legislatures by allowing them to win in districts with relatively few votes. This is an advantage that Democrats running in statewide and national races do not have. Compared to Republicans, Democratic House candidates tend to win in lower-turnout areas. Since Democrats have traditionally done well among lower socioeconomic groups and since lower socioeconomic characteristics are strongly correlated with nonvoting, lower socioeconomic districts tend to elect Democrats, sometimes by large vote percentages but still with a relatively small number of actual votes because of the lower district turnout. As a result, compared to the Republican vote, the Democratic vote for the House is divided among districts in such a way that it elects more Democrats. Because House and state legislative elections are decided entirely by the vote within particular districts, the fate of these candidates is not directly affected by the size of the district turnout.[9] It only matters that a candidate receive more votes than any of his or her competitors, whether the "more" is of a huge number or a small number of voters. If votes for an office only matter within the confines of a district, the fact that turnout is low in the district and the party's winning candidate receives fewer actual votes than the winning candidates in other districts does not matter.

While all that matters to House candidates is that they receive a plurality of the district vote, regardless of district turnout; this is not all that matters to candidates running for higher office. At the state level, where governors and senators are elected and where Electoral College votes for president are decided, congressional (or state legislative) district boundaries do not matter, and they do not limit the impact of low turnout on the aggregate vote. Governors and senators are decided by how many votes the candidates receive, not by how many congressional districts they carry. Thus, unlike a party's House candidates (or its state legislative candidates), it matters greatly to a party's presidential, senatorial, and gubernatorial candidates whether turnout is high or low in the party's stronghold districts.[10]

This district-turnout explanation may explain more than why Democratic House candidates (and state legislative) outperformed Democratic candidates for higher offices. It may also help to explain why Democrats dominated the House for so long. It suggests that there has been a Democratic tilt to the House electoral system. This tilt has been based on Democrats winning a disproportionate number of low-turnout districts. Because of the low turnout in these districts, Democrats have expended relatively few votes to win these cheap seats. The theory of cheap seats will be more fully elaborated shortly.

The Electoral System and the Democratic Majority

The Democratic record in House elections from 1954 to 1992 is certainly impressive. However, the record of Democratic victories does not per-

Table 2.8
The Overrepresentation of the Democratic House Vote, 1954–1992

Election	Democratic Vote Percentage	Democratic Seat Percentage	Difference
1954	52.8	53.3	+.6
1956	51.2	53.8	+2.6
1958	56.7	64.9	+8.2
1960	55.1	60.0	+4.8
1962	52.9	59.4	+6.6
1964	57.8	67.8	+10.0
1966	51.4	57.0	+5.6
1968	51.0	55.9	+4.9
1970	54.7	58.6	+3.9
1972	53.2	55.8	+2.6
1974	59.2	66.9	+7.7
1976	57.4	67.1	+9.7
1978	54.8	63.7	+8.9
1980	51.5	55.9	+4.4
1982	56.4	61.8	+5.2
1984	52.5	58.2	+5.6
1986	55.0	59.3	+4.4
1988	54.2	59.8	+5.6
1990	53.3	61.5	+8.1
1992	53.1	59.4	+6.4
Mean	54.2	60.0	+5.8

Note: The Democratic vote percentages were calculated from volumes of *The Statistical Abstract of the United States,* with corrections being made for the inclusion of the District of Columbia, not counting Liberal Party votes for Democratic Party candidates in New York before 1960, estimates of turnout in uncontested districts in states in which that turnout is not reported, and several other minor discrepancies. Note that the actual vote calculated here is usually slightly more Democratic (a mean difference of about three-tenths of a percentage point more Democratic) than that reported by Ornstein et al. (1990, table 2-2).

fectly reflect the Democrats' success in attracting votes. The Democratic Party's share of votes for the House is smaller than its share of seats. Table 2.8 presents for comparison the percentages of both votes and seats won by Democratic House candidates.

As the table demonstrates, while Democrats have won a majority of votes, as well as seats, in each of the 20 elections from 1954 to 1992, their share of seats in each of these elections has consistently been larger than their share of votes. Over this period, the Democratic share of votes has ranged from a low of 51 percent in Eisenhower's 1956 reelection to a high of 58.5 percent in the post-Watergate election of 1974. Over the same period, Democrats never occupied fewer than 53.3 percent of the seats (1954) and after the Johnson landslide of 1964 held 67.8 percent of the seats. Although they never received as much as 60 percent of the votes for the House in any election in the past 40 years, they held 60 percent or more of the seats following 8 of the 20 elections of the Democratic dynasty.

In a plurality-rule, single-member-district electoral system, such as that used to elect most House members, the party winning a majority of the national vote normally wins an even larger share of legislative seats.[11] Under the plurality-rule system, unlike various proportional representation methods, the party with a plurality of votes systematically receives an even larger proportion of seats. This is a long acknowledged characteristic of the plurality system, originally dubbed "the cube law"—the ratio of seats split between two parties supposedly being a cubic function of the ratio of votes between the parties. While modern analysis indicates that the "cube law" is not a hard and fast law and that the precise translation of votes to seats (including how many seats each party could expect with 50 percent of the vote) varies from one plurality-rule electoral system to another, these sophisticated analyses have supported the cube law's general description of the S-shaped relation between a party's proportion of seats and its proportion of votes (Rae, 1971; Tufte, 1973; Taagepera and Shugart, 1989, 166).

The cube-law description of the relationship between seats and votes is depicted by the S-curve shape in figure 2.1. The curve is in contrast to the diagonal, which reflects a system of perfect proportional representation in which parties receive the same share of seats as their share of votes. The steepness of the slope in the middle of the vote distribution reflects the responsiveness of the electoral system. *Responsiveness* refers to the expected change in a party's share of seats from a specified change in votes. Plurality-rule systems, compared to proportional representation systems, are very responsive. For example, a 10 percentage point gain in the vote for a party (from 50 percent to 60 percent) would produce an equivalent 10 percentage point seat gain in a perfectly proportional representation system but would produce a much larger (27 percent) change in a plurality-rule system (assuming the cube-law relationship). Note that the responsiveness of the electoral system is symmetric between the parties. In the above example, whether the Democrats or the Republicans were the party in question, either would benefit equally by being the majority vote-getting party in the plurality-rule system and either would suffer equally by being the minority vote-getting party.

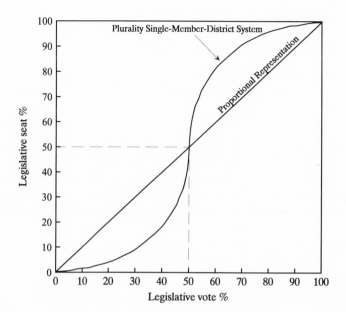

Figure 2.1
The Relationship between Seats and Votes in Plurality and Proportional Representation Electoral Systems

Why is the plurality-rule system responsive? Why does it overrepresent the party with the most votes? We will address this question more fully in chapter 4, but, for now, the plurality-rule system overrepresents the stronger party because it causes the minority vote-getting party to waste a larger portion of its vote in losing candidacies. A majority party does not waste many of its votes. It can even win in districts in which it receives less than its average vote percentage. The minority party, on the other hand, not only receives fewer votes but wastes many of those that they do receive. The minority vote party can even lose (and thereby wastes votes) in districts in which its vote percentage actually exceeds its average vote percentage. Thus, a minority party wastes votes on losing candidates because it wastes votes in districts where its vote falls short of its average *plus* some districts where its vote actually exceeds its average, only not by enough to establish a plurality.

For instance, what would happen if Democrats received 57 percent of the national vote and the Republicans received 43 percent? If the vote were uniformly distributed across all districts in the country, Democrats would win all of the districts. No votes cast for Democrats would have been wasted (they all would have won some representation), and all votes cast for Republicans would have been wasted (they would not have received any representation). But because of all of the sociological bases of the vote, the national vote is not distributed evenly. Each party has pockets of strength and areas of weakness. With 43 percent of the vote nationwide, Republicans would waste votes in any district in which it received 43 percent of the vote or less, but would also waste votes in districts in which it performed better than its typical showing but not enough better to achieve a majority. Assuming some variation in the distribution of the Democratic vote, Democrats would only waste votes in districts in which they did much more poorly than their national average. Votes for Democrats would only be wasted where a Democratic district vote percentage falls a full 7 percentage points below its national average of 57 percent. As a result, the plurality-rule system provides many more opportunities for the minority party to waste its votes, and this produces system responsiveness.

The responsiveness of the plurality-rule electoral system is one reason why Democrats were overrepresented or received a larger share of seats than votes; however, it is not the only possible means by which a party can be overrepresented. The electoral system can also be biased in favor of a party. The nature and causes of partisan bias in an electoral system will be explored in some detail in chapter 4. However, we should note at this point that bias in an electoral system is operationally defined as the proportion of seats above or below 50 percent when parties (in a two-party system) receive an equal number of votes. In an unbiased system, each party should receive 50 percent of the seats when it receives 50 percent of the votes. In a biased system, if both parties received the same vote, one party would win a larger share of seats. By definition, a biased electoral system is asymmetric in its treatment of the parties.[12]

While the responsiveness of an electoral system is produced by the minority party wasting a larger share of its votes on losing candidates, electoral system bias appears when the average winning candidate of one party receives more votes than the average winning candidate of the opposition party. A party is favored in an electoral system when it expends fewer votes in its victories than its opposition expends in its successful candidacies. Given a constant number of unwasted votes (votes not wasted in losing causes), a party would rather spend fewer, rather than more, votes per victory. As the analysis in later chapters will show, bias in the electoral system is one reason that Democrats win a larger share of seats than votes, and this may have contributed to the longevity of the Democratic House majority. The single-member-district, plurality-rule electoral system, the way in which votes are counted to award seats to the parties, is biased in favor of the Democratic Party, and this helped Democrats maintain their majority in the House of Representatives (and also in most state legislatures).

❑ The Cheap-Seats Thesis ❑

How were Democrats able to maintain their large majorities in the House for so many years? There are several plausible explanations. Democratic majorities certainly could not have survived without a good deal of public support for Democratic candidates in general. Democrats were, indeed, the more popular party. Moreover, increased ticket splitting in the late 1960s allowed Democratic congressional candidates to protect their vote majorities against national political tides often favoring Republicans and electing several Republican presidents. However, the vote majorities that the electorate provided for Democrats may be only part of the explanation for the Democratic Party's long-term dominance of the House. Democrats may have become entrenched as the House majority whether or not voters really wanted them to. The electoral system and the lack of a real choice for many voters also contributed to the Democratic dynasty.

The argument advanced here is this: *the Democratic Party has been particularly and continuously successful in House elections in part because the electoral system (owing to a constellation of interrelated political, social, economic, and geographic conditions) is biased in its favor.* Democrats maintained a House dynasty not only because of the number of voters casting Democratic ballots but also because of the distribution of its votes around the nation. The organization of its votes into a particular arrangement of congressional districts was critical to the maintenance of the Democratic majority. The electoral system favored Democrats because the party was able to extend the "purchasing power" of its votes over a larger number of seats. It was able to do this because it won a disproportionate share of very-low-turnout seats, the cheap seats. The evidence in the following chapters will show that Democratic victories in these low-turnout districts were a consistent feature of elections over the past 40 years. Even in 1994, when Republicans finally ended the Democratic reign of the House, Democrats won a large portion of the low-turnout districts and this buffered their losses. As a result of Democrats prevailing in low-turnout districts, the average number of votes for winning Democratic congressional candidates falls well below that for Republican winners. Consequently, if Democratic and Republican candidates across the country received the same number of votes, Democrats would win a significantly greater number of seats.

There are several possible reasons for a Democratic cheap-seats bias in the electoral system, but the most plausible involves the conjunction of five factors:

1. the system of single-member, equal-population congressional districts;
2. the socioeconomic basis of the Democratic and Republican coalitions;
3. the association of socioeconomic class with turnout;
4. the socioeconomic homogeneity of housing patterns; and
5. the reflection of these neighborhoods in drawing district boundaries.[13]

A critical condition for the cheap-seats thesis is the institution of the single-member, equal-population congressional district system. The single-member district system, though not a constitutional requirement, is the prevailing method for apportioning a state's allocated number of seats to the House. This has not always been the case. Multimember districts, in either the form of statewide at-large elections or separate multimember districts, were used by many states up until the 1840s (Congressional Quarterly, 1985, 678). Multimember districts, in the form of statewide at-large districts sometimes layered over individual districts, were traditional arrangements in Connecticut (ending in 1960), Hawaii (1968), New Mexico (1966), North Dakota (1960), Texas (1958), and Washington (1956) and were often used in other states before the 1950s to select representatives until redistricting plans could be worked out. At-large districts in states having two or more representatives were prohibited by federal statute in the late 1960s (Congressional Quarterly, 1985, 693).

The equal population characteristic of our electoral system was also not always the case. While the Constitution apportioned seats to the states according to their populations, it was silent on not only whether those seats had to be assigned to electoral districts (single or multimember) but, if districted, whether the population in the districts had to be equal. Substantial malapportionment was common through the 1960s. The Supreme Court declared malapportionment impermissible by extending the one-person, one-vote principle to congressional districting in their ruling in *Wesberry v. Sanders* in 1964 and reinforced this standard nearly 20 years later in their ruling in the case of *Karcher v. Daggett* (Congressional Quarterly, 1985, 696). While neither the single-member-district arrangement nor the equal-district-population rule were original to the American electoral system, they are now political ground rules that are firmly in place and serve as the first ingredient in the cheap-seats thesis.[14]

The second and third ingredients in the cheap-seats thesis are the characteristics of the Democratic and Republican coalitions and their relation to turnout. Compared to the Republican coalition, the Democratic coalition has consisted of sociodemographic groups that do not turn out at high rates. Democrats have been more likely to be on the lower rungs of the socioeconomic ladder and also are more likely to be from southern states (Axelrod, 1972; Stanley et al., 1986; Erikson et al., 1989). Less-educated and lower-income citizens, as well as southerners, are less likely to vote (Wolfinger and Rosenstone, 1980).

Most important from the standpoint of the cheap-seats thesis, the partisan characteristics associated with turnout are also associated with where people live and (because of the single-member-district system) where they vote. Poor and working-class citizens are likely to live in neighborhoods apart from middle- and upper-class citizens, who vote at higher rates. Neighborhoods are not perfectly homogeneous in terms of class, but most neighborhoods can be generally characterized as consisting of poor or working-class or middle-class or wealthy residents. In light of the proximity of residents with similar characteristics (education, income, and regional location) related to both turnout and partisanship, combined with the tradition of creating congressional districts with some geographic compactness and contiguity, as well as observing community boundaries (Butler and Cain, 1992, 65), it does not require intricate gerrymandering to produce an electoral bias.[15] Because the Democratic coalition contains low-turnout groups that are geographically concentrated, the equal population, single-member-district electoral system allows Democrats to win many low-turnout districts and thereby win more seats nationally than Republicans would have won with an equal number of votes.

The particular argument posed here to explain a pro-Democratic electoral system bias in modern American congressional elections is an application of a larger proposition about bias in single-member-district, plurality-rule electoral systems. A more generalized form of the electoral system bias proposition can be stated as: *single-member-district electoral systems apportioned by population are biased in favor of parties representing lower socioeconomic groups.*[16] The logic of this proposition is that lower socioeconomic groups turn out to vote at lower rates and that the single-member-district electoral system reduces the partisan impact of this low turnout by confining its implications within the districts.

A hypothetical case illustrates the point. Assume a homogeneous lower socioeconomic district and a homogeneous upper socioeconomic district (of equal size populations) in a party system based on a strong class cleavage. Further assume that voting-age citizens of the lower socioeconomic class turn out at significantly lower rates than do those who are better off. The electoral outcomes in these two districts will be one representative of the lower-class party and one representative of the upper-class party, regardless of the turnout in the two districts. Because of the district organization of the votes, the lower-socioeconomic-class party is not hurt at all by the low turnout of its adherents and the upper-socioeconomic-class party is not helped at all by the higher turnout of its supporters. All that matters to electing the two representatives is the vote division *within* each district rather than the actual number of total or pooled votes for each party.

The thesis can be stated in an even more general form: *any party whose adherents have characteristics associated with low turnout and are geographically concentrated by these characteristics will benefit from a districting system that reflects these geographic concentrations.*[17] As previously stated, the pertinent characteristics were socioeconomic, but the logic holds regardless of the particular characteristic associated with partisan voting, turnout, and geographic concentration. So long as district boundaries are drawn with respect for established communities, with concern for geographic compactness and contiguity, and without regard to normal turnout levels in the proposed districts, the single-member-district electoral system should favor the party with low-turnout characteristics that tend to be also concentrated geographically.[18] The party of low-turnout characteristics will be advantaged by winning the cheap seats.

From this discussion, it should be clear that the single-member-district electoral system is not inevitably biased in favor of the Democrats. It is the combination of factors linking a characteristic of potential voters, in this case socioeconomic status, to turnout and to partisanship, and the geographic concentration of that characteristic so that it is reflected in differences among districts, that makes a single-member-district electoral system biased. If socioeconomic status were uncorrelated with turnout, or with partisanship, or with housing patterns, or if districts were drawn in such a way that there were no aggregate socioeconomic differences among districts, then the single-member-district system would not generate electoral bias based on turnout differences.[19] However, the cheap-seats thesis claims that in modern American politics all of these necessary ingredients are present and, as a consequence, the single-member-district electoral system for the House is biased in favor of the Democratic Party.

❑ Overview ❑

The record of Democratic electoral success in the House from 1954 to 1992 is impressive. The four-decade-long Democratic majority was impressive, whether compared to the longevity of prior House majorities or to contemporary Democratic successes in other offices. The Democratic House majority over the 40 years preceding its collapse in 1994 was unprecedented historically, sizable by any standard, and resilient to a variety of countervailing conditions.

One perspective on the Democratic House majority set it in the context of the party's success in seeking other political offices over this era. Democrats were quite successful, pretty much across the board. They won a majority of elections for most offices throughout this period. From Senate seats to governorships to state senate and state house seats, Democrats usually won a majority of elections. The glaring exception to this Democratic ascendancy was the White House. In presidential elections, Republicans held their own with the Democrats. Some went so far as to claim that Republicans had an "electoral lock" on the White House. Barring unusual circumstances, such as the emergence of populist third-party candidates (such as Ross Perot) or scandals on the order of Watergate, Republicans seem to have had a clear edge in presidential elections (Will, 1988).

Less obvious, but more telling, was the variation in Democratic success below the presidential level. Democrats were most consistently successful in seeking offices that represented districts rather than entire states. The success of Democrats in state legislative elections comes close to matching their impressive record in House races. While very successful in Senate and gubernatorial elections, the Democratic record in these races falls short of the party's near perfect record of majorities in the House and state legislatures over the past 40 years. The pattern is telling. These comparisons provide a clue to determining why Democrats dominated the House of Representatives. There appears to be something about districted offices that helps the chances of Democrats being elected and hurts the prospects of Republican victories. This brings us to the third point of the chapter.

What is it about districted offices that helps Democrats? It may be that districting provides the party with an opportunity to win a number of cheap seats. Because of demographic links between partisanship, turnout, and district boundaries, Democrats regularly win many seats with relatively small numbers of votes, at bargain-basement prices (in terms of votes spent for a victory). Because of this, Democrats acquire more seats per vote than Republicans. Put differently, because of the system of congressional districts and the nature of the two parties' coalitions, the electoral system has been biased in favor of the Democrats. This thesis will be investigated at length in the following chapters. However, other explanations have also been offered for the Democratic dynasty, and we now turn to them.

3

□□□□□□□□□□□□□□□□□□□□□□□□□□□□□□□

Voters, Parties, and Candidates

How did Democrats dominate the House of Representatives for so many years? How did they preserve their majority through so many elections in an otherwise competitive two-party system? Party leaders had their ideas about this. As one might expect, Democrats and Republicans did not see eye to eye. Many Republicans thought that the system was rigged to give Democrats, especially Democratic incumbents, an advantage.[1] Through a combination of shameless partisan gerrymandering and the crafty exploitation of incumbency perquisites, including everything from pandering to constituents through pork-barrel politics to stuffing campaign coffers with PAC money to abusing the franking privilege by running permanent taxpayer-financed campaigns, Republicans figured Democrats overwhelmed and undermined the democratic electoral process. By whatever mix of shenanigans, Republicans figured that "the fix was in."

Democrats had a quite different interpretation. Many regarded their continuing majority as testimony to the Democratic Party's successful representation of the American public. Voters filled the House with Democrats election after election because Democrats were more sensitive to the concerns of the average voter. Republicans were responsive to the monied interests, the "fat cats," while Democrats responded to the needs of the average working guy, and this was reflected at the polls—at least as the Democrats saw it.

Like the debate among politicians, the explanations offered by political scholars who addressed the subject differ on one central question: Did the Democratic Party's extended control of the House reflect the will of the voters?[2] At one end of the spectrum are explanations that trace the

45

Democratic dynasty directly to the voters (recall figure 1.2). At the other end are claims that the Democratic majority was not so much a product of voters freely voting Democrats into office as a political system that made the survival of the Democratic majority all but inevitable. Still other theories occupy a middle ground, claiming that the Democratic majority was a result of both voters favoring Democrats and a political context that enhanced the prospects of a Democratic House.[3]

The *intentional explanations* for the era of Democratic dominance, the first set of theories, claim that the long tenure of the Democratic majority reflected the will of the voters working through the democratic process. A majority of voters, year in and year out, chose a majority of Democratic House candidates in fair and competitive elections. A number of reasons have been advanced to explain why voters sent Democrats to the House, but all boil down to this: Democrats controlled the House because the American voters wanted it that way. The Democratic House resulted from the democratic system working as intended.

Other theories claim quite the opposite, that the Democratic dynasty was the result of a breakdown in democracy. The Democratic majority was not in place so long because citizens wanted it that way but because the arrangements of the electoral system made it a foregone conclusion. The Democratic dynasty was an artifact of the electoral system and not a reflection of the public's will. At the most extreme is the claim that the electoral system was consciously rigged, through the gerrymandering of congressional district lines, to subvert the will of the people in order to keep Democrats in power. In a more charitable vein, the electoral system may have naturally worked to the advantage of a party under certain conditions and the Democratic Party just happened to have the necessary characteristics. The Democratic advantage may simply have been an unintended consequence of the electoral system. No rigging was required. From either perspective, these *institutional explanations* of the Democratic dynasty differ greatly from the intentional explanations. The Democrats were *not* an entrenched majority in the House because voters wanted it that way. Democrats controlled the House because the electoral system installed them in the majority, regardless of whether the electorate wanted them in control or not. In short, Democracy (as in, rule by the Democrats) was at the expense of democracy.

Who or what was responsible for the Democratic dynasty? The first set of theories says that the voters were responsible. The second claims that the political system was responsible. There are still other possible culprits or heroes (depending on your point of view). *Contextual explana-*

tions claim that characteristics of the candidates tilted the process toward the Democrats. Strictly speaking, the Democrats were in the majority because a majority of the electorate decided to vote for congressional Democrats, but these vote decisions were steered toward the Democrats. For instance, a voter may have to decide between an incumbent Democratic representative who has lavished government largess on constituents and an inexperienced Republican challenger running an underfunded campaign. If the voter opts to return the Democrat to office and thereby helps to renew the Democratic majority in the House, in one sense the Democratic majority is a product of the electorate's decision. But that is only part of the story. The voter, in this instance, has not been offered a full and fair choice between the parties. If the Republican candidate had enjoyed the same kind of government and campaign resources as the Democratic incumbent, if the campaign were conducted on a level playing field, perhaps voters would have decided differently.

While it is possible that a single explanation accounts for the sustained Democratic majority, it seems more likely that the Democratic dynasty was a result of a mix of several causes. There is no reason to assume that the Democrats attained their record by only one route or to think that the suggested causes are mutually exclusive. Although the principal point of this book is that there were substantial institutional reasons for the Democratic majority, it is also quite possible that there is merit also to the intentional and contextual explanations.

The purpose of this chapter is to examine these noninstitutional explanations. The intentional explanations trace the Democratic majority to a single source, the voters. Voters, according to this explanation, either simply wanted Democrats in office or were especially interested in having Democrats in Congress. The principal contextual explanation traces the Democratic majority to congressional candidates. According to this explanation, while the Democratic seat majority was based on its vote majority, that vote majority was not simply the expression of the free will of voters choosing between the parties' congressional candidates in a fair campaign. We turn first to the voters and the parties as possible contributors to the Democratic dynasty.

❑ Voters and Parties ❑

Although there is controversy about what sustained the Democratic majority, one central fact is indisputable: Democratic congressional candidates won a majority of votes cast in each congressional election from

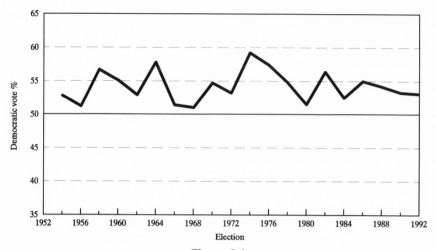

Figure 3.1
The Democratic Congressional Vote, 1954–1992

Note: The Democratic congressional vote is the percentage of the two-party vote. See the note to table 2.8

1954 to 1992. As Fiorina observed prior to the 1994 election, Republicans *"should not* win a majority of House seats because they do not receive a majority of House votes" (1992a, 16). The congressional two-party vote percentage cast for Democratic candidates in elections over this period is charted in figure 3.1. The Democratic congressional vote in elections during this period typically fluctuated around 54 percent and never dipped below 50 percent. There is little question that Democratic congressional voters were the foundation for the Democratic dynasty. However, the Democratic vote may not be the whole story behind the Democratic seat majority.

The Voice of the People

From one perspective, the consistent success of Democratic congressional candidates in winning the support of a majority of voters from 1954 to 1992 should not be surprising. Democrats consistently outnumbered Republicans among those identifying with a political party during this period. On average, Democratic Party identifiers constituted about 53 percent of the voting public (ranging from approximately 48 to 60 percent), while about 37 percent of voters identified with the Republicans (ranging from approximately 34 to 45 percent).[4] With professed Democrats outnumbering Republicans in each election (typically by almost a three-to-two margin), and with the inclination of partisans to support their own (even though defection rates have been higher among Democrats), a consistent Democratic majority in the congressional vote might well be expected.

This simple explanation of Democratic dominance, however, does not explain the disparity of Democratic success in seeking different offices. If the public was so generally disposed to support Democrats, why did Democrats not have the same lock on the White House and the Senate that they had on the House? Why did Democrats more consistently win a majority of votes in House races than for elections for other offices? One reason may be the composition of the parties' coalitions. The Democratic coalition may be better suited to running in local rather than national contests. Tensions exist within all coalitions, but they have traditionally been greater within the more diverse Democratic coalition than among Republicans.[5] Poking fun at the many divisions and routine turmoil within the Democratic Party, humorist Will Rogers said, "I belong to no organized political party—I am a Democrat" (Henning, 1992, 65). One persistent point of division within the Democratic coalition has been the inclusion of both generally liberal minority groups and generally conservative white southerners. Within congressional districts, however, this tension is often greatly reduced. In predominantly minority districts, Democratic candidates can tailor their appeals to the more liberal constituency. In predominantly white southern suburban districts, Democrats can stake out a more moderate or conservative stance. In seeking higher office with a broader constituency, the intraparty tensions are less often defined away by district lines. Appeals to one part of the Democratic constituency made in statewide or national races may cost candidates support from other constituencies within the party. These unavoidable tradeoffs in dealing with the Democratic coalition across district boundaries are likely to be more severe than those faced within less heterogeneous districts, an advantage for House Democratic candidates.[6]

It may also be the case that some voters have been more receptive to Democratic candidates for Congress than for other offices.[7] A number of reasons have been advanced for why a small but strategically important minority of voters split their tickets to vote for Democratic congressional candidates (Alesina and Rosenthal, 1989, 1995; Jacobson, 1990, chap. 6; Fiorina, 1992a, 64–82, 1992b, 1992c, 1994; Petrocik, 1991; and Ingberman and Villani, 1993). Some ticket splitters may be trying to obtain moderate policies in voting for Democratic congressional candidates and Republican presidential candidates. Barone and Ujifusa (1987) and Alesina and Rosenthal (1989, 1995) argue that these moderate split-ticket voters vote for congressional Democrats, who generally favor more liberal policies, to balance the more conservative inclinations of Republican presidential candidates. Others may vote with the intention of creating political gridlock. If voters distrust both political parties, they may want a Democratic Congress and a Republican president to keep each other in check (Fiorina, 1991). Jacobson (1990) offers a different motivation for split tickets, with the congressional vote going to the Democrat. He suggests that the basis of these votes lies in the mutually exclusive policy preferences by some voters and the policy stands of the parties. Voters want government officials to say yes to their special or local interests (more likely from Democrats), while at the same time saying no to the special interests of others (more likely from Republicans).[8] Congressional representation focuses on local interests, where voters want more government largess. This is right up the Democratic alley. Presidential politics, on the other hand, tends to focus on broader interests, where voters often want more government restraint. This is better turf for Republicans (Petrocik, 1991). Other factors might also come into play that would help to explain why Democratic congressional candidates as a group have fared so well, but the basic fact is that, for the 40-year period from 1954 to 1994, they consistently fared well at the polls.[9]

After reviewing the partisan congressional vote history, one might be tempted to say that the puzzle of the sustained Democratic congressional majority is no puzzle at all. Democrats won a majority of seats year in and year out because they won a majority of votes year in and year out. Thus, the Democratic majority in the House reflected the will of the people. It is as simple as that. What is the mystery?

A Desired Dynasty?

There are a couple of catches to the argument that the Democratic majority simply reflected the desires of the electorate. First, a majority vote for Democratic candidates does not necessarily indicate that a majority freely favored a Democratic majority in the House over a Republican majority. Democrats may have won a majority of votes because of votes influenced by reasons other than those involved in offering a fair choice between the parties. Democratic candidates may have received many votes for reasons entirely unrelated to the character, perspectives, and quality of its candi-

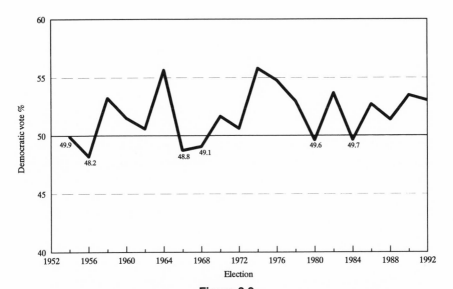

Figure 3.2
The Democratic Congressional Vote in Contested Districts, 1954–1992

Note: The Democratic congressional vote is the percentage of the two-party vote in districts with candidates of both major parties.

dates relative to Republican opponents. Most obviously, in light of the fact that there have been more Democratic than Republican incumbents, the benefits of incumbency may have provided an extra push in the Democratic direction for a critical number of voters (again, recall figure 1.2). In addition, the greater number of uncontested Democratic candidates, restricting voter options to a Democratic vote or abstention, may have helped to produce Democratic majorities by default rather than by voter choice. The Democratic congressional vote in contested districts suggests that the total Democratic vote (in figure 3.1) may have exaggerated Democratic popularity. In districts in which voters had a choice between a Democrat and a Republican, Republicans received a majority of the vote in six elections from 1954 to 1992 (1954, 1956, 1966, 1968, 1980, and 1984). Figure 3.2 presents the Democratic House vote in contested districts. While there is certainly selection bias in examining just contested seats (Republicans being highly unlikely to do very well in the seats that they left uncontested to Democrats, thus inflating the Republican vote percentage), national Democratic vote majorities appear to be inflated by the absence of Republican candidates on the ballots in many districts.

Second, on close inspection, the history of the Democrats' popular support is less overwhelming than it first appears. Although Democrats outnumbered Republicans, Democratic Party identification often hovered at just over half of the electorate. In several elections in the 1980s, Democratic partisanship dropped below 50 percent.[10] This sometimes marginal majority, combined with the greater defection rates of Democratic identifiers and the fact that Democratic candidates have not been quite as successful in other offices (especially the presidency), should temper claims that the continuity of the Democratic House majority rested on public support alone.

A closer inspection of the Democratic congressional vote also suggests that reasons other than the electorate's support for the Democratic Party may have contributed to the party's success in the House. Although it is true that the Democrats won a majority of congressional votes, as well as seats, in each election from 1954 to 1992, their national vote margin was occasionally quite narrow. In 4 of the 20 elections in this period, Democrats received 51.5 percent or less of the national vote. The narrowest Democratic congressional vote majority was in 1968, an election in which Democrats received 51 percent of the vote. Democratic congressional vote majorities were also slim in 1956 (51.2 percent), 1966 (51.4 percent), and 1980 (51.5 percent). In another three elections, the Democratic vote majority was under 53 percent. These modest Democratic vote majorities were in the 1954 (52.8 percent), 1962 (52.9 percent), and 1984 (52.5 percent) elections. In light of the narrow Democratic popular-vote victories in 7 of the 20 elections, it is quite possible that any number of elements in these elections, when combined with a strong base of Democratic partisanship, may have made the difference between a Republican or a Democratic popular-vote majority. As we shall see shortly, the Democratic Party enjoyed several advantages that might have been sufficient to maintain a Democratic House majority in these close elections.

Finally, in examining the narrow Democratic popular-vote majorities, it is difficult to imagine that Democrats would not have maintained a majority of seats even if their vote share had dropped below 50 percent. For instance, Democrats in 1968 won a bare majority of votes (51 percent), but quite a healthy majority of seats (55.9 percent). Would the Democrats have lost 5.9 percent of seats in the House (about 26 seats) if they had lost just 1 percent of the vote? Very unlikely. Democrats maintained sizable seat majorities following several other elections (1962, 1966, 1980, and 1984) in which their popular-vote majorities were modest to narrow. Everyone would admit that the single-member-district sys-

Table 3.1

The Expected Democratic Seat Percentages and the Necessary Swing Ratio
to Obtain the Observed Democratic Seat Percentages in Five Elections

| Election | Vote | Democratic Percentage | | | Swing Ratio Necessary to Obtain Observed Seat Percentage |
| | | Seats | | | |
		Actual	Expected	Difference	
1962	52.9	59.4	55.8	+3.6	3.2
1966	51.4	57.0	52.1	+4.9	5.0
1968	51.0	55.9	51.5	+4.4	5.9
1980	51.5	55.9	52.3	+3.6	3.9
1984	52.5	58.2	53.8	+4.4	3.2

Note: Expected seat percentages assume no partisan bias and are based on Jacobson's estimates of the conversion rate of votes to seats, or the swing ratio (1990). Jacobson's estimate of the swing ratio (or responsiveness) from 1946 to 1964, using the national vote division, is approximately 2. This indicates that a party should expect to gain about 2 percent of seats for every additional 1 percent of the vote it receives (1990, table 5.5). After 1964, the swing ratio dropped to approximately 1.5. The necessary swing ratio assumes no partisan bias and is computed by subtracting 50 percent from both the actual percentage of seats and votes and then taking the ratio. For example, in 1962 assuming no bias (a party would win 50 percent of the seats with 50 percent of the vote), Democrats won 59.4 percent of the seats with 52.9 percent of the vote. Since the swing ratio is the ratio of seat change to vote change, the swing ratio in this case is 3.2 ((59.4 − 50)/(52.9 − 50) = 3.24).

tem exaggerates majorities, or causes the minority vote party to waste a greater portion of its votes in losing causes. However, the Democratic Party's share of seats in these cases was much greater than what we would expect from only the magnification of majorities by the responsiveness of the single-member-district system. The normal amplification of the vote majorities would have produced much smaller seat majorities than what we actually observed. With vote percentages in the 51-to-53 percent range, Democrats should have won seats in the 52-to-56 percent range (226 to 244 seats)—not in the 56-to-59 percent range (a 13-to-17 seat difference). The expected seat percentages in these five elections, computed from the actual vote and Jacobson's estimates of the magnification factor or swing ratio (1990, 86), are presented in table 3.1. The table also presents the swing ratio that would have been necessary to produce the observed seat percentages (supposing an unbiased electoral system).[11]

On the basis of the observed vote and existing swing-ratio estimates, it appears that the Democrats won about 3.6 percent to 4.4 percent more seats in these five elections than one would have expected based on the normal amplification of a vote majority. This suggests that Democrats would have won a majority of seats in each of these elections even if they had failed to obtain a majority of the popular vote.[12] The size of the "necessary swing ratios" to obtain the actual percentage of seats also raises doubts about the neutrality of the House electoral system. Whereas Jacobson estimates the pre-1966 swing ratio at about 2 percent of seats for every additional percentage of the vote and about 1.5 after 1964, the swing ratios that would have been necessary to obtain the Democratic seat shares in the five elections in table 3.1 were well over 3. In two years, the "necessary swing ratios" were equal to or greater than 5, more than three times larger than the estimated swing ratio! These unrealistic swing ratios suggest only one thing: *the premise on which these swing ratios were calculated, that the electoral system was neutral, is wrong.*

While congressional Democrats undoubtedly received a great deal of public support over the last 40 years, the continuity of the Democratic majority was based on more than votes alone. True, during this period Democrats won a majority of votes in each election, albeit a narrow majority in several. However, these vote majorities do not necessarily mean that Democratic majorities survived because the voters wanted it that way. A number of factors having little to do with voter judgments about the parties' relative governing capacities may have thrown enough votes to Democratic candidates to assemble a Democratic vote majority. Moreover, Democrats probably would have won a majority of seats in at least 5 of the 20 elections from 1954 to 1992, even if they had fallen short of a popular-vote majority. Democratic votes, cast for whatever reasons, may have been *sufficient* for the preservation of the Democratic House majority, but they may not have been *necessary* to its survival.

❏ The Candidates ❏

The theory that the Democratic dynasty in the House was simply the product of the intentions of a majority of voters who wanted Democrats to represent them in Congress is open to challenge on a number of grounds. As already noted, Democrats most likely would have won a majority of seats even without a majority of votes. In addition, Democratic vote majorities did not necessarily mean that a majority of voters wanted to be represented by Democrats. The link between the vote and the intentions of voters involves several assumptions about the choices offered to voters.

In this section, we turn to two candidate-related factors that boosted the number of votes that congressional Democrats received—incumbency and uncontested districts.[13] While both incumbency and the lack of opposition in a district can be traced to past votes and anticipation of future votes in a district, both bestow on a party's candidate additional or bonus votes that have little to do with any preference that these voters might have for Democratic rather than Republican candidates. To the extent that the Democratic majority rests on these votes, it reflects more about the political system than the free will of the voters.

Incumbency attracts votes. As a rule, congressional candidates can expect to receive additional votes when they are incumbents.[14] Some voters are drawn to the incumbent, regardless of party, through a variety of reasons associated with the advantages of incumbency. Incumbents tend to be better known, better positioned to take credit for government programs, and better financed to run campaigns than their challengers. Others vote for the incumbent simply out of inertia, giving the current occupant the benefit of any minor doubt. These advantages translate into votes. Because there were more Democratic than Republican incumbents, some portion of the Democratic vote majority was a product of votes cast because of incumbency. These votes attracted by incumbency are votes that would have been cast for incumbents of either party. To the extent that the Democratic vote majority has been based on votes generated by incumbency, it undermines the idea that the party's seat majority simply reflects the free will of the electorate expressed through a fair and unbiased electoral process.

Congressional Democrats also received a number of votes by default. In uncontested districts voters can only choose to vote for the sole available congressional candidate or abstain from voting for that office. What do votes for these unchallenged congressional candidates reveal about the preferences of voters? It is hard to argue that these votes necessarily indicate a preference for representation of the party posting a candidate. Because a majority, sometimes an overwhelming majority, of uncontested districts in elections between 1954 and 1992 involved Democratic congressional candidates without Republican opposition, Democrats nationally enjoyed an advantage over Republicans. As in the case of incumbency-based votes, to the extent that the Democratic vote majority is based on votes that it received by default, the vote cannot be read simply as having reflected voter sentiment for representation by Democrats.

The Democratic Advantage in Incumbency

Given the advantages of incumbents and the propensity of voters to vote for incumbents, even from the opposing party, it is clear that the party with more incumbent candidates has an advantage over the opposing party. The aggregate of the incumbency advantages of individual candidates should show up in national vote totals. Since more Democratic candidates than Republican candidates have enjoyed incumbency status, the national Democratic congressional vote totals have been inflated over what the vote they would have been without the incumbency boost. In this section we examine the extent of the Democratic incumbency advantage. After we also examine the advantage Democrats had enjoyed in uncontested seats, we will determine the extent to which this dual candidate advantage (incumbency and uncontested seats) was responsible for sustaining the party's dynasty.[15]

The Democratic incumbency advantage from 1954 to 1992 rested on two indisputable facts: *(1) more incumbents seeking reelection were Democrats than Republicans, and (2) incumbency itself is generally worth votes, regardless of the incumbent's party.*[16] Not only were more Democratic candidates incumbents because more incumbents are Democrats, but in every election from 1954 to 1992, Democratic incumbents were more likely to run for reelection than Republican incumbents (Gilmour and Rothstein, 1993, 348–49).[17] In view of these two facts, there is no doubt that some portion of the Democratic vote and seat majorities were a result of incumbency. The only real question is how much of the Democratic vote was based on the party's incumbency advantage. Was the dynasty preserved because of incumbency? Put differently, how many votes did the Democratic Party receive because of its incumbency advantage and how many votes would it have received if it did not enjoy this advantage?

Table 3.2 presents the number of Democratic and Republican incumbents running for reelection from 1954 to 1992. As expected, throughout this period a majority of incumbents running in each election (with the single exception of 1954) were Democrats. Moreover, much as you would expect, given their substantial seat majorities, the Democratic lead in incumbents running in the general election was also usually substantial. In this period, there were typically anywhere from 70 to 90 more Democratic incumbents running than Republican incumbents. Rarely

Table 3.2

The Incumbency Advantage as a Democratic Party Advantage, 1954–1992

Election Year	Democratic Incumbents Running	Republican Incumbents Running	Net Democratic Incumbent Seat Advantage
1954	196	205	−9
1956	218	186	+32
1958	219	168	+51
1960	267	135	+132
1962	238	151	+87
1964	231	160	+71
1966	275	130	+145
1968	230	175	+55
1970	221	170	+51
1972	221	154	+67
1974	220	163	+57
1976	252	128	+124
1978	249	128	+121
1980	248	143	+105
1982	215	168	+47
1984	254	154	+100
1986	232	159	+73
1988	245	163	+82
1990	247	158	+89
1992	211	136	+75
1994	225	157	+68

Source: Gary Jacobson supplied data up to 1992. The 1994 data were calculated from *Congressional Quarterly* (22 October 1994). The numbers include incumbents running against other incumbents. This occurred in 3 cases in 1952, 7 in 1962, 1 in 1966, 4 in 1968, 1 in 1970, 2 in 1972, 6 in 1980, and 5 in 1992.

did the Democratic incumbency advantage slip below 50 incumbents, and on several occasions there were over 100 more Democratic than Republican incumbents seeking reelection. As long as incumbency is worth something, and there is a good deal of research to indicate it is of substantial value, the national Democratic vote must have been boosted by the fact that more of its candidates ran as incumbents.[18]

The Democratic Uncontested-Seat Advantage

In addition to the incumbency advantage, Democrats enjoyed an advantage over Republicans in the number of seats that were won by default. Like the incumbency advantage, the uncontested-seat advantage boosted the national Democratic congressional vote above what it would have been if it had reflected the will of the voters choosing between Democratic and Republican representation. Of course, districts are usually uncontested for a reason; the prospects for a successful challenge is so remote that prospective challengers are discouraged from making a futile run. Nevertheless, even if a challenge were futile, it is safe to say that some citizens who happen to reside in uncontested Democratic districts would vote for a Republican congressional candidate if that option were available. It is probably also safe to say that, while some of these would-be Republican congressional voters simply do not vote, at least at the congressional level, others cast a meaningless vote for the lone candidate on the ballot. Thus, if uncontested seats boost a party's vote totals above what voters would have given the party if they had a choice between the parties and if Democrats had more uncontested districts than Republicans, then some portion of the Democratic vote merely reflected the lack of a choice presented to voters rather than the choice of the voters. How large was the Democratic uncontested-seat advantage, and how much did this advantage contribute to the Democratic vote?

The number of uncontested seats for each party in elections from 1954 to 1992 is presented in table 3.3. As the table indicates, Democrats held a consistent edge over Republicans in uncontested seats. The median Democratic advantage was 40 seats, though unopposed Democrats outnumbered unopposed Republicans by more than 60 in several elections. In recent years, the Democratic uncontested-seat advantage declined and, as we will see in chapter 7, Republicans in 1994 actually had an uncontested-seat advantage over Democrats. However, throughout the era of continuous Democratic control of the House, Democrats were well on their way to a seat majority before a single ballot had been cast and some votes added to the Democratic totals by default rather than by choice. The question is how many?

The Democratic Candidate Advantage

Two factors enter into calculating the vote boost that Democrats received from their candidate advantage: (1) the number of seats in which each of

Table 3.3
Uncontested Congressional Districts, by Political Party, 1954–1992

Election Year	Total Uncontested Congressional Districts (Percentage)	Unopposed Party		Democratic Uncontested Net Seat Advantage
		Democrats	Republicans	
1954	86 (20)	84	2	+82
1956	72 (17)	69	3	+66
1958	97 (22)	96	1	+95
1960	79 (18)	76	3	+73
1962	51 (12)	50	1	+49
1964	42 (10)	41	1	+40
1966	57 (13)	53	4	+49
1968	48 (11)	41	7	+34
1970	63 (14)	58	5	+63
1972	54 (12)	46	8	+38
1974	60 (14)	58	2	+56
1976	52 (12)	46	6	+40
1978	70 (16)	51	19	+32
1980	56 (13)	41	15	+26
1982	58 (13)	47	11	+36
1984	68 (16)	54	14	+40
1986	74 (17)	56	18	+38
1988	81 (19)	61	20	+41
1990	84 (19)	48	36	+12
1992	31 (7)	18	13	+5
1994	52 (12)	16	35	−19

Source: Calculated from Congressional Quarterly's *Guide to U.S. Elections,* 2d ed. (1985), and *Congressional Quarterly Weekly Reports* for 1988, 1990, and 1992. The percentages are of all districts that were uncontested.

the parties had a candidate advantage (uncontested seats or incumbents) and (2) the percentage of votes that a party could typically expect because of a candidate advantage, the vote value to a party of an individual district being uncontested or defended by an incumbent. Using these two quantities, we can calculate the extent to which Democratic vote has been boosted by the party's candidate advantages. The benefit to the party is the product of the individual vote value of an advantage and the number of districts in which they have that advantage.

We address first the number of districts in which Democrats and Republicans had candidate advantages that could have affected the district's vote. The numbers of uncontested and incumbent districts (tables 3.2 and 3.3), however, require some adjustment before calculating the impact of the candidate advantage. The two advantages often overlap in the same districts. The single candidate in uncontested districts is usually an incumbent. Thus, the count of the uncontested-seat and incumbency advantages should be combined in order to avoid double counting.[19] If the unopposed candidate and incumbency advantages were analyzed separately, we would exaggerate the total vote inflation from a party's candidate advantage. A party gets a boost for every uncontested district and for every incumbent running in a contested district, but it is unrealistic to assume that a party would gain an additional boost if one of its unopposed candidates also happened to be an incumbent. In order to examine the total candidate advantage of the Democratic Party simultaneously, we combine the two types of advantages to indicate the Democratic advantage in uncontested seats and the additional Democratic advantage of incumbency in contested seats.

Table 3.4 presents the number of unopposed candidates for each party (the same as in table 3.3) and the number of incumbents in each district who ran in contested districts. Observe that the Democratic Party consistently enjoyed an advantage in uncontested seats and since 1960 also enjoyed advantage of more incumbents in contested seats (with only one minor exception, 1974). In assessing the impact of these candidate advantages on the parties' vote, it is reasonable to assume that each uncontested seat has more of an impact than each contested incumbent seat; since with only one candidate on the ticket, voters are forced to vote for one party's candidate if they are to vote at all. The question that we must now address is how many votes does each of these candidate advantages mean to the parties' total votes? Are the candidate advantages enough to make it appear that a majority of voters wanted Democratic candidates when really they either were steered that way by incumbency or were offered no alternative to the Democratic candidate?

What difference does the lack of an opponent mean to the vote in an uncontested district? How many votes does a party forgo in leaving an opposing candidate unchallenged? Put differently, if a seat that had been uncontested instead was contested by two major-party candidates, how would the vote have changed? Certainly there would be many differences from one previously uncontested seat to another, but we would expect that turnout in the typical district would increase and that the number of votes for the party that had left the seat unopposed would increase considerably.[20] There is no expectation that the party that had left the

Table 3.4
The Democratic Candidate Advantage, 1954–1992

Election Year	Unopposed Candidates: Incumbents and Open Seats			Contested Incumbents		
	Dem.	Rep.	Net Seat Advantage	Dem.	Rep.	Net Seat Advantage
1954	84	2	+82	119	202	−83
1956	69	3	+66	153	183	−30
1958	96	1	+95	127	167	−40
1960	76	3	+73	194	130	+64
1962	50	1	+49	180	150	+30
1964	41	1	+40	191	159	+32
1966	53	4	+49	224	126	+98
1968	41	7	+34	192	167	+25
1970	58	5	+63	166	165	+1
1972	46	8	+38	179	146	+33
1974	58	2	+56	161	162	−1
1976	46	6	+40	210	122	+88
1978	51	19	+32	205	109	+96
1980	41	15	+26	212	128	+84
1982	47	11	+36	170	158	+12
1984	54	14	+40	201	140	+61
1986	56	18	+38	178	142	+36
1988	61	20	+41	185	144	+41
1990	48	36	+12	199	122	+77
1992	18	13	+5	196	125	+71

Note: A positive net seat advantage indicates an advantage for the Democrats. The number of unopposed candidates are from table 3.3. The number of contested incumbents are calculated from the total number of incumbents (in table 3.2) and the number of unopposed incumbents. The number of unopposed incumbents were provided by Gary Jacobson (personal correspondence, 5 April 1993).

seat uncontested would be competitive by offering a candidate, but by running a respectable candidate, someone who would do little personally either to attract or repel voters, the party should draw a significant number of votes. Just how many is difficult to say. However, it is probably safe to say that it would be roughly similar to the number of votes received by the lower tier of losing candidates. A cautious, yet realistic, estimate is that these candidates would, on average, receive about 20 percent of the vote.

One method of assessing the impact of uncontested seats is to examine the district vote before and after the seat was uncontested. With respect to unopposed incumbents who constitute most of the unopposed candidates, Jacobson (1993) recently noted that, "In elections from 1946 to 1990, the mean vote for incumbents in the current election who had been opposed in the previous election was 70.6 percent, while the mean vote for incumbents in the previous election who were unopposed in the current election average had been 71.2 percent. These figures are downwardly biased, of course—incumbents should attract opponents more frequently when their anticipated support is lower—but surely not enough to make 100 percent a plausible assumption" (50). This suggests that a party may forgo, on average, almost 30 percent of the vote by leaving the opposition party unchallenged. However, given Jacobson's caveat that this 30 percent figure likely overestimates the impact of the uncontested circumstance, since challengers are more likely to appear when a candidate is more vulnerable (e.g., postredistricting), and the fact that a number of districts are uncontested over several elections, we will place a slightly reduced vote value of the uncontested-seat advantage. We assume that a party, on average, would receive about 23 percent of the vote by posting a candidate in a district that otherwise would have been left uncontested.[21]

As we estimate it, the entire vote that a party would receive by contesting a currently uncontested seat is from an increase in turnout in the district rather than at the expense of the other party. This assumption is based on observed drop-off rates between contested and uncontested districts in presidential election years and a set of assumptions about the distribution of a district's vote in the uncontested and contested situations. First, on the basis of an examination of turnout drop off in on-year elections between presidential and congressional voting, turnout increases by about 30 percent when a district is contested. In presidential election years from 1956 to 1988, the mean turnout drop off in uncontested districts between presidential and congressional voting was about 27 percent. On the basis of the national data for presidential and congressional turnout, drop off in contested districts would appear to be approximately four percent. The net drop-off difference in uncontested seats is then 23 percent, indicating that the uncontested status of the district depresses turnout by 23 percent. Reorienting this to the gain produced by changing a district from the uncontested to the contested status amounts to a 30 percent boost. That is, a 23 percent turnout decline in changing from a contested to an uncontested seat is equivalent to a 30 percent turnout increase in changing from an uncontested to a contested seat. Second, the analysis also assumes a rough equivalence between the vote a party won by default when its seat was uncontested and the additional votes it would gain by increased turnout when the other party mounted a challenge. In an uncontested seat, a party will receive some votes that would have gone to the opposition if that option were available on the ballot to these voters. If the seat were contested, the party would lose these votes. On the other hand, in an uncontested seat, a party fails to receive some votes because the lack of a contest keeps some voters home. If the seat were contested, the party would gain these votes. We assume that these two votes are roughly equivalent.[22]

There are many estimates of the vote value of incumbency and its increase in recent years (see Erikson, 1971, 1972; Cover, 1977; Cover and Mayhew, 1981; Born, 1979; Payne, 1980; Collie, 1981; Alford and Hibbing, 1981; Garand and Gross, 1984; Alford and Brady, 1993; Gelman and King, 1990; and Krashinsky and Milne, 1993). Initial estimates of the vote value of incumbency were based on vote changes between elections. These studies examined both the district vote for a candidate before and after he or she was an incumbent (the sophomore surge) and a party's vote in a district before and after an incumbent voluntarily leaves the seat (the retirement slump). With respect to the apparent effect of incumbency when an incumbent first runs for reelection (the sophomore surge), Cover and Mayhew (1981) found that incumbency increased the vote by 2.3 percentage points in elections from 1962 to 1966 and 6.8 in elections from 1968 to 1978. When the advantage of incumbency was lost to a party, it typically experienced a vote loss similar in magnitude to its vote gain after its candidate ran as an incumbent. Following an incumbent's retirement, the party's vote typically slumped by 2.5 percentage points in elections from 1962 to 1966 and by 7.8 percentage points in elections from 1968 to 1978 (Cover and Mayhew, 1981; Jacobson, 1992, 29).

A more sophisticated analysis of the incumbency advantage conducted by (Levitt and Wolfram, 1996) has produced similar estimates. By their estimation, incumbency was worth 3.4 percentage points of the vote in contested elections from 1948 to 1958, 4 percentage points from 1960 through 1968, 6.8 percentage points from 1970 through 1978, and 8 percentage points from 1980 through 1990.[23] Rather than reinventing the wheel, we will use these estimates of the vote value of incumbency to determine how much the Democratic Party's advantage of having more incumbents has inflated the Democratic congressional vote.

Having the number of uncontested and contested incumbent seats for both parties established, as well as the vote value of these two candidate

Table 3.5
The Democratic House Vote and the Simulated Vote, Removing the
Incumbency and Uncontested Seat Advantages, 1954–1992

	Democratic House Vote Percentage		
Election	Actual	Without Candidate Advantages	Difference
1954	52.8	51.6	−1.2
1956	51.2	50.2	−1.1
1958	56.7	54.3	−2.4
1960	55.1	52.7	−2.4
1962	52.9	51.5	−1.4
1964	57.7	56.5	−1.3
1966	51.4	**49.2**	−2.2
1968	51.0	50.0	−.9
1970	54.7	53.6	−1.1
1972	53.2	51.8	−1.3
1974	59.2	57.7	−1.5
1976	57.4	55.0	−2.4
1978	54.8	52.6	−2.2
1980	51.5	**49.7**	−1.8
1982	56.4	55.3	−1.1
1984	52.5	50.5	−2.1
1986	55.0	53.3	−1.6
1988	54.2	52.6	−1.6
1990	53.3	51.9	−1.5
1992	53.1	51.7	−1.4
Mean	54.2	52.6	−1.6

Note: The elections in which the Democratic Party's vote percentage would have slipped below a majority without the party's candidate advantages are indicated in boldface.

advantages, we can now determine their aggregate impact on the congressional vote. Has the Democratic Party received a majority of the congressional vote because their candidates have enjoyed the advantages of more often running unopposed or with the privileges of incumbency?

The effects of candidate advantages for each party are presented in table 3.5. The table presents the division of the two-party vote with and without these advantages. The aggregate vote effect of incumbency and uncontested seats for each party was calculated as the product of three values. The first is the estimated vote percentage advantage for each type of advantage (e.g., in the 1950s incumbency was worth 3.4 percent of the vote in a contested district). The second value is the mean number of votes cast in districts won by each party. The product of these values is the number of votes attracted to a party because of a candidate advantage in one of its typical districts. For example, for Democrats in 1956, incumbency was worth about 3.4 percent of the vote in each district. Since there were about 135,030 votes cast in the average contested district won by a Democrat that year, a 3.4 percent boost amounts to about 4,591 extra votes for each Democratic incumbent. To determine the aggregate effect, this must be multiplied by the number of districts in which the party enjoyed this advantage (see table 3.4). Since there were 153 Democratic incumbents running in the 1956 election, the Democrats attracted about 702,423 additional votes because of incumbency (153 x 4,591). Of course, Democrats also received additional votes because of incumbency, and these must also be taken into account.

Once the aggregate votes associated with the parties' candidate advantages were calculated, they were applied to the total national vote to determine the total vote that the parties would have received had neither party enjoyed these advantages.[24] The adjustment amounts to a simulation of the national vote if all seats were contested and neither party had a net incumbency advantage over the other. In calculating the total vote without these advantages, the votes a party attracted because of incumbent advantages are subtracted from its total vote and added to the opposing party's total vote. The votes attributable to uncontested seats are simply added to the opposing party's total vote, since the vote boost associated with contesting the seat, as noted above, comes to a party in the increased turnout in a district. The figures and calculations involved in this simulation are presented in appendix A.

As the figures in table 3.5 indicate, candidate advantages consistently benefited the Democrats in House elections. Typically, their incumbency and uncontested-seat advantages added about 1.5 percentage points to the Democratic national vote. The net effects of these advantages ranged from a pro-Democratic benefit of slightly less than 1 to 2.5 percentage points. Even though this might appear to be a small effect, *candidate advantages were apparently large enough to determine which party received the majority of congressional votes in two elections, 1966 and 1980.* In both cases, Democrats received a majority of the two-party congressional vote because many of their candidates in contested districts were incumbents and many others won election without opposition. The analysis suggests that without these benefits Republicans would have won narrow vote majorities in both years. Moreover, in other elections, the Democratic vote majority would have been reduced considerably had they not enjoyed these candidate advantages. The Democratic share of the national two-party vote would have dropped to 52 percent of the vote or less in fully half of the elections since 1954 without the aid of incumbency and the absence of Republican challengers in many districts.[25]

Returning to the main point, this analysis of the parties' candidate advantages suggests that the Democratic lock on a majority in the House was not simply a function of voters freely choosing representation by Democrats in open contests on a level playing field. Although it is indisputably true that Democrats won a majority of the congressional vote in each election from 1954 to 1992, it is also true that these majorities were consistently padded by the presence of a greater number of Democratic incumbents and the absence of Republican challengers in many districts. In at least two cases (1966 and 1980), these Democratic candidate advantages were apparently enough to provide Democrats with vote majorities that they otherwise might not have won.

❏ Overview ❏

Two different explanations of the Democratic dynasty were examined in this chapter. The first claims that Democrats maintained their House majority because voters wanted it that way. That is, the Democratic House majority was a result of voters freely expressing a preference for representation by Democrats rather than by Republicans. There is certainly some evidence for this. Democratic congressional candidates won a majority of the vote in each election from 1954 to 1992. However, in several elections these vote majorities were quite small, and a majority vote does not necessarily indicate that voters freely chose Democrats. If voters have no choice, as is the situation in uncontested districts, or if a party receives a sizable vote simply because more of its candidates enjoy the advantages of incumbency, the party's vote majority may not reflect the support of the voters for that party's candidates.

This raises a second explanation for the Democratic dynasty. Some speculate that the Democrats won a majority of seats because more Democratic candidates ran without Republican opposition and more ran as incumbents, with all the advantages of holding office. The analysis indicated that there is something to this explanation as well. Regardless of party, running without opposition or running as an incumbent typically attracts additional votes. Democrats consistently had more candidates running unopposed than Republicans, and, with only a couple of exceptions, Democrats also had more incumbents running in contested districts than did Republicans. On the basis of the analysis, these Democratic-candidate advantages were responsible for anywhere from 1 to 2.5 percentage points of the national Democratic presidential vote, enough that they probably were responsible for Democratic vote majorities in 1966 and 1980.

The analysis also suggests the plausibility of a third explanation of the Democratic dynasty, that the electoral system has been biased in favor of the Democratic Party. An examination of the five elections in which Democrats won narrow vote majorities reveals that their seat majorities remained substantial. Some discrepancy between seat and vote majorities can be expected because of the responsiveness of the single-member-district plurality-rule system. However, in these several close elections, Democrats won seat majorities far in excess of what could be expected from the responsiveness (or swing ratio) of the electoral system alone. In at least these five elections, a quarter of the congressional elections held between 1954 and 1992, the Democratic majority vote, however motivated, was not required for Democrats to win a majority of seats. Moreover, Republicans were denied a majority of contested seats in four of the six post-1954 elections in which they received a majority of the vote in contested districts (1966, 1968, 1980, and 1984). The Democratic share

Table 3.6

Four Elections in Which Democrats Won a Majority of Seats
with a Minority of the Vote in Contested Districts

	Contested Districts	
Election	Democratic Vote Percentage	Democratic Seat Percentage
1966	48.76	51.07
1968	49.09	51.95
1980	49.64	53.32
1984	49.66	53.95

Source: Computed from district returns as reported in Congressional Quarterly's *Guide to U.S. Elections,* 2d ed. (1985).

of votes and seats in contested districts in these four elections is presented in table 3.6. This suggests the possibility of partisan bias in the electoral system.

We next turn to the issue of partisan bias. Has the electoral system been biased in favor of the Democratic Party? How has partisan bias been measured and what has prior research found? Did bias in the electoral system help to preserve the Democratic majority in the House for 40 years?

4

□□□□□□□□□□□□□□□□□□□□□□□□□□□□□□

Bias in the Electoral System

The cheap-seats thesis claims that the translation of votes into House seats has favored the Democratic Party and that this bias was important to the Democratic House majority. Was the electoral system biased? Did it favor Democrats? If so, by how much? Did it make the difference between a Democratic and a Republican majority in the House? This chapter lays the foundation for addressing these questions.[1]

The foundation consists of three matters regarding partisan bias in the electoral system—its definition and measurement, previous findings of electoral system bias, and the proposal of an alternative measure of bias. We first return to the issues of the conceptualization and operationalization of bias, matters addressed in a preliminary way in chapter 2. What does partisan bias mean, and how is it measured? After defining terms and evaluating the different approaches to its estimation, the current state of research on bias in the House electoral system is reviewed. Research on bias in the House electoral system has failed to reach consensus. Some find a Democratic electoral system, others a Republican system. What is the basis for these conflicting findings and which should we believe? The answer lies, I will argue, in the use of two different measures of the congressional vote in estimating bias. One measure is appropriate, while the other produces faulty estimates. Finally, on the basis of a theoretical model of partisan bias, an alternative measure that avoids several problems found in previous measures is developed.

But first things first. Before offering a critique of the literature and proposing an alternative measure of bias, a few basics should be pinned down. What do we mean by partisan bias in an electoral system, and how has past research measured it?

Table 4.1

Hypothetical Examples of Electoral Systems with and without Partisan Bias

Electoral System Case	Democratic Party (%)		Republican Party (%)		Partisan Bias
	Votes	Seats	Votes	Seats	
A	50	50	50	50	None
B	60	75	60	75	None
C	60	75	60	60	Democratic
D	20	15	20	10	Democratic
E	80	100	80	90	Democratic

Note: The examples do not assume that the two parties receive their votes in the same election year. Obviously, in cases A, C, and E, they could not, since the vote totals would exceed 100 percent. The examples assume either that the electoral system translating one party's votes into seats in one election year is the same electoral system responsible for translating the other party's votes into seats at a later election or that the treatment of the parties could be deduced from simulated votes (the hypothetical, or Butler, method).

❑   The Concept and Measurement of Partisan Bias   ❑

As conventionally defined and as used here, *partisan bias in an electoral system is the difference between the proportion of seats that the political parties would be awarded if they were to receive identical shares of the national vote* (see Niemi and Deegan, 1978; and Grofman, 1983). In an unbiased electoral system, there is no difference. If Democrats win Y percent of seats with X percent of the vote, Republicans would also win Y percent of the seats with the same X percent of the votes. A few examples, presented in table 4.1, illustrate this. Case A illustrates an unbiased electoral system. In this case, either party wins half the seats if it receives half of the votes. Case B is also an unbiased system, even though it deviates from proportional representation. In case B, regardless of which party receives 60 percent of the vote, that party wins 75 percent of the seats. By contrast, cases C, D, and E illustrate biased electoral systems. In case C, the Republicans are awarded 60 percent of the seats for their 60 percent of the vote, while the Democrats are awarded 75 percent of the seats with the same vote share. This indicates a pro-Democratic partisan bias in the electoral system, since Democrats and Republicans are awarded different shares of seats even though they received an identical proportion of the vote. What is crucial to the matter of partisan bias is that party labels should not matter in the awarding of seats. If 60 percent of the vote translates into 75 percent of the seats, it should do so for whichever party has received the 60 percent of the vote. An unbiased electoral system may well treat parties with different vote totals differently in awarding seats, but if it treats parties with the same vote totals differently, it can no longer be said to be unbiased.

Partisan bias in an electoral system may exist at any level of support for the parties. If one party wins a larger share of seats than another party with an equal number of votes, whether the number of votes is few or many, there is partisan bias. Take case D. If the Democrats win 15 percent of the seats with 20 percent of the vote while the Republicans win only 10 percent of the seats with 20 percent of the vote, there is bias in favor of the Democrats. At the other end of the spectrum (case E), if the Democrats win every seat by receiving 80 percent of the vote and the Republicans (presumably in another election year) win only 90 percent of the seats after receiving an equivalent 80 percent of the vote, there is again electoral system bias in favor of the Democrats. In both cases, partisan bias is reflected in the fact that equal vote totals for the parties are not accorded equal treatment in the awarding of seats.

Although partisan bias may be present at any division of the vote, and while a number of measures of bias are possible (Taylor and Johnson, 1979, 338–42; Grofman, 1983), bias is conventionally measured at the 50 percent of the vote mark.[2] That is, if the Democrats and the Republicans were to split the vote equally, each receiving precisely 50 percent of the vote, what would be the division of seats between the parties? Bias is indicated when both parties, having equally divided the vote, do not also equally divide the seats. If an even-vote split results in Democrats winning 53 percent and Republicans 47 percent of the seats, the electoral system is biased by 3 percentage points (53 percent − 50 percent) in favor of the Democrats. That is, the electoral system is biased to the point that Democrats win 3 percent more of the seats than they would have won in an unbiased electoral system.

The conventional method for estimating bias uses regression analysis (or a nonlinear estimation technique, such as logit analysis).[3] The party's share of the congressional vote is specified as the independent variable and its share of congressional seats as the dependent variable. On the basis of the estimated intercept and slope, the expected seat share for the party when it receives 50 percent of the vote can be calculated. The difference between the expected seat share, based on the regression, and 50 percent is the measure of partisan bias. If the expected seat share exceeds 50 percent, the electoral system is biased in that party's favor (the party whose seat and vote shares are used in the regression). If the expected seat share is less than 50 percent, the system favors the other party.[4]

While there is general agreement on measuring bias at the 50 percent vote point in the estimated relationship between votes and seats, there are differences over how partisan bias at this vote point should be estimated and what data are most appropriate to use in evaluating the electoral system. Niemi and Fett (1986) nicely assess the different approaches used in estimate characteristics of electoral systems, both responsiveness (or the swing ratio) and partisan bias. They note that there have been two general approaches to assessing electoral system characteristics, the historical (multiyear) approach and the hypothetical (single-year) approach. The two approaches employ different data in estimating the relationship between the proportion of seats and votes that parties receive.

The historical, or multiyear, approach assesses the relationship between the actual aggregate percentage of seats and votes won by a party over some set of elections. That is, a regression analysis with the Democratic share of the vote as the independent variable and the Democratic share of seats as the dependent variable may be estimated with actual national election results from one election year to some later election year. The regression results may then be used (as described above) to estimate partisan bias.

Because the historical approach requires estimation over some series of elections, it confronts a tradeoff. On the one hand, estimates of partisan bias (and responsiveness) are generally more reliable if they are based on a greater number of elections. At the extreme, the historical method cannot be used on a single election and is very unreliable when applied to a pair of elections (Niemi and Fett, 1986, 77–78). So, from a reliability standpoint, the more elections used in estimating bias with the historical approach, the better. On the other hand, there are reasons to believe that partisan bias may not be static, that the consequences of the electoral system may change through the years. Gerrymandering, malapportionment, migration, and other factors may cause change in the bias of an electoral system over time. Immediately after reapportionment and redistricting, an electoral system may benefit one party, and, 10 years later, after demographic shifts, the system may favor the opposition party. These changes may be inappropriately "averaged out" in the historical approach's single estimate of bias for a series of elections.

An alternative to the historical approach is the assessment of electoral system characteristics by using hypothetical data from a single election. This approach, first suggested by Butler (1951), begins with the known data point of the actual share of seats and votes won by a party in the election. Additional data points (seats matched with votes) are generated by simulation. The standard simulation assumes a uniform vote swing across districts. That is, it assumes that an additional percentage of the vote for a party nationally would add an additional percentage point of the vote to that party's actual vote in each district. To the extent that the additional vote percentage for a party would have made a difference in the party winning the district's seat, the seat shares are adjusted accordingly for the simulated case. For example, consider the case of a party that actually received 55 percent of the national vote and 60 percent of the seats. If an additional 1 percent of the vote in each district would have carried eight more seats for the party (or 1.8 percent of the seats), then, on the basis of the assumption of a uniform vote swing across districts, the party would have hypothetically won 61.8 percent of the seats if it had received 56 percent of the vote. Additional hypothetical election results are simulated by calculating the share of seats a party would have won across a range of national vote percentages. This provides sufficient data to then run a regression analysis of votes on seats. The partisan bias can then be calculated as the expected seat percentage for a party if it had received half of the votes.

The hypothetical approach avoids the problem of assuming a single or constant partisan bias across a long series of elections. When this method is used, bias is estimated for each election year separately. However, this approach has problems of its own. The principal problem is the simulation. As Niemi and Fett observe, the single-year approach may be criticized "on the grounds that it is hypothetical. It is a measure of what might have been, not of what actually happened" (1986, 81). The assumption of a uniform vote swing across districts is a simple assumption, but probably inaccurate. If a party loses or gains votes, it is unlikely to lose or gain them evenly across all districts. It might be easier for a party to gain a percentage of the vote in a competitive district than one solidly in the other party's column or solidly in its own. If true, rather than assume that a one percentage point gain in the national vote translates into a one percentage point vote gain in each district, we might assume that it translates into a vote gain of two or three percentage points in competitive districts and only a fraction of a percentage point in noncompetitive districts. If the uniform-vote-swing assumption is used for the simulation when actual vote gains or losses would have been distributed differently, then electoral system characteristics (including partisan bias) could be misestimated.[5]

While both the historical and hypothetical approaches have their shortcomings, both approaches have been used to assess the characteristics (including the partisan bias) of the congressional electoral system. What have they found?

❑ Estimates of Partisan Bias ❑

Prior research has failed to reach a consensus regarding electoral system bias. Four principal studies of bias are considered here—Tufte (1973), Jacobson (1990), Brady and Grofman (1991), and King and Gelman (1991; Gelman and King, 1990).[6] The findings range from the observation of a consistently pro-Democratic bias to a strong but diminishing pro-Republican bias. On the one hand, Tufte's (1973) seminal analysis of the partisan bias in the electoral system found a regular pro-Democratic bias. In this, his findings square with the explanation of the Democratic dynasty proposed here. On the other hand, more recent work by King and his associates (King and Browning, 1987; King and Gelman, 1991), suggests a pro-Republican bias over much of this period and is thus very much at odds with the partisan-bias explanation of the Democrats' success in elections to the House. In order to determine the basis for these conflicting findings, we should review these analyses closely.

Prior Research

Like several earlier examinations of the relationship between votes and seats (Dahl, 1956; March, 1957), Tufte's analysis of the congressional electoral system both was based on historical electoral data and produced evidence of a pro-Democratic partisan bias.[7] Tufte examined a number of "triplets," or sets of three consecutive national elections. The votes-to-seats regression estimates indicated a consistent pro-Democratic electoral system bias of varying magnitudes throughout most of this century.

Using this same methodology, I extend Tufte's analysis to include elections up to 1988.[8] These estimates of partisan bias are presented in table 4.2. The estimates agree on one point: the electoral system in House elections has been consistently biased in favor of the Democrats. While consistently biased in favor of the Democrats, the degree of pro-Democratic electoral system bias has varied. The erratic estimates or

Table 4.2
Tufte's Estimates of Partisan Bias, 1942–1988

Election Period "Triplets"	Percentage of Votes to Elect 50 Percent of Seats for the Democrats	Estimated Pro-Democratic Partisan Bias (%)
1942–46	48.1	+1.9
1948–52	49.5	+.5
1954–58	50.1	−.1
1960–64	47.4	+2.6
1966–70	42.1	+7.9
1972–76	49.8	+.2
1978–82	46.3	+3.7
1984–88	36.0	+14.0
Grand Mean	46.2	+3.8
Pre-1964 Mean	48.8	+1.2
Post-1964 Mean	43.6	+6.5

Note: The partisan bias estimates from 1942 to 1970 are from Tufte (1973, table 6). Estimates from 1972 to 1988 were computed from regressions estimated by the author. The data used in the regressions are the two-party vote and seat percentages computed from Ornstein et al. (1990, tables 1-18 and 2-2).

variability of Tufte's results are due, in part, to the fact that the analysis examines only three elections at a time.[9] However, despite this variability, Tufte found the system favorable to the Democrats in all but one of the 11 election triplets after 1906. Moreover, the single exception of contrary results (1954–58) was negligible (one-tenth of 1 percent). The extent of Democratic bias generally appeared moderate in magnitude. From 1954 to 1970 (the last election in Tufte's series), the average bias in Tufte's analysis was about 3.5 percent of seats in favor of the Democrats (1973, 550; and a bias of 3.8 percent of seats updated through 1988). That is, if the Democrats won exactly 50 percent of the national congressional vote, they would win 53.5 percent of the seats in the House. Translating this bias into seats, Democrats typically obtained approximately 15 more seats than they would have won in an unbiased system, a swing of about 30 seats from the Republicans to the Democrats. The mean bias of the updated series indicates an even slightly greater pro-Democratic bias (+3.8 percent, or 17 seats).

Tufte suggests several plausible sources of this bias. Bias, he notes, could have been produced by "gerrymandering, differential turnout

Table 4.3
Jacobson's Estimates of Partisan Bias, 1946–1988

Congressional Vote Percentage Measure	All Districts	
	1946–1964	1966–1988
National Vote	2.1% Democratic	3.9% Democratic
Mean District Vote	14.6% Republican	.5% Republican

Source: Jacobson (1990, table 5.5 and p. 93). The bias estimates for the mean district vote were calculated by the author from the third equation in Jacobson's table 5.5.

Note: Jacobson also estimated partisan bias only in contested congressional districts. Using the mean district vote in these contested districts, he found a 7.2 percent pro-Republican bias from 1946 to 1964 and a .6 percent pro-Democratic bias from 1966 to 1988 (1990, 93).

across districts, and the population sizes of electoral districts" (548). Malapportionment, the existence of districts with different-sized populations, appeared to be a substantial source of the bias. According to Tufte, Republicans carried a disproportionate number of large population or oversized districts prior to reapportionment in the 1970s. On the basis of this finding, he concludes that "Republican seats were more expensive in terms of votes than Democratic seats" (548). Democrats controlled the House not just because they won more votes but because it took Democrats, on average, fewer votes than Republicans to win a seat. Democrats won the cheap seats.

Jacobson's (1990) analysis of partisan bias is really two analyses, one essentially concurring with the above findings of a pro-Democratic bias and another very much at odds with that conclusion. His estimates, based on historical data from 1946 to 1988, are displayed in table 4.3. Examining the relationship between the national congressional vote and seats (for all districts), Jacobson (1990) reports a 2 percent pro-Democratic partisan bias in elections between 1946 and 1964 (9 seats) and nearly a 4 percent pro-Democratic partisan bias (17 seats) from 1966 to 1988 (93). In the second part of his analysis, Jacobson examined the mean district vote, rather than the aggregated national vote, and reached a very different conclusion. He found that the electoral system was biased to the advantage of Republicans, not Democrats, until the mid-1960s. Since the late 1960s, however, the electoral system has been essentially neutral toward the parties, according to this estimate. Using the mean district vote, Jacobson's analysis indicates a startling 14.6 percent Republican advantage from 1946 to 1964. This bias shrank to a near negligible level of a half of a percentage point Republican advantage in elections since the mid-1960s.[10]

Unlike the previous historical data based studies, Brady and Grofman (1991) adopted the hypothetical approach (the Butler method). They simulated election results 10 percentage points above and below the actual election returns, estimated a logit regression, and used the regression estimates to determine the expected proportion of seats for a party if it had received 50 percent of the vote. They then estimated the characteristics of the congressional electoral system from 1850 to 1980. Their estimates of partisan bias in the post–World War II period are presented in table 4.4. The results generally suggest a minor pro-Democratic bias, finding the electoral system to have favored the Democrats in 11 of the 18 elections from 1946 to 1980. While their estimates indicate that bias nationally favored Democrats in elections since 1968, overall bias was quite erratic and regionally based. Brady and Grofman's regional analysis indicates that the electoral advantage Democrats enjoyed nationally was primarily located in the South and that the electoral system outside the South was actually biased in favor of Republicans, though this advantage has been quite small since the mid-1960s.

King and his colleagues also are at odds with Tufte's finding of a pro-Democratic electoral system bias. In their state-by-state analysis of elections from 1950 to 1984, King and Browning (1987) find partisan bias in individual states but no general pattern of bias for either party.[11] In a more expansive examination of partisan bias over time, King and Gelman (1991) conclude that the electoral system has and continues to favor Republican candidates.[12] These estimates of bias are produced from a modified hypothetical vote analysis in which vote swings are simulated on the basis of district characteristics rather than simply assumed to be uniform across all districts, as previous hypothetical analyses had done. On the basis of this more sophisticated and realistic vote simulation, they conclude, "Whereas the overall electoral system in the nonsouthern states moved from severe Republican bias to moderate Democratic bias, the deeper patterns beneath the configuration of incumbents and their electoral advantages reveal an electoral system that has remained severely biased toward the Republican party for all elections in the past four decades. Only the particular existing pattern of incumbents keeps the system biased in favor of the Democrats" (129).

Table 4.5 presents King and Gelman's (1991) estimates of partisan bias for elections from 1946 to 1984. Two sets of estimates are presented,

Table 4.4
Brady and Grofman's Estimates of Partisan Bias, 1946–1980

Election	Estimated Pro-Democratic Partisan Bias (%)	
	All Districts	Non-South
1946	−2.5	−6.3
1948	+4.7	−1.8
1950	−2.8	−6.6
1952	+4.2	−5.0
1954	+1.0	−8.4
1956	−1.0	−5.8
1958	+1.2	−6.5
1960	+1.0	−2.6
1962	−.5	−2.6
1964	−1.5	−5.8
1966	−5.2	−1.0
1968	+.7	−1.4
1970	+4.0	−.8
1972	+2.0	−.4
1974	+3.0	−2.7
1976	+4.7	−.5
1978	−.1	−.4
1980	+.8	−1.1
Grand Mean	+.8	−3.3
Pre-1964 Mean	+3.8	−5.1
Post-1964 Mean	+1.2	−1.0
Percentage of Elections with Pro-Democratic Bias	57.9	0

Source: Brady and Grofman (1991).

an estimate of overall bias and an estimate of bias that controls for incumbency. The overall measure, probably the more appropriate of the two, indicates an electoral system heavily tilted toward the Republicans until the mid-1960s and very slightly pro-Democratic in recent years.[13] While this diverges a good deal from many of the previous estimates of bias, King and Gelman's second series is even more at odds with them. This series indicates a very strong pro-Republican bias that, though weakened in recent years, remains of substantial help to the Republicans.

Has the electoral system been biased? The results are all over the

Table 4.5

King and Gelman's Estimates of Partisan Bias, 1946–1984

Election	Estimated Pro-Democratic Partisan Bias (All Districts) (%)	
	General Estimate	Estimate with Incumbency Effect Removed
1946	−7.2	−8.5
1948	−6.4	−7.0
1950	−5.7	−8.7
1952	−5.9	−8.0
1954	−6.5	−9.0
1956	−5.3	−8.7
1958	−3.9	−7.6
1960	−4.5	−8.9
1962	−2.5	−7.0
1964	−3.5	−5.7
1966	+.7	−7.0
1968	+.2	−6.5
1970	+.1	−3.5
1972	+.3	−4.2
1974	−2.3	−3.9
1976	+.4	−5.0
1978	+1.1	−3.8
1980	+1.5	−2.5
1982	−.2	−2.4
1984	+3.4	−4.3
Grand Mean	−2.3	−6.1
Pre-1964 Mean	−5.1	−7.9
Post-1964 Mean	+.5	−4.3

Sources: The figures were obtained from Gary King. The first column reflects the reported estimates of partisan bias in King and Gelman (1991, fig. 8).

Note: King and Gelman's published estimates measured partisan bias in terms of the seat margin due to bias and is thus twice the magnitudes reported above. For example, King and Gelman report partisan bias in 1946 to increase the seat gap by about 15 percentage points. This is roughly twice the 7.2 percentage point value reported above. Also, the published estimates included 1986. From their fig. 8, the overall bias in 1986 was only slightly less pro-Democratic than it was in 1984.

place. Tufte finds a consistent Democratic bias. Jacobson produces different results depending on the congressional vote measure used. One set
of estimates, concurring with Tufte's analysis, finds a moderate pro-
Democratic bias. Jacobson's second set of estimates finds a strong pro-
Republican bias that has declined to near neutrality in recent years.
Brady and Grofman find mixed results with Democratic bias in the South
and Republican bias elsewhere. King and Gelman find substantial change
over time, with the system becoming more biased in favor of the Democrats in recent years. However, they also find that, if incumbency effects
are taken into account, the electoral system is significantly biased in favor
of the Republicans.

Two Measures of the Congressional Vote

Why do these studies reach such divergent conclusions? Jacobson's dual
analysis provides a clue. *The reason for conflicting estimates of partisan bias is
the use of different measures of the congressional vote.* Assessments based on
nationally aggregated congressional actual votes, including Tufte's analysis and Jacobson's initial analysis, find a pro-Democratic bias. On the
other hand, assessments based on the aggregate district vote percentages
(e.g., the mean district vote percentage in an election year), including the
research by King and Gelman, Campagna and Grofman, and Jacobson's
final analysis, conclude either that the system has been unbiased or has
actually favored Republicans.

The implications of using the two different measures are evident
in the estimates of partisan bias in table 4.6. Seats-vote regressions are
estimated for elections from 1954 to 1992. Because of autocorrelation,
the regressions are estimated with a two-stage Cochrane-Orcutt pseudo-
generalized least-squares technique. The most important result of this
analysis is the difference in the estimate of partisan bias. Consistent with
previous research, the regression using the partisan split of the national
vote indicates a considerable (3.6 percent) pro-Democratic partisan bias.
This bias added approximately 16 seats to the Democratic majority, not
enough alone to account for Democratic majorities (except in 1954), but
enough to provide a considerable boost and to be of help in sustaining
these majorities.[14] The regression using the mean district partisan-vote
division, on the other hand, indicated a much more nearly neutral electoral system.[15]

Both the findings of previous research and those in table 4.6 raise

Table 4.6

The Relationship between Two Measures of the Democratic Party's
House Vote and Its Share of House Seats, 1954–1992

Independent Variable: Measure of the Two-Party Congressional Vote	Dependent Variable: Democratic Two-Party % of House Seats	
	(1)	(2)
Democratic Share of the National Two-Party House Vote	1.53 (.17)	—
Mean Two-Party District Vote for Democratic House Candidates	—	1.16 (.22)
Constant	−23.02 (7.07)	−6.97 (7.91)
Number of Cases	20	20
R^2	.81	.61
Adjusted R^2	.80	.59
Standard Error of Estimate	1.82	2.74
Durbin-Watson	1.62	1.35
Expected Democratic Percentage of Seats when Democratic Vote Equals 50%	53.63	51.03
Democratic Partisan Bias (%)	+ 3.63 (+15.8 seats)	+1.03 (+5.7 seats)

Note: Standard errors are in parentheses. Because of autocorrelation in the OLS analysis, a two-stage Cochrane-Orcutt pseudo-GLS analysis was used to generate these coefficients (Ostrom, 1978). The first-order autocorrelations for each equation (.246 and .382, respectively) were used in the partial differencing of the lagged variables. The intercept has been converted to its OLS equivalent.

two natural questions: Why do different measures of the congressional vote produce different estimates of partisan bias, and which measure is more appropriate for estimating bias? Since conclusions about partisan bias may rest on whether the congressional vote for a party is calculated as its percentage of the total national vote or its mean percentage of district votes, we first ought to determine which measure is more appropriate.[16] As both Taylor and Johnson (1979, 341–42) and Gudgin and Taylor (1979, 56) have argued, the contention here is that *the national vote measure is the appropriate measure.*[17] Moreover, the mean district vote can be quite misleading (see Erikson, 1972, 1236–37).[18] If the regression using the national vote rather than mean district vote is the appropriate one

Table 4.7

Comparison of Turnout Effects on Nationally Aggregated and Mean
District Congressional Votes, Using Two Hypothetical Districts

Hypothetical Congressional District	District Vote Percentage and Total Vote for Candidate of Party		
	Democratic	Republican	Total Votes Cast
District A			
Percent	80%	20%	
Votes	80,000	20,000	100,000
District B			
Percent	20%	80%	
Votes	60,000	240,000	300,000
Aggregated Party Vote:			
Total Vote	140,000	260,000	400,000
Percentage of Total Vote	35%	65%	
Mean District Vote Percentage	50%	50%	

Note: The mean district-vote percentage is computed by summing the district percentages (a sum of 100 percent for each party, in this particular case) and dividing by the number of districts. For example, Democrats won 80 percent of the vote in District A and 20 percent in District B, so their mean district-vote percentage is 50 percent ((80 + 20)/2).

for estimating bias, partisan bias is substantial (as indicated in table 4.6) and should be a significant component in any explanation of the four-decade-long Democratic House majority.

The mean district vote measure is problematic for measuring bias because it weights all districts equally, regardless of the number of voters in them. Given the great variance in district size and turnout, the assumption of equal weighting is quite erroneous. It is especially dangerous if one party does disproportionately well in high-turnout districts while the opposing party's strength is in lower-turnout districts.[19]

The insensitivity of the mean district vote to different turnout rates and the problems this can create for studying partisan bias are illustrated by examining two hypothetical districts in table 4.7. District A is a low-turnout district won handily by the Democratic congressional candidate. District B is a high-turnout district won just as easily by the Republican candidate. In the area encompassed by the two districts, Republican voters greatly outnumber Democratic voters (260,000 to 140,000). This fact is reflected in the percentage of the total vote accorded each party (65 percent Republican to 35 percent Democratic). However, the mean district vote suggests something different. The mean district vote, by failing to take into account the smaller number of voters in District A, indicates that the parties are of equal strength. Clearly, the mean district vote indicates parity only because it is completely insensitive to the turnout differential between the two districts.[20]

While these hypothetical districts make the point well enough, in that the mean district vote departs significantly from the actual national vote, the point is sharpened by considering a more extreme case. Suppose a system in which the Democrats and Republicans evenly split the total national congressional vote. Suppose further that because of severe malapportionment, gerrymandering, or turnout differences that each Democratic voter was in a separate district by him- or herself and all Republican voters were grouped into a single district. The system would thus comprise numerous districts where Democrats received 100 percent of the district vote and a single district in which Republicans received 100 percent of the district's vote. With an increasing number of districts, the mean district vote approaches 100 percent for the Democrats and 0 percent for the Republicans. Voters in the one purely Republican district matter less and less to the mean district vote with each additional single-voter Democratic district. Similarly, with an increasing number of districts, the proportion of seats for each party approaches 100 percent for the Democrats and 0 percent for Republicans. When the mean district votes and the seat shares for the parties are compared, it would appear that the system was unbiased and perfectly proportional. However, we know that it is, in fact, severely biased in favor of the Democrats. Despite having won only half of the total national congressional vote, Democrats receive nearly all of the seats. As this extreme example illustrates, using the mean district vote in examining partisan bias may produce very erroneous conclusions.

The fact that the two measures of the congressional vote differ in theory does not necessarily mean that they differ in practice. However, they do. As figure 4.1 shows, the mean district congressional vote consistently overstates the Democratic vote and thus makes it appear as though Democrats are deserving of more seats in an unbiased system. For elections from 1954 to 1992, the mean district vote for Democrats exceeded their national vote percentage in every election. The difference was typically more than three percentage points and in several elections exceeded six percentage points.[21] This difference reflects two factors: the very real turnout differences across districts and the partisan complexion of these districts. For example, in the 1988 elections, there were 23 contested

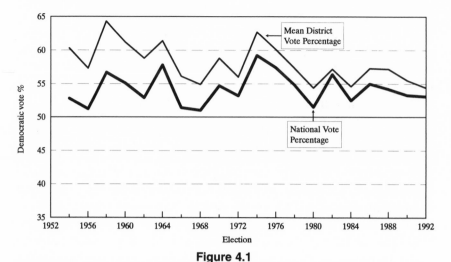

Figure 4.1

The Mean District Vote and the National Congressional Vote for Democrats, 1954–1992

Note: The congressional votes are two-party votes. See the note to table 2.8.

districts (mainly Democratic districts) that cast fewer than 150,000 congressional votes each. At the other end of the spectrum were 36 districts which cast more than 250,000 congressional votes each. In each of these districts, turnout was at least two-thirds again the total vote in the low-turnout districts. In light of these differences, *counting each district equally essentially counts individual voters quite unequally.*[22] A voter from a low-turnout district carries much more weight in the mean district measure than his or her counterpart in a high-turnout district. Because of this, if the voter from the low-turnout district happens to vote differently from the typical national voter, the mean district vote measure will poorly reflect how voters are voting nationally.

Because the mean district vote ignores differential turnout rates across districts, since turnout varies so greatly across districts and since, as Tufte observed (1973, 548), turnout differences are an important source of bias in the electoral system, the mean district vote is an inappropriate measure of a party's appeal in the electorate. It should not be used to examine partisan bias in the electoral system. Using the mean district vote as a measure of a party's success in winning votes essentially eliminates, by faulty operationalization, an important source of potential partisan bias—differential turnout rates. It even leads to incorrect conclusions about which party is advantaged by the electoral system. Since the mean district vote always exaggerates the actual vote of the party carrying low-turnout districts, its use creates the appearance that the party is being inadequately rewarded in seats for its share of the vote.

The conflicting findings regarding partisan bias by studies examining actual votes rather than the percentage of district votes may be explained in a similar fashion. Consider Fiorina's explanation of the pro-Republican bias found in the King and Gelman study: "The greater geographic concentration of Democratic voters in urban areas makes it more likely that their votes will be wasted in excess majorities for Democratic candidates" (1992a, 18). While true in one sense, the statement is wrong in another. True, the concentration of votes makes it more likely that Democratic vote percentages will be wasted in excess majorities, suggesting a pro-Republican bias as found by King and Gelman. However, while Democrats pay a higher price per victory in the percentage of the district vote, they do not necessarily pay a higher price per victory in terms of the actual number of votes cast. While Democratic candidates in urban districts run up large majorities in percentage terms, they are not especially impressive in actual votes, because the turnout in these districts is so low. When turnout in a typical district is on the order of 250,000 votes, a district won with only 40,000 votes cast for the winner is a cheap seat even if those 40,000 votes were 100 percent of those voting in that district.[23]

❑ An Alternative Measure of Partisan Bias ❑

The electoral system studies that have been reviewed differ in many respects, but they are essentially similar in their approach to estimating partisan bias. Whether examining time-series or cross-sectional data, using the national congressional vote or the mean district vote, they first estimate the relationship between votes and seats and then identify partisan bias by the expected seat share for a party when the parties divide the vote evenly.[24] If, for instance, the seats-votes regression indicates that a party is expected to receive 55 percent of the seats when it receives 50 percent of the national vote, partisan bias in the electoral system is estimated at 5 percent in favor of the party.

This study proposes an alternative approach to measuring partisan bias. The method builds on Tufte's observations about the sources of partisan bias: "If, in the aggregate of all districts, low-turnout or small districts are aligned with a particular party, there will be bias in the seats-votes curve since that party is winning seats with relatively small numbers of votes" (1973, 548). An electoral system, thus, is biased in favor of a party to the extent that one party expends fewer votes per victory (unwasted votes) than the opposing party.[25] This alternative approach calculates the extent of partisan bias in an election produced by the electoral system allowing one party to win "seats with relatively small numbers of votes." The method calculates the mean number of votes each party expends in obtaining a victory, the mean number of unwasted votes. The extent of bias can then be directly calculated by comparing the number of unwasted votes per victory for a particular party with the mean number of unwasted votes for victorious candidates generally.

Before examining the alternative measure in detail, an example might be useful. Consider again the hypothetical districts we examined earlier in table 4.7. Recall that the Democrats received 80,000 votes in low-turnout district A (80 percent of the district's vote), while the Republicans received 240,000 votes in high-turnout district B (80 percent of that district's vote). Suppose that an electoral system was composed only of districts of these two types and that there were three districts of type A for every one of type B, as presented in table 4.8. The simple arithmetic indicates that the two parties would evenly divide the national vote in this system. For every four districts (three of type A and one of type B) Democrats would receive a total of 300,000 votes, of which 240,000 were cast in three winning causes and 60,000 were wasted in a lost cause (a district B). For every set of four districts, Republicans would also receive a total of 300,000 votes. Only because of the way these Republican votes are organized into districts, 60,000 were cast in three losing causes and 240,000 were cast in a single winning effort. Thus, in this hypothetical electoral system, when the vote is split evenly, Democrats win three-quarters of the seats. This is because the partisan bias in the electoral system exacts a smaller than average number of unwasted votes from Democrats for a victory (80,000 per victory) and a larger than average number of unwasted votes from Republicans for a victory (240,000 per victory). If districts were redrawn so that both parties "spent" the mean number of votes for a victory (120,000), both parties would be as equally represented in the legislature as they were in the polling booths.[26]

The unwasted-vote measure of partisan bias can best be understood by revisiting the electoral system's basic characteristics of responsiveness and partisan bias and the factors that affect them. The principal point is that partisan bias can be measured by examining unwasted votes because all of the factors affecting partisan bias exert their effect by changing the

Table 4.8
A Hypothetical Electoral System

Hypothetical Congressional District	District Vote Percentage and Total Vote for Candidate of Party		
	Democratic	Republican	Total Votes Cast
District A1	80%	20%	
	80,000	20,000	100,000
District A2	80%	20%	
	80,000	20,000	100,000
District A3	80%	20%	
	80,000	20,000	100,000
District B	20%	80%	
	60,000	**240,000**	300,000
Total Vote	300,000	300,000	600,000
Percentage of Total Vote	50%	50%	
Seats Won	3	1	
Percentage of Total Seats	75%	25%	
Total Unwasted Votes	240,000	240,000	480,000
Mean Unwasted Vote	80,000	240,000	120,000
Pro-Democratic Partisan Bias (percentage of seats)	25%		

Note: Unwasted votes (indicated in bold) are votes cast for candidates who won election. At 80,000 unwasted votes per victory, Democrats would win three seats (75 percent of all seats) with half of all unwasted votes (240,000/80,000 = 3). Partisan bias equals the percentage of seats won in excess of 50 percent with 50 percent of unwasted votes. In this case, bias is 25 percentage points pro-Democratic (75 − 50 = 25).

mean number of unwasted votes for the parties. Responsiveness, on the other hand, is a function purely of wasted (and not unwasted) votes.

Causes of Responsiveness and Partisan Bias

Why are electoral systems more or less responsive, and why are they biased toward or against a party? As discussed briefly in chapter 2 and presented in table 4.9, the electoral system characteristics of responsiveness and partisan bias involve quite different mechanisms and reflect different aspects of the vote. Responsiveness, the rate by which votes translate into seats, is a function of a party wasting votes in losing causes. In the single-member-district, plurality-rule system, the party with the minority of the vote generally wastes a larger portion of its votes in losing

Table 4.9

The Mechanisms of Responsiveness and Partisan Bias in Electoral Systems

Electoral System Characteristic	Symmetry	Mechanism by Which One Party Is Underrepresented
Responsiveness (Swing ratio)	Symmetric	A party wastes a larger share of its votes in districts that it loses than does the opposing party in districts that it loses.
Partisan Bias	Asymmetric	A party expends more votes in districts that it wins than does the opposing party in districts that it wins.

Note: Symmetry refers to whether parties receiving the same national share of the vote would receive the same national share of seats.

Table 4.10

How the Minority Party Wastes More of Its Votes in Losing Causes

	District Vote Above or Below the Party's National Vote Percentage				
	Below		Equal to National Party Vote %	Above	
	$\geq m$	$<m$		$<m$	$\geq m$
Majority Party	Loss	Win	Win	Win	Win
Minority Party	Loss	Loss	Loss	Loss	Win
Party Wasting Votes	Both Parties	**Minority Party**	**Minority Party**	**Minority Party**	Neither Party

Note: m is the margin of the majority party's national two-party vote above 50 percent. Thus, the majority party's vote = 50% + m, and the minority party's vote = 50% − m. For instance, if $m = 5$, the majority party would have received 55 percent and the minority party, 45 percent of the two-party vote. The majority party would need to fall short of its national vote by 5 percent or more in order to lose a district. The minority party would need to exceed its national vote by 5 percent or more in order to win a district.

causes. As a consequence, the party with a majority of the vote wins a larger share of seats than its vote share and the responsiveness of the electoral system is greater than one.

The reason why minority parties waste a larger portion of their votes is illustrated in table 4.10. The table presents the five possible circumstances of a party's district vote relative to the national vote and national vote margin (*m*) for both the majority and minority parties. The national vote margin refers to the difference between the national vote and an even division of the vote. In any district a party may receive (1) exactly its national vote percentage, (2) more than its national vote percentage but not in excess of its national vote margin, (3) more than its national vote percentage by more than its national vote margin, (4) less than its national vote percentage but less than its vote margin, or (5) less than the national vote and less than the national vote margin.[27] At extreme deviations from the national vote percentages, either both parties waste their votes or neither does. When a party falls well short of its national vote, whether it is in the majority or not nationally, it wastes whatever votes it obtains. When a party does exceedingly well in a district, its votes are not wasted. In the middle ground, however, differences are evident. The majority party wins districts, and therefore does not waste votes, so long as its district vote does not fall short of its national margin. The minority party, on the other hand, wastes votes even when its district vote exceeds its national vote percentage, but not by more than the margin of its loss. Thus, the majority party wastes votes in only one of the five situations, while the minority party wastes votes in four of the five.

Figure 4.2 presents a causal model explaining the level of responsiveness in an electoral system. The immediate cause of electoral system responsiveness is the relative proportion of votes wasted on losing congressional candidates. The greater the disparity between the parties in the proportion of votes they waste in losing causes, the greater the electoral system's responsiveness. The disparity in wasted votes is in turn affected by the level of competition in congressional districts. As observed from table 4.10, to the extent that districts are concentrated in the middle categories (generally competitive districts), only the minority party wastes votes. System responsiveness would be at its peak when one party barely carries every district and nearly half of all votes are wasted or cast in losing causes for one of the parties. A slight tilt of the vote in the opposite direction would cause an electoral avalanche. Finally, the level of competition in congressional districts is a function of the level of national competition between the parties, especially when party votes are distributed more uniformly across the nation and gerrymandering is designed to dilute minority party votes in districts so that the party falls just safely short of a majority in any district (termed *cracking* by Butler and Cain [1992, 87]).

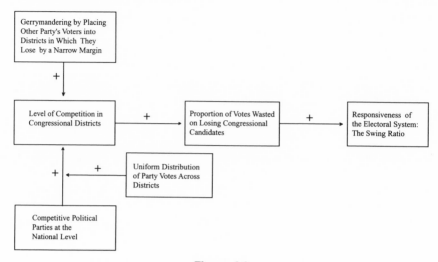

Figure 4.2
A Causal Model of Responsiveness in Electoral Systems

In contrast to responsiveness, partisan bias depends on the distribution of unwasted rather than wasted votes. Figure 4.3 is a causal model indicating the possible influences on the mean number of unwasted votes for a party and how this affects partisan bias. Many of the elements included in the model were originally identified by Tufte (1973, 548–49). A system can be biased in favor of a party by reducing the mean number of unwasted votes per victory for that party and raising the mean number of unwasted votes per victory for the opposing party.[28] That is, bias is generally produced by one party winning relatively cheap seats. How is such a partisan difference in the mean unwasted votes created? As the model indicates, a party can win with fewer votes if it wins districts where there are relatively few votes cast (so long as it does not win these districts with unusually high percentages of the vote), and these low-turnout districts are a product of there being few voting-age citizens residing in the district (malapportionment) and low turnout among those who are eligible to vote.[29] While the model offers an explanation of how gerrymandering, vote margins, differential turnout, and malapportionment affect the partisan bias of an electoral system, the most important aspect of this model for our purposes is that bias is only directly determined by altering the mean number of unwasted votes per victory expended by each party.[30]

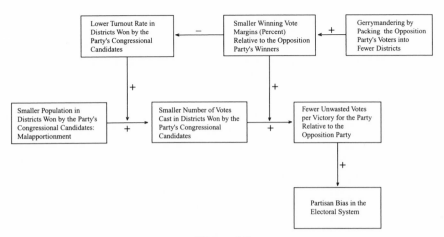

Figure 4.3
A Causal Model of Partisan Bias in Electoral Systems

Note: Arrows pointing to other arrows specify interaction effects.

For measurement purposes, we can take advantage of the fact that the principal factors affecting partisan bias are funneled through the difference in the mean number of votes that parties expend in their victories. Unwasted votes have the great advantage that they can be counted. Because they can be counted, we can calculate partisan bias directly and sidestep many of the estimation problems encountered by conventional approaches to measuring bias. Moreover, we can obtain a measure of partisan bias in every election year without resorting to simulating the vote with all of the assumptions that such a method entails. It does require that we assume that both parties at an even division of the national vote would waste a similar share of their votes in losing causes. This assumption is reviewed in detail in appendix B, and, although there have been some exceptions, the data generally conform to the assumption. Finally, and quite importantly, unlike the historical measure of partisan bias, the unwasted-vote measure does not require bias to be a constant. It is quite plausible that bias might vary with the distribution of the vote, and this could have important political implications. If, for instance, partisan bias is greater when the party is doing well at the polls, it would only be adding seats to an already large majority. On the other hand, if partisan bias is greater when a party is not doing as well in the vote, it may make a substantial difference, perhaps even determining which party has a controlling majority in the legislature.

Measuring Partisan Bias with Unwasted Votes

Having established the rationale for the approach, we can now outline the procedures for calculating partisan bias with unwasted votes. There are five steps. The first is to calculate the mean number of votes cast for each party in the seats that it won and the mean number of votes cast at the district level for the winning candidate, regardless of party. The second is to calculate the total number of unwasted votes. The third step is to divide the total number of unwasted votes in half, to determine how many unwasted votes each party would have received if the vote were evenly divided. The fourth step is to divide this half of the total unwasted votes by the mean number of unwasted votes per victory for the party being examined. This indicates how many seats the party would have won if it had received 50 percent of the vote, on the assumption that it was "paying" for seats at its rate of unwasted votes per seat rather than the opposing party's rate or the mean rate. Finally, the number of seats the party would have won at its unwasted votes rate can then be divided by the total seats to put it in terms of percentages and subtracted from 50 percent to indicate the direction and extent of bias.

To follow up on the earlier example from table 4.8, the first step calculates the mean number of unwasted votes for Democrats, Republicans, and the system as a whole. As the table indicates, the mean numbers of unwasted votes per victory are 80,000 for Democrats, 240,000 for Republicans, and 120,000 overall. The second step, the calculation of the total number of unwasted votes, indicates that there were 480,000 unwasted votes cast in these four districts. Half of this total, the third step, would be 240,000 votes. Applying the fourth step, if the Democrats had received 240,000 unwasted votes and paid 80,000 unwasted votes per victory, they should receive three of the four, or 75 percent, of the total seats. Finally, considering that Democrats would have won 75 percent of the seats with half of the unwasted votes, this hypothetical electoral system is biased by 25 percent of the seats in favor of the Democratic Party.[31]

❏ Overview ❏

This chapter reviewed the concept, measurement, and previous estimates of partisan bias in electoral systems and offered an alternative approach to its measurement. The concept of partisan bias in an electoral system is straightforward: it is the asymmetric treatment of political parties in the conversion of votes into seats. Operationally, it is the difference between the proportion of seats that the political parties would win if they were to receive the same number of votes nationally. In an unbiased system, political parties that receive the same number of votes receive the same number of seats. By convention, the measurement of partisan bias in a two-party system compares the proportion of seats that the parties would win if each had half of the national vote.

The existing research on partisan bias in the electoral system for the House in the last several decades has failed to reach a consensus regarding the extent or direction of bias. The findings are amazingly disparate. Some find Democratic bias, others find Republican bias, and still others find no consistent bias for either party. While there are many methodological differences among these studies that may have lead them to reach different conclusions, the principal reason for the lack of a consensus finding is the difference in the measurement of the congressional vote used. Some studies examine the mean district vote percentage (or a variant thereof) and others the total national vote. The analysis of hypothetical electoral systems demonstrates that *the mean district vote is an inappropriate measure for assessing bias.* Because it implicitly weights each congressional district equally, regardless of the actual number of votes cast in the district, the mean district vote measure of the congressional vote produces very misleading estimates of partisan bias. From a different perspective, the mean district vote is an inappropriate measure to assess the partisan bias of the electoral system because it is itself a product of that system. Redraw district lines and you get a different mean district vote, without a single change in an individual vote. To assess the effects of the system on the awarding of seats, you need a vote measure that is unaffected by how the system organizes votes.

Appropriate estimates of partisan bias can be obtained by conventional analysis of the relationship between the partisan division of the total national vote and seats. Such an analysis indicates that the Democrats have typically enjoyed a partisan advantage over Republicans of about 15 to 16 House seats (3.6 percent of seats). That is, if both Democrats and Republicans evenly divided the vote, based on the seat-vote relationship of elections in recent decades, Democrats would be expected to win 233 seats and Republicans 202 seats. This alone would not have accounted for the Democratic House majority, but it suggests that the electoral system has worked substantially to the advantage of Democrats.

In the final part of the chapter, an alternative measure of partisan bias was proposed. Unlike the hypothetical method, this measure does not entail strong assumptions about how additional votes might have

affected election results and, unlike the historical method, it allows a separate reading of bias in each election year. This method is based on the
unwasted votes cast for each party. Unwasted votes are votes cast for winning candidates. An examination of both responsiveness and partisan
bias, the two central characteristics of electoral systems, suggests that responsiveness results from one party having a larger share of its votes cast
for losing candidates (wasted votes) than the opposing party, while partisan bias results from one party expending more unwasted votes per victory than the opposing party. By recognizing this basis for partisan bias,
a straightforward method was devised to calculate directly the degree of
electoral bias in an election year.

This method for calculating partisan bias will be applied to House
election returns from 1954 to 1992 in the next chapter and to the dramatic 1994 election in chapter 8. The results concur with the basic findings of the conventional historical method using the total national vote.
The electoral system has been biased in favor of the Democrats. As the
cheap-seats thesis contends, the electoral system is biased because Democrats win a disproportionate number of very-low-turnout seats. This provided an important foundation for four decades of Democratic Party
control of the House.

5

□ □

The Price of a Seat

$\mathbf{D}$o many House Democrats sit in cheap seats? Put differently, have winning Democratic candidates, on average, received fewer votes than winning Republican candidates? Without a doubt, they have. The analysis will show that many House Democrats have been elected in districts with very low vote totals. Having won a substantial number of low-turnout districts and spent relatively few unwasted votes for these victories, Democrats consistently have enjoyed a significant advantage over Republicans.

The evidence from contested elections between 1954 and 1992 indicates that Democrats consistently won an overwhelming majority of low-turnout districts. As a result, the average number of votes cast in Democratic victories (Democratic unwasted votes) was much lower than that for winning Republicans. This provided the basis for partisan bias in the electoral system. *There has been not one price for victory, but two, and Democrats have paid the lower price.* If the two parties had expended the same number of unwasted votes per victory, as would have been the case in an unbiased system, the House would have been significantly more Republican.

To begin the unwasted-vote analysis, we turn first to the matter of turnout in congressional districts. At least one notion of representative government requires that an electoral system come as close as practically possible to the equal representation of the nation's citizens. As Butler and Cain (1992, 67–68) observed, this equality of representation is central to the democratic principles of majority rule and popular sovereignty. Constitutional features such as state boundaries and extraconstitutional features such as the fixed number of representatives in the House are obstacles to designing a system that is perfectly equal in its representation of citizens. However, with due consideration for these constitutional and extraconstitutional impediments, there is now a considerable body of law strictly applying the principle of equal representation, or "one person, one vote," to the reapportionment of representatives and the redrawing of district boundaries.[1] The more basic principle lying behind one person, one vote is that districts should be nearly equal in size so that the ballot of each voter has an equal opportunity of influencing the election of a representative. While the standard of equally sized districts in a formal sense (equal populations) is now firmly entrenched, it is less evident that districts are effectively equal in size. It would be merely a constitutional nicety rather than a guarantee of popular sovereignty to insist that districts be equally populated, if the numbers of actual voters in districts varied widely, with very few casting ballots in some districts while huge numbers voted in other districts in one election after another. This raises the question: How much disparity among congressional districts has there been in the number of votes actually cast? Are there cheap seats to be had?

❏ **Turnout in Congressional Districts** ❏

There are cheap seats. Despite strenuous efforts to ensure that districts are equal in population, districts vary greatly in their effective size, as measured by the actual number of votes cast. In 1990, for instance, there was one district (the Third District of Minnesota) where nearly 300,000 citizens cast ballots, while in another contested district (the Eighteenth District of New York) just over 40,000 voters made it to the polls—an enormous 7.5-to-1 disparity. In 1992, after reapportionment (so district population differences should have been as small as feasible), there were nearly 360,000 ballots cast in Maine's First Congressional District, while there were just over 50,000 ballots cast in California's Thirty-third District—a 7.2-to-1 disparity.[2] As Dodd and Oppenheimer (1985), Oppenheimer (1989), and Ornstein (1990) have observed, these huge differences are by no means restricted to a few extreme districts in a couple of isolated election years. There are many districts that regularly record small turnouts and others that regularly record high turnouts.

Table 5.1 presents some descriptive statistics regarding variation in district turnout, the effective size of the district. It displays the total number of congressional votes cast at both the twentieth and the eightieth percentiles of the turnout distribution for contested elections from 1954 to 1992. To assist comparison, the percentage-point difference between

Table 5.1

Variation of Total District Turnout in Contested Seats, 1954–1992

	Total Turnout in Contested Districts				
Election	20th Percentile	80th Percentile	Percentage Difference	Standard Deviation	N
1954	86,500	143,100	+65	36,068	346
1956	112,200	188,600	+68	46,899	356
1958	91,100	156,100	+71	42,604	334
1960	117,500	208,800	+77	58,788	353
1962	93,300	164,400	+76	43,650	366
1964	125,400	197,600	+58	46,443	386
1966	99,100	160,800	+62	36,261	374
1968	129,500	191,900	+48	36,987	385
1970	105,300	165,100	+57	35,317	372
1972	144,900	205,000	+41	34,073	380
1974	100,800	156,000	+55	33,555	374
1976	150,800	208,500	+38	35,161	383
1978	106,500	165,300	+55	36,512	365
1980	158,700	223,100	+41	45,740	377
1982	127,600	179,800	+41	33,133	376
1984	177,900	232,900	+31	35,931	367
1986	119,600	172,900	+45	33,549	361
1988	177,000	231,700	+31	38,726	354
1990	123,400	183,000	+48	41,313	350
1992	196,000	261,000	+33	44,625	405

Note: The mean percentage difference is 52 percent. Only single-member-district seats contested by both of the major parties are included. Seats uncontested by a major-party candidate, multimember districts, seats won by third-party or independent congressional candidates, and at-large seats (except those for one-district states) are excluded. The total district turnout measure is the total number of votes cast for any congressional candidate in the district.

these percentiles is also presented. Since the table includes only contested elections, the number of districts falling below the twentieth percentile or above the eightieth percentile differs slightly from election to election, but there are usually about 70 districts in the low- and high-turnout categories (about 140 districts in total). Thus, the comparison of the bottom and top quintiles involves a substantial number of districts. The table also presents the standard deviations of the total district vote in these elections.

There are large turnout differences across districts. The differences

Table 5.2

Turnout in Seven Congressional Districts in New York and
the Two Congressional Districts in Maine, 1990

	Maine			New York	
District	Winning Party	Turnout	District	Winning Party	Turnout
1	Democrat	278,459	6	Democrat	60,641
2	Republican	238,502	8	Democrat	78,042
			9	Democrat	54,644
			10	Democrat	76,431
			13	Democrat	59,003
			18	Democrat	40,796
			19	Democrat	74,761
Total Votes Cast		516,961			444,318
Total Districts		2			7

between the bottom and top turnout quintiles of districts are considerable. Turnout in the top quintile of districts is about 50 percent greater
than turnout in the bottom quintile. There are about as many votes cast
in two districts at the eightieth percentile size as three districts of the
twentieth percentile size. Standard deviations tell the same story. There
is great variation around the average district turnout in each election
year. While district turnout grew with population growth over the years,
the typical turnout of a contested district was about 175,000 in presidential election years and 135,000 in midterms. Standard deviations of about
40,000 voters, thus, represent a large difference between low- and high-
turnout districts. One standard deviation from the mean district vote
amounts to roughly a quarter of the district's votes. In terms of votes cast,
not population estimates, many congressional districts are very unequal.

The magnitude of turnout differences is illustrated in more stark
terms in table 5.2. The table contrasts Maine's two electoral districts with
the seven lowest-turnout districts in New York for 1990. Over half a million ballots were cast in the two districts in Maine, while fewer than
450,000 votes were cast in seven New York districts combined. That is,
about 70,000 fewer New Yorkers sent three and a half times as many
representatives to Washington than a greater number of Maine voters.
From the standpoint of votes cast, the Maine districts were extremely

expensive, while the New York seats were bargain-basement cheap. Several of these cheap New York seats cover much of the Queens borough of New York City and together are an interesting example of cheap seats from the 1980s.

New York's Cheap Borough

The Sixth, Seventh, Eighth, and Ninth Districts of New York cover the Queens borough of New York City.[3] Although some of these districts were uncontested in several elections during the 1980s, when the Republicans mounted a challenge, the seats were won cheaply. In comparison to other contested districts around the country, turnout in the Queens districts was low, and the seats were won with relatively few votes. All four districts have consistently elected Democrats to the House over the years and this continued throughout the 1980s. Joseph Addabbo represented the Sixth District from 1960 until his death in 1986.[4] In 1986, the Sixth elected Floyd Flake, who won reelection into the 1990s. The Seventh District was represented by Benjamin Rosenthal from 1962 until his death in 1983. He was succeeded by Gary Ackerman, who, like Flake, was reelected into the 1990s. James Scheuer was first elected in 1964 and, despite several substantial redistrictings, has won each election since. He is currently serving in his sixteenth term. The Ninth District was initially represented in the 1980s by Geraldine Ferraro. She first won election in 1978 and represented the district until her nomination as Walter Mondale's vice presidential running-mate in 1984. She was succeeded by Thomas Manton, who has been reelected since (in the district now numbered the Seventh).

As a group, the Democratic delegations from Queens during the 1980s were decidedly liberal. The Americans for Democratic Action (ADA) ratings, an index of liberalism in roll-call voting, for the representatives in these districts seldom fell below 80 percent and often was in the 90s for several representatives. Ferraro and Manton, who represented the more politically competitive Ninth District (numbered the Seventh in the 1990s), were the least extreme in their records and often had liberal ratings in the high 60s and 70s. The delegation was even more politically homogenous in its support of organized labor positions. The ratings of these representatives on the AFL-CIO roll-call index rarely fell below 90 percent.

Ethnically and racially, the Queens' districts were diverse. The Sixth District (southern Queens) was about 50 percent African American. The

Seventh and Eighth Districts (eastern and central Queens and northern Queens, respectively) had large Jewish populations. The Ninth (western Queens) had a large Catholic ethnic population, including many of Italian, Irish, and Greek ancestry. The Seventh, Eighth, and Ninth Districts also had Hispanic populations of between 15 and 20 percent. Each district also had significant numbers from the groups that predominate in adjoining districts. For instance, the Sixth and Seventh Districts also had a significant Catholic ethnic community, the Eighth included a significant number of African Americans, and the Sixth included a significant number of Jews and WASPs. Queens was also diverse economically. There were affluent areas and poor areas. But the borough as a whole is best typified as working class. As Barone and Ujifusa (1990, 827) observed about the Ninth, it was the Archie Bunker district of the 1970s and the *Moonstruck* district of the 1980s. Both allusions raise images of a colorful, crusty, working class, old-line-labor Democratic constituency.

Elections in the four districts of Queens were not closely contested on a regular basis. In the five elections after the 1980s redistricting (1982 to 1990), each of the four districts was left uncontested by Republicans at least once. The Eighth was uncontested by Republicans in three of the five elections. However, of the 12 contested races in Queens over this period, Democrats were held under 70 percent in 5. They exceeded 80 percent only once. Although the four districts are by no means competitive (although the Ninth was a district that Republicans had real hopes of gaining), and Republicans have not regularly mounted high-powered campaigns against the entrenched Democrats, they nonetheless occasionally had credible showings.

The turnout in the four districts of Queens regularly placed them near the bottom of turnout rankings among all contested districts. Each of the 12 contested elections held in these districts during the 1980s was in the lowest quintile of turnout. The districts often ranked among the 10 lowest in turnout (of contested seats). In 1990, turnout in the Ninth ranked third from the bottom and turnout in the Sixth District ranked fifth from the bottom (of 349). In 1986, three of Queens' districts ranked in the bottom 10 of turnout (of 360). In the 12 contested elections among these districts in the 1980s, the highest turnout ranking relative to other contested district was fiftieth from the bottom. Even at this high point, nearly 86 percent of contested districts that year had higher vote totals. The low turnout in Queens was also evident from conventional measures. Turnout as a proportion of registered voters was about

8 to 10 percentage points less than it was for New York State as a whole.[5] These were clearly cheap seats.

□ Population and Turnout Differences □

Some differences in district turnout are created by seats being apportioned to states, and the limit on the total number of seats. Following the reapportionment in the 1990s, Montana and Wyoming were each apportioned a single seat, even though Montana had a population of over 800,000 and Wyoming had a population of under 500,000. District population disparities are also found in multiseat states. After the reapportionment based on the 1990 census, the average district in Kansas had over 620,000 people, while the average Oklahoma seat had a population of less than 530,000.[6] These population differences can be the basis for significant turnout differences among districts. However, even within the same state with equally populated districts, turnout differences among districts can be large. In the 1992 elections in California, for instance, the combined number of votes cast in the five districts with the highest turnout was nearly three times the total vote cast in the five California districts with the lowest turnout.[7]

District turnout disparities, in themselves, do not create partisan bias. Indeed, they are not absolutely necessary for the creation of bias in an electoral system. However, as the causal model of partisan bias (figure 4.2) in the last chapter suggested, these turnout differences set a context in which bias may develop. If there is a partisan association with district turnout (in the actual number of voters), there is a distinct possibility that there will also be a difference between the parties in the number of votes they receive per victory, and this is the basis for partisan bias.

□ Party Victories and District Turnout □

Turnout differences among districts only have implications for the parties if one party is disproportionately successful in winning high- or low-turnout seats. If both parties did equally well in low- and high-turnout districts, the parties would be paying roughly the same price (in unwasted votes) for a seat, and these turnout differences would not matter much, at least in terms of representation of the parties. On the other hand, if the success of the parties correlates with the number of voters in districts, there may be significant partisan repercussions. If a party wins many low-turnout districts, it may also expend fewer votes for these victories, thus extending the purchasing power of its votes. Since the hypothesis is that partisan bias in the electoral system has helped Democrats, we might expect Democrats to have done well in the lower-turnout districts and Republicans to have been more successful in the higher-turnout districts. They have.

Democrats have been much more successful in low-turnout districts than have Republicans. The consistently disproportionate success of Democrats in low-turnout districts is evident in table 5.3. The table groups contested districts into quintiles by their total turnout in the particular election year for elections from 1954 to 1992.[8] After grouping districts into the five turnout categories, the percentage of winning Democratic candidates is calculated at each turnout level. To illustrate, in 1956 Democrats won 75 percent of contested seats among districts ranked in the bottom fifth of turnout and only 29 percent of seats ranked in the top fifth of turnout. Democrats have had their greatest success in the districts with the lowest turnouts. The highest rate of Democratic success is in districts in the bottom quintile of turnout. This is true for each of the 20 election years. Democrats typically won 4 of 5 of the very-lowest-turnout districts. Democrats won nearly 9 of 10 of these very-low-turnout districts in some years. In the second turnout quartile, Democrats usually won about 3 of 4 districts. In the middle-to-high-turnout districts, Republicans and Democrats competed nearly evenly, with Republicans winning in these districts just slightly more often than Democrats.

The correlation and logit coefficients in table 5.3 tell a similar story, without grouping the districts by turnout categories. In every election from 1954 to 1992, there was a significant correlation between whether the district elected a Republican and the total number of ballots cast in the district. The correlations quite consistently fell within the .2-to-.3 range. Logit analyses were also conducted with the party winning the seat (Republicans coded 1) as the dependent variable and the total turnout in raw votes as the independent variable. These logits indicated that the probability of the district electing a Republican rose by about three to four percentage points with every additional 10,000 votes cast in the district.[9] All of these coefficients were statistically significant and corresponded closely with parallel regression analyses.

Examination of both the grouped data and statistical analysis of ungrouped data reveals a clear and consistent pattern. In every election over this period, Democrats won a larger share of seats in the lowest turnout category than in any other. In more than half of the elections, the

Table 5.3

The Relationship between the Party of the Winning Congressional
Candidate and District Turnout in Total Votes, 1954–1992

Year	Percentage of Districts Won by Democrats in Districts Grouped (in Quintiles) by Total District Turnout in Votes					Association between Total District Turnout and the Election of a Republican Representative	
	Low				High		Logit
	1	2	3	4	5	r	Derivative
1954	61	49	34	32	38	.23	.033
1956	75	54	35	34	29	.32	.039
1958	76	49	53	54	42	.19	.022
1960	84	52	39	48	37	.29	.027
1962	81	48	49	45	39	.26	.033
1964	82	70	54	57	57	.22	.024
1966	77	49	38	41	49	.22	.032
1968	69	64	48	43	37	.26	.039
1970	78	61	43	44	38	.29	.045
1972	70	61	49	38	41	.25	.039
1974	82	65	55	52	56	.19	.028
1976	87	63	65	54	52	.26	.038
1978	88	64	56	51	51	.26	.036
1980	84	53	44	43	43	.30	.037
1982	79	56	53	52	56	.16	.025
1984	77	57	41	46	51	.21	.032
1986	72	65	42	53	47	.17	.026
1988	84	53	60	46	38	.30	.043
1990	89	70	55	53	47	.26	.033
1992	83	57	53	52	54	.21	.026
Mean	79	58	48	47	45		

Note: Only single-member-district seats contested by both of the major parties are included. The total district-turnout measure is the total number of votes cast for any congressional candidate in the district. A table entry is the percentage of seats won by Democratic candidates at a particular level of turnout in a given election year. For example, Democrats in 1954 won 61 percent of contested districts in the lowest quintile of voter turnout measured by total votes cast. The correlation (r) is between the total district turnout and a dummy variable indicating whether the Republican won. The logit derivative indicates the change in the probability of the Republican congressional candidate being elected for every additional 10,000 votes cast in the district. Thus, for every additional 10,000 votes in a district in 1954, the likelihood that the district elected a Republican increased by 3.3 percentage points. All logit coefficients were statistically significant at $p < .01$.

Table 5.4

Contested Congressional Districts with Highest
Total Congressional Voter Turnout, 1990

Rank	State and District	Total Vote	Winning Candidate	Political Party
1	Minnesota, 3	292,228	Ramstad	Republican
2	Maine, 1	278,459	Andrews	Democrat
3	Massachusetts, 10	258,022	Studds	Democrat
4	South Dakota, AL	257,298	Johnson	Democrat
5	Minnesota, 6	254,954	Sikorski	Democrat
6	California, 14	249,051	Doolittle	Republican
7	Florida, 9	244,666	Bilirakis	Republican
8	North Carolina, 4	240,057	Price	Democrat
9	Maine, 2	238,502	Snowe	Republican
10	Oregon, 1	238,259	AuCoin	Democrat
11	Arizona, 3	237,297	Stump	Republican
12	Florida, 14	236,304	Johnston	Democrat
13	Texas, 10	235,455	Pickle	Democrat
14	Florida, 6	234,009	Stearns	Republican
15	North Dakota, AL	233,973	Dorgan	Democrat
16	Florida, 11	232,961	Bacchus	Democrat
17	California, 37	232,082	McCandless	Republican
18	Arizona, 4	231,238	Kyl	Republican
19	California, 1	230,261	Riggs	Republican
20	Massachusetts, 6	229,461	Mavroules	Democrat

Seats Won by Each Party: Democrats 11
Republicans 9

Note: At-large statewide districts are indicated by AL. Also, only the 350 seats contested by congressional candidates of both major parties in 1990 are examined. The single district won by a candidate without a major-party affiliation (Vermont-AL) is excluded.

Democrats were next most successful in the second-to-lowest turnout group of districts. The pattern supports the thesis that the electoral system allowed Democrats to win a substantial number of cheap seats.[10]

The districts listed in tables 5.4 and 5.5 put some names with the numbers. Table 5.4 lists the 20 highest-turnout districts in 1990, the actual number of voters casting ballots for the House in those districts, and the winning congressional candidates and political parties. Table 5.5 provides the same information for the 20 contested seats with the lowest total turnout.

The list of the highest-turnout districts, districts with turnout near

Table 5.5
Contested Congressional Districts with Lowest
Total Congressional Voter Turnout, 1990

Rank	State and District	Total Vote	Winning Candidate	Political Party
331	California-31	83,987	Dymally	Democrat
332	Tennessee-9	83,640	Ford	Democrat
333	California-30	78,083	Martinez	Democrat
334	New York-8	78,042	Scheuer	Democrat
335	Tennessee-4	77,272	Cooper	Democrat
336	West Virginia-4	76,894	Rahall	Democrat
337	New York-10	76,431	Schumer	Democrat
338	New York-19	74,761	Engel	Democrat
339	Mississippi-4	70,891	Parker	Democrat
340	Mississippi-2	70,671	Espy	Democrat
341	Maryland-7	70,157	Mfume	Democrat
342	California-25	68,717	Roybal	Democrat
343	Michigan-13	67,817	Collins	Democrat
344	Mississippi-1	67,318	Whitten	Democrat
345	California-29	64,672	Waters	Democrat
346	New York-6	60,641	Flake	Democrat
347	New York-13	59,003	Solarz	Democrat
348	New York-9	54,644	Manton	Democrat
349	New Jersey-10	52,305	Payne	Democrat
350	New York-18	40,796	Serrano	Democrat

Seats Won by Each Party: Democrats 20
Republicans 0

Note: These lowest turnout districts are from the 350 seats contested by congressional candidates of both major parties in 1990.

or in excess of 230,000 voters (listed in table 5.4), illustrates that no party has had a monopoly on these districts and that no clear thread runs through them. Of the 20 districts, Democrats won 11 and Republicans won 9. In terms of district characteristics, the highest-turnout districts tended to be in high-growth areas (such as Florida) and in predominantly white, northern nonurban areas.

There is also diversity at the other end of the turnout spectrum, districts with turnout below 85,000 voters. Many of these districts were urban with sizable minority populations. Eleven districts were either in New York City or Los Angeles.[11] African Americans made up a third or more of the district's population in 10 of the 20 districts. Several low-turnout districts also had large Hispanic populations. In addition, as one might expect of an election just prior to reapportionment, several low-turnout districts were in areas that had lost population since the last remapping.

❑ Unwasted Votes and the Price of Victory ❑

Did the typical House Democrat win with fewer votes than the House Republican? Was the mean number of unwasted votes in a party's victories smaller for Democrats than for Republicans? Although the link between the success of the parties and the turnout in congressional districts is a good reason to suspect that Democrats paid a lower price (in votes) for their victories, it is logically possible that they did not. If Democrats had won by larger vote margins in these low-turnout districts, they might not have paid a smaller price for their victories than the Republicans, even though they often won in lower-turnout districts. To illustrate, if a Republican won a high-turnout district (200,000 votes) with 51 percent of the vote and a Democrat won a low-turnout district (120,000 votes) with 85 percent of the vote, each would have received the same number of votes in his or her victory (102,000 votes).

In fact, Democrats did pay a lower price in votes for their victories in most elections than did Republicans.[12] Democrats won many seats with low vote totals. The evidence is presented in table 5.6. While the pattern is not quite as sharp or as consistent as the partisan association with turnout, it is nevertheless clear in most election years. As in table 5.3, districts are grouped into quintiles based on the number of votes received by the winning candidate (unwasted votes). Among districts falling in the bottom 20 percent range of the number of votes for the winning candidate, Democrats typically won about 7 of 10 times. In several years, including 1990, Democrats won about 8 of 10 of these districts. In the next-to-lowest category of unwasted votes, Democrats typically won nearly 6 of 10. In the three highest categories of unwasted votes, Democrats and Republicans were often quite competitive, or Republicans had a slight edge.

As in the earlier analysis of the partisan association with district turnout, table 5.6 also presents a systematic analysis of the association between the number of votes cast for the winning candidate in a district and the party of the winning congressional candidate. Table 5.6 offers the correlations, based on ungrouped district data, between the winning party and the number of votes cast for the winning candidate of the district. It also presents the results of logit analyses for each election. In the

Table 5.6

The Relationship between the Party of the Winning Congressional Candidate
and the Total Votes Cast for the Winning Candidate, 1954–1992

Year	Association between the Percentage of Districts Won by Democrats in Districts Grouped (in Quintiles) by Total District Votes for the Winning House Candidate					District Vote for the Winning Candidate and the Election of a Republican	
	Low 1	2	3	4	High 5	r	Logit Derivative
1954	55	51	24	41	43	.13	.031
1956	73	49	44	28	32	.30	.059
1958	66	48	50	55	55	.04	.009
1960	74	55	37	52	41	.19	.029
1962	77	47	47	55	38	.22	.043
1964	74	56	50	78	62	.04	.006
1966	71	46	55	56	27	.25	.056
1968	71	57	52	48	31	.29	.067
1970	65	64	39	55	42	.17	.039
1972	61	61	47	51	38	.18	.039
1974	70	51	57	65	67	−.01	−.002
1976	81	62	65	57	57	.16	.033
1978	82	68	56	56	47	.22	.045
1980	67	68	52	45	35	.29	.051
1982	67	53	58	55	63	.04	.008
1984	71	68	47	47	38	.26	.052
1986	61	57	51	64	47	.07	.014
1988	75	61	60	44	42	.24	.043
1990	81	71	56	51	53	.19	.037
1992	67	64	60	49	58	.12	.020
Mean	70	58	50	53	46		

Note: Only single-member-district seats contested by both of the major parties are included. The total district vote for the winning candidate is the actual number of votes cast for that candidate. A table entry is the percentage of seats won by Democrats among all winning candidates receiving a particular range of votes in a given election year. For example, Democrats in 1954 won 55 percent of the contested districts in the lowest quintile of total votes cast for the winning candidate. The correlation (r) is between the number of unwasted district votes and a dummy variable indicating whether the Republican won. The logit derivative indicates the change in the probability of the Republican congressional candidate being elected for every additional 10,000 unwasted votes cast in the district. Thus, for every additional 10,000 unwasted votes in a district in 1954, the likelihood that the district elected a Republican increased by 3.1 percentage points. The coefficients were statistically significant ($p < .01$), except in 1958, 1964, 1974, 1982, and 1986.

logit analyses, the party of the congressional candidate winning the district (Republicans coded 1) is the dichotomous dependent variable, and the number of votes cast for the winning candidate (in units of 10,000 votes) is the independent variable. As expected, with one exception, the correlations and logit analyses indicate that in districts where the winning candidate received a relatively larger number of votes, that candidate was more likely to be a Republican. The relationship between the party winning the seat and the number of unwasted votes cast in the district is statistically significant in 15 of the 20 elections examined. In most elections, the relationship was substantial. The logit analyses suggest that for every additional ten thousand unwasted votes cast in a district, the probability of the district winner being a Republican increased by about four to six percentage points.

It is worth noting that the relationship between the number of unwasted votes and the party winning the district faltered in five elections. In 1958, 1964, 1974, 1982, and 1986, the associations fell short of statistical significance. In 1974, the association was actually in the opposite direction, though not statistically significant and very nearly zero. This is a matter that we will return to later in this chapter and address fully in the next; however, at this point, we might note that a common thread runs through these years: each had an election in which Democrats did especially well. From 1954 to 1992, the national Democratic congressional vote reached or exceeded 55 percent on seven occasions (see table 2.8), and the elections noted above constitute five of these seven. The association between the number of unwasted votes in a district and the party winning the seat, an association that forms the basis for partisan bias in the electoral system, was weakest when Democrats were doing well. The other side of this coin, the more politically interesting side, is that the association and, as we will shortly see, partisan bias were stronger when the Democrats were doing relatively less well nationally. This is a matter that will be addressed at greater length in chapters 6 and 7.

The basic point, however, is that, while both parties have won some seats with low vote totals, Democrats consistently got the better bargains. A comparison of an equal number of the lowest-turnout districts won by each party in 1992 illustrates the Democratic advantage. In the 67 lowest turnout districts won by Democrats in 1992, they cumulatively received just under seven million votes. By contrast, in an equal number of the lowest-turnout districts won by Republicans that year, Republicans received a total of more than 8.35 million votes, over 1.35 million more votes than Democrats for the same number of victories in the same elec-

tion. The vote difference is about what it would have taken to have
elected an additional 9 or 10 Republicans in 1992.[13]

❑ The Extent of Bias ❑

Having established the turnout and unwasted vote basis for partisan bias,
we can now turn to the calculation of bias. As outlined at the end of the
last chapter, there are five steps in calculating bias through unwasted
votes: (1) compute the mean number of unwasted votes per victory for
each party and overall, (2) compute the total number of unwasted votes,
(3) compute an even division of all unwasted votes, (4) calculate (on the
basis of steps 1 and 3) the number of seats a party would have won if it
received half of the unwasted votes and expended votes per victory at
that party's rate, and (5) convert this number of seats into a percentage,
and subtract 50 percent from it, to obtain the percentage of seats attributable to bias produced by the parties winning seats with different numbers
of unwasted votes.

The first step in calculating bias is demonstrated in table 5.7. The
table presents the mean number of votes cast for winning congressional
candidates for contested districts from 1954 to 1992, for all winning candidates and also for the winning candidates of each party. As one would
expect on the basis of the earlier analysis, with a single exception (1974),
the mean number of votes cast for winning Republican candidates consistently exceeded the mean number of votes cast for winning Democratic
candidates. Consistent with the cheap-seats explanation of the Democratic dynasty, fewer votes were expended in Democratic than in Republican victories. By exacting a greater price for victory from Republicans
than from Democrats, in most elections, the electoral system has been
biased in favor of Democrats.

Sometimes the differences between the parties were rather minor,
but in some cases they were substantial. In 1958, 1964, and 1982, for
instance, typical Republican winners did not receive many more votes
than did typical Democratic winners. In these three elections, the difference of means was less than 2,200 votes, which accounts for less than 3
percent of the mean Democratic winning vote. In most elections, however, the differences were sizable. Typical Republican winners received
more than 10,000 more votes than typical Democratic winners in eight
election years, and in several of these cases this amounted to the mean
Republican winning vote being more than 15 percent greater than the
mean Democratic winning vote.

Table 5.7

Mean Number of Votes for Winning Democratic and Republican
Congressional Candidates in Contested Elections, 1954–1992

| | Contested Seats | | | | | |
| | Democrats | | Republicans | | All Contested Seats | |
Year	Seats Won	Mean Winning Votes	Seats Won	Mean Winning Votes	Total Seats	Mean Winning Votes
1954	148	65,109	198	70,422	346	68,150
1956	161	82,079	195	99,779	356	91,774
1958	183	74,731	151	76,776	334	75,656
1960	183	93,572	170	106,535	353	99,815
1962	192	75,120	174	86,622	366	80,588
1964	247	98,897	139	101,052	386	99,673
1966	191	76,145	183	88,281	374	82,083
1968	200	93,725	185	108,057	385	100,612
1970	197	82,052	175	89,709	372	85,654
1972	196	106,638	184	114,889	380	110,634
1974	232	80,815	142	80,508	374	80,699
1976	246	111,393	137	119,220	383	114,192
1978	226	82,897	139	93,769	365	87,037
1980	201	113,318	176	131,932	377	122,007
1982	222	97,540	154	99,277	376	98,251
1984	199	126,556	168	140,189	367	132,797
1986	202	96,910	159	100,191	361	98,355
1988	199	130,884	155	144,639	354	136,907
1990	219	93,048	131	103,306	350	96,887
1992	241	135,151	163	142,803	404	138,238

Note: Seats uncontested by a major-party candidate, multimember districts, seats won by third-party or independent congressional candidates, and at-large seats (except those in one district states) are excluded from these calculations.

The implications of these differences are clarified with an example. Consider 1988. The average vote for Democratic winners in 1988 was about 131,000 votes, while the average vote for Republicans was nearly 14,000 votes greater. If the Democrats had received the same number of unwasted votes in this election but because of districting arrangements expended the same number of unwasted votes per victory as Republicans, they would have won about 19 fewer seats. Of course, in an unbiased electoral system, each party would expend an equal number of votes per victory, on average.

The second and third steps involve the calculation of the total unwasted vote and an even division of that vote. The total unwasted vote in any election can be obtained by multiplying the total number of contested districts by the mean number of unwasted votes in contested districts. The results of the third step, the number of unwasted votes that each party would have received if the parties evenly divided the total vote, are presented in table 5.8. The table also presents the mean number of unwasted votes per Democratic victory in each election (taken from table 5.7) and, taking the fourth step, divides the even split of unwasted votes by this Democratic rate of unwasted votes per victory. The result is the number of seats the Democrats would have won had they evenly divided the total vote but paid their lower unwasted-vote rate for each victory. This is the number of contested seats that Democrats would have been expected to win if the national congressional vote had been equally divided.[14] For example, half of the unwasted votes cast in 1988 amounted to a bit over 24.2 million votes. With 24.2 million unwasted votes and a victory rate of 1 seat for every 130,884 unwasted votes, Democrats would have won approximately 185 seats.

The final step in calculating partisan bias is the conversion of seats that Democrats would have won with half of all unwasted votes into a percentage of all contested seats. Table 5.9 reports these percentages. The number of seats that the Democrats would have won with 50 percent of the vote (from table 5.8), given their rate of unwasted votes per victory, is divided by the total number of contested seats in the election (from table 5.7) to produce the percentage of seats that Democrats would have won. Because an unbiased system should award a party half of the seats for half of the votes, 50 percentage points are subtracted from this percentage to indicate the percentage of seats awarded to a party because of bias in the electoral system. For example, the 185 seats that Democrats could have been expected to win with half of the 1988 vote amounts to 52.3 percent of all contested seats (185/354 = 0.523), a bias of 2.3 percent of the contested seats in favor of the Democrats. This amounts to an 8-seat bias in favor of the Democrats or an inflation of their seat margin over Republicans of 16 seats.

The mean bias in the system has been about 2.4 percent of the contested seats. This is in the same ballpark as the earlier regression estimate of partisan bias using the national congressional vote (table 4.6). With approximately 382 contested seats in a typical election, partisan bias

Table 5.8

Number of Contested Seats Democrats Would Have Won Based
on an Even Division of the Vote and the Mean Number of
Unwasted Democratic Votes per Victory, 1954–1992

Year	Half of Unwasted Votes in Contested Districts	Mean Number of Unwasted Votes per Democratic Victory	Contested Seats That Democrats Would Have Won with Half of the Unwasted Votes
1954	11,789,850	65,109	181
1956	16,335,750	82,079	199
1958	12,634,500	74,731	169
1960	17,617,300	93,572	188
1962	14,747,650	75,120	196
1964	19,236,900	98,897	194
1966	15,349,550	76,145	202
1968	19,367,800	93,725	207
1970	15,931,650	82,052	194
1972	21,020,350	106,638	197
1974	15,090,650	80,815	187
1976	21,867,900	111,393	196
1978	15,884,300	82,897	192
1980	22,998,500	113,318	203
1982	18,471,250	97,540	189
1984	24,368,150	126,556	193
1986	17,753,100	96,910	183
1988	24,232,500	130,884	185
1990	16,955,250	93,048	182
1992	27,924,116	135,151	207

Note: Seats uncontested by a major-party candidate, multimember districts, seats won by third-party or independent congressional candidates, and at-large seats (except those for one district states) are excluded from these calculations. The number of contested seats that Democrats would have won had they won half the votes is computed by dividing the number in the first column by the one in the second. The half of the total national unwasted votes in contested districts is rounded to the nearest 50 votes.

typically shifted about 9 or 10 seats in the Democratic direction, inflating the Democratic seat margin over Republicans by 18 to 20 seats. However, as noted previously, there was a good deal of variation around the typical degree of bias. In the 1974, post-Watergate, election, the electoral system actually favored the Republicans, though just barely, and in several other elections (1958, 1964, 1982, and 1986) bias favored the Democrats by less than 1 percent of contested seats. On the other hand, the system worked

Table 5.9

Extent of Partisan Bias Resulting from the Different Expenditure of Votes per Seat for Democratic and Republican Congressional Candidates, 1954–1992

Year	Percentage of Contested Seats That Democrats Would Win with 50 Percent of the Unwasted Vote	Percentage Partisan Bias from Unwasted Votes
1954	52.3	+2.3 Democratic
1956	55.9	+5.9 Democratic
1958	50.6	+.6 Democratic
1960	53.3	+3.3 Democratic
1962	53.6	+3.6 Democratic
1964	50.4	+.4 Democratic
1966	53.9	+3.9 Democratic
1968	53.7	+3.7 Democratic
1970	52.2	+2.2 Democratic
1972	51.9	+1.9 Democratic
1974	49.9	+.1 Republican
1976	51.3	+1.3 Democratic
1978	52.5	+2.5 Democratic
1980	53.8	+3.8 Democratic
1982	50.4	+.4 Democratic
1984	52.5	+2.5 Democratic
1986	50.8	+.7 Democratic
1988	52.1	+2.1 Democratic
1990	52.0	+2.0 Democratic
1992	51.1	+1.1 Democratic
Grand Mean	52.4	+2.4 Democratic
Pre-1964 Mean	52.7	+2.7 Democratic
Post-1964 Mean	52.0	+2.0 Democratic

Note: The Democratic seat percentage at 50 percent of the vote in contested seats was determined by calculating the total number of unwasted votes in contested seats and dividing that in half, to determine how many votes constituted 50 percent in each election (unwasted votes are those cast for winning candidates, only unwasted votes are counted to avoid mixing issues of bias and responsiveness). This 50 percent of the total vote was then converted into Democratic seats by dividing the number of votes constituting 50 percent by the mean number of votes received by winning Democratic candidates. The number of Democratic seats was then converted into a percentage by dividing it by the total number of contested seats and translating that proportion into a percentage. In calculating the means, pre-1964 includes the 1964 election.

considerably more to the advantage of Democrats at other times. In 1956, 1962, 1966, 1968, and 1980, the electoral system favored Democrats by more than 3.7 percent of the contested seats, inflating the Democratic seat margin over Republicans by nearly 30 seats.

❑ The Partisan Division of an Unbiased House ❑

The analysis of partisan bias to this point has assessed bias at the point at which each party receives exactly half of the vote. An alternative is to calculate the extent of partisan bias at the actual vote divisions for the parties. Rather than applying the rate of Democratic unwasted votes per victory to a hypothetical, even division of unwasted votes, the prevailing systemwide rate of unwasted votes per victory (a party-neutral rate) can be applied to the actual number of votes for winning Democratic candidates. We can thus determine how many fewer seats Democrats would have won in an unbiased system that exacted the same number of votes per victory from both parties. This measure of partisan bias allows us to go beyond the question of whether partisan bias exists, to the more central question of this study: did partisan bias contribute significantly to the maintenance of the Democratic dynasty in the House?

The effects of partisan bias in particular elections are presented in table 5.10. The table presents the actual distribution of seats to the parties resulting from an election and the distribution that would have resulted if the parties expended an equal number of votes for each victory. The latter is what would have resulted from an unbiased electoral system. The difference between actual election results and those of an unbiased electoral system indicates the impact of partisan bias in the system. The data necessary to calculate the results of an unbiased system appear in table 5.7. By multiplying the number of seats won by Democrats and their mean number of unwasted votes per victory, we arrive at the total number of unwasted votes. This is then divided by the mean number of unwasted votes for all contested seats, to obtain the number of seats that Democrats would have won if both Democrats and Republicans paid the same price in votes for a victory. To demonstrate, on the basis of their number of victories and the mean number of unwasted votes per victory, Democrats received over 26 million unwasted votes in 1988 ($199 \times 130,884 = 26,045,916$). If the system were designed so that Democrats expended the mean number of votes for a victory (136,907 in 1988), they would have won 190 seats ($26,045,916/136,907 = 190.2$) rather than the 199 that they actually won because of their winning cheap seats. In 1988, then, partisan bias gave

Table 5.10

Actual Party Distribution of Seats in the House of Representatives and the Distribution of Seats without Partisan Bias in the Electoral System, 1954–1992

Year	Actual Seat Division		Seat Division without Partisan Bias		Difference in the Number of Democratic Seats
	Democrats	Republicans	Democrats	Republicans	
A. Contested Districts					
1954	148	**198**	141	**205**	−7
1956	161	**195**	144	**212**	−17
1958	183	151	181	153	−2
1960	183	170	172	**181**	−11
1962	192	174	179	**185**	−13
1964	247	139	245	141	−2
1966	191	183	177	**197**	−14
1968	200	185	186	**199**	−14
1970	197	175	189	183	−8
1972	196	184	189	**191**	−7
1974	232	142	232	142	0
1976	246	137	240	143	−6
1978	226	139	215	150	−11
1980	201	176	187	**190**	−14
1982	222	154	220	156	−2
1984	199	168	190	177	−9
1986	202	159	199	162	−3
1988	199	155	190	164	−9
1990	219	131	210	140	−9
1992	241	163	236	168	−5
Mean	204	164	196	172	−8.1
B. All Districts					
1954	232	203	225	210	−7
1956	234	201	217	**218**	−17
1958	283	153	281	155	−2
1960	262	175	251	186	−11
1962	258	176	245	189	−13
1964	295	140	293	142	−2
1966	248	187	234	201	−14
1968	243	192	229	206	−14
1970	255	180	247	188	−8
1972	242	192	235	199	−7
1974	291	144	291	144	0
1976	292	143	286	149	−6

continued

Table 5.10 (*continued*)
Actual Party Distribution of Seats in the House of Representatives and the
Distribution of Seats without Partisan Bias in the Electoral System, 1954–1992

Year	Actual Seat Division		Seat Division without Partisan Bias		Difference in the Number of Democratic Seats
	Democrats	Republicans	Democrats	Republicans	
			B. All Districts		
1978	277	158	266	169	−11
1980	243	192	229	206	−14
1982	268	167	266	169	−2
1984	253	182	244	191	−9
1986	258	177	255	180	−3
1988	260	175	251	184	−9
1990	267	167	258	176	−9
1992	258	176	253	181	−5
Mean	263	173	254	181	−8.1

Note: Republican seat majorities are indicated in bold. The seat division without partisan bias was determined in two steps for each party: (1) the number of seats won by a party was multiplied by the mean number of votes cast for that party's winning candidates to determine the party's total number of unwasted votes, and (2) the party's total number of unwasted votes was then divided by the overall mean number of votes cast for winning House candidates to determine how many seats the party would have won if both parties expended the same number of votes per successful candidacy. The actual seat division for all districts is from Ornstein et al. (1990), except for 1992, which was computed from election returns reported in Congressional Quarterly. The unbiased seat division of the entire House is calculated by adding the number of uncontested and multimember seats for each party to the calculated number of contested seats it would have won in an unbiased electoral system.

nine seats to the Democrats that would have gone to Republicans in an unbiased system.

Like the prior analysis, the figures in table 5.10 indicate a consistent Democratic bias in the electoral system. With the single exception of 1974, Democrats won more seats than they would have in a neutral electoral system. Typically, partisan bias shifted about eight or nine seats in the Democratic direction. However, again, there was considerable variance. During the period of the Democratic dynasty, from 1954 to 1992, the Democrats gained more than 10 seats through partisan bias in seven elections. More important from the standpoint of preserving the Democratic majority, *partisan bias was responsible for Democrats winning a majority of contested seats in six elections between 1954 and 1992.* Without bias, Republicans would have won a majority of contested seats in 1960, 1962, 1966, 1968, and 1980.[15] This is in addition to the two elections, 1954 and 1956, in which Republicans actually won majorities of the contested seats despite the electoral system's bias against them in those years. Thus, if the electoral system were unbiased, Republicans would have won a majority of contested seats in 8 of the 20 election years (40 percent). In 11 of the remaining 12 elections (1974 being the exception), the elimination of electoral bias would have narrowed the Democratic margin over Republicans in contested seats.

The second part of table 5.10 indicates the effect of partisan bias on the partisan composition of the entire House of Representatives, not just the contested seats. In this part of the table, election results from uncontested and multimember districts are added to the results of contested seats. As these figures indicate, partisan bias in the electoral system, by itself, was generally insufficient to sustain the Democratic majority. The removal of bias in the electoral system may have produced a razor-thin Republican majority in only one election, 1956.[16] In other elections, although the removal of partisan bias would have narrowed the Democratic majority, sometimes quite substantially (e.g., 1966, 1968, and 1980), the other factors working to the party's advantage (its incumbency advantage and uncontested-seat advantage), as well as the support for Democratic candidates by the voters, were enough to keep the Democratic majority in place. This is not to minimize the importance of partisan bias to the Democratic dynasty. It suggests instead that the Democratic majority did not depend on any single factor alone, even one that benefited them as significantly and as consistently as the partisan bias of the electoral system.

❑ **Partisan Bias and Incumbency** ❑

Although the pro-Democratic bias found in the preceding analysis is significant and consistent, it is also underestimated. Some portion of partisan bias in prior elections carries into future elections through the effects of incumbency.[17] Because Democrats systematically won more seats than would have been the case in an unbiased system, they had additional incumbents seeking reelection, and, through the various advantages of their office, these Democratic incumbents attracted an additional number of votes. As noted in chapter 3, estimates of the vote value of incumbency indicate that it was worth about four percentage points of a district's vote in the 1950s and rose to about nine percentage points of the vote by the 1980s (Levitt and Wolfram, 1996). Since partisan bias produces more incumbents and incumbents produce more votes, the vote totals that we use in our analysis of a given election year have already been influenced to some extent by partisan bias in prior elections.[18]

Because partisan bias consistently favored Democrats, as already demonstrated in the analysis of individual election years, the consideration of carryover partisan bias effects from prior years should indicate that the general electoral system's bias was even more favorable to Democrats. The logic is as follows. Some number of Democratic incumbents enjoy their incumbency by virtue of partisan bias in a prior election, and this is not necessarily limited to only the bias of the last election. These Democrats receive the generally larger vote that incumbents are able to attract rather than the smaller vote that they would have received had they run as challengers. In essence, there is an incumbency multiplier effect to partisan bias that has not been incorporated into the above calculations and, if incorporated, would indicate an even stronger pro-Democratic bias.[19]

The estimation of the additional votes and seats derived from partisan bias in the immediately prior election involves a number of calculations and several assumptions. The analysis, in some detail, is presented in appendix C. The analysis indicates that some effects of partisan bias in past elections are carried into later elections via incumbency; however, these effects are marginal.

The marginal nature of these carryover effects is due, in part, to the stability in the location of bias. That is, the very-low-turnout districts in the current election were very likely the very-low-turnout districts in prior elections. Correlations of the number of unwasted votes in districts won by Democrats in adjacent election years illustrates this stability. Four pairs of elections were examined: 1954–56, 1964–66, 1974–76, and 1984–86. For each pairing, all districts that were contested in both election years were examined. In each of the four pairs of elections, the number of unwasted votes in a district in one election year was strongly and positively correlated with the number of unwasted votes in that district in the next election (.84 in 1954–56, .63 in 1964–66, .65 in 1974–76, and .69 in 1984–86). This indicates substantial continuity in the location of the cheap seats, so earlier bias was not helping to elect many candidates that bias in the current election would not have helped anyway. In addition, carryover effects are marginal because many of the votes that Republicans would have gained if there had not been bias in earlier elections are votes that would be cast for losing Republican candidates.

The bottom line is that incumbency typically boosts the number of seats linked to partisan bias by about two or three seats. Adding this carryover effect of bias in previous elections to partisan bias in the current election indicates that the electoral system generally deviates by about 10 to 12 seats from neutrality.

❑ Overview ❑

The electoral system systematically worked to the advantage of Democrats. The origin of this advantage is the great disparity in turnout among districts. It was not at all unusual for turnout in one district to be more than half again the turnout of another. Most importantly, the evidence indicates that Democrats have done especially well in the low-turnout districts. With the exception of only one election since the 1950s (1974), fewer votes have been cast for the average winning Democratic candidate than for the average winning Republican candidate in each election year from 1954 to 1992. Democrats obtained a greater payoff from their votes or won additional seats because they won a significant number of seats with very few votes, the cheap seats. This was the basis of the pro-Democratic partisan bias in the electoral system.

After considering the extent to which incumbency carries forward the effects of prior partisan bias into later elections, it appears that partisan bias typically shifted about 10 to 12 seats away from the Republicans and to the Democrats. Among contested seats, this bias was sufficient to turn a Republican majority into a Democratic majority in six elections, in addition to the two election years (the 1954 and 1956 elections) in which Republicans won an outright majority of contested seats despite a pro-Democratic electoral system bias. In 1956, without the bias of the electoral system, Democrats might have narrowly lost their seat majority. Otherwise, however, the Democratic cheap-seats advantage was not by itself sufficient to account for the Democratic majority in all seats (both contested and uncontested), although it significantly narrowed the Democratic majority on several occasions. In an unbiased electoral system, a Republican majority would have been within reach in several elections since 1954.

The analysis also indicates that there was a fair degree of stability in the location of bias. The number of unwasted votes at the district level were positively correlated across elections. The mean interelection correlation of unwasted votes in districts was about .7. Despite this stability and despite the consistency with which bias favored the Democrats, there was also a good deal of variation in partisan bias.[20] In some elections (1958, 1964, 1974, 1982, and 1986), partisan bias was minimal and in others (1956, 1962, 1966, 1968, and 1980), large. This is the issue that we turn to next. Why has bias varied? We know that, in an immediate sense, electoral system bias is the result of one party disproportionately winning low-turnout districts, but in a broader sense what causes this? What factors systematically affect bias, causing it to be larger in some elections and smaller in others?

6

□ □

The Changing Price
of a Seat

Despite the consistency with which the electoral system has tilted in favor of the Democratic Party, the extent of this bias has varied greatly. In one election (1974), the system was nearly neutral. In five others (1958, 1964, 1974, 1982, and 1986), it tilted only slightly toward the Democrats (less than 1 percent, or fewer than four seats). At other times, Democrats benefited greatly from the system. In five elections (1956, 1962, 1966, 1968, and 1980), the electoral system favored Democrats by at least 3.5 percent of contested seats (more than 15 seats).[1] Other year-by-year estimates, including studies reviewed in chapter 4, have also found considerable variation in bias. This variability is the principal subject of this chapter. What accounts for variation in the extent of partisan bias in the electoral system?

One might initially presume that bias is a stable or fixed feature of an electoral system and that any variation in estimates of bias reflects errors in its estimation. The presumption that partisan bias is constant over some series of elections is a premise of many time-series or historical estimates of bias (as was the case in table 4.6).[2] Bias, however, is not necessarily a constant. It is certainly not a constant by definition. The defining characteristic of partisan bias is only that its effect on the conversion of votes into seats is *asymmetric* with respect to the parties. It is conceivable for an electoral system to be biased in favor of the Democrats in one election year and biased in favor of the Republicans at the next. Partisan bias is not necessarily a stable trait of an electoral system.

There are several reasons to suppose that change in partisan bias is not only possible but that it is likely. Change in bias should be expected because the characteristics of the electoral system affecting bias—its electoral laws and their implementation, district boundaries, population growth and migration, turnout rates, and party loyalties—change over time, some from one election to the next. Electoral laws tend to be stable, and district boundaries seldom change more than once every decade, but the other elements of the electoral system change more often. Turnout rates fluctuate. Party loyalties can be dramatically influenced by short-term forces and occasionally shift more substantially. Population growth and migration are constantly changing parameters on the political landscape. These changes can affect the bias of the electoral system.

❑ Influences on Partisan Bias ❑

In recent years, four conditions may have affected partisan bias. First, a variety of legal and socioeconomic developments may have caused a general decline in the partisan bias of the electoral system. In particular, the more stringent application of the one-person, one-vote principle to congressional reapportionment and the 1965 Voting Rights Act may have equalized turnout among districts and thereby reduced bias. Second, because the extent of partisan bias is sensitive to the way votes are organized into districts, periodic partisan gerrymandering may have affected bias. Bias may have been greatest immediately following redistricting and deteriorated as shifting populations and political preferences undid the effect of the remapping. Third, if partisan bias is a consequence of socioeconomic backgrounds linking Democratic preferences and nonvoting, it may have been smaller in higher-turnout elections. That is, if bias is a result of the nonvoting neighbors of Democratic voters reducing the price (in votes) of Democratic districts, it should be reduced on the occasions when these usually inactive and likely Democratic neighbors turn out to vote. Finally, the size of the Democratic Party's vote may have affected the extent of partisan bias. If in good Democratic years Democrats gain votes disproportionately in their lower-turnout districts, partisan-turnout differentials should decline, the difference in the mean number of unwasted votes should also decline, and consequently the extent of partisan bias should be reduced.

Sociolegal Changes and Partisan Bias

There are three plausible sociolegal changes that may have caused partisan bias to decline over the past 40 years. The first involves the laws governing the apportioning of districts. Bias may be smaller because of more stringent rules regarding the equal population size of districts and greater efforts to ensure equality. Certainly one factor that would account for turnout differences among districts and the resulting bias is the significant disparity in the populations of districts (recall figure 4.2). Since the 1970s, following the Supreme Court's one-person, one-vote reapportionment ruling in the 1964 case of *Wesberry v. Sanders* and its subsequent rulings requiring minimal district size differences in state reapportionment plans, the population sizes of districts were greatly equalized.[3]

The effect of these changes in reapportionment standards can be seen by comparing intrastate differences in district populations before and after *Wesberry*. In the reapportionment of districts following the 1960 census (pre-*Wesberry*), the population size of districts differed greatly in a number of states. For instance, following redistricting for the 1960s, one district in Illinois had a population of only 279,000, while another had a population of 553,000.[4] In Colorado, one district contained only 196,000 people, while another had 654,000. In Michigan, the smallest district contained a population of only 177,000, while the largest was 803,000, and these intrastate differences were not particularly unusual. The tremendous intrastate differences among districts in the 1960s and before, however, were not permitted in the 1970s. For instance, following the redistricting of the early 1970s, the smallest district in Illinois had a population of 460,000 and the largest just slightly more at 466,000.[5] In Colorado, the smallest district was 439,000 and the largest 442,000. In Michigan, the district population differences similarly shrank to a nearly negligible 3,000 residents. Cox (1981, 23) calculated that the national average percentage point deviation of congressional district populations from the average district size in a state ranged from 14 to 22 percent in the 1950s and early 1960s. In the early 1970s, on the other hand, the national average deviation within a state was less than one percentage point, almost nonexistent. Across the nation, the reapportionment of the 1970s, under a new judicial scrutiny, greatly equalized the population sizes of districts within states.

In view of the reduction of population differences among districts, the proportionate difference between the number of voters casting ballots in districts may have also been reduced. That is, some of the turnout differences among districts in the 1950s and 1960s may have reflected large population differences among districts, differences that were greatly reduced by the rules guiding reapportionment in the 1970s. Smaller turnout differences may have also reduced the difference between the parties in their mean number of unwasted votes, thereby reducing bias. As already noted, district turnout differences are often the reason for unwasted-vote differences between the parties, the basis of electoral system bias. Thus, reducing turnout differences by equalizing district populations may reduce partisan bias.

The reapportionment criteria of the 1970s may not have been the only factor reducing partisan bias. Another set of legal and social changes that might have reduced partisan bias was the civil rights movement. Because of the Voting Rights Act of 1965 and a series of court rulings, voter registration for blacks became a less imposing or discriminatory process, and a larger percentage of voting-age black Americans registered to vote, especially in southern states. Additionally, because of the civil rights movement, more blacks became politically active. With both the easing of voter-registration demands and the mobilization of black Americans, turnout among minorities increased significantly in the 1960s and 1970s. While black turnout was increasing, turnout among whites was declining.[6] Thus, the turnout difference between black and white Americans shrank.[7] This narrowing of the racial turnout gap should have also reduced turnout differences between historically low-turnout southern and northern inner-city districts with large minority populations and predominantly white districts with historically higher turnout. This should have increased the price in votes of the cheap seats and thereby reduced the partisan bias of the electoral system.

Beyond the legal changes associated with reapportionment and minority voting rights, a further sociopolitical change might have also reduced partisan bias. Changes in the socioeconomic class makeup of the political parties may have contributed to a reduction in partisan bias over time. As Abramson et al. (1994) well document, the association between socioeconomic status and partisan voting has eroded a good deal since the 1950s, although Democrats continue to draw more support among the less educated and less affluent segments of society. With the deterioration in the association between party voting and class, Democratic candidates may be doing a bit better in higher-socioeconomic, higher-turnout districts, and Republican candidates may be doing a bit better in lower socioeconomic, lower-turnout districts than they historically did. Thus, several legal and socioeconomic partisan changes may have caused a trend toward a less biased electoral system.

On the other hand, during the time in which changes in the legal and socioeconomic aspects of the electoral system may have diminished partisan bias, demographic changes may have served to increase bias. Two demographic changes in particular may have heightened district

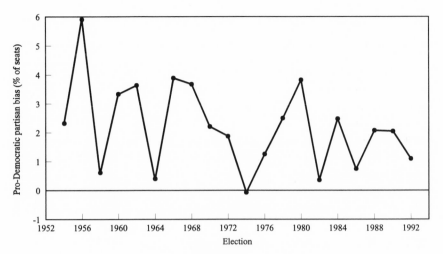

Figure 6.1
Trend in Partisan Bias, 1954–1992

turnout and partisan differences and, thus, increased bias. The first development is the large-scale immigration of lower socioeconomic groups, especially Hispanics, primarily settling in inner-city neighborhoods. Many of these immigrants were illegal aliens, and many of them are included in population counts used in establishing district boundaries. These illegal aliens, while contributing to the population count, do not contribute to the district's vote count, since as noncitizens they are ineligible to vote. The second demographic change relevant to partisan bias is the "white flight" to the suburbs. A number of racial, life-style, transportation, and economic developments caused a significant migration of the white middle class to the booming suburbs in the 1960s and 1970s. This may have also increased the district turnout differences between the parties and thereby increased partisan bias. Thus, there are both reasons to suppose that partisan bias favoring the Democrats may have decreased and countervailing reasons to suppose that bias may have increased throughout this period.

Figure 6.1 plots the partisan bias of the electoral system since 1954. As the figure shows, there is no strong trend. Bias has fluctuated erratically. For instance, the electoral system strongly benefited Democrats in 1962, very weakly benefited them in 1964, and then again strongly benefited them in 1966. Despite this volatility, there is some evidence suggesting that partisan bias may be marginally smaller in recent years.

Before 1972, partisan bias exceeded 3 percent in 6 of the 10 elections. After 1972, partisan bias only reached that level on one occasion (1980). More systematically, a regression using an over-time, or temporal, countervariable indicates that partisan bias has been reduced by about a tenth of a percentage point in each election.[8] An alternative regression using a dummy variable for elections after the 1970s reapportionment indicates that partisan bias is about 60 percent of its prior level.[9] Thus, while certainly not a strong or consistent trend, there is some evidence to suggest that the electoral system is now working slightly less to the Democratic Party's advantage than it once did. Presumably, changes in the electoral rules for reapportionment and the weakening of the class basis of partisanship, changes that should have weakened partisan bias, were sufficient to more than offset the demographic shifts that might have bolstered bias in the electoral system.

Redistricting and Partisan Bias

Of the many possible sources of partisan bias, political folklore would probably hold partisan gerrymandering in the decennial redistricting process as the most pernicious. Republican and journalistic anecdotes abound of cases in which Democratic state legislators, governors, and even judges have designed, enacted, or imposed districting lines to maximize Democratic clout. There is certainly reason to give these stories and complaints some credence as general causes of partisan bias. As noted in chapter 2, Democrats have controlled a majority of state legislatures throughout this period and in many states have often had complete control of the executive and legislative branches of government. They have had ample opportunity to influence, if not actually draw, district boundaries. Naturally, political self-interest would lead the party to take advantage of these redistricting opportunities. Thus, there is good reason to hypothesize, as many Republicans have, that redistricting provided the Democratic tilt to the electoral system.

There are also good reasons, however, to suppose that redistricting has not been responsible for bias. First, although the Democratic Party controlled many redistricting plans, they have had to compromise with Republicans at many others, and, in some cases, Republicans controlled the power to redistrict. Democratic redistricting successes may have been muted by the necessity to compromise and partially offset in the aggregate by Republican successes elsewhere. Second, even where Democrats controlled the process, there are competing demands in the drawing of district lines. While the party would like to maximize its seats, its incumbents would like lines drawn to ensure their safe reelection, even at the expense of the party in adjoining districts. Racial concerns to ensure the possibility of the election of racial minorities, a concern fortified by the Voting Rights Act, also compete with partisan goals. Third, as noted in chapter 4, there are two ways a party can gain additional seats through redistricting. One way is to pack its opponent's voters into a few districts, increasing the partisan difference in the mean number of unwasted votes and, thus, partisan bias. However, a party can also gain an advantage by splitting up the opposition vote so that it falls just short of a majority in many districts (the strategy termed "cracking" [Butler and Cain, 1992, 87]), thus increasing the responsiveness of the electoral system. That is, even intentional and successful gerrymandering may not take the form of increased partisan bias (Abramowitz, 1983). Finally, even when state Democrats attempt to pack Republican voters into a few districts, they are not likely to meet consistently with success. Standard redistricting criteria, such as the contiguity and compactness of districts, and the geographic distribution of partisans place some constraints on gerrymandering. Moreover, gerrymandering, even when relatively unconstrained, is an inexact science. Voters cannot always be counted on to behave as anticipated.[10]

The effects of redistricting on bias are examined through several regressions. Each attempts to account for variation in the electoral systems' bias favoring the Democrats in elections from 1952 to 1992. The first specification includes a single dummy variable taking a value of 1 for each election immediately following a redistricting. The construction of this variable was complicated by the fact that states have been redistricted at irregular intervals and different times. Although states have usually been redistricted following the decennial census and national reapportionment of seats, some delayed, and the court rulings regarding the one-person, one-vote principle caused further redistrictings in the mid-1960s. From 1952 to 1990, there are six elections in which a significant number of states (17 or more) redrew district lines (Cox, 1981, table 1). These postredistricting elections were in 1952, 1962, 1966, 1968, 1972, and 1982. If redistricting consistently boosted pro-Democratic partisan bias in the electoral system, there should be a significant positive coefficient for this dichotomous variable. A second specification included a countervariable that increased by 1 for each election after an election until the next redistricting. If the effects of redistricting erode with time, we should expect a significant negative coefficient for this

Table 6.1
The Effects of Redistricting on Partisan Bias, 1952–1992

Independent Variables	Dependent Variable: Democratic Electoral Bias (%)		
	(1)	(2)	(3)
Post-Redistricting Election	.70	—	—
	(.75)		
Post-Redistricting Counter	—	.01	—
		(.25)	
1952 Election	—	—	3.09
			(1.62)
1962 Election	—	—	1.52
			(1.62)
1966 Election	—	—	1.77
			(1.62)
1968 Election	—	—	1.56
			(1.62)
1972 Election	—	—	−.24
			(1.62)
1982 Election	—	—	−1.76
			(1.62)
1992 Election	—	—	−1.02
			(1.62)
Constant	2.12	2.33	2.12
R^2	.04	.00	.39
Adjusted R^2	.00	.00	.07
Standard Error of Estimate	1.62	1.66	1.56

Note: $N = 21$. Standard errors are in parentheses. The partisan bias percentages are presented in table 5.9. The 1952 election was added to the analysis as the major redistricting election of the 1950s. Partisan bias in 1952 was 5.2 percent in favor of the Democrats.

countervariable. Finally, the effects of redistricting were gauged with a set of dummy variables reflecting each of the six postredistricting elections separately. This specification acknowledges that all redistricting efforts may not have had the same effect.

Table 6.1 presents the redistricting regression results. They suggest that widespread gerrymandering does not systematically account for the Democratic advantage in the electoral system.[11] Although both general redistricting indicators (in equations 1 and 2) had their expected sign (indicating redistricting may have helped Democrats, if it helped either party), neither approached conventional standards of statistical significance.[12] The third regression, examining individual redistricting years, suggests that redistricting may have helped Democrats in the 1950s ($p <$ .04, one-tailed). However, since the 1950s, redistricting effects have not approached statistical significance, although redistricting coefficients were in the expected pro-Democratic direction until the 1970s. The bottom line, reinforced by the anemic proportions of explained variance in bias, is that the Democratic Party's advantage in redistricting appears to play an inconsequential role in the aggregate pro-Democratic partisan bias in the electoral system.

The fact that general redistricting effects are not in evidence does not indicate that gerrymandering does not, from time to time and place to place, have an effect. Moreover, some redistricting effects are masked by other developments that may have biased the electoral system. Redistricting in California illustrates both localized redistricting consequences and the problem of detecting them. Probably no state in recent history was as carefully gerrymandered as California was in the 1980s. With the support of a Democratic governor and state legislature, Democratic Congressman Phil Burton masterfully devised a plan to advantage the Democratic Party. The plan, as Butler and Cain (1992, 104) summarize it, displaced some Republican incumbents and put others into the same district while at the same time creating new Democratic districts and strengthening existing Democratic seats.

Despite vehement Republican protests and the admiration of Democratic politicians for Burton's artistry in sculpting the plan, hard evidence of the plan's effectiveness is elusive. The problem is that the post-Burton system does not look substantially more biased in favor of the Democrats than the pre-Burton system. Nonetheless, the California electoral system was biased in favor of the Democrats in the elections following implementation of the Burton gerrymander. In 1982, Democrats won 28 of 45 seats (62 percent) with less than 52 percent of the statewide vote. The average winning Democrat received just over 100,000 votes, while the average winning Republican received nearly 120,000. The unwasted-votes analysis indicates that the electoral system in California favored Democrats by 3.7 percent of the seats in 1982. However, because of the severe malapportionment that had developed among the state's districts over the course of the 1970s, the pre-Burton electoral system was at least as biased in favor of the Democrats as the post-Burton system.[13] In 1980, prior to the Burton plan, Democrats won a majority of seats (22 of 43, or 51.2 percent) with a minority of the statewide vote (46.7 percent). The typical Democratic winner received 104,182 votes while the typical

Republican winner received 143,735, nearly 40,000 more votes. The unwasted-vote analysis indicates that California's electoral system in 1980 favored Democrats by 9.3 percent of the state's districts.[14] In short, redistricting may produce electoral system bias in particular cases, even if this effect does not stand out clearly from preexisting bias. However, there is no clear evidence of a generalized gerrymandering basis for partisan bias.

Turnout and Partisan Bias

While gerrymandering is probably not a basis for the general partisan bias in the system, it is possible that bias, based on disparities in turnout, might be affected by the extent of voter turnout. Partisan bias may be minimized with increases in turnout. According to conventional wisdom, if nonvoters voted, the great majority would vote for Democrats. This view is grounded in the relationship of socioeconomic class to both partisanship and turnout. Those on the lower socioeconomic rungs are less likely to vote (Verba and Nie, 1972; Wolfinger and Rosenstone, 1980; Rosenstone and Hansen, 1993; and Leighley and Nagler, 1992), but those that do vote tend to identify with and to vote for Democrats (Axelrod, 1986; Stanley et al., 1986; and Erikson et al., 1989). The supposition is that if the nonvoting poor and working class were to show up at the polls, they would vote for Democrats at a rate similar to that of the poor and working class who now vote. If so, if the nonvoters are in large measure a cadre of unmobilized Democratic votes, the pro-Democratic bias of the electoral system should decline in high-turnout elections. As the electorate swells, Democratic votes should be disproportionately added in traditionally low-turnout, lower socioeconomic districts, where Democrats have enjoyed their electoral system advantage. With these newly mobilized Democratic voters added to the electorate, the mean number of unwasted votes for winning Democratic candidates should rise to the mean for Republican winners, and the pro-Democratic electoral system bias should shrink. Bias should decline with a higher price in votes for the now not-quite-so-cheap seats.

Although conventional wisdom anticipates bias to decline with rising turnout, there are both theoretical reasons and empirical findings to suggest this should not occur. First, social characteristics and backgrounds, though significantly related to political predispositions and vote choices, are far from determinative (Abramson et al., 1994; Stanley et al., 1986; and Erikson et al., 1989). There is a good deal of political diversity within most sociodemographic groups, and, while many groups have distinct political leanings, few would now argue, as the authors of *The People's Choice* did a half century ago, that "a person thinks, politically, as he is, socially" (Lazarsfeld et al., 1944, 27). Second, while many nonvoters have sociological similarities to Democratic voters, Campbell (1960) and De-Nardo (1980) argue that their political distinctiveness is more telling. Nonvoters and occasional or peripheral voters tend to be less interested in politics and have less firmly held political beliefs and preferences. As DeNardo puts it, "Peripheral voters are just as fickle inside the voting booth as they are about getting to it" (1980, 418). In the absence of firm standing commitments, they are especially likely to be swayed by the po-litical winds of the campaign and cannot be counted upon by either party (Petrocik, 1981).[15] Moreover, empirical examinations of presidential vo-ting indicate that if nonvoters voted, they would divide their votes very much like current voters (Teixeira, 1992a, 1992b; Calvert and Gilchrist, 1993).[16] This may also be the case in congressional voting. An examina-tion of the reported preferences of nonvoters in surveys conducted in elections from 1978 to 1990 indicates that they would not have voted consistently and substantially more Democratic than actual voters.[17] Fi-nally, regressions on elections from 1936 to 1992 indicate that the Demo-cratic congressional vote does not increase with rising turnout, whether or not controls are included for the election being an on-year election.[18] On the basis of these theoretical reasons and empirical findings, there are good reasons to suspect that nonvoters are not systematically inclined to vote Democratic. Thus, we should not expect the Democratic vote to increase with increasing turnout, even in low-turnout Democratic strong-holds. Nor should we expect increasing turnout to reduce the unwasted-vote gap between Democratic and Republican winners and thereby shrink electoral bias.

The evidence indicates that bias does not decrease with higher voter turnout. The plot of electoral system bias and national voter-turnout rates in figure 6.2 demonstrates that there is no close association between turnout and bias. To the extent that there is any relationship, contrary to expectations, it appears to be positive rather than negative. However, this apparently slightly positive association is probably spurious. Since there is a general downward trend in turnout over this period, some effects of the sociodemographic downward trend in bias is misattributed to turn-out.[19] In any case, the evidence does not support the notion that bias declines with rising turnout. Increased turnout apparently does not equalize unwasted votes between the parties by awakening a reserve of Democratic peripheral voters.

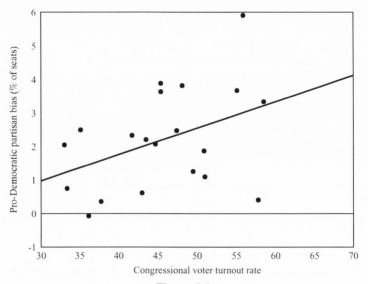

Figure 6.2
Partisan Bias and Congressional Turnout, 1954–1992

The Congressional Vote and Partisan Bias

If the variability of partisan bias is not explainable by redistricting or turnout and only slightly reflects a downward trend, presumably traceable to changing rules governing redistricting and a weakening of the socioeconomic basis of partisanship, what accounts for variation in bias from one election to the next? One possible explanation is that bias depends on support for Democratic candidates and varies with that support. But why? How does this work? It begins with the plausible assumption that the cheap seats held by Democrats are the seats that they are least likely to lose. Thus, in years in which the public mood is least sympathetic to Democrats, their losses tend to be in moderate- and higher-turnout districts. This increases the partisan-turnout and unwasted-vote gaps and, therefore, the extent of partisan bias. In addition, in bad years for Democrats, they may be more likely to lose votes in their middle- and higher-turnout districts just because there are more votes there to lose. In contrast, in good years for Democrats, their seat gains may come in moderate- to high-turnout districts, since they already hold a large majority of the very-low-turnout districts. They may also gain votes both by conversion and slightly higher turnout in the cheap seats,

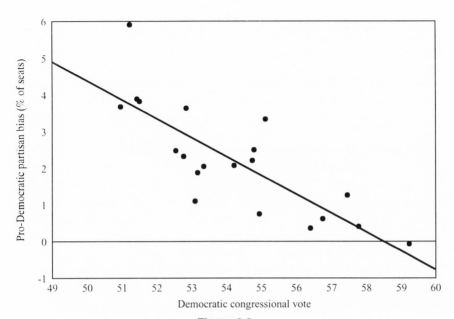

Figure 6.3
Partisan Bias and the Democratic House Vote, 1954–1992

making them not quite as cheap as they had been. Both of these changes narrows the partisan-turnout and unwasted-vote differences, thus reducing partisan bias. The two parties come closer to paying the same market price, in votes, for a victory.

What does the evidence show? Was the pro-Democratic bias of the electoral system greater in elections in which Democrats received a smaller share of the vote? In chapter 5 we observed that partisan bias was smallest in years in which the Democratic vote was relatively strong and was greatest when the Democratic vote barely reached a majority. In the seven elections since 1954 in which Democrats received at least 55 percent of the national vote, the mean partisan bias of the electoral system favored them by less than 1 percent of contested seats. On the other hand, in the five elections during this period in which Democrats received no more than 52.5 percent of the vote, partisan bias typically favored them by about 4 percent of contested seats.

The electoral system's bias is plotted against the national Democratic congressional vote in figure 6.3. As is evident from this plot, there is a pronounced negative association between the Democratic vote and the extent of pro-Democratic bias in an election. A bivariate regression indicates that bias is reduced by 0.6 of a percentage point with every additional percentage point of the congressional vote for Democrats ($r = -.86$). The evidence could not be much stronger: *partisan bias for Democrats in the electoral system is inversely related to the national vote for Democrats.*

Table 6.2 offers some insight into the basis for the inverse relationship of partisan bias and the national vote. The table examines the victory rates of Democratic congressional candidates in contested districts with different levels of turnout and districts won with different amounts of votes cast for the winning candidate (unwasted votes). Districts are grouped in quintiles both by the number of votes cast and by the number of unwasted votes cast in the district. The victory rates in these groupings were reported in tables 5.3 and 5.6, respectively. The national Democratic two-party congressional vote is the independent variable explaining successful election outcomes in each category.

With respect to turnout, as one might expect, the table indicates that as Democrats do better nationally, they register gains in both low- and high-turnout districts. Coefficients are positive and statistically significant ($p < .05$, one-tailed) in each category. For every additional percentage point of the national vote, Democrats win an additional 1 percent of the lowest turnout districts. However, also as expected, in good years, Democrats are likely to register even larger gains in middle- and higher-turnout districts. For every additional percentage point of the national vote, Democrats can expect to win approximately an additional 2 percent of seats in middle- and high-turnout districts. By picking up two high-turnout districts for every one additional low-turnout district with each percentage point gain in the vote, the proportion of Democratic victories that are in the cheap seats is reduced.[20]

The fact that Democrats registered greater gains in middle- and high-turnout districts in good Democratic years should reduce the disparity between the parties in the number of votes that each expends to win a seat. The second half of table 6.2 indicates that this was indeed the case. The pattern of coefficients in the unwasted-vote categories is even stronger than the turnout pattern. As the Democratic national vote increased, it made a negligible difference in districts won with few votes but an increasingly great difference in districts won with a relatively large number of votes.[21] The Democratic vote coefficient in the two lowest unwasted-vote categories of districts were small (less than .4) and not statistically significant ($p < .05$, one-tailed). In the middle and higher categories of unwasted votes, however, Democratic victory rates increased substantially when Democrats did well nationally. The coefficients were

Table 6.2

The Democratic Congressional Vote and Success in Districts, by District Turnout and Number of Unwasted Votes, 1954–1992

| | Dependent Variable: Percentage of Seats in Category Won by Democratic Candidates | | | | | | | | | |
| | Turnout Category | | | | | Unwasted-Votes Category | | | | |
Independent Variable	Low 1	2	3	4	High 5	Low 1	2	3	4	High 5
Democratic Share of the National Two-Party House Vote	1.01 (.66)	1.12 (.66)	2.08 (.70)	2.10 (.49)	1.87 (.68)	.39 (.70)	−.35 (.78)	1.07 (.90)	2.99 (.72)	4.19 (.60)
Constant	23.94	−2.76	−64.20	−66.85	−55.91	49.27	76.55	−7.56	−109.39	−181.21
R^2	.12	.14	.33	.51	.30	.02	.01	.07	.49	.73
Adjusted R^2	.07	.09	.29	.48	.26	.00	.00	.02	.46	.72
Standard Error of Estimate	6.82	6.75	7.16	5.02	6.99	7.22	7.98	9.28	7.38	6.18

Note: N = 20. The Democratic congressional vote is the party's share of the two-party national vote. The turnout and unwasted-vote categories are as used in tables 5.3 and 5.6, respectively. They reflect the quintiles of contested districts in each year on the turnout and unwasted-vote variables. Turnout categories are based on the actual number of total votes cast in districts. Standard errors are in parentheses.

statistically significant ($p < .01$, one-tailed) in regressions on districts in the two highest categories of unwasted votes. In other words, this was where the action was. The Democratic national vote made little or no difference in low-unwasted-vote districts. They carried a large majority of these districts under any circumstances (recall table 5.6). The Democratic vote made a big difference, however, in districts won with big votes. Among districts with the highest number of unwasted votes, Democrats won more than 4 percent more of these seats with every additional percentage point of the national vote. In times favorable to the Democrats, they were more likely to win in higher-turnout districts and win by larger margins. Both of these effects add a considerable number of noncheap seats to the cheap-seat base for the Democrats. The mix should mean that the average number of votes expended by Democrats in victories comes closer to that of Republicans. The bottom line is that, in good years for Democrats, the electoral system comes closer to partisan neutrality, but in bad years for Democrats, the electoral system was heavily biased in the Democratic Party's favor.

The effects of the congressional vote on bias is estimated within the context of trend, turnout, and redistricting effects in table 6.3. The regressions indicated that the conclusions based on the bivariate analyses stand intact. There has been a slight downward trend in partisan bias. Redistricting and overall turnout have negligible effects on aggregate bias. Finally, and most important, bias is inversely related to the vote for Democrats.[22] When Democrats received a larger vote, bias declined. They registered gains in uncheap seats. Conversely, when Democrats received a smaller vote, bias increased. For every additional percentage point of the national Democratic vote, the electoral system's partisan bias is reduced by about 0.5 percent of the seats in the House.

A caveat to this pattern is in order, however. While, empirically, the pro-Democratic bias of the electoral system increases with a declining Democratic vote, this cannot, logically, extend indefinitely. At the extremes, when one of the parties receives all or none of the votes, there can be no bias. Hypothetically, if either party received zero votes, the system would award that party 0 percent of the seats, and if either party received all of the votes, it would win all of the seats. There would be no bias at these extremes, because the organization of the vote at these extremes is irrelevant to the outcome. In terms of the present situation, as their vote declined, Democrats would eventually lose even the cheap seats (thereby reducing bias). Conversely, with a rising Democratic vote, they would eventually win the "high-rent" districts (again reducing bias).

Table 6.3
Influences on Democratic Electoral Bias, 1954–1992

Independent Variables	Dependent Variable: Democratic Electoral Bias in Contested Seats (%)				
	(1)	(2)	(3)	(4)	(5)
Democratic Share of the	−.54	−.54	−.51	−.53	−.52
National House Vote	(.08)	(.09)	(.08)	(.08)	(.09)
Post-Redistricting	−.67	−.64	—	—	—
Election	(.40)	(.45)			
National Turnout	.03	.03	—	—	—
	(.03)	(.03)			
Year Counter	−.04	—	−.04	—	—
	(.016)		(.015)		
Post-1964	—	−.51	—	−.86	—
		(.46)		(.42)	
Constant	99.41	30.39	115.00	31.31	30.18
R^2	.81	.76	.76	.72	.65
Adjusted R^2	.75	.70	.73	.68	.63
Standard Error of Estimate	.75	.83	.79	.85	.93
Durbin-Watson	2.38	2.12	2.46	2.11	1.65

Expected Democratic Partisan Bias when the Democratic Vote Equals 50%:

Equation 3 (with Year = 1972)	$30.2 - (.508 \times 50) = 4.8$
Equation 4 (post-1964)	$30.5 - (.526 \times 50) = 4.2$
Equation 5	$30.2 - (.516 \times 50) = 4.4$
Democratic Partisan Bias	+4.2% to +4.8% of contested seats (+15.5 to +17.7 seats) or +3.6% to +4.1% of all seats

Note: N = 20. The Democratic congressional vote is the party's share of the two-party national vote. The Democratic partisan bias is the percentage of seats that the Democratic Party would have won with 50 percent of the unwasted congressional vote minus 50 percent (the percentage it would have won in an unbiased system). Partisan bias percentages are presented in table 5.9. An average of 368 seats were contested in elections since 1954. Standard errors are in parentheses.

Considering these logical constraints on the relationship between the Democratic vote and the extent of bias, we should be very cautious in extrapolating likely levels of bias under Republican-vote majorities. Nevertheless, in the middle of the vote distribution, where the parties vie for control of the House, the system has been most favorable to Democrats when they have been down on their luck.

This caveat aside, the analysis suggests that the earlier time-series estimate (see table 4.6) understated the extent of bias when both parties evenly split the vote. This underestimation goes beyond that involved with prior incumbency inflating the vote. The reason for this second underestimation is the assumption that partisan bias has been a fixed characteristic of the electoral system over the last four decades. Because of this assumption, the estimated bias is similar to the average bias for the period (at the average vote) rather than the bias present when the vote is evenly divided. If the effects of the slight downward trend and the congressional vote are taken into account, the electoral system midway through this period (1972) was biased by 4.5 percent of contested seats (about 17 seats) in favor of the Democrats rather than the 3.6 percent of all seats (15 to 16 seats) found in the time-series analysis of table 4.6 or the 2.4 percent of contested seats (about 9 or 10 seats) average bias found table 5.9.[23] The calculations are presented in table 6.3. In 1990 the bias was only slightly less (4 percent of seats or about 15 seats). After considering the incumbency multiplier effect, as we examined it in chapter 5, the partisan bias favoring Democrats has probably been in the neighborhood of 18 to 22 seats. This, however, does not alter the basic finding: although bias in the electoral system alone was not sufficient to preserve the Democratic House majority, it was consistently in the Democrats' favor, contributed substantially to the maintenance and size of their majority, and was greatest when the Democratic majority was most threatened.

❑ The Swing Ratio When Bias Varies ❑

The fact that partisan bias varies inversely with the congressional vote has important implications for the estimation of the swing ratio, the responsiveness of the electoral system. Recall that responsiveness is the characteristic of the electoral system in which the representation of parties is affected by one party wasting more of its votes in losing candidacies than the opposing party. Whereas partisan bias entails asymmetric deviations from proportional representation, responsiveness entails symmetric deviations from proportional representation in which a party would receive Y proportion of seats if it received X proportion of votes, regardless of whether the party in question was the Democratic or Republican Party. Conventional longitudinal estimates of responsiveness have been based on the faulty assumption that partisan bias is fixed. Since partisan bias is not constant, and, moreover, since it is affected by the congressional vote, previous estimates of responsiveness may be off the mark.

Table 6.4
The Swing Ratio with and without an Adjustment
for Unwasted-Vote Bias, 1954–1992

| | Dependent Variable: Democratic Two-Party Share of Seats (%) | | | |
| | Unadjusted | | Adjusted for Partisan Bias | |
Independent Variable	(1)	(2)	(3)	(4)
Democratic Share of the	1.53	1.96	1.97	2.53
National Two-Party House	(.17)	(.33)	(.18)	(.31)
Vote				
Post-1964	—	32.10	—	43.01
		(21.92)		(20.21)
Post-1964 × Democratic	—	−.58	—	−.78
House Vote		(.40)		(.37)
Constant	−23.02	−46.71	−48.48	−79.59
R^2	.81	.83	.88	.90
Adjusted R^2	.80	.79	.87	.88
Standard Error of Estimate	1.82	1.90	1.85	1.75
Durbin-Watson	1.62	1.62	1.76	1.78

Note: N = 20. Standard errors are in parentheses. Because of autocorrelation, a two-stage Cochrane-Orcutt pseudo-GLS analysis was used to estimate these coefficients (Ostrom, 1978). The first-order autocorrelations for the equations were .246, .156, .194, and .102, respectively. These were used in the partial differencing of the lagged variables. The intercepts have been converted to the OLS equivalent. The adjustment for partisan bias entailed calculating the Democratic share of seats if there had been no partisan bias as calculated in table 5.10 (for all districts).

An accurate estimate of the swing ratio requires the examination of the seat-vote relationship while taking the variability of partisan bias into account. Since the extent of partisan bias has already been calculated and the division of the House without partisan bias has likewise been calculated, the relationship of the parties' division of the vote to the unbiased division of seats can be examined directly. Table 6.4 presents the regressions of votes on seats, both unadjusted and adjusted for partisan bias. The adjustment for partisan bias is the share of seats that the Democrats would have won if there were no electoral bias. These were calculated and presented earlier in table 5.10. Since the one-person, one-vote rulings and the growth of the incumbency advantage may have reduced the responsiveness of the electoral system, bringing it more in line with a proportional representation system, regressions allowing for a change in responsiveness were also examined. These regressions included an interaction term of the vote with a dummy variable for post-1964 elections and a separate additive term for these elections.

Once the effects of partisan bias are taken into account, the electoral system appears to be more responsive than previously estimated. The estimated responsiveness without an adjustment for partisan bias indicates that Democrats could expect to gain about 2.3 seats for every additional percentage point of the vote in elections before 1964 and about 1.5 seats for every percentage point of the vote after 1964.[24] The estimates of responsiveness are greater in both cases in which adjustments for partisan bias are made. Before 1964, the responsiveness of the electoral system caused about 2.5 seats to shift for every percentage point of the vote. After 1964, responsiveness caused about a 1.7 seat shift for every percentage point of the vote. In both periods, estimates of the swing ratio were about 25 percent greater after adjusting for variation in partisan bias.[25]

❑ The Basis of Cheap Seats ❑

The reason why the electoral system has consistently favored the Democrats since at least the mid-1950s is clear: *the electoral system has been biased because Democrats have consistently carried a large majority of low-turnout congressional districts—the cheap seats.* The mix of cheap seats in the Democrats' portfolio of seats also explains why bias has varied. Bias is greater in bad years for the Democrats, when a larger share of the seats that they continue to hold are the cheap seats. Conversely, bias is smaller in good Democratic years, when Democrats add higher-turnout districts to their base of cheap seats. This raises the average number of votes for winning Democrats closer to that of the average winning Republican. While the phenomenon of cheap seats explains why the system is biased in favor of the Democrats and why this bias has varied in different election years, several questions about cheap seats themselves remain. Why do cheap seats exist, and why do Democrats win the lion's share of them? Are cheap seats intentionally created? Are they avoidable, or are they an inevitable and natural product of a constitutional system that apportions congressional seats by population rather than by voters? Essentially, these questions revolve around one central question—who or what is responsible for there being cheap seats? Who created the cheap seats? The Democrats? The Constitution? Or, is there some other reason why some seats are so cheap?

Republicans are inclined to believe that cheap seats are the intentional product of Democratic gerrymandering. We have seen, however, that there is little evidence to support this claim. Democrats are not so controlling, skillful, and single-minded as to be able to manipulate the system to their advantage on such a widespread and consistent basis. While Democratic gerrymandering is undoubtedly successful in many cases, and while redistricting effects may be masked by other demographic trends (as in California in the 1980s), there is no clear evidence that cheap Democratic seats depend on successful Democratic gerrymanders.

An alternative explanation of cheap seats, a view sometimes adhered to by Democrats, is that cheap seats are an inevitable outgrowth of the constitutional system set in place by the framers. The Constitution provided that seats in the House of Representatives would represent the people, not only those that voted. Article 1, Section 2 of the Constitution, specifying provisions for membership in the House, and subsequently Section 2 of the Fourteenth Amendment (ratified in 1868) indicate that "representatives shall be apportioned among the several states according to their respective numbers, counting the whole number of persons in each state." In other words, the House is supposed to represent people, not only voters. If in the process of creating equally populated districts, some districts contain many fewer voters than other districts, that is just the price of creating the constitutionally mandated equal population districts. What matters is that district populations, following the decennial census and reapportionment, are as nearly equal as possible.

But there are two faults with the notion that cheap seats spring naturally from constitutional arrangements.[26] First, the Constitution's principle of representation in the House being based on population refers to the apportionment of seats to the states and not directly to how these seats should be awarded within the separate states. Second, the creation of congressional districts within states does not prohibit in any way the creation of districts that are also likely to be more nearly equal in their numbers of voters.

Constitutional provisions apportioning representation to the states according to their populations did not require equal population, single-member districts for the election of representatives within the states. The Constitution was silent regarding whether a state's representatives should be elected at-large or in districts. While Madison had indicated in the 56th *Federalist* a preference for districted elections, the mode of election was left to state legislatures and the merits and constitutionality of both forms were publicly debated (Zagarri, 1987, 105–12). Many states in the nineteenth century and some in the twentieth century held at-large or multimember district elections for House seats. In 1824, for instance, about half of the states with more than one representative to the House elected their representatives through either an at-large system or through a mixture of single-member and multimember districts.[27] Some states (New Mexico and Hawaii) even into the 1960s were using at-large electoral systems. Thus, since the Constitution, at least as it was interpreted for some time, did not require single-member districts within the states, and since turnout disparities can only emerge from the single-member-district system (or some districting system), it is difficult to place the blame for cheap seats with the Constitution.

While not directly mandated by the Constitution, equal population, single-member districts have become the prevailing mode of awarding seats.[28] Are cheap seats a natural outgrowth of the equal population, single-member-district system? The answer is no. Districting systems of some sort are logically necessary for turnout differences to exist, and single-member-district systems (whether requiring equal populations or not) provide the greatest opportunity for these differences. However, there is no reason why they would inevitably produce districts with consistently large turnout differences. It is certainly logically possible to draw single-member-district lines within a state so that each district is equally populated *and* has an equal expected number of voters. Redistricting plans regularly take a variety of considerations besides population into account—compactness, community boundaries, and geographic contiguity, among other factors—the expected turnout in an area could be taken into account as well. Given the considerable stability in relative district turnout (and unwasted votes) that were observed in chapter 5, it seems practically possible to make reasonably reliable estimates of expected turnout in districts. While consideration of expected turnout would not guarantee an equal number of voters in districts, it could greatly reduce the huge differences among districts that have provided the basis for cheap seats. Moreover, the "equal protection" clause, the basis for demands of equally populated districts, would provide a strong foundation for requirements that districts be effectively equal in size as well as nominally equal (or equally populated).

If Democratic gerrymandering and the equal population, single-member-district system are not the cause of cheap seats, what is? The answer is geography, the fact that people with traits associated both with Democratic voting and with a failure to vote at all tend to live in the same areas and that the redistricting criteria of geographic compactness, contiguity, and respect for community boundaries tend to leave these areas intact when constructing district lines. In elections in the 1950s, for instance, the low-turnout contested districts tended to be geographically located in southern states. In 1954, for instance, nearly half of the lowest-turnout districts were in the South, despite the fact that barely 10 percent of all contested seats were in that region.[29] While many low-turnout districts continue to be found in the South, in more recent years a larger number of low-turnout districts have been in urban areas with large minority populations.[30] Of the lowest-turnout quintile of contested districts in 1990, less than a third were in the South (20 of 70, or 29 percent). An equal number of cheap seats were in New York City and Los Angeles alone. Eleven districts in New York City and nine districts in the Los Angeles area were in the lowest-turnout category in 1990. Whether in the rural South of the 1950s or the inner cities of the 1990s, cheap seats were created because district lines respected neighborhoods and the sociodemographic characteristics (socioeconomic status, regional culture, race) of residents in these neighborhoods predisposed some in these areas to vote Democratic and others not to vote at all.

❏ Overview ❏

Although the electoral system was not the sole reason for Democratic dominance in the House, it was an important ingredient. Without bias in the electoral system, Democratic majorities in several elections would have been tenuous. Chapter 5 demonstrated that partisan bias in the electoral system has been significant and consistently beneficial to the Democrats. This chapter demonstrated not only that the electoral system has been biased, but that bias varies in such a way that it was especially important to sustaining the Democratic majority up to 1994.

While electoral system bias was important to the Democratic majority over the last four decades, it has varied greatly. It has ranged from near neutrality in the 1974 election to a minor bias of four or five seats in some years (e.g., 1964, 1982, and 1986) to the severe bias in excess of a dozen seats at other times (e.g., 1956, 1966, 1968, and 1980). In this chapter, we explored several issues related to this variation. Did it reflect a trend related to the advent of the one-person, one-vote judicial rulings on redistricting? Did it reflect varying successes in partisan gerrymandering? Did it diminish with rising turnout, when previously nonvoting citizens with suspected Democratic proclivities flocked to the polls? Did it reflect the distribution of the congressional vote itself, where vote gains and vote losses came from? More specifically, did bias decline as the Democratic vote rose and, in doing so, raise the average price (in votes) of seats won by Democrats?

While a number of factors were plausible causes of varying levels of bias, most of these "likely suspects" had little or no effect. There was a slight downward trend in the extent of bias, perhaps related to the malapportionment rulings or perhaps related to the civil rights movement, but, whatever the mix of causes, this downward trend was only slight. There is no evidence that Democratic gerrymandering was effective enough on a widespread basis to have produced greater electoral system bias for their party. Contrary to what we might expect if gerrymandering effects were pervasive, bias was not greater immediately following the redrawing of district lines. There is also no evidence to suggest that Democratic cheap seats were a result of would-be Democratic voters who just did not bother to vote. If cheap seats were cheap just because Democrats were benefiting from a quasi-proxy voting system in which voters simply reflected the sentiments of their nonvoting neighbors, bias should have diminished on occasions when turnout surged and the somnambulant (would-be Democratic) neighbors awoke long enough to vote—but it did not.

There is only one condition strongly linked to variation in partisan bias—the congressional vote itself. Partisan bias was strongly and inversely related to the national congressional vote for Democrats. Bias was greatest when the Democratic vote was at its ebb and a larger portion of Democratic seats were cheap. On the other hand, the system was least biased when Democrats were doing well and gaining ground in high-turnout, competitive districts (as we observed in table 6.2).

The association of the congressional vote to partisan bias has important implications for understanding how the Democrats were able to maintain their dynasty in the House. Electoral bias was greatest when Democrats needed it most—when the voters provide them with only a slim vote majority. Thus, bias played an even greater role in maintaining the Democratic majority in the House than we first estimated. This relationship also explains why Democrats were so overrepresented in 1962, 1966, 1968, 1980, and 1984 (as we observed in chapter 3, table 3.1), each a fairly close election in terms of the national Democratic congressional vote.[31] The relationship between bias and the vote also confounded estimates of the swing ratio that commonly assume that bias is fixed. After adjusting for the relationship between bias and the vote, a reestimated swing ratio was greater than previous estimates.

This chapter also examined the causes of partisan bias in a deeper sense. Was it caused by intentional partisan maneuvering in the drawing of districts? Is it an inevitable outgrowth of the constitutional arrangement awarding districts on the basis of population rather than potential or actual voters? The answer to both questions is no. Cheap seats are a product of socioeconomic housing patterns and respect for geographic compactness and contiguity in the drawing of district lines.[32] They are also a product of failing to take into account likely turnout differences when constructing districts. Nevertheless they are a fact of political life and the basis for a Democratic tilt to the electoral system.

However caused, electoral system bias contributed to Democratic House majorities from 1954 until the Republican revolution of 1994. The system was consistently biased in favor of the Democrats and was particularly biased when Democrats needed help most. But did the electoral system also work to the Democratic Party's advantage before 1954 and did it continue to tilt in favor of the Democrats in 1994? These are the questions addressed in the next two chapters. First, was the electoral system prior to 1954 also biased in favor of the Democrats, or has bias been more distinctively a feature of the political system from 1954 to 1992?

7

□ □

The Historical
Perspective

There is no question that the electoral system worked to the benefit of the Democratic Party over the past 40 years and that it did extra duty when times were relatively tough for Democrats. Their lean vote majorities at these times were well fattened into substantial seat majorities by a favorable electoral system, and, although this process alone may not have preserved the Democratic seat majority in the House, it certainly helped. The consistent bias of the electoral system over the past 40 years raises a question of whether this bias was peculiar to the recent period or was present in earlier elections.

Some might suppose that if electoral system bias were partly responsible for the Democratic dynasty, it must have been absent or, at least, less pronounced in elections before 1954.[1] However, this need not be the case, so long as the claim is that bias helped to preserve the Democratic majority and not that the majority was dependent on bias alone. The bias in the electoral system that helped the Democrats from 1954 to at least 1992 may also have helped them before 1954. Although the thesis that bias in the electoral system helped to preserve the Democratic dynasty in the House is unaffected by whether bias predated the Democratic majority, it may still be useful to gain some greater historical perspective on the effects of this electoral system. Did the electoral system before the 1950s also favor the Democratic Party? Was it more or less biased than the system from 1954 to 1992?

❏ Cheap Seats before 1954 ❏

There are several reasons to suppose that partisan bias favoring the Democrats before 1954 was equal to, if not greater than, bias in more recent

146

years. All of the key factors responsible for creating bias were even stronger in the 1930s and 1940s. The class basis of partisan associations was stronger then. The class basis of turnout was no less strong then than now. Turnout in the then solidly Democratic South was especially low compared to turnout in other regions. In short, predominantly lower socioeconomic and southern districts were even more likely to have both more Democrats and more nonvoters. This provides the arithmetic for Democrats winning seats with fewer unwasted votes. In addition, disparities in district populations were greater in this era predating the one-person, one-vote court rulings. Although this variance could conceivably work to either party's favor, Democratic control of state governments controlling redistricting might have produced district lines favorable to Democratic congressional candidates.[2]

Table 7.1 presents Democratic victory rates in contested district elections in the nine national elections from 1936 to 1952. The districts are grouped by their turnout and by the number of votes cast for the winning candidate. Districts in the top half of the table are divided into quintiles by their total turnout (see table 5.3). Districts in the lower half of the table are divided into quintiles by the number of votes cast for the winning candidate in the district. The entries are the percentage of districts in a particular quintile won by a Democratic Party candidate. For instance, Democrats won 94 percent of the lowest-turnout districts in 1936 and only 22 percent of the highest-turnout districts in 1952.

In the elections from the mid-1930s to the early 1950s, Democrats won most of the cheap seats, just as they have done in elections since. Whether we examine district turnout or the total votes cast for the winning candidate (the unwasted votes), Democrats typically won about three of four of the cheap seats. In each election from 1936 to 1952, as in elections since, the Democrats' best showings among contested districts were in the lowest turnout and unwasted-vote categories.[3] They consistently won a large majority of these cheap seats. The range of Democratic victories in these low-turnout districts was from about two-thirds of the seats to better than 90 percent. Democrats did not have anything approaching this consistent rate of success in higher-turnout districts. In fact, Democrats typically won fewer than half of the seats in each of the four higher turnout and unwasted-votes categories. Democratic congressional majorities in this period were, thus, largely dependent on their winning the cheap seats and their great holding of uncontested seats, mostly in the then "Solid South."

Table 7.2 presents the extent of partisan bias and its basis in unwasted votes for the parties in the nine national elections from 1936 to

Table 7.1

The Association between the Party of the Winning Congressional
Candidate, District Turnout, and Unwasted Votes, 1936–1952

Year	Percentage of Districts Won by Democrats in District-Turnout Quintiles					Association between Total District Turnout (or the Vote for the Winning Candidate) and the Election of a Republican Representative	
	Low 1	2	3	4	High 5	r	Logit Derivative
1936	94	70	64	73	82	.08	.006
1938	80	49	45	35	48	.04	.019
1940	81	46	45	45	62	.32	.003
1942	81	32	29	25	29	.18	.026
1944	74	49	33	38	49	.12	.013
1946	74	30	19	22	19	.32	.054
1948	79	51	47	39	62	.18	.021
1950	66	56	27	26	39	.27	.039
1952	60	49	25	36	22	.25	.030
Mean	77	48	37	38	46		

Year	Percentage of Districts won by Democrats in District Unwasted-Vote Quintiles						
	Low 1	2	3	4	High 5	r	Logit Derivative
1936	91	60	69	79	85	−.01	−.002
1938	82	49	43	35	48	.02	.035
1940	76	57	34	46	65	.35	.002
1942	81	37	32	13	33	.19	.048
1944	72	46	31	39	53	.09	.017
1946	76	31	22	19	16	.35	.103
1948	76	46	47	46	62	.09	.020
1950	69	43	36	30	35	.26	.063
1952	66	39	31	31	25	.27	.057
Mean	77	45	38	38	47		

Note: See tables 5.3 and 5.6 for this analysis of elections from 1954 to 1992. The unwasted-vote quintiles divide districts into five groupings of approximately equal number on the basis of the number of votes cast in the district for the winning congressional candidate.

Table 7.2

Unwasted Vote Bias in Contested Elections, 1936–1952

| | Contested Districts | | | | | | |
| | Democrats | | Republicans | | | | |
Year	Seats Won	Mean Winning Votes	Seats Won	Mean Winning Votes	Half of Unwasted Votes in Contested Districts	Contested Seats That Democrats Would Have Won with Half of Unwasted Votes	Percentage Partisan Bias from Unwasted Votes
1936	269	66,328	82	65,324	11,599,400	175 (49.8)	+.2 Republican
1938	169	55,425	158	63,242	9,679,550	175 (53.4)	+3.4 Democratic
1940	187	73,594	149	74,997	12,468,300	169 (50.4)	+.4 Democratic
1942	122	42,029	191	51,519	7,483,900	178 (56.9)	+6.9 Democratic
1944	168	67,993	178	73,144	12,221,200	180 (51.9)	+1.9 Democratic
1946	112	42,251	232	61,939	9,551,000	226 (65.7)	+15.7 Democratic
1948	191	66,645	152	71,101	11,768,300	177 (51.5)	+1.5 Democratic
1950	141	58,302	188	70,554	10,742,300	184 (56.0)	+6.0 Democratic
1952	129	82,298	207	96,244	15,269,550	186 (55.2)	+5.2 Democratic
Mean Partisan Bias							+4.5 Democratic
Median Partisan Bias							+3.4 Democratic

Note: Numbers in parentheses are percentages. Seats uncontested by a major party candidate, multimember districts, seats won by third-party or independent congressional candidates, and at-large seats (except those for one district states) are excluded from these calculations. The half of total unwasted votes is rounded to the nearest 50 votes. The number of contested seats that the Democrats would have won if the parties evenly split the vote can be calculated by dividing half the unwasted votes in contested districts by the mean number of unwasted votes for Democratic candidates. This number of seats can then be converted into the percentage of all contested seats in that election. Since a neutral system would award 50 percent of seats for half of the unwasted votes, any percentage of seats awarded that is greater than 50 percent reflects partisan bias in the electoral system.

1952.[4] The data indicate that the magnitude of the pro-Democratic electoral system bias in elections before 1954 was about as great or even slightly greater than in post-1954 elections. With but one exception, the electoral system was biased in favor of the Democrats throughout this period. The sole exception was the 1936 election, and, in this case, as in the 1974 exception of the post-1954 era, the electoral system was quite nearly neutral. The electoral system bias from 1936 to 1952 boosted Democratic numbers in the House by an average of about 15 seats and, though incumbency advantages were not so great in those days, the incumbency-multiplier effect undoubtedly made the typical pro-Democratic bias even a bit greater.

As in more recent elections, Democrats in these pre-1954 elections carried a large majority of low-turnout districts, the cheap seats. In every election from 1938 to 1952, more votes were cast for the typical Republican candidate winning an election than for the typical Democratic winner. However, while the magnitude and basis of partisan bias before and after 1954 were similar, the location of the cheap seats was not. As we have already seen (recall table 5.5), many cheap seats in more recent elections have been northern inner-city districts with large minority populations. By contrast, in the earlier elections most cheap seats were in the South and its bordering states. For example, in the 1942 election, 15 of the 20 contested congressional districts with the lowest turnout (each won by a Democrat) were in southern or border states.[5]

The 1950 election offers an unusual opportunity to see directly the effects of partisan bias. In this election, half of the national two-party congressional vote was cast for Democratic candidates and half for Republican candidates. Despite this even division of the vote, Democrats won 234 seats in the House (54 percent). Republicans won only 199 seats (46 percent).[6] Uncontested seats account for some of the overrepresentation of Democrats. In 1950, there were 92 Democrats who were elected without major-party opposition. In contrast, only seven Republicans had free rides. In the contested districts of the 1950 election, Democrats did not do as well, but they fared better than they might have in a less hospitable electoral system. The national Democratic vote in contested districts fell short of a majority (48 percent) and in the median contested district the Democratic candidate received slightly less than 50,000 votes, while the Republican candidate received almost 57,500 votes, a division of 46.5 percent versus 53.5 percent. Democrats also failed to carry a majority of the districts, taking only 141 of the 329 contested (43 percent). As in most elections, Democrats in 1950 typically expended fewer votes to win a seat than did Republicans. The typical winning Democratic candidate won with fewer than 60,000 votes. The typical Republican winner, on the other hand, received in excess of 70,000 votes. Democrats won 31 of the 35 contested districts with the lowest turnout, while Republicans won 23 of the 35 contested districts with the highest turnout.[7] If both parties had expended the same number of votes for a contested seat victory in 1950, Democrats would have won 15 fewer seats and Republicans 15 more.[8] The difference can be put in stark relief by examples at the extremes. At one extreme, a Democratic candidate won in the Twelfth District of Texas in 1950 with just over 13,000 votes of fewer than 17,000 votes cast. At the other extreme, a Republican won in the Twenty-second District of Ohio with nearly 220,000 votes of more than 350,000 cast.[9]

❑ **Bias in Good and Bad Years** ❑

Not all elections in this period were like 1950. As in more recent elections, there was a good deal of variation in bias in elections between 1936 and 1952. In several years, bias was nearly absent. In four of the nine elections (1936, 1940, 1944, and 1948), bias shifted fewer than seven seats to the Democratic column. In other elections, however, it was large. In 1942, 1946, 1950, and 1952, Democrats won at least 17 additional seats because of the electoral system. At the extreme, bias accounted for the election of at least 27 additional Democrats in the 1946 midterm, a 54-seat partisan swing.

The variation in bias in this pre-1954 period can be explained in much the same way as more recent variation in bias. Bias in the electoral system is greatest in the bad years for Democrats (when they need it most) and smallest in their good years. Of the nine pre-1954 elections examined, pro-Democratic bias was smallest in the three elections in which Democratic congressional candidates nationwide captured at least 53 percent of the vote (1936, 1940, and 1948). In contrast, bias most strongly benefited Democrats in the three elections in which Democrats received 50 percent (1950) or less of the national vote (1942 and 1946).[10]

The two extreme election years in this period best illustrate the association of the congressional vote and electoral system bias.[11] The 1946 election marked the low point of the national Democratic vote from 1936 to 1992 (45.3 percent of the vote). This was also the peak (15.7 percent of contested seats) of the electoral system's Democratic bias. In 1946, the typical Republican winner received almost half again as many votes as did the typical Democratic winner. Democrats in 1946 won only about one of five of the moderate-to-high-turnout districts, yet they continued to do well in their low-turnout strongholds—winning three of four of the lowest-turnout districts. Despite this strong electoral system tilt in their favor, Democrats lost control of the House in 1946, winning only 188 seats and only 112 of the contested seats. However, without bias, Democrats in 1946 would have been in an even more depleted minority.

The 1936 election stands in sharp contrast to 1946. In 1936, the national Democratic vote was at a high point (58.5 percent), a level only approached in the post-Watergate election of 1974, and the electoral system's pro-Democratic bias was at a low. The electoral system in 1936 was nearly neutral. As table 7.1 shows, Democrats in 1936 won about 9 of 10 of the lowest-turnout districts (which was not too far from usual), but they also did exceedingly well in high-turnout areas. They won nearly three out of four of the moderate- to high-turnout districts.[12] As in the post-1954 period, when Democrats did well nationally they added higher-turnout districts to their win column, and the vote for the typical winning Democratic candidate more nearly equalled that of the typical Republican winner. In these good Democratic years, a smaller portion of winning Democrats were sitting in the cheap seats.

❏ The Cheap Seats of the 1940s ❏

Where were the cheap seats before the 1950s? Cheap seats could be found in most parts of the country. A listing of seats falling in the lowest quintile of both turnout and unwasted votes in 1942, a total of 56 districts, finds 17 different states represented. Nevertheless, and despite the large number of uncontested districts in the region, a majority of contested cheap seats were in southern and border states.[13] In 1942, even though only 45 districts in these states were contested, and this amounted to only 14 percent of all contested districts nationally that election year, more than half of the districts in the lowest quintiles of turnout and unwasted votes were from these states. While the average vote for a winning candidate in a contested district outside the South in 1942 was about 52,000 votes, winning candidates in contested southern districts typically received less than half this number of votes.[14]

Table 7.3 presents the 17 districts that fell into both the lowest-turnout quintile and lowest-unwasted-vote quintile in each of the five elections following reapportionment in the 1940s. There may have been equally cheap seats during this period that failed to make the list because they were uncontested at some point during the decade, but these 17

Table 7.3

The Consistently Cheap Seats of the 1940s

State	District	Democratic Vote Percentage in Year				
		1942	1944	1946	1948	1950
Florida	5	71	68	61	71	77
Kentucky	5	61	58	51	66	63
Kentucky	7	51	53	41	61	56
Maryland	1	56	51	49	48	43
Maryland	3	73	74	64	71	66
Maryland	4	49	59	57	65	58
Nevada	AL	54	63	41	51	53
North Carolina	1	93	91	89	93	93
Ohio	5	36	32	40	48	43
Ohio	10	36	36	33	42	35
Ohio	11	39	46	39	49	47
Oklahoma	2	51	58	63	71	66
Oklahoma	6	58	60	66	74	67
Oklahoma	7	70	71	79	79	67
Oklahoma	8	39	42	45	58	46
South Dakota	2	28	31	26	34	40
Virginia	9	64	56	55	52	58
Seats Won by:						
Democrats		11	12	9	12	11
Republicans		6	5	8	5	6

Note: AL indicates an at-large statewide district. Any district uncontested in any of the five election years was dropped from the list. The 17 districts listed were contested districts in the lowest quintile of both district turnout and unwasted votes in each of the five elections from 1942 to 1950.

districts illustrate both the cheap seats of this era and the continuity of cheap seats.[15] These seats ranked near the bottom in both turnout and unwasted votes in each election from 1942 to 1950. The so-called "Fighting Ninth" Congressional District of Virginia is, in many ways, a good example of a cheap seat in the 1940s.

The "Fighting Ninth" of Virginia

The Ninth Congressional District of Virginia was composed of 12 counties in the state's southwestern corner along the Kentucky and West Virginia borders.[16] As Barone et al. (1972) wrote about the district in a later decade, the district is "really part of Appalachia. [It] is a virtually all-white coal mining area, where the hills, scarred by strip-miners, are dotted with the crude homes of the impoverished mountaineers who live here" (852). In 1930 the district elected John W. Flannagan Jr., a Democrat. Flannagan served nine terms in the House, winning reelection throughout the 1930s and 1940s until he retired in 1948.[17] Flannagan faced serious challenges from a Republican candidate in each election. Although he won each bid, Flannagan received less than 60 percent of the district vote in five of his nine races and never received more than two-thirds of the vote (Cox 1981, 1116–23). He was succeeded in the Ninth by Thomas B. Fugate, also a Democrat, who won the 1948 election by a narrow margin and served two terms.

The Ninth District of Virginia, although unusually competitive for a cheap seat (hence the "fighting" of the Fighting Ninth), was typical of many cheap seats of the 1930s and 1940s in that it was southern, poor, and was consistently won by Democrats. It was also consistently cheap. The total vote in the Fighting Ninth was never much more than half the vote of the typical contested district and often less than half. In 1942, for instance, the average turnout in contested districts nationally was over 79,000 votes, more than three times the 26,189 votes cast in Virginia's Ninth District. That year, the Democrat, Flannagan, went to Washington on the basis of fewer than 17,000 votes.[18] Of the 311 representatives who faced a major-party opponent in 1942, only 12 won with fewer votes than Flannagan.[19]

❑ Overview ❑

The effects of the electoral system before 1954 were examined in this chapter. The electoral system from 1936 to 1952, like that of the more recent period, was generally biased in favor of the Democrats. It played a role in inflating Democratic House majorities since at least the mid-1930s. In all but one of the nine pre-1954 elections examined, typical Democratic winning congressional candidates won with fewer votes than did typical Republican winners. There was no appreciable bias in the 1936 election and a negligible amount in 1940. In general, however, the pre-1954 electoral system was biased in favor of the Democrats by at least as much as the post-1954 system. The bias was based on the Democratic control of the cheap seats. They regularly won about three quarters of the cheap seats, a large percentage of which in this era were in southern and border states.

As in more recent elections, bias was greatest in bad years for the Democrats, when they most needed the help. When the going got rough for the Democrats, the first districts to go were the higher-turnout districts (1946). In tough times, they were able to hold most of their low-turnout strongholds, like Virginia's Fighting Ninth. Even in 1946, the worst year of the period for Democrats, they still won three of four of the cheapest seats.

The fact that electoral system bias in the 1936 to 1952 period looks much like that of more recent times in many ways should be expected. All the fundamentals to the relationship, the basis for cheap seats—the sociodemographic links to partisanship and turnout and electoral districting arrangements—were in place before 1954. Analysis of elections from 1936 to 1952 adds to the reliability of the post-1954 findings. Electoral system bias favoring the Democrats was evident in 27 of the 29 national elections from 1936 to 1992. The Democratic dynasty that truly began in the 1930s was built on a popular base of electoral support but was also magnified by the incumbency advantage and augmented by a large number of uncontested seats and by victories in a solid block of low-turnout districts—the cheap seats. Only the heavy midterm seat losses for the highly unpopular Truman administration in 1946 and the substantial coattails of Republican presidential candidate and national hero Dwight Eisenhower in 1952 were able briefly to interrupt Democratic dominance of the House over the sixty years from 1932 to 1992.[20] The evidence, before 1954 as well as since, lends support to the cheap-seats thesis. To a great extent, though by no means entirely, the Democratic Party was successful in maintaining its majority in the U.S. House of Representatives because the electoral system was biased in its favor.

But that majority came to a close, or was at the very least interrupted again, by the 1994 election. What happened? Congressional Democrats had enjoyed 40 years of popular support, winning popular vote majorities in 20 straight elections. Moreover, as the preceding chapters demonstrated, throughout this period the system had also worked to the Democrats' advantage. They benefited from incumbency, from more uncontested seats, and from an electoral system tilted in their favor and magnifying their vote majorities into even larger seat majorities. Moreover, as we have seen in the past, bias in the electoral system tended to increase when Democrats were not doing so well at the polls. Thus, with Democrats failing to attract a majority vote in 1994, bias should have been especially in their favor. If so, why was it insufficient to preserve the Democratic majority in 1994? Was the system strongly biased in favor of the Democrats, or was it, for some reason, more neutral in 1994? Were there still cheap seats to be had in 1994, and did Democrats continue to occupy them? We now turn to that fateful midterm election of 1994 to explain which elements that had sustained the Democratic majority for 40 years finally gave way to a Republican majority.

8

□□□□□□□□□□□□□□□□□□□□□□□□□□□□□

The Collapse of the Democratic Dynasty

The November 1994 midterm election brought an abrupt end to the Democratic dynasty in the House. For the first time in 40 years, a Republican majority was elected to the House of Representatives. The election sent 230 Republicans, 204 Democrats, and 1 independent to the House. With 218 members needed for a House majority, Republicans had a 13-seat majority—a small majority, but a majority nonetheless, and enough to elect a Republican speaker, set the rules, and organize the House committee system. For four decades, a Democratic House majority could be taken for granted. No longer. The unthinkable was now not only thinkable, it had happened.

The 1994 midterm was a disaster for Democrats. Midterm elections are often interpreted as 435 individual elections playing 435 distinct campaigns with 435 separate outcomes. But there was a single, unmistakable national story in 1994: the election was a stinging defeat for the Democrats. Since 1958, Democrats had never held fewer than 242 seats, a 25-seat majority at their low point. 1994 left them with 38 fewer seats than their worst showing in more than three decades. Adding insult to injury, among the defeated Democratic candidates was the Democratic House speaker, Tom Foley of Washington. Republicans, who had been unable to top their strongest showing of 192 seats in more than three decades, not only broke the 192-seat ceiling but exceeded it by nearly 40 seats. And if that were not enough, the post-election party switches of several conservative southern Democratic House members to the Republicans compounded the bad news for Democrats.

❑ Democratic Losses in Perspective ❑

The Democratic Party's loss of 52 House seats was the most severe loss for either party in several generations.[1] In the first half of the century elections frequently produced sweeping partisan change. About a third of elections between 1900 and 1950 (9 of 26 elections) produced party shifts of 50 or more seats. Several moved more than 75 seats between the parties.[2] Although generally less volatile than the earlier half of the century, there have been a few elections since 1950 that produced substantial changes in the partisan balance of the House.[3] However, electoral changes have generally been smaller in more recent decades. There have been 22 elections between 1950 and 1992. In these 22 elections, the median net seat change between the parties from one election to the next was only 15 seats. Interelection change has been even more limited since the mid-1970s. In the nine elections from 1976 to 1992 the median change was only 10 seats. In this context, the 1994 election stands out. No party since 1948 had lost as many House seats in a single election year as the Democrats did in 1994.

While the magnitude was surprising, some Democratic seat losses in 1994 were expected. In 32 of the 33 midterm elections since 1862, the president's party had lost seats in the House.[4] In the 12 midterm elections from 1946 to 1990, the president's party lost seats in each midterm and sustained an average loss of about 26 seats. In some midterm elections (1962, 1986, and 1990) the losses were minor, fewer than 10 seats. In other elections (1946, 1958, 1966, and 1974), however, the president's party suffered major casualties, with losses of as many as 45 to 55 seats. But whether few or many, midterm losses for the president's party are a fact of American political life, and in 1994 a Democrat occupied the White House.

Despite the expectation of Democratic losses, there were at least three reasons to think that they would be moderate, more on the order of 20 seats or so rather than more than 50. First, as table 8.1 indicates, presidential party losses from 1946 to 1990 had averaged only about 26 seats and had been even smaller in most recent midterms. Over the previous two decades, spanning the six midterm elections from 1970 to 1990, the mean midterm seat loss for the president's party was only about 19 seats, and only once (the 1974 Watergate midterm) did losses exceed 25 seats.[5] Presumably the increased advantage of incumbency and the weakened allegiances of partisans had restrained national partisan electoral swings.

Table 8.1
Midterm Seat Losses for the President's Party, 1946–1990

	Midterm Elections	
	1946–66	1970–90
Mean Seat Loss	−33.8	−19.1
Median Seat Loss	−38.3	−13.5
Largest Seat Loss	−55.5	−48.5
Losses of More than 25 Seats	4 of 6 (67)	1 of 6 (17)

Note: Numbers in parentheses are percentages.

Second, modest Democratic losses were expected in 1994 because the Democratic presidential victory in 1992 had been relatively narrow (Campbell, 1993). Nearly as regular as the midterm loss of seats for the president's party is the rule that midterm losses are inversely related to the size of the prior presidential victory. That is, presidents who win popular-vote landslides and carry a large number of congressional candidates into office on their coattails usually suffer bigger losses in the midterm when their party's candidates run without the benefit of presidential coattails. In contrast, presidents elected with modest vote pluralities usually sustain smaller losses.[6] Since President Clinton won with just 43 percent of the popular vote in 1992 (53.5 percent of the two-party vote compared to the post-1944 average of about 55 percent for the winner), large midterm presidential losses were unexpected.

Finally, large Democratic losses in 1994 were unexpected, because of President Clinton's standing with the public. To some extent, midterm elections are referendums on the president. A popular president can reduce his party's midterm loss, while casualties can be heavier under an unpopular president. Presidential approval ratings going into midterm elections average in the mid-50s. That is, in a typical midterm election since 1946, about 55 percent of the public indicate that they approve of the way that the president is handling his job. These ratings generally run into the mid- to high 60s on the positive side and to the low 40s on the negative side (though Nixon's approval rating just prior to his resignation and the 1974 midterm sank to the mid-20s). President Clinton's approval ratings before the 1994 midterm hovered in the low 40 percent range. These were low ratings and foreboded somewhat greater-than-usual Democratic losses, but they were not appallingly low and gave no sign of the Democratic catastrophe that would follow.[7]

This chapter addresses two questions regarding the fall of the Democratic dynasty in the 1994 midterm election. First, why did the Democratic House majority collapse? What caused the surprising end of the Democratic majority that had survived four often politically tumultuous decades and that had not been seriously threatened in more than three decades? Second, what was the role in the 1994 election of the structural factors that had supported the Democratic majority for so long? What role did the Democratic Party's incumbency advantage play in the election? Did uncontested seats continue to add to the Democratic column, or did Democrats lose this advantage? Did the electoral system continue to work to the advantage of Democrats? Were there cheap seats in 1994, and did Democrats continue to dominate them as they had for most of the previous six decades?

In the end, all of the structural advantages of the Democratic House majority could not protect it from the completion of the Republican realignment. The Republican realignment that began with the Republican "southern strategy" of the 1960s took several decades to dismantle long-standing political allegiances and local Democratic Party defenses and to build a Republican base from scratch in the once solid Democratic South. It also took decades because of several detours along the way, including the Watergate debacle and a disengaged president who reneged on his "read-my-lips" no-new-taxes pledge to the voters. In 1994 the realignment appeared finally to have come to fruition. Although Republican gains in presidential voting and in party identification had been evident for some time, they were fleeting and modest at the congressional level—until 1994. Based in no small measure on the movement toward the Republican Party of conservative white southerners and white males nationally, the long-awaited, slow-moving, fitful Republican realignment finally arrived.

The completion of the Republican realignment took place with most, but not all, of the structural advantages that had helped to maintain the Democratic majority over the years in place. The Democratic Party lost control of the House, despite continuing to enjoy an incumbency advantage over the Republicans. In 1994, as in each election from 1956 to 1992, there were more Democratic incumbents than Republican incumbents running, and, despite a groundswell of complaints against Congress and the overwhelming popularity of term-limits proposals, incumbency remained an asset to candidates. As in past years, most incumbents fared better than most challengers. However, while Democrats continued to enjoy greater benefits from incumbency and would have suffered greater losses without it, they did not have their usual uncontested-seat advantage over Republicans. In 1994, for the first time in more than 40 years, Republicans held a greater number of uncontested seats than Democrats.

Democrats also lost their House majority despite the electoral system's bias in their favor. As in nearly every election since at least the mid-1930s, the electoral system favored the Democrats in 1994. Because of their domination of the lowest-turnout districts, the cheap seats, Democrats paid a lower price for their victories. Had the electoral system been neutral between the parties in 1994, Democrats would not only have lost control of the House to the Republicans, but they would have lost many more seats than they did, and Republicans would have taken control of the House with a significantly larger majority. Even with this considerable electoral system advantage, however, the Democratic majority was not protected from the Republican tide of 1994.

❑ The Voters Spoke ❑

Why did the Democratic House majority collapse in 1994? Several potential reasons for the Democratic dynasty's collapse can be ruled out. First, it was not caused by generalized anger at congressional incumbents. Not a single Republican incumbent in the House was defeated, and most Democratic incumbents were reelected. Second, 1994 was also not simply a swing back to the Republicans after the defeat of President Bush in the 1992 presidential election. While many voters indicated their displeasure with the Republican incumbent that year by voting for his opponents, who collectively received 62.6 percent of the vote, President Clinton won the election with only a minority of the popular vote, and the rejection of President Bush was not by itself large enough to account for such a massive swing back to the Republicans in 1994.[8] Finally, the Democratic 1994 collapse was also not simply a referendum, an emphatic rejection of President Clinton and his administration's performance in office. While the president's unpopularity was a component of the election, his public standing would have had to have been much worse to account for the Democratic debacle.

It is difficult to interpret the 1994 election results as anything other than a partisan statement by the voters. The Democrats lost their seat majority in the House in 1994 because they lost their popular-vote majority.

For the first time since 1952, Republicans received a majority of the popular vote in House elections (52.4 percent). Moreover, 1994 was generally a Republican year. Republican gains were not confined to the House. Republicans won across the board. They won 21 of the 35 Senate seats up for election (60 percent) and with it the control of the Senate that they had lost in 1986. They also won 24 of the 36 governorships at stake (67 percent). The Republican tide also swept over state legislative contests. For only the second time since 1954 (recall table 2.6), Republicans controlled a majority of upper chambers of state legislatures, albeit a bare majority of 25 to 24. Similarly, for only the second time since 1954, Republicans gained control of a majority of lower state legislative chambers, although again by the slimmest of margins, 24 to 23 chambers (with two ties). This is a particularly interesting continuity in light of our discussion in chapter 2 of the similarity of House and state legislative election results over the past 40 years.[9]

❑ **The Republican Realignment** ❑

Was the Republican sweep in 1994 a temporary rejection of the Democrats, based on public reactions peculiar to the circumstances surrounding that election, or part of a more permanent partisan shift toward the Republicans, a partisan realignment?[10] There is considerable evidence that Republican gains in 1994 reflected a deepening and spreading of a Republican realignment that had begun some 20 years earlier. It was part of a realignment very unlike the model critical realignment of the 1930s, when Democrats during the Great Depression displaced the earlier Republican majority largely through the mobilization of new Democratic voters over a period of about eight years.[11] The Republican realignment began in the 1960s with a first step that, ironically, strengthened the Democratic majority. It developed slowly and erratically over the next several decades. The realignment moved at a glacial pace because it suffered several interruptions and setbacks along the way (including the Watergate scandal), required the building of a Republican Party in southern states where Democrats historically dominated and Republicans were politically inconsequential, and was driven by the slower process of converting the partisan predispositions of voters rather than mobilizing previously inactive citizens.

There are many facets to the Republican realignment. It is an intricate realignment involving shifts in partisan loyalties along many regional, social, and demographic lines. This said, it is also a simple realignment or, more accurately, a simplifying realignment. It is primarily a conservative realignment in which the parties have been sorted out more clearly on ideological grounds. Overlaid on the ideological structure of the new partisan alignment is a racial division, although it would greatly oversimplify matters to suggest that the realignment was primarily about racial polarization. Nevertheless, the initial step of the realignment was the movement of African Americans toward the Democratic Party. The support of the Democratic Party for the civil rights agenda and for an expanded social welfare state, along with the advance of the civil rights movement and the adoption of the Voting Rights Act, mobilized great numbers of African Americans and drew them closer than ever to the Democratic Party (Carmines and Stimson, 1989). Turnout among African Americans increased substantially in the late 1960s and into the 1970s, especially in southern states, and Democratic presidential candidates could now count on receiving nearly 9 of 10 of their votes.

The Realignment in the South

The developments of the 1960s, while immediately beneficial to the Democrats, also eventually extracted from them a higher political price. The move of the national Democratic Party toward the left in civil rights and domestic issues more generally provided the foundation of a Republican effort to convert conservative Democrats nationally and, more particularly, the Republican southern strategy to break the solid Democratic South.[12] The presence of conservative white southerners in the more liberal national Democratic coalition had been uneasy for some time. The Dixiecrats, led by then-Democratic Senator Strom Thurmond of South Carolina, bolted from the 1948 Democratic convention. The more conservative southern state Democratic Parties and the near invisibility of the Republican Party in southern states preserved the allegiance of many white southerners for the Democrats. The southern Democratic candidacies of Jimmy Carter and Bill Clinton also forestalled Republican inroads. Nevertheless, these circumstances merely delayed the inevitable.

Given the prevalence of one-party systems across the South and the conservatism of these Democratic Parties, Republican inroads were initially limited to presidential elections. The early rumblings that Democrats might not be able to take the South for granted appeared in 1948 with Strom Thurmond's Dixiecrat candidacy. Every Democratic presidential candidate in the 17 elections from 1880 to 1944 had carried Arkansas, Louisiana, Mississippi, Alabama, Georgia, and South Carolina.

Six other southern states were almost as dependably Democratic.[13] In 1948, four of these states voted for Thurmond. While most returned to the Democratic fold in the next several elections, five defected to Goldwater in 1964. The Democratic presidential lock on the South had clearly ended by 1968. In the 1968 presidential election, Alabama Governor George Wallace, running as a third-party candidate, carried five southern states, and Republican candidate Richard Nixon carried six states in the region. Since 1968, the South has generally voted Republican in presidential elections. Southerners returned to the Democrats temporarily in 1976, in the aftermath of Watergate and with a southerner (former Georgia Governor Jimmy Carter) heading the Democratic ticket, and had some success in 1992, with a Democratic ticket of two southerners (former Arkansas Governor Bill Clinton and Tennessee Senator Al Gore Jr.), but, otherwise, Republican presidential candidates have dominated. Of the 997 electoral votes cast by the 12 southern states in the seven presidential elections from 1968 to 1992, 756 were cast for Republican presidential candidates (76 percent), and only 194 were cast for Democratic candidates (19 percent).[14] Moreover, Republican strength in the region has grown while the electoral voting strength of the region has also grown.[15]

Below the presidential level, Democrats continued to dominate for some time. In 1968, with the southern presidential shift to Republicans well underway, Democrats won more than three out of four southern congressional seats, and Republicans conceded about a quarter of southern districts without even mounting token opposition.[16] Republicans were still a small minority of the southern congressional delegation a decade later. Of the 114 southern members elected in 1978, 82 were Democrats (72 percent) and 32 were Republicans. This division in the region was a major reason for divided government nationally.

Because of its twists and turns and detours, many election analysts doubted that a realignment was underway, instead devising explanations for idiosyncratic Republican presidential victories and holding to a view that partisan dealignment rather than realignment was in process.[17] Others concluded that a realignment had taken place but that it was a split-level or "two-tiered" realignment with Republicans becoming the first or "sun" party in presidential voting, while Democrats maintained their primacy below the presidency (Ladd, 1989). Another variant on this interpretation claimed that the realignment was "hollow," marked by a continuing dealignment or a discounting of the importance of partisanship by the electorate that permitted greater split-ticket voting (Wattenberg, 1990).[18] The 1994 election suggests that these conclusions were premature. The realignment appeared hollow or two-tiered only because it was a work still in progress.

While Republicans continued to post anemic congressional showings in the South, they nevertheless gradually built a base in southern state legislatures through the 1970s and 1980s, developing a pool of potential candidates with political experience for future congressional races. After the 1964 election, Republicans held fewer than 5 percent of seats in the lower chamber of state legislatures in six southern states and exceeded 12 percent of seats in only two southern states.[19] Ten years later, Republicans still held fewer than 15 percent of the seats in most southern states.[20] However, over the late 1970s and early 1980s, Republicans made substantial inroads in many southern states. After the 1984 election, although Republicans held fewer than 15 percent of the seats in five southern state legislatures, they held more than 30 percent of the seats in five other southern states.[21] By the 1992 election, Republicans held over 30 percent of state legislative seats in seven southern state legislatures, more than 20 percent of the seats in another three southern states, and more than 10 percent of seats in the two remaining states.[22] Republicans were now a presence in southern politics and could put forward to voters viable and experienced candidates for the House. They now had to be taken seriously.

Republican state-legislative gains in the South over the 1970s and 1980s paid congressional dividends in the 1990s. Democrats had maintained their southern congressional strength years after they had lost the region in presidential voting, but this changed dramatically in 1994. In 1994 Republicans won a majority of southern House districts.[23] They won 15 of 23 seats in Florida, 8 of 12 seats in North Carolina, 7 of 11 seats in Georgia, and 5 of 6 seats in Oklahoma. Republicans gained even in the Texas congressional delegation where Democrats outnumbered Republicans by nearly 2 to 1, since they had been outnumbered by 11 to 1 as recently as the mid-1970s.[24]

Race, Gender, and Realignment

The conservative Republican realignment not only altered regional voting patterns but, like past realignments, altered the party loyalties of sociodemographic groups. The New Deal realignment was most distinguished by sizable class differences in party voting, but it also affected religious and ethnic group allegiances (Petrocik, 1981; Erikson et al., 1989). The current Republican realignment also reflects the changing partisan loyalties of a variety of groups. The most fundamental group shift in the current realignment is racial (Carmines and Stimson, 1989). Although black voters were more Democratically inclined than white voters before the 1970s, the average racial gap in presidential voting was only about 25 percentage points from the 1940s to 1960.[25] Since 1964, it has been twice as large. While the racial gap is an important part of the story regarding the current realignment, it does not help us to explain the 1994 congressional results. The racial gap in congressional voting in 1994 was about 50 percentage points, about 10 to 15 points higher than in the four previous congressional elections, but about the same as in the 1984 election that left the Republicans in the minority (Ladd, 1995, 48–49).

A second, less consistent but perhaps equally important, group shift in the current realignment may have been the emergence of a gender gap. Prior to the 1970s, there were very small and fluctuating differences in the party voting of men and women. In a number of elections since the 1970s, however, there have been pronounced differences, with men more inclined to vote for Republicans and women more inclined to vote for Democrats (Bowman, 1995). Although these differences look minor when compared with the racial gap, the fact that each group constitutes roughly half of the electorate makes the differences important.

A common misconception of the gender gap is that Republicans have a problem attracting the support of women. However, neither logic nor empirical analysis supports this view. The gender gap is not a problem for Republicans; it is a problem for Democrats. Democrats have a problem with males. Given that no gender gap was evident before the 1970s, that the Democrats were the majority party of that era, and that the public as a whole has moved away from this Democratic majority, the only interpretation consistent with this arithmetic is that males have been moving away from the Democratic coalition.

Table 8.2 presents the history of the gender gap in both presidential and House elections from 1968 to 1994. Far from signalling Republican problems, the gender gap appears intimately connected to Republican success. The last national Republican victory in presidential or House voting without a significant gender gap was 1968. Since that election, the gender gap dividing line between Republican success and failure is remarkably clear. Since 1968, Republicans have lost every election in which the gender gap was less than six percentage points.[26] Conversely, Republicans won whenever the gender gap was equal to or greater than six percentage points. This includes the 1994 House election. Con-

Table 8.2
The Gender Gap and the Republican Realignment, 1968–1994

Year	Election	Republican Vote (%) Male	Female	Gender Gap	Republican Victory	Did Republicans Win with a Gender Gap of 6 Percent or Greater and Lose When the Gap was Smaller?
1968	Presidential	55	53	+2	Yes	No
	Congressional	48	48	0	No	Yes
1970	Congressional	46	45	−1	No	Yes
1972	Presidential	68	61	+7	Yes	Yes
	Congressional	43	44	−1	No	Yes
1974	Congressional	37	39	−2	No	Yes
1976	Presidential	48	48	0	No	Yes
	Congressional	42	43	−1	No	Yes
1978	Congressional	42	43	−1	No	Yes
1980	Presidential	55	47	+8	Yes	Yes
	Congressional	44	47	−3	No	Yes
1982	Congressional	44	41	+3	No	Yes
1984	Presidential	62	56	+6	Yes	Yes
	Congressional	53	48	+5	No	Yes
1986	Congressional	47	44	+3	No	Yes
1988	Presidential	57	50	+7	Yes	Yes
	Congressional	46	41	+5	No	Yes
1990	Congressional	46	43	+3	No	Yes
1992	Presidential	38	37	+1	No	Yes
	Congressional	47	44	+3	No	Yes
1994	Congressional	57	46	+11	Yes	Yes

Source: The congressional votes in 1978 and from 1982 to 1994 are from Ladd (1995, 48–49, 54). The data were originally collected by Voter News Service (for 1994), Voter Research and Surveys (1990 and 1992), and CBS News/*New York Times* (1984, 1986, and 1988). The presidential votes from 1976 to 1992 are from Bendyna and Lake's analysis (1995) of CBS News Exit Polls (1976, 1980, 1988), CBS News/*New York Times* Exit Polls (1988), and the Voter Research and Surveys Exit Poll (1992). The ABC Polls for 1980, 1984, and 1988 are close to the CBS results, although they indicate an eight-point rather than six-point gap in 1984. Both presidential and congressional votes from 1968 to 1974 are from Miller and Traugott (1989), based on the National Election Studies and their predecessor national election surveys. These percentages are based on the two-party rather than total vote. The Gallup Poll breakdown of the 1968 presidential vote which separated out Wallace supporters also found no gender gap for Republican candidate Richard Nixon. The Mitofsky International Exit Poll indicated an eight-point gender gap in 1994 (Ladd 1995, 156).

gressional Republicans had a gender gap consistently since 1982. However, it exceeded six percentage points in 1994 for the first time. In fact, one survey indicated that the gender gap in 1994 was nearly twice that margin.

Whether the emergence of the gender gap, the inroads of Republicans in the South, and other Republican regional and socioeconomic gains indicate the deepening and widening of a permanent partisan realignment or fleeting reactions to the specific political circumstances of 1994 is impossible to say with complete certainty at this point. However, it is quite clear that the Democratic loss of the House in 1994 reflects, in one way or the other, the decisions of the electorate. The voters spoke. What remains to be seen is whether the candidate context in the 1994 campaign and the electoral system skewed the 1994 election outcome. Did the system, including incumbency advantages, uncontested-seat advantages, and the organization of votes into seats, make the displacement of the Democratic majority easier or more difficult?

❑ The Candidate Context in 1994 ❑

In previous elections, Democrats had a head start toward a House majority by virtue of more of their candidates running as incumbents, with all the advantages and opportunities that incumbency entails, and because more Democratic candidates than Republican candidates were unopposed. Since incumbency is typically worth additional votes for a candidate and since more Democratic candidates than Republican candidates were incumbents, Democratic congressional candidates nationally received a bonus vote from incumbency. Similarly, since being unopposed is worth some additional votes and prevents the opposition from obtaining votes it otherwise would have received if voters and potential voters in the district had been afforded an opportunity to choose between opposing candidates and since more Democratic candidates than Republican candidates in past elections have been unopposed, the Democratic congressional vote nationally was larger than it would have been if all voters faced a real choice. As I showed in chapter 3, these advantages typically added a couple of percentage points to the Democratic vote and probably salvaged Democratic vote majorities in two election years (1966 and 1980). Did they continue to work to the Democratic Party's favor in 1994? Incumbency did, but Democrats lost their uncontested-seat advantage.

Incumbency

As in each election since 1956, Democrats had an incumbency advantage in 1994. As usual, a majority of incumbents running for reelection were Democrats. There were 225 Democratic incumbents and 157 Republican incumbents, giving Democrats a net incumbency advantage of 68 seats. Although this was a smaller net seat advantage than in the prior five elections, it was not unusually small. The net party difference in running incumbents had been closer to even in seven elections since 1956 and, in an absolute sense, was still strongly to the advantage of the Democrats.

Although there were unquestionably more Democratic than Republican incumbents running in 1994, there is a question of whether incumbency was still an asset to a candidate? Public cynicism in 1994 was strong. Public regard for professional politicians was about on par with that of used car salesmen. Was incumbency worth as many votes as in previous elections? Did the political earthquake of 1994 signal a collapse in the value of incumbency, or did it survive, despite the public protestations against Washington insiders?

Incumbency was not devalued in 1994. The 1994 election was not a revolt against incumbents. As evidence of this, we need look no further than the fate of Republican incumbents. Not a single Republican incumbent in the House, the Senate, or a governorship was defeated for reelection. There were a number of Democratic incumbents who went down to defeat, including 2 incumbent Senators, 5 incumbent Governors, and 34 incumbent House members.[27] However, even with a strong Republican tide running against them, most Democratic incumbents in the House survived. Of the 225 incumbent Democrats running, 191 (85 percent) were reelected. In addition, Jacobson (1995) estimated the Gelman-King index of incumbency value at about 10 percentage points, about normal for recent election years. Thus, the Democratic share of the 1994 vote, as in past years, was padded by votes received because of incumbency, and the Republican vote share was diminished to the same extent.

Uncontested Seats

If the partisan implications of the incumbency advantage reflected the pro-Democratic status quo, the partisan consequences of uncontested seats marked a sharp departure from politics as usual. The usual Democratic advantage in uncontested seats not only disappeared in 1994, but a Republican advantage emerged. For the first time in this century, uncontested Republicans outnumbered uncontested Democrats. There were 35 uncontested Republicans in 1994 and only 16 uncontested Democrats, a 19-seat net Republican advantage.

This Republican advantage in uncontested seats may be additional evidence of a Republican realignment. The realignment not only shifted votes, generally and more particularly among some sociodemographic groups and in some regions of the country, but it apparently opened up some districts to the possibility of electing a Republican and closed the possibility of electing a Democrat in other districts. Along the same lines as the realignment in voting, the number of uncontested Republican seats began rising in the late 1970s and the growth of uncontested Republican seats has been strongest in the South. About two-thirds of uncontested Republican seats in 1994 were in southern states. Nine uncontested Republican seats were in Florida alone, and another five were in Texas.

With uncontested seats favoring Republicans and contested incumbent seats favoring Democrats, the overall impact of the candidate context in 1994 was minor. Applying the same sort of analysis as outlined in appendix A for earlier elections indicates that the Democratic share of the national vote would have declined by only about a half of a percentage point (from 46.2 percent to 45.7 percent) and the Republican share would have increased by an equal amount (rising from 53.8 percent to 54.3 percent) if there had been no uncontested seats and if neither party had received votes due to incumbency.[28]

❑ The Electoral System in the 1990s ❑

In nearly every election of the past six decades, the electoral system favored the Democratic Party. Although this bias was not the sole basis for the extraordinary success of Democrats in House elections, it was an important component of that record. Moreover, bias was greatest when Democratic fortunes were at their ebb. So what happened in 1994? With the ripening of the Republican realignment working against Democrats, public opinion running against the incumbent Democratic president, and Democrats losing their long-held advantage in uncontested seats, Democratic fortunes in 1994 were certainly at their ebb. Did the Democratic dynasty in the House end in part because they also lost their electoral system advantage in 1994, or did Democrats lose the House despite an electoral system still strongly biased in their favor?

With three different approaches, this analysis makes five separate estimates of partisan bias in the House electoral system in the 1990s. The three approaches are the historical approach, a modified hypothetical approach, and the unwasted-vote approach. First, the analysis estimates bias from the aggregate national vote and seat percentages over the last several elections. As in Tufte's (1973) earlier analysis, bias is estimated from a seats-votes regression of the last three elections.

The next three estimates of bias are based on a district-level analysis. These are achieved by a modification of the hypothetical vote method (Niemi and Fett, 1986) discussed in chapter 4. The second and third estimates are derived using of a uniform partisan seat analysis of the 1992 and 1994 elections, respectively. Recall that this technique adds an increment to one party's vote percentages in each district and subtracts an equivalent percentage from the other party and then recomputes the seat totals on the basis of the new hypothetical votes. The modification introduced here is that the hypothetical vote percentages are translated into votes (rather than percentage of votes) in each district and then aggregated nationally. Partisan vote percentages are incrementally adjusted uniformly across all districts until the total national vote is evenly divided between the parties.[29] At that point, with a hypothetical even division of the national vote, the winners of each seat are determined on the basis of the district vote adjusted by the uniform-vote-percentage swing. These are then aggregated to determine the percentage of seats each party would have won at an even vote division. This technique was also used to generate estimates of bias in contested districts in elections from 1954 to 1992 and are reported in appendix B.

The fourth method further modifies the district-level analysis of the hypothetical vote swing by examining the 1992 and 1994 elections together. Rather than assuming a constant or uniform vote swing in each district or simulating a likely vote swing through modeling of district characteristics (King and Gelman, 1991; Jackman, 1994), the approach interpolates the swing from the actual vote swing between the two elections. The interpolation is achieved by iteratively examining proportions of the actual vote swing from 1992 to 1994. For instance, if the Democratic vote percentage in one district dropped by 20 percent from the 1992 to the 1994 election (and increased by an equal amount for Republicans) and dropped by 6 percent in another, half of that actual vote swing would amount to a 10 percentage point swing in the first case and a 3 percent swing in the second district. Proportionate swings are examined iteratively until the proportionate swing produces an even division of the national vote. The percentage of seats that would have been won with this swing is then determined. With the vote evenly split, bias is indicated

Table 8.3
Votes and Seats for the Party Receiving the Majority of the House
Vote in the 1990, 1992, and 1994 Elections

| | | All Congressional Districts | | | Contested Districts | |
| | | Percentage of the Vote | | | | |
Year	Majority Party	Unadjusted	Adjusted	Percentage of Seats	Percentage of Votes	Percentage of Seats
1990	Democrats	54.1	53.7	61.5	53.5	62.5
1992	Democrats	52.6	52.7	59.4	52.7	59.9
1994	Republicans	53.6	53.8	53.2	51.7	51.3

Note: Vote percentages are of the two-party vote. Seat percentages divide seats won by third-party candidates evenly between the parties. The adjusted vote takes into account an estimated vote for the winning party in uncontested districts in which the vote is unreported. Some states do not report the vote count for uncontested districts, while others do. The estimated vote in nonreporting districts is the mean vote for that year in uncontested districts in states in which the vote is reported. The 1994 vote is the official vote reported in *Congressional Quarterly Weekly Report* (15 April 1994, p. 1090).

by any deviation from an equal division of seats. The final measure of bias in the 1994 is an application of the unwasted-vote measure of bias. Unwasted votes are examined for both contested districts and for all districts.

The five measures arrived at substantively the same conclusion: as it had over most of the past 60 years, the electoral system in 1994 remained significantly biased in favor of the Democrats. Bias estimates ranged from just under 3 percent (about 12 seats) to just over 4 percent of seats (or about 19 seats) in favor of the Democrats.[30]

National Election Results and Bias

The 1994 election had many political consequences and at least one important analytical consequence. Prior to 1994, estimates of recent electoral system bias required extrapolation from the string of elections that had produced Democratic vote majorities. With 1994, for the first time since 1954, we have a case falling on the other side of the even vote division and are in a position to make a more certain estimate of bias based on interpolation from these elections rather than extrapolation.

Table 8.3 presents the election results, the two-party seat and vote percentages, for the 1990, 1992, and 1994 elections, for all districts, and for contested seats only. In the case of all districts, two vote percentages for each election are presented, the actual reported result and an adjusted vote that takes into account a simulated vote in uncontested districts that do not report vote totals. Most, but not all, states report the election results of uncontested elections. Reported vote totals thus underreport the vote for parties carrying these unreporting districts. The likely vote in these unreporting districts is simulated as the mean reported vote in uncontested seats where the vote was reported.[31]

The results of these three elections so clearly demonstrate electoral system bias that they almost make a more systematic analysis unnecessary. In terms of the national vote, the 1994 election was nearly a mirror image of 1990 and 1992. In 1990 and 1992, Democrats won modest vote majorities of 53.7 and 52.9 percent, respectively, of the two-party vote (adjusted). In 1994, Republicans won a similarly modest vote majority of 53.8 percent. However, this is where the similarity ends. The elections were not at all similar in the proportion of seats that were won by the majority party. The similarity of vote percentages and the contrast of seat outcomes makes the electoral system's bias obvious. *With their two modest vote majorities, Democrats won about 60 percent of the seats. With their equally modest vote majority, Republicans won only 53.2 percent of the seats.* The bias is plain. With nearly equal vote totals, Democrats won 6 to 8 percent more House seats. If Republicans had been treated by the electoral system in 1994 in the same way that Democrats had been treated, Republicans would have held between 61 and 62 percent of the House after the 1994 elections.[32] Instead of only 230 members in the Republican majority, a majority smaller than any Democratic majority in 40 years, there would have been a very formidable Republican majority of between 265 and 269 members.

Figure 8.1 graphs the seat and vote election outcomes of the three elections and plots the associated linear regression. This further extends Tufte's analysis of election triplets discussed in chapter 4. The regression estimates fit the three elections perfectly! The seat-vote regression estimates indicate a 4.2 percent pro-Democratic bias to the electoral system. If both parties had evenly divided the vote, Democrats would have been expected to win 54.2 percent of the seats. The tilt of the electoral system can also be seen from another perspective—the share of the vote necessary to change the House majority, the critical vote. In order for Republicans to have won a majority of seats in the House, they would have had to have held the Democrats to less than 47.9 percent of the two-party vote.

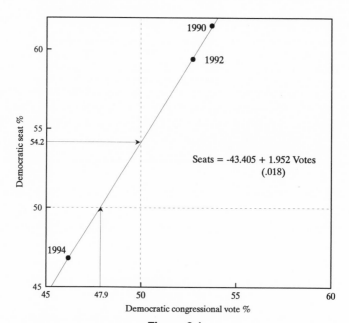

Figure 8.1
The National Estimate of Electoral System Bias, 1990–1994

Note: The percentages are of all congressional districts. The vote is the adjusted vote from table 8.3. The adjustment takes into account unreported votes in uncontested districts. The estimated regression line has an adjusted R^2 of 1.00 and a standard error for the equation of .105.

District Election Results and Bias

A second approach to estimating bias is based on an examination of district-level election results. There are five steps in estimating bias through this modified hypothetical vote method. First, district vote percentages are incrementally adjusted away from the party with the majority vote. In 1994, since the Republicans won a vote majority, Republican district vote percentages are incrementally adjusted downward and Democratic district vote percentages are adjusted upward by the same amount. In 1992, since Democrats won a vote majority in that election, vote percentages in each district are subtracted from Democratic candidates and added to Republican candidates. Second, these hypothetical vote percentages are then converted to hypothetical district vote totals. The adjusted district vote percentages are then multiplied by the total district vote to obtain the number of district votes that the parties would have received at the adjusted district vote percentages. Third, these hypothetical votes are then summed for all districts and compared. Further adjustments are made until the hypothetical aggregated national vote is evenly divided between the parties. Fourth, at this point, when the national vote would have been evenly split, the winning party in each district is determined by using the adjusted or hypothetical district vote percentages. Finally, these hypothetical victories are then aggregated nationally to determine the proportion of seats that a party would have won with half the national vote. Any deviation from a 50-50 split in seats indicates electoral system bias.

This modified hypothetical vote method of estimating bias is applied in three ways to assess the electoral system of the 1990s. The first two of these use a uniform-vote-percentage swing in generating hypothetical votes for the 1992 and 1994 elections. That is, the same percentage swing (toward the minority party and away from the majority party) is used in each district. The third application takes advantage of the change in the party winning the majority of the congressional vote. Rather than using the same vote percentage swing for each district, this application uses the information about each district's actual swing from 1992 to 1994. Proportions of the actual vote-percentage swing in each district are incrementally used to generate hypothetical votes until the national vote total is evenly split. The seat division based on these hypothetical votes is then calculated. As in the other applications, any deviation from a even division of seats at this point indicates electoral system bias.

The three applications of the modified hypothetical vote measure examine all congressional districts except the at-large district in Vermont won by an independent candidate. In order to examine all remaining districts, two modifications to the election returns from 1992 and 1994 were required. First, because some states do not report vote results in uncontested districts, there were no votes in 14 districts in 1992 and 13 districts in 1994.[33] Since votes were cast in these districts for one party's candidate, the election results would more accurately reflect voter decisions if we could approximate these unreported votes. These votes were simulated using the reported presidential vote in these districts and the turnout drop-off from the presidential level to the congressional level in the uncontested districts in which the vote was reported.[34] Second, a simulated vote for the party leaving a seat uncontested was calculated. By definition, one party wins 100 percent of the two-party vote in an uncontested district and the party failing to make a bid receives no votes.

As we discussed in chapter 3 and as Jacobson has argued elsewhere (1993, 50), this vote division does not accurately gauge voter support for the two parties. Even a nominal candidate for the losing party in these districts would have attracted some votes. To better gauge voter support, a simulated vote for the party leaving the seat uncontested was calculated.[35]

The 1992 Analysis. The uniform-partisan-vote-swing analysis of the 1992 election essentially asks two questions: (1) what percentage of the vote in 1992 would Democrats have had to have lost and Republicans gained in each congressional district in order for the national vote to be evenly divided, and (2) if the Democrats had lost these votes and Republicans had gained them, how many seats would each party have won? The answer to this second question amounts to asking whether bias existed in 1992. With an even division of the vote, a deviation from an even division of seats indicates bias in the electoral system. Bias in the 1992 election does not necessarily indicate bias in 1994. However, 1992 was the immediately prior election, and both elections are organized by the 1990s reapportionment.

Table 8.4 presents the vote swings necessary to achieve an equal division of the vote in each of the three applications, including the 1992 analysis. The table also presents the seat division that would have resulted at this even split of the vote. For 1992, the national two-party vote was evenly divided, with about a 2.8 percent swing in each district's vote percentage toward the Republicans and away from the Democrats. With this vote swing, Democrats would have won 233 seats and Republicans would have won only 201 seats. With an even division of the national vote produced by a uniform swing of the vote across all districts, Democrats would have won 53.7 percent of the seats and Republicans would have won 46.3 percent, indicating a pro-Democratic bias of 3.7 percent of the seats.[36]

The 1994 Analysis. In 1994, as table 8.4 indicates, convergence on an even division of the national vote was achieved after approximately a 3.0 percent swing of the vote away from the Republicans and toward the Democrats. With this even division of the national vote, Democrats would have won 229 seats and Republicans would have won only 205 seats. This amounts to a 2.8 percent pro-Democratic bias in the system. If the 1994 election had been a dead heat, Democrats would have won a seat majority. Moreover, the seat majority that Democrats would have won in a dead-heat election would be about as large as the seat majority that Re-

Table 8.4

Three District Analyses of Partisan Bias in the 1990s

Election	Method for Vote Examination and the Increment of the District Vote Percentage that Produced an Even Partisan Division of the National Two-Party House Vote	Seats		Percentage Partisan Bias
		Democrats	Republicans	
1992	Uniform Partisan Vote Swing: +2.82 percentage points in each district to Republicans and from Democrats	233	201	3.7
1994	Uniform Partisan Vote Swing: +2.95683 percentage points in each district to Democrats and from Republicans	229	205	2.8
1992 and 1994	Proportional Partisan Vote Swing: .48663 of district vote swing from 1992 to 1994, subtracted from district Democratic vote percentage, and added to the district's Republican vote percentage for 1992	235	199	4.1

Note: In each case, the adjusted district vote was multiplied by district turnout to obtain the number of votes for each party in a district. These were then aggregated to the national vote. In the case of the combined 1992 and 1994 proportional vote-swing estimation, the adjusted percentages were multiplied by the district's average turnout for the two election years.

publicans actually won in 1994 with their very real vote majority of between 53 and 54 percent of the two-party vote.

The 1992–1994 Analysis. The uniform-vote-swing assumption in the 1992 and the 1994 analyses is simple and straightforward; however, it is undoubtedly unrealistic. Votes may be nearly fixed in some districts and very fluid in others. A vote swing is unlikely to be equal in all districts. In fact, although the mean district vote swing from 1992 to 1994 was about 5.7 percentage points toward the Republicans, many districts varied significantly from this average. The standard deviation of the vote swing between elections was about 8.4 percent of the vote. While Republicans gained ground in more than three-quarters of congressional districts

(331 seats), Democrats actually won a higher percentage of votes in about a fifth of all districts (86 seats).[37]

The assumption of a proportionate swing is more realistic than the uniform-vote-swing assumption in simulating the distribution of additional votes. The realism comes from using the actual district vote swings and represents an improvement on the more sophisticated vote simulations (King and Gelman, 1991; Jackman, 1994) as well as the simpler uniform-vote-swing simulations. The proportionate-swing method uses data from a pair of elections and is particularly applicable when the party winning the vote majority changed, as it did from 1992 to 1994, and when both elections are reasonably close to the even-vote mark.[38] Rather than examining uniform-vote-percentage swings from one election to the next, it examines proportions of the actual vote swing that occurred between the elections. Proportions of the swings were iteratively examined until the national party votes converge at an equal national vote division.[39] Table 8.5 demonstrates the major iterations in narrowing in on the even national vote division. The parties would have equally shared the national vote when each district's vote swing was just short of half of its actual swing from 1992 to 1994. At this point, 235 Democrats (54.1 percent of seats) and 199 Republicans (45.9 percent of seats) would have been elected, reflecting a 4.1 percent pro-Democratic bias in the system. Again, the electoral system is such that Democrats would have won as many or more seats in a dead-heat election than Republicans won with almost a 54 percent vote majority.[40]

District Turnout and Partisan Bias

With four different estimates of bias indicating that the electoral system continued to work to the Democratic Party's advantage in 1994, we should expect that Democrats continued to dominate in the lower-turnout districts and to receive fewer votes in their typical victory. This was indeed the case. Table 8.6 examines the turnout and unwasted-vote quintiles of contested districts in 1994, as we previously examined for earlier elections. As the table indicates, Democrats won a majority of seats only among the very-lowest-turnout districts. Democrats in 1994 won four out of five of the lowest-turnout districts. This was typical. The average success of Democrats in these districts over the previous 40 years was 79 percent. Democrats and Republicans almost evenly divided the next-to-the-lowest-turnout quintile. However, districts with average to high

Table 8.5

The Proportionate-Vote-Swing Analysis of the 1992 and 1994
Elections to the U.S. House of Representatives

Percentage of Actual District Vote Swing from 1992 to 1994	Interpolated Election Results			
	National Vote Percentage		Seats	
	Democrats	Republicans	Democrats	Republicans
0	52.8	47.2	258	176
10	52.2	47.8	257	177
20	51.6	48.4	252	182
30	51.1	48.9	246	188
40	50.5	49.5	240	194
48.663	*50.0*	*50.0*	*235*	*199*
50	49.9	50.1	234	200
60	49.4	50.7	232	202
70	48.8	51.2	220	214
80	48.2	51.8	217	217
90	47.6	52.4	207	227
100	47.1	52.9	204	230

Source: Election return data were obtained from *Congressional Quarterly Weekly Reports* (1993 and 1995).

Note: The proportion of the district vote swing necessary to obtain an equal division of the national House vote is italicized. This proportionate or interpolated hypothetical vote method involves six steps. First, each district's actual vote swing from 1992 to 1994 is calculated. Second, a proportion of this percentage-point swing is added to the 1992 district vote percentage to create a hypothetical vote percentage for each party in each district. Third, using each district's mean turnout (in raw votes) for the 1992 and 1994 elections, each district's hypothetical vote percentage is converted to hypothetical votes for each party. Fourth, these hypothetical votes in each district are summed to determine the national vote percentages for each party at the particular proportion of vote swing. These steps are repeated iteratively until the national votes for the two parties converge. At that point, on the basis of each district's hypothetical vote percentages, the party that would have won each district at that critical vote swing is determined and aggregated. Since the interpolated national vote is evenly divided at this point, any deviation of the national partisan seat division from 50 percent indicates electoral system bias.

turnouts split about 60-40 in favor of Republicans. The pattern of partisan success in districts grouped by the number of unwasted votes was similar to the turnout pattern. Democrats were most successful in the lowest category of districts grouped by the number of votes cast for the winning candidate. The parallel logit analyses of the ungrouped districts further support the finding that Democrats were more successful in 1994

Table 8.6
The Relationship of the Party of the Winning Candidate to
District Turnover and Unwasted Votes, 1994

District Grouping	Percentage of Districts Won by Democrats in Districts Grouped in Quintiles by Turnout and Unwasted Votes					Association between the Total District Turnout (or Unwasted Votes) and the Election of a Republican Representative	
	Low 1	2	3	4	High 5	r	Logit Derivative
Total District Turnout in Votes	80	46	40	34	44	.23	.036
Unwasted Votes	68	57	44	43	32	.25	.063

Note: Unwasted votes in a district are those cast for the winning candidate in the district.

in districts with lower turnout and with fewer votes cast for the winning candidate.

Tables 8.7 and 8.8 list the cheap and the expensive seats of 1994. At one end of the spectrum, in table 8.7, are those contested districts that were won in 1994 with fewer than 70,000 votes. There were 32 such districts, about 8 percent of all contested seats. Four of these seats were won with fewer than 50,000 votes. These are the cheapest seats of 1994, and nearly all of them were won by Democrats. Democrats won 30 of the 32 seats (94 percent) in "the under-70 club." As in past years, in 1994 Democrats dominated the cheap seats.[41]

Although Democrats won the overwhelming number of cheap seats, they did not generally win them with an overwhelming proportion of the vote. Many of these cheap seats were seriously contested. Twenty-three of the 30 cheapest Democratic cheap seats in 1994 were won with less than 70 percent of the vote. More than half of these, 16 of the 30, were won with less than a 60 percent vote for the winning Democratic candidate.

The cheap seats of 1994 were of several types. The list reflects considerable geographic diversity, comprising 12 different states. There are

Table 8.7
Winning House Candidates in Contested Districts Who
Received Fewer than 70,000 Votes in 1994

State	District	Democratic Vote Percentage	Votes for Winning Candidate	Total Votes Cast	Party of the Winning Candidate
California	30	70.1	43,943	66,425	Democrat
Texas	29	73.4	44,102	60,054	Democrat
Illinois	4	75.2	46,695	62,079	Democrat
Texas	16	57.1	49,815	87,224	Democrat
California	46	39.4	50,126	87,721	Republican
California	31	59.1	50,541	85,467	Democrat
California	26	66.0	55,145	88,138	Democrat
California	20	56.7	57,394	101,230	Democrat
No. Carolina	12	65.8	57,655	87,588	Democrat
Indiana	10	53.5	58,573	109,571	Democrat
California	42	51.1	58,888	115,205	Democrat
California	50	61.6	59,214	104,451	Democrat
Texas	20	62.5	60,114	96,149	Democrat
Texas	15	59.9	61,527	104,366	Democrat
Texas	5	51.4	61,877	123,616	Democrat
New York	11	90.4	61,945	69,700	Democrat
Texas	25	53.7	61,959	118,529	Democrat
Arizona	2	65.6	62,589	100,446	Democrat
No. Carolina	7	51.6	62,670	121,519	Democrat
No. Carolina	8	52.4	62,845	119,985	Democrat
Florida	3	57.7	63,845	110,740	Democrat
Kentucky	1	49.0	64,849	127,236	Republican
Texas	24	52.8	65,019	123,081	Democrat
Texas	27	59.4	65,325	110,018	Democrat
Georgia	2	66.2	65,383	98,812	Democrat
California	35	78.1	65,688	84,078	Democrat
No. Carolina	1	61.0	66,827	109,429	Democrat
Kentucky	3	50.2	67,663	152,492	Democrat
New Jersey	13	73.8	67,688	95,467	Democrat
Mississippi	2	58.0	68,014	126,692	Democrat
New York	6	80.4	68,596	85,271	Democrat
Indiana	1	56.5	68,612	121,532	Democrat

Districts Won by Democratic Candidates: 30 of 32 (93.8%)

Source: The data were compiled from the official 1994 election returns in *Congressional Quarterly Weekly Report,* 15 April 1995, 1090–97.

Table 8.8
Winning House Candidates in Contested Districts Who
Received More than 140,000 Votes in 1994

State	District	Democratic Vote Percentage	Votes for Winning Candidate	Total Votes Cast	Party of the Winning Candidate
South Dakota	AL	62.0	183,036	305,922	Democrat
Minnesota	3	26.4	173,223	236,531	Republican
Massachusetts	10	68.8	172,753	251,240	Democrat
Montana	AL	53.5	171,372	352,133	Democrat
Kansas	1	22.6	169,531	219,008	Republican
Oregon	3	78.9	161,624	222,822	Democrat
Oregon	4	66.8	158,981	238,149	Democrat
New York	22	26.6	157,717	214,781	Republican
Alabama	6	20.9	155,047	196,222	Republican
Nebraska	3	21.3	154,919	196,862	Republican
Missouri	2	31.3	154,882	230,287	Republican
Michigan	11	30.9	154,696	226,792	Republican
Minnesota	8	65.7	153,161	233,271	Democrat
New York	27	25.5	152,610	204,770	Republican
California	47	25.8	152,413	212,623	Republican
Texas	6	22.6	152,038	201,012	Republican
Ohio	2	22.6	150,128	193,858	Republican
Arizona	5	29.8	149,514	220,771	Republican
Ohio	17	77.4	149,004	192,491	Democrat
Washington	7	75.1	148,353	197,444	Democrat
New York	21	68.3	147,804	220,674	Democrat
Florida	19	66.1	147,591	223,370	Democrat
Massachusetts	9	69.8	146,287	209,656	Democrat
Massachusetts	7	64.4	146,246	226,920	Democrat
Michigan	2	24.0	146,164	192,153	Republican
Arizona	3	29.9	145,396	207,335	Republican
Colorado	3	30.4	145,365	208,792	Republican
Michigan	4	25.8	145,176	198,517	Republican
California	4	36.3	144,936	236,323	Republican
Idaho	2	25.0	143,593	191,529	Republican
Maryland	8	29.7	143,449	204,109	Republican
California	48	23.3	143,275	195,241	Republican
Virginia	1	24.0	142,930	192,468	Republican
Nevada	2	31.5	142,202	223,932	Republican
Massachusetts	5	69.9	140,725	201,459	Democrat
Washington	8	23.9	140,409	184,574	Republican
Missouri	6	66.1	140,108	211,817	Democrat

Districts Won by Democratic Candidates: 14 of 37 (37.8%)

Source: The data were compiled from the official 1994 election returns in *Congressional Quarterly Weekly Report,* 15 April 1995, 1090–97.

Note: AL indicates a statewide at-large district.

also some concentrations. Seventeen of the cheapest seats were in southern or border states. Eight of these were in Texas and four were in North Carolina. Many of the very-cheap-seat districts were majority-minority districts, either Hispanic or African American. Of the 32 districts listed in table 8.7, 12 were majority Hispanic and 6 were majority African American. Several of these very cheap seats (the Twelfth District in North Carolina and the Third District in Florida) were highly controversial, geographically noncompact, racially gerrymandered majority-minority districts, districts drawn over extensive areas in order to increase the likelihood of electing African American candidates. In addition to the southern districts, another 8 of the 32 cheapest seats were urban California districts.

At the other end of the spectrum are districts won with at least twice as many votes as 1994's under-70 club. Table 8.8 lists the 37 seats won with at least 140,000 votes cast for the winning candidate in the election, the over-140 club.[42] Republicans won most of these high-turnout, high-unwasted-vote districts. They did not, however, dominate in the same way that Democrats dominated at the low end. Democrats won 14 of the 37 most vote-expensive seats, a distinct, but not inconsequential, minority.

California's Thirty-first District

A good example of a cheap seat in the 1990s is the Thirty-first District in California. It ranked sixth from the bottom of contested districts in terms of the number of votes cast for the winning candidate in 1994. Fewer than 51,000 voters, about 59 percent of district voters, elected Matthew Martinez, returning the Democratic incumbent to Washington for a seventh term. Total district turnout was also low. Fewer than 86,000 votes were cast in the district in 1994. The district was in the lowest quintile of both turnout and the number of votes for the winning candidate in both 1992 and 1994. Located in East Los Angeles County and the surrounding communities of the San Gabriel Valley, the district's ethnic composition is nearly 60 percent Hispanic and about a quarter Asian (Duncan, 1993, 195). Economically, it has been described as a middle-income area.

Prior to electing Martinez in a special election in 1982, the district had been represented by George Danielson, also a Democrat. Danielson was first elected in 1970 (the district was then the Thirtieth) and won reelection for six terms, before accepting a judgeship. Prior to Danielson, the district (then the Twenty-ninth) was represented by George

Brown. Brown, also a Democrat, was elected in 1962 and was reelected to four terms before deciding to make a run for the Democratic Senate nomination.

Although the Thirty-first is unquestionably a cheap seat and has elected Democrats consistently since at least 1962, it has not been conceded to Democrats by Republicans. Republicans have contested the district in each election for the past 30 years. The challenges have also been more than nominal. Although Democrats have won at least the last 18 elections in a row (since 1962), they have never won more than 75 percent of the vote and often have been held under 60 percent. The current Democratic incumbent has won four of his seven terms with under 60 percent of the vote.[43]

The district's representatives over the years have been decidedly left of center. The current incumbent typically has ADA ratings of between 80 and 95 percent and his AFL-CIO ratings have been consistently over 90 percent, and frequently 100 percent, in favor of organized labor's positions. His ACU ratings (a conservatism index) are usually in the single digits.

Unwasted Votes and Bias

As a consequence of Democratic cheap seats in 1994 and Republican success in moderate- to high-turnout districts, the typical winning Democrat received far fewer votes than did the typical winning Republican. Table 8.9 presents the unwasted-vote measure of partisan bias for the 382 seats that were contested in 1994. Republicans winning contested districts in 1994 received, on average, about 12,800 more votes than did Democratic winners. This is about 13 percent more votes than winning Democrats typically received. If unwasted votes were equally divided and rates of unwasted votes per victory remained unchanged, with 98,392 unwasted votes for a Democrat securing that candidate's election, Democrats would have won about 204 (53.3 percent) of the 382 contested seats. This reflects a pro-Democratic bias of 3.3 percent of contested seats. As should be expected, given the inverse relationship of the Democratic vote and pro-Democratic bias of the electoral system, the extent of bias in 1994 was greater than usual. Of the 12 elections from 1970 to 1992, electoral system bias favored Democrats only once (1980) by as much as it did in 1994 (see table 5.9). Electoral system bias in 1994 was at least a third greater than it was in 11 of the 12 previous elections.

Although the unwasted-vote analysis concurs with the aggregate na-

(table 6.3) also concurs with these findings. They placed bias at between 3.6 percent and 4.1 percent of all seats.[45]

The electoral system bias that had helped maintain the Democratic majority for 40 years, though evident once again in 1994, was insufficient to preserve that majority in the 1994 election. It nevertheless played an important role in shaping the election results. Had there been no bias in 1994, Republicans would have won between 242 and 249 seats in the House rather than the 230 that they actually won. Conversely, rather than holding 204 seats in the minority, a system without bias would have reduced the Democratic minority to between 185 and 192 seats. Taking the midpoint of 1994 bias estimates, a pro-Democratic bias of 15 seats, the Republican seat majority would have been more than twice as large had the electoral system been neutral. The actual election results left Republicans with 230 seats, a 13-seat majority. An unbiased system would have elected about 245 Republicans, a 28-seat majority. While Republicans had a majority in either case, 15 more Republicans and 15 fewer Democrats might have made a difference on many important House votes.

❑ Overview ❑

With the possible exception of Newt Gingrich, the results of the 1994 election took everyone by surprise. The biggest surprise was that voters ended the 40-year reign of the Democratic majority in the House by electing a Republican majority. The end of the Democratic majority, a majority not seriously threatened for several decades, was understandably surprising. Democrats lost their majority in the House because they lost their vote majority and there are many indications that this change was the maturation or completion of a gradual Republican realignment.

Less noticed, though equally surprising to those believing in the neutrality of the electoral system, was the small size of the Republican seat majority. While it is in one sense impressive that the Republicans were able to elect a majority, the Republican majority of 230 seats (later added to by Democratic party-switchers) was smaller than any Democratic majority in the previous four decades. More interesting, the Republican majority was not small because voters provided them with a narrow vote majority. The Republican vote majority was no narrower than the Democratic majority in the two previous elections. The Republican seat majority was small because of bias in the electoral system. In past elections, electoral system bias inflated the Democratic *majority*. Matters were only slightly different in 1994. In 1994, the electoral system inflated the Democratic *minority*. As they had for most of the past 60 years, Democrats won the cheap seats in 1994. They paid a lower price in votes for their victories than Republicans paid, and the result was a closer seat division of the House than would have been the case with a neutral translation of the 1994 votes into seats. There would have been 12 to 19 seats more in the Republican majority and 12 to 19 fewer seats in the Democratic minority if the electoral system had been unbiased.

Although certainly not widely recognized, the 1994 election came close to creating a democratic crisis. Political commentators frequently raise the undemocratic specter of one presidential candidate winning a popular-vote majority and the other candidate winning an Electoral College majority. The 1994 elections nearly produced a similar crisis for the House. If Democrats had received only 1.7 percent more of the 1994 vote, bringing their share of the two-party vote to 47.9 percent, the potential undemocratic consequences of electoral system bias would have been realized. With only a 47.9 percent minority share of the vote, Democrats would have won a majority of seats. Even with a majority of the two-party congressional vote and over 4 percent more of the vote than the Democrats nationally, Republicans would have been left once again in the House minority. The strength of the Republican tide in 1994 averted this situation. The Democratic vote was held shy of the critical 47.9 percent. However, the electoral system remains in place and with it the possibility that the Democrats could regain control of the House without winning a majority of the vote.

9

□ □

Representation and Cheap Seats

The evidence is overwhelming: the electoral system for the U.S. House of Representatives is biased in favor of the Democratic Party. With only a few exceptions, the electoral system has been biased in favor of the Democrats over the 40-year-long reign of the Democratic dynasty in the House. As the preceding analysis demonstrated, the electoral system has favored Democrats in 28 of the 30 congressional elections between 1936 and 1994. The best estimates indicate that bias has amounted to about 3.5 to 4 percent of all seats, or a swing from one party to the other of anywhere from 13 to 18 seats.[1] That is, at an even division of the vote, Democrats would continue to hold control of the House with anywhere from 230 to 236 seats.

The reason for this bias is clear: many Democratic representatives sit in the cheap seats. These seats are cheap primarily because of their low turnout (rather than especially narrow victory margins). Democratic success in these cheap seats is based on a steady constellation of politics, economics, geography, and electoral districting arrangements. The relation of socioeconomic status to turnout, vote choice, and housing patterns is at the root of the matter. Less-educated citizens are the least likely to vote, and, through several party systems, poorer citizens (who also tend to be the less educated) who vote are more likely to vote for Democrats. Since housing patterns reflect household incomes and congressional districts reflect these concentrations of citizens of similar socioeconomic backgrounds, the districts that tend to have low turnout also tend to elect Democrats. The pattern was the same whether examining the predominantly working-class, poor white Protestant rural "Fighting Ninth" District in the Appalachian corner of Virginia in the 1940s (chapter 7), the set of four ethnically, religiously, and racially diverse urban districts in the Queens borough of New York City in the 1980s (chapter 5), or the predominantly Hispanic, urban Thirty-first District in the East Los Angeles area of California in 1994 (chapter 8). In many respects, these were very different districts. Yet they also had important things in common. Many residents of these districts were poor or working class. Turnout in these districts was usually very low, and the candidates who won these districts did so with relatively few votes. In each case, the winning candidate was a Democrat.

❑ Consequences ❑

This chapter explores the consequences of the bias created by Democratic dominance of the cheap seats. One of its principal consequences is that it helped to prolong Democratic control of the House. Bias alone may have provided the difference between the parties in one election during this era, the 1956 election in which Democrats maintained control of the House despite Eisenhower's reelection (table 5.10). In conjunction with the Democratic Party's incumbency and uncontested-seat advantages, bias also may have been critical to preserving the Democratic House majority in the 1966 and 1980 elections. Table 3.5 in chapter 3 indicated that the Democratic vote majority probably would have evaporated without their incumbency and uncontested-seat advantages in these two elections. However, as the analysis of chapter 8 indicated, because of electoral system bias, Democrats could maintain their seat majority so long as their national vote did not fall below approximately 48 percent. Without their candidate advantages in 1966 and 1980, Democrats probably would have lost their vote majorities (receiving 49.2 and 49.7 percent, respectively) but would have preserved large enough of a vote minority to keep their seat majority—because of the electoral system bias in their favor.[2]

Although the Democrats' electoral system advantage was only occasionally necessary to the maintenance of the Democratic dynasty in the House, it contributed more routinely to the inflation of the Democratic majority. The analysis reported in chapter 5 indicates that, in the typical election over the last 40 years, about 8 to 10 additional Democrats were elected, and an equal number of Republicans were denied election, because of electoral system bias.[3] This is a considerable impact. Moreover, though the extent of bias varied from one election to the next, with one exception, bias was in the Democratic direction.

Even if usually falling short of determining control of the House, bias certainly buttressed the Democrats' control, and this must have affected relations between the parties. For Democrats it meant security in their firmly ensconced majority. For some Democrats, this sense of security may have developed into a feeling of heady invincibility, perhaps arrogance. For Republicans, the consistently augmented Democratic majority meant frustration. An arrogant majority and a frustrated minority are not likely to work very well together, and many believe that they did not. Democrats may have felt little reason to accommodate a Republican minority, and Republicans may have found their bargaining position too weak to bother with compromise. Beyond these strategic or psychological effects, the pro-Democratic bias in the House electoral system, when combined with the neutral or pro-Republican electoral systems for the Senate (Oppenheimer, 1989; Oppenheimer and Sandstrum, 1995) and the presidential Electoral College, probably increased the frequency of divided government in modern American politics.[4] In several ways, then, the bias of the House electoral system may have had a hand in the governmental pathologies known as *partisan gridlock*.

The consistent electoral system bias favoring Democrats and the basis for this bias in the turnout disparities among congressional districts may have had wide-ranging consequences beyond helping to preserve the Democratic House majority and fueling partisan gridlock. The existence of cheap seats dominated by one party and the bias that it produces raise several issues of representation. The issues of representation are at four levels of aggregation: the representation of the public as a whole, the representation of constituencies at the district level, the representation of groups in the process, and the representation of individual voters.

There are several questions relating to how well the House as a whole has represented the views and perspectives of the American public. Has bias in the electoral system skewed the ideological perspective of the House? Has bias in the electoral system and its effect of dampening the apparent swing ratio of elections (thereby blunting the amount of electoral change that would be produced by a swing of votes) caused voters to become more frustrated with the political process and skeptical of its fairness? At a second level, how have cheap seats affected the representation of constituencies? Has it caused overrepresentation of those voters who happen to live in low-turnout districts, or has it amounted to a system of proxy voting in which the whole public, nonvoters as well as voters, are represented? At a third level, have cheap seats caused the overrepresentation of some groups in society? Would the elimination of cheap seats disadvantage economically underprivileged groups in society, including racial minorities? Finally, at the individual level, the existence of cheap seats raises questions about the equality of political representation. Can a system that permits turnout disparities on the order of seven to one, seven voters in one district for every one voter in another, be said to be a politically equitable system? Can an institution whose membership is based on such political inequities rightfully call itself the "House of the People"? In addition to addressing these issues of representation, we will also explore several possible reforms that would eliminate or at least greatly reduce the number of cheap seats and their effects.

❑ Representing the Electorate ❑

The consequences of cheap seats extend beyond partisanship to policy and possibly to the public's attitudes toward politics and its support for the government. By affecting who serves in government, it affects what policies the government adopts, and, because cheap seats skew the political process from the general viewpoint of the public, public sentiment may be less supportive than it might otherwise be.

Ideology and Public Policy

The policy consequences of cheap seats are directly related to its partisan consequences.[5] By adding to the number of Democrats and subtracting from the number of Republicans in the House, cheap seats, and the electoral bias they created, have tilted the House to the left. Since Democrats as a rule are more liberal than Republicans, adding Democrats to the House adds liberals, and this makes a difference to the kinds of public policies that are able to win congressional approval.

The ideological tilt of the cheap seats is examined following two elections, 1984 and 1990. As in the earlier analysis, the contested districts in these two election years are grouped into quintiles by both the total number of votes cast in the election and the number of votes cast for the winning candidate (the unwasted votes). Unlike the earlier analysis, which reported the percentage of Democrats winning in each quintile, table 9.1 reports the median liberalism score of representatives elected from districts in particular quintiles. The liberalism score is based on the ratings of the Americans for Democratic Action (ADA), a liberal interest group, and the American Conservative Union (ACU), a conservative interest group. Both ratings evaluate representatives' roll-call voting on about 19 or 20 votes in a session. The scores are the percentage of votes supporting the liberal (ADA) or conservative (ACU) position. ACU scores

Table 9.1
Ideological Bias of the Electoral System, 1984 and 1990

	Median Liberalism Rating of Representatives in Contested Districts Grouped in Quintiles by District Turnout and Unwasted Votes					Association between the Total District Turnout (or Unwasted Votes) and the Liberalism Rating of the Representative	
	Low 1	2	3	4	High 5	r	Slope (Standard Error)
Total District Turnout in Votes:							
Post-1984 Election	68	62	28	48	52	−.15	−.14 (.05)
Post-1990 Election	85	56	50	41	40	−.24	−.20 (.04)
District Unwasted Votes:							
Post-1984 Election	62	69	48	50	28	−.16	−.20 (.07)
Post-1990 Election	78	61	50	40	53	−.16	−.21 (.07)

Note: $N = 362$ in 1984, and $N = 345$ in 1990. The unwasted votes in a district are votes cast for the winning candidate in the district. The ratings of representatives who filled vacancies occurring after the 1984 and 1990 elections were excluded. The liberalism rating has a hypothetical range from 0 (most conservative) to 100 (most liberal). The index in 1990 is based on the ADA and the ACU ratings of congressional roll-call votes in 1991. The value is obtained by adding the ADA index to 100 minus the ACU index of conservatism and dividing by 2. Subtracting the ACU index from 100 has the effect of converting the conservatism index to a liberalism index, which can then be averaged with the ADA index. The post-1984 ratings are based on roll-call votes cast in 1986. The post-1990 ratings are based on roll-call votes cast in 1991. The ADA and ACU ratings are those reported in the Congressional Quarterly's *CQ Almanac* for 1987 and 1992, respectively. The slope is an OLS estimate of the effects of turnout or votes for the winning candidate (in thousands of votes) on the liberalism rating of representatives.

have been reversed, by subtracting them from 100, to make them comparable to the ADA liberalism score. The liberalism index is calculated as the average of a representative's ADA score and the reversed ACU score and, thus, ranges from 0 (most conservative) to 100 (most liberal). The session examined in 1984 was 1986, the second year of the two-year term for those elected in 1984. The session examined for 1990 was 1991, the first year of the two-year term for those elected in 1990.

As table 9.1 indicates, the representatives from the cheap seats, as a group, are more liberal than those elected from higher-turnout districts.

The representatives from the lowest-turnout districts in 1984 had a median liberalism rating of 68 percent, slightly higher than those from the second quintile and much higher than those with average or high turnouts. In terms of unwasted votes, the typical cheap-seat representative in 1984 had a voting record slightly less liberal than those in the second quintile, but was much more liberal than members from higher-turnout districts. The results in 1990 show even greater differences. The median liberalism score of representatives from the lowest-turnout districts in 1990 was 85 percent, nearly 30 percentage points more liberal than the median score in any of the higher-turnout quintiles. The ungrouped correlations and the regressions of the liberalism index also indicate that representatives for the lower-turnout and lower-unwasted-vote districts tend to be more conservative. The regression coefficients indicate that a 25,000-vote difference in the number of votes cast for the winning candidate (about one standard deviation) produces about a five-point difference on the liberalism index.[6]

Although one might suspect that Democrats who sit in the cheap seats are more liberal than Democrats from high-turnout areas, there is little evidence of this. For instance, in the 1990 analysis, the median liberalism score among Democrats in the bottom-turnout quintile was the same as in the highest-turnout quintile; both had a very liberal median score of 87.5 percent. There was also no relationship between turnout or unwasted votes and liberalism among Democrats in the 1984 analysis. The Democrats who sit in the cheap seats are no more or less liberal than those from higher-turnout areas, but they are definitely more liberal than typical Republican members. Thus, because cheap seats add Democrats to the House and because Democrats typically are more liberal in their roll-call voting (and those from the cheap seats are certainly no less liberal than Democrats generally), cheap seats have produced a more liberal House of Representatives than would have been elected under a neutral electoral system.

Behind the ideological ratings are real roll-call votes that decide public policy issues, or at least what the House of Representatives has to say about these issues. The difference in ideological ratings caused by electoral system bias, thus, has real policy consequences. The full extent of these consequences is difficult to pin down, however, because we are dealing with counterfactuals and the legislative process can sometimes take alternate routes to the same result. With a different partisan and ideological mix, different coalitions become possible, different deals and compromises become feasible, and the votes of different legislators become critical. Where once party leaders not needing a vote might "free" the representative to vote with his or her constituency and please the folks back home, a closer vote might cause party leaders to call for greater party loyalty.

Recent Congresses have had many examples of razor-thin margins on roll-call votes. A few may illustrate the impact of electoral system bias.[7] One example was the Democratic tax bill of 1992 (H.R. 4210) sponsored by then-chairman of the House Ways and Means Committee, Democrat Dan Rostenkowski. The bill raised taxes on upper-income taxpayers by creating a new and higher tax bracket and adding a 10 percent surtax on millionaires. The revenues raised by these additional taxes would be used to fund a small and temporary tax credit for middle-class taxpayers (a $400 tax credit for couples and a $200 tax credit for individual filers). In addition, the bill contained various economic-stimulus provisions, including the indexing of capital gains. The fight over this legislation was very partisan. Democrats claimed it offered much-needed tax relief for the middle class. Republicans claimed it was just another Democratic "soak-the-rich" scheme. The vote on H.R. 4210 was identified by Congressional Quarterly as one of 16 "key votes" of 1992. The bill passed the House by a vote of 221 to 210. A six-vote swing would have shifted the majority of those voting. The bill passed on the strength of its Democratic Party support. Of the 265 Democrats voting, 219 (83 percent) voted for passage, and only 46 (17 percent) opposed it. Republicans were nearly unanimous in their opposition to the bill. Only 1 of the 165 Republicans voting voted with the Democrats for passage. Although in the end President Bush vetoed the bill, the House had expressed its will.

What would have happened if the electoral system in 1990 had not been biased in favor of the Democrats? As we calculated in chapter 5, the electoral system was biased by nine seats in favor of Democrats in 1990. Assuming that the nine Democrats serving because of system bias voted like Democrats generally (a split of about 7.5 in favor to 1.5 opposed) and that the Republicans who would have been elected had there been no bias voted like other Republicans (virtually unanimous in opposition), the expected vote on H.R. 4210 would have been about 213 or 214 in favor to about 217 or 218 against.[8] This vote would have defeated the bill.

A similar bill a year later offers another case of an important vote in which electoral system bias may have been decisive. This was the 1993 Budget Reconciliation Bill, H.R. 2264. The bill initially voted on in the House was proposed to reduce the budget deficit through a varied mix of tax increases and spending cuts or freezes. On the revenue side, there was a tax-rate increase on higher-income taxpayers (including Social Security benefits), a federal energy tax, an increased corporate income tax rate, and revenues that would be generated by auctioning off the public radio spectrum.[9] The bill also included several provisions that reduced revenue, principally through preferences for lower-income taxpayers and incentives for economic growth.[10] On the spending side, savings were made in Medicare spending and in a large number of discretionary programs.[11] The bill was controversial on many fronts, not the least of which was the energy tax. With an all-out lobbying effort from the White House and promises of changes during Senate consideration, the bill narrowly passed the House in late May by a vote of 219 to 213. The vote was partisan. Democrats divided 218 in favor to 38 against. Not a single Republican voted for the bill (0 to 175). The president won a narrow victory, one that he might not have won if the partisan composition of the House had been even slightly more Republican. A different version of the bill narrowly passed the Senate a month later, also without a single Republican vote.[12]

The conference report version of the bill was voted on in early August. In most respects the bill out of conference was similar to that originally passed by the House in May. The most important difference was the energy tax provision. Instead of a broad-based energy tax, the bill provided for an increased federal gasoline tax at the pump. Democrats defended the bill on the grounds of deficit reduction and fairness, claiming that upper-income taxpayers would bear most of the burden. Republicans attacked the bill for raising taxes, which would slow economic growth, hitting the middle class with the increased gas tax, and failing to make significant spending cuts in domestic programs. They also attacked the retroactive provision of the income-tax increases as unfair. Lobbying, on both sides, was every bit as intense as on the initial vote and the final votes, in both the House and Senate, were even closer.

The conference report on H.R. 2264 passed the House by a single vote, 218 to 216.[13] As close as this appears, this one-vote margin actually understates how close this vote was. Congressional Quarterly described the scene of the vote:

> As the 15-minute nominal limit on the vote expired, the count was tied at 210-210. For several more moments, the tally seesawed back and forth, with Democrats winning one moment and losing the next. Finally all attention centered on freshman Marjorie Margolies-Mezvinsky, D-Pa., who had announced to the largely Republican constituents in her suburban Philadelphia district that she would oppose the plan, just as she had the first time in May.

But leaders told her they would lose without her, and, with the terror-struck demeanor of someone being marched to her own hanging, she walked into the well of the House and signed one of the green cards required to register a yes vote after time had expired and the electronic voting apparatus has been shut off. (Hager and Cloud, 1993, 2127)

This vote was as partisan as the first. Democrats divided 217 in favor (including Representative Margolies-Mezvinsky) and 41 against. The one independent in the House (Representative Sanders of Vermont) voted, as he usually does, with the majority of Democrats. Republicans were again unanimous in their opposition, all 175 voted against the bill. The bill went on to the Senate, where a positive vote from Vice President Gore was required to break the 50-50 tie vote. President Clinton later signed the bill into law and, a year and half later, Marjorie Margolies-Mezvinsky lost her reelection bid.

How would H.R. 2264 have fared in an unbiased electoral system? In the 1992 elections, the extra mileage that Democrats got out of their cheap seats amounted to about five extra Democrats and five fewer Republicans. Without these extra Democratic votes in the House and with these additional Republicans, the prospects of the 1993 Reconciliation bill passing, at least in the form that it passed and without the hunting down and arm-twisting of other reluctant but persuadable Margolies-Mezvinskys, would be remote.[14] The bias of the electoral system made the difference.[15]

Bias probably affected the outcome of these and other especially close and partisan votes, but most votes are neither so close nor so partisan. Yet, whether or not bias determined the outcome of particular pieces of legislation, it most certainly affected legislation. Making sizable shifts in the partisan composition of the House, as bias did, cannot help but change coalition-building strategies, agendas, and the nature of compromises—the substance of legislation. Changing the party balance in the House changes who needs to be won over for passage or defeat of a bill. It changes who holds leverage in the House and what they can exact as concessions for their votes. At the margins, at the very least, partisan bias shifted legislation to the left, and removing it would have moved policy in a more conservative direction.

Civic Attitudes

Partisan bias in the electoral system may also have affected public opinion generally regarding the political system and more specifically regarding

Congress. Although we can only speculate, partisan bias may have had a hand in the decline of civic attitudes over the past 40 years, even if only indirectly through its bolstering of the long-tenured Democratic majority.[16] Among the most important of those civic attitudes suffering a decline were feelings of external political efficacy, the sense that the political system is open to citizen influence. In addition, feelings of support for and approval of the political system and its institutions, a sense that those in the system can be trusted to do what is right much of the time, may have indirectly suffered because of electoral system bias.[17]

Public support for Congress, while fluctuating from the 1950s through to the 1990s, generally declined over this period (Keene and Ladd, 1992; Patterson and Magleby, 1992). In reviewing two different survey measures of public esteem for Congress from 1963 to 1985, Patterson and Caldeira (1990) found that favorable ratings of congressional performance (indicating Congress was doing an "excellent" or "pretty good" job) dropped from the mid–40 percent range in the 1960s to the high–20 percent to mid–30 percent range in the 1970s and 1980s.[18] Patterson and Caldeira observed a similar decline in the numbers expressing confidence "in the people running Congress." In the 1960s, roughly 40 percent declared great confidence in Congress. In the 1970s and 1980s, this number had dropped into the mid-teens. By 1992, Congress was held in such low repute that only 18 percent of Americans indicated that they approved of the way Congress was doing its job.[19]

Partisan bias in the electoral system may have indirectly contributed to the decline in public support for Congress in five different ways. First, by reducing the responsiveness of the electoral system and tilting congressional politics to the left, partisan bias may have contributed to declining sense of political efficacy. Because of bias, the voting public was represented by a Congress more Democratic and more liberal than what it voted for.[20] In addition, because electoral system bias has increased with the Democratic vote, the system seemed unresponsive to changes in the public's vote. Democrats won large seat majorities when they received large vote majorities but also, because of their domination of the cheap seats, Democrats still won fairly large seat majorities when their vote majorities were modest or even narrow. Variation in support for Democrats did not seem to matter much. They won sizable House majorities regardless. Thus, by both adding to the distortion between votes and seats and muting partisan change in the House, electoral system bias may have eroded feelings among the public that they exercised control of the government through the electoral process.[21] Since political efficacy has been shown to be the most important factor affecting individual evaluations of Congress (Patterson et al., 1992, 328–29), if bias in the electoral system depressed feelings of political efficacy, it may also account indirectly for the public's less supportive evaluations of Congress.

Second, by expanding and securing the Democratic House majority to the point that it seemed unassailable, bias in the system may have contributed to a partisan backlash against Congress. Because of the long tenure of the Democratic majority in the House, Congress as an institution may have been considered by some as tantamount to an arm of the Democratic Party. Democrats may not have had an objection to this and felt that the system was working well. However, among Republicans and perhaps some independents, this meant diminished support for Congress as a political institution. Where they would normally support institutions of the government, they felt less friendly to an arm of the opposition party. As one might expect in this regard, even after controlling for a variety of factors affecting public support for Congress, Republicans have been less supportive of Congress than Democrats (Patterson et al., 1992).[22]

Third, by increasing the political independence of the Democratic majority in the House and by increasing the likelihood of divided government, electoral system bias may have increased conflict between the president and Congress and, thereby, lowered public esteem for Congress. The public finds political gridlock and partisan bickering in government distasteful and this may well be reflected in their evaluations of Congress. This is consistent with Patterson and Caldeira's (1992) finding that there is "some tendency for public esteem for Congress to be higher when the president and Congress are in the hands of the same party and congressional support for the president is high" (38).

Aside from normal partisan posturing, the role of divided government and an emboldened Democratic majority in the politicization of ethical and policy disputes may have cost Congress as an institution some support. Although we can only speculate about the extent of the relationship, a large and entrenched Democratic majority may have seen partisan advantage in emphasizing presidential scandals and interpreting policy differences as scandals (e.g., Watergate and Iran-Contra). Congress as an institution may have suffered in the eyes of those seeing the Democratic majority as using congressional powers for narrow partisan political gain.

Finally, although we can only speculate, by enlarging and securing the Democratic majority in the House, bias in the electoral system may have established a context conducive to congressional scandals and, thereby, indirectly caused the public to think less of Congress. A seemingly permanent congressional majority may have been more prone to scandals. Security in power breeds arrogance and carelessness. Again, we may only speculate, but one is left wondering whether the entire history of congressional scandals in recent decades (Abscam, Speaker Jim Wright's book deal, the House check-bouncing scandal, and several other individual indiscretions) would have occurred if the Democratic majority had been less firmly entrenched. Certainly these scandals did nothing to add to the reputation of Congress among the public.

❑ **Representing the District** ❑

How well does the electoral system represent the constituencies of congressional districts? In particular, are constituencies in cheap-seat districts well represented? Because actual district turnout is rarely, if ever, complete, the question of whether decisions made by voters represent the broader constituency (including nonvoters) is a question for all districts. The voting fraction of any district decides who represents the entire constituency. But as that active fraction shrinks, as it does in very-low-turnout, cheap-seat districts, the potential for misrepresentation rises.

One defense of the equal-population, single-member-district system is that it represents the interests of all residents of a district—regardless of whether they vote, are registered to vote, pay taxes, are old enough to vote, or are even citizens. The argument is that the Constitution and, more generally, democratic principles require that all people, not just voters, should be accorded representation. Cheap seats may not be problematic from this perspective. They may not be a problem if the views of the voters in these districts also reflect the views of the nonvoters. If they do, election results would be unchanged if everyone voted. To take this argument further, cheap seats may not only be a nonproblem but may be a remedy to the misrepresentation that would result if only voters were represented without organizing them into districts. By allowing voters in low-turnout areas to speak for (and effectively vote on behalf of) their nonvoting neighbors, the views of these nonvoters weigh into the election results. Since it is important to the stability and legitimacy of the system to represent everyone, the districting system compensates for the failure of many to participate in the electoral process. Because of single-member districts and the similarities of district residents, the views of nonvoters can be counted even though they do not officially register those views at the ballot box.

But are the votes of the few representative of the preferences and interests of the many nonvoters? Put differently, is the cheap-seats system effectively a system of proxy voting, where actual voters reflect the concerns of their neighboring nonvoters, or is it misrepresentative, in which district lines arbitrarily magnify the independent voting strength of some voters and dilute the voting strength of others (those living in high-turnout areas)?

The answer to these questions turns on an important counterfactual that has long been a matter of dispute: if the nonvoters voted, how would they vote?[23] Since most nonvoters never vote in any election, how they would vote if they were to vote is a matter that we can only speculate about. Nevertheless, two possibilities seem plausible: (1) a district's nonvoters might vote like the district's voters or (2) alternatively, nonvoters nationally might vote like voters do nationally.[24] Because one party currently does appreciably better in the low-turnout districts in a system of equally populated districts, both possibilities cannot be true. The arithmetic does not add up.[25] If nonvoters were to vote like their voting neighbors, the national vote would become more Democratic because these nonvoters would come disproportionately from the now-low-turnout Democratic strongholds and, assuming that they voted like their neighbors now vote, they would add significantly to the Democratic column. If, on the other hand, the national vote did not change as a result of getting nonvoters to turn out, then the new voters in the once-cheap seats would have to be less Democratic than their neighbors who now vote.

The two scenarios can also be cast in terms of the two measures of the congressional vote: the mean district percentage and the nationally aggregated percentage. If nonvoters were to turn out and vote like the voters in their districts, the national Democratic vote percentage would rise to the party's mean district percentage. Returning to figure 4.3, this means that, if everyone voted and the previous nonvoters voted like their voting neighbors did, the Democratic national congressional vote would typically have increased by about 3 percentage points and, in some elections (since 1954), by as much as 7.5 percentage points. It is worth observing that Democrats would gain no seats with these additional votes, because each party's vote share in a district would be unchanged under this scenario. Democratic vote totals would rise nationally because many of their additional votes are located in the formerly cheap-seat districts already carried by Democrats. However, whereas they won these districts on the cheap under incomplete turnout, they now win them by paying roughly the same price in votes per victory as Republicans. It is also worth noting that while this scenario is favorable to the Democrats, the increase in the Democratic vote that would result from nonvoters voting like their districts is well short of what is usually imagined by hopeful Democrats expecting nonvoters to be a large reservoir of would-be Democratic voters. On the other hand, if everyone voted and those previously not voting voted for the parties in the same proportions as voters did nationally, the mean district vote for Democrats would decline to their national vote percentage. This would typically amount to a decline of about three percentage points in the mean district vote but would entail a decline of more than six percentage points in several elections.[26] In short, with complete turnout, the two measures of the congressional vote would converge under either view of the current nonvoter. Under the first view of the nonvoter, the national vote moves or converges on the mean district vote and, under the second view, the mean district vote converges on the national vote percentage.

The conventional view is that nonvoters would vote like their voting neighbors and that Democrats would benefit from increased turnout. This supposition is based on the socioeconomic and demographic similarities of nonvoters and Democrats. Both groups are more likely to be working class or poor. Both groups are likely to be racial or ethnic minorities. Accordingly, it is assumed that because of these similarities, if nonvoters voted that they would disproportionately vote for Democrats. If so, there is reason to believe that the nonvoting neighbors in low-turnout districts would vote very much like the few who now vote. The current system is then not a system of misrepresentation but a system that amounts to proxy voting. If the nonvoters voted accordingly, the Democratic vote would increase but their seat holdings would not, because their cheap seats would no longer be cheap.

If, on the other hand, nonvoters were similar to voters nationally in their preferences, the proxy-voting interpretation of electoral system bias breaks down. While nonvoters and voters in a district often share socioeconomic similarities, they are politically distinct. There is good reason to suppose that nonvoters of lower socioeconomic backgrounds are less Democratically inclined than voters of a similar status and, to whatever degree Democratic, probably less dependable in their partisan inclination. There is a good deal of research sustaining this view. A number of studies suggest that the nonvoters nationally are similar to voters in their issue positions, partisanship, or vote preferences (Verba and Nie, 1972; Wolfinger and Rosenstone, 1980; Leighley and Nagler, 1992; Teixeira, 1992a, 1992b; Calvert and Gilchrist, 1993; Verba et al., 1993; and Erikson, 1995).[27] Related research also indicates that nonvoters are less politically anchored, more open to the short-term influences of the particular campaign and less dependably partisan for either party (Campbell, 1960; DeNardo, 1980, 1986; and Petrocik, 1981). These views of the nonvoter are consistent with the analysis indicating that bias was not smaller when turnout increased (which would have been expected if high-turnout electorates were composed of additional peripheral Democratic voters) and that the Democratic House vote (1936 to 1992) was unrelated to national turnout rates over those years (chapter 6).

The reason that adding nonvoters to the electorate may not add to the Democratic vote is that nonvoters as a rule are politically less interested, more volatile, and more easily swayed by the particular conditions surrounding specific campaigns. Thus, if previous nonvoters voted like voters nationally, district vote percentages would be shifted toward the national vote. In many cases, the vote in previously cheap seats would become significantly less Democratic than they had been when turnout was low. However, given that a majority of the national vote cast was Democratic in elections up to 1994, if nonvoters were to divide their votes similarly, district votes would not tip previously Democratic seats to the Republicans. Democrats would continue to carry even their cheap-seat districts.[28] Only the additional volatility of the preferences of these new voters might have helped Republicans carry a few of the marginal, formerly cheap seats.

Ironically, where the mobilization of nonvoters might have made the biggest difference to election outcomes was in 1994. If nonvoters had voted and had cast their votes in the same proportions for the parties as national voters did, Republican seat gains might have been even greater than they were. A simulation of the impact of adding nonvoters to the 32 cheapest seats in 1994, those in the under–70 club (table 8.6), indicates that Republicans might have gained as many as 18 of these seats if the newly added voters divided their votes as national voters had (53.8 percent Republican to 46.2 percent Democratic).[29] Many of these districts were marginal Democratic victories at their low turnout levels. At complete turnout, and with the assumption that the nonvoters would have tilted toward Republicans as voters did nationally, Republicans would have narrowly won these districts. Of course, there is uncertainty regarding the votes of these newly added voters and perhaps they would not have tilted as much toward the Republicans as those actually casting ballots in 1994 did, but, even if Republicans had carried half or even a third of these seats, the turnout of nonvoters might have made a significant difference in 1994, a difference unexpected by the conventional wisdom.

Although there is a good deal of evidence that nonvoters are not dependably Democratic voters (even the district-similarity scenario would only shift the vote a few percentage points) or politically like the voters in their districts, there is no way of knowing with much certainty how nonvoters would vote if they were mobilized. As with any counterfactual, the implications of perfect turnout cannot be properly considered in isolation. If everyone voted, many things would change. Candidates and parties might stake out different positions. Campaign resources might be differently distributed. Everything would be thrown up in the air, and no one knows how that would affect the voters' decisions. Even district lines would undoubtedly be altered under full turnout. It is, therefore, impossible to say to what extent the Democratic bias in the electoral system amounts to proxy voting, allowing for the representation of many for nonvoting Democrats in low-turnout districts, or to what extent this bias amounts to the misrepresentation of the nonvoters. The only way to know with much certainty which party would benefit from nonvoters voting is if they actually voted. However, based on the two likely scenarios of how they might vote (like district or like national voters) and with the exception of the 1994 election, whatever misrepresentation might be created by turnout differences among districts would generally appear to be small.

In the final analysis, we know only two things with certainty. First, we know that the electoral system is an advantage for Democrats. Even if bias in the electoral system amounts only to an informal system of proxy voting (with voters in low-turnout districts wielding the influence of their like-minded but nonvoting neighbors), it is a major advantage for the Democrats to win seats in the House without having to get their supporters to the polls. If all of the nonvoters voted, and voted Democratic enough to preserve current Democratic seats, there would be no bias from cheap seats or turnout differentials. But the facts are they do not vote and we do not know how they would have voted if they had (this is why we hold elections), and Democrats hold on to the seats anyway. Because of the single-member-district system, the impact of a party's no-shows is confined to the district, and, if they win the district anyway, the failure of would-be Democratic voters to turn out costs the party nothing in congressional representation. Second, dealing quite strictly with the reality of votes as cast and seats as decided, not with the "what ifs" of what might have happened if everyone voted or if somehow the system were able to tap the will of silent nonvoters, the electoral system has been consistently and substantially biased in favor of the Democrats.

❑ Racial Politics and Representation ❑

Any discussion of the fair representation of voters in American politics must address the representation of racial groups. Many aspects of the American electoral system throughout history have been shaped by and have affected racial politics. The electoral system has been used at different times both to exclude and to empower African Americans. Perhaps no one in recent times has drawn as much public attention and controversy to the racial issues of electoral systems as Lani Guinier.

In her book *The Tyranny of the Majority,* Guinier issued a stinging indictment of the American political system in general and the principle of majority rule in particular. She argues that the American electoral system, based on its use of the majority-rule principle, unfairly dilutes the full due representation of minorities. She argues that a more democratic system would afford minorities their fair share of representation *and* power in the political process. While her argument applies to the treatment of any permanent political minority, it is particularly pertinent to racial minorities.[30] Guinier argues that the single-member-district, winner-take-all electoral system facilitates white dominance, a tyranny of an unrestrained and permanent white majority. She finds geographically determined single-member districts to be an arbitrary way to organize votes into seats and one that dilutes the impact of minority interests. According to Guinier, the bottom line of feeding the racial divisions of American politics into the single-member-district, plurality- or majority-rule system is that "blacks may vote, but it is whites who will govern" (1994, 22).[31]

Although insightful on several matters, there is much to criticize in Guinier's argument. Her reading of Madison, from whom she takes the warning of the potential for majority tyranny and whom she counts as an ally, ignores his equal concern for the tyranny of minorities and his dedication to broadly popular government. Her interpretation of the American constitutional order as majoritarian overlooks the many impediments to majority rule.[32] Her perspective of American political divisions as exclusively racial, with a politically homogeneous white majority oppressing a politically homogeneous African American minority, is both simplistic and extreme. As reactions to the O. J. Simpson murder trial verdict painfully reminded us, racial divisions are unquestionably important in American life, political and otherwise. However, there are many other important, cross-cutting divisions as well. Among others, the nation confronts economic class, gender, regional, religious, and a variety of ideological divisions. For instance, though both Senator Ted Kennedy and House Speaker Newt Gingrich are of the same racial background, Kennedy has much more in common politically with Senator Carol Mosely-Braun from Illinois, who is African American, than with Gingrich. Moreover, although African Americans are a permanent racial minority, until 1994 they had been an important part of an entrenched political majority for six decades.

Guinier's remedy for what she perceives as the system's shortcomings is every bit as extreme as her perspective on the nation's political divisions. She rejects the theory of "black electoral success," the effort to get more African Americans elected to office through the advantageous drawing of district boundaries and the creation of "majority-minority districts" (districts with a population majority of racial minority voters), as being inadequate to assure political power over public policy formation. By the same logic, she would presumably also reject the proportional representation of African Americans, since that would also leave them in a minority position within a majority-rule system. Instead, Guinier advocates a form of power sharing under "the principle of taking turns," a principle that would lead to public policy careening from left to right and back again—an unwise, unworkable, and fundamentally undemocratic government.

While there is much to take issue with, Guinier's assertions regarding the plurality-rule, single-member-district electoral system are most important to this study.[33] Guinier claims that the majority- (or plurality-) rule, single-member district is in principle unfair to minorities and causes them to be underrepresented. In this, she parts company with the conventional view. The conventional criticism of the single-member-district, plurality-rule system is that it is not unfair to racial minorities in principle but that it has been abused in practice. It has been used against minorities historically, but there is nothing inherent in the single-member-district system that caused this. The people who controlled the electoral system chose to use it as a tool of discrimination. Through racial gerrymandering, the impact of the votes of racial minorities had been diluted. The impact of African American votes was minimized in the drawing of districts, either by packing those voters into a few districts so they would only influence a few elections or by spreading the votes among several districts so they would be inconsequential.

With the Voting Rights Act of 1965, its subsequent renewals, and related judicial rulings, reformers have sought to rectify the past discrimination of electoral systems (Ball et al., 1984; Parker, 1990; Grofman et al., 1992). As in all areas of racial discrimination, there is disagreement about what a fair system would entail. Some would argue for a race-blind system, treating racial minorities like all other minorities. Others argue for greater affirmative action, requiring that districts be drawn to maximize the prospects of electing candidates who are from racial minority groups. This view promotes the creation of as many racial majority-minority districts as possible, even at the expense of geographic compactness (allowing district lines to encompass scattered areas of a state in order to build a majority of minority voters). In their "preclearance" of state redistrictings, the Justice Department in the 1980s and early 1990s apparently adopted this so-called max-black policy. The Supreme Court, on the other hand, through its rulings in the cases of *Shaw v. Reno* and *Miller v. Johnson,* took a more moderate position.[34]

Whether one accepts a race-neutral or an affirmative-action view of electoral system reform or something in between, it is generally accepted that the single-member-district, plurality-rule electoral system can be made fair to minorities. Guinier, however, is not part of this consensus. From her perspective, the effort to make the plurality-rule, single-member district fair to minorities amounts to tinkering with a fundamentally flawed system. Reformers might succeed in making the system less unfair than it was, but they cannot elevate it to her standard of political justice.

There is an element of truth to Guinier's charge against the *plurality-rule* aspect of the electoral system, but her charge is fundamentally wrong with respect to the *single-member-district* aspect of the system. As to plurality rule, on the one hand, she is correct in asserting the familiar charge that the plurality-rule system underrepresents minorities of all sorts, including racial minorities. However, the equally familiar defense of plurality rule is that its magnification of majorities allows for more stable and effective government, a benefit thought to outweigh the underrepresentation of minorities. Moreover, as Guinier acknowledges, her complaints on behalf of African Americans are not constrained to racial minorities. They could have been made with equal force for Republicans or for any minority from right-wing to left-wing extremists. Thus, as well as underrepresenting African Americans, the plurality-rule system may disadvantage views anathema to those of a majority of African Americans. In addition, from another perspective, the plurality-rule system may be seen to have worked to the advantage of African Americans. Although a racial minority, African Americans have also been an important part of the Democratic Party's political majority, a majority that benefited from the magnifying effects of the plurality-rule system.

While Guinier is only partly right regarding the impact of the plurality-rule system on African American interests, her assertions as they apply to single-member districts are outright wrong. African Americans, like any minority (including Republicans until 1994), are underrepresented by the plurality-rule system compared to proportional representation but are not underrepresented as a result of districting arrangements. Quite to the contrary, the single-member-district system, which permits the existence of cheap seats and the overrepresentation of its voters, significantly augments the representation of African Americans. *While most cheap seats are not majority-minority districts, most majority-minority districts are cheap seats.* In 1994, 17 (63 percent) of the 27 contested majority-minority districts were in the lowest-turnout quintile.[35] A large majority of districts with significant, though less than majority, African American populations were also in the lowest two quintiles of turnout.[36] The proportion of a district's population made up of African Americans was strongly and negatively associated with district turnout (in terms of actual votes). Every percentage point of a district's black population reduced expected turnout in 1994 by about a thousand votes. Rather than causing the underrepresentation of African Americans, the single-member-district system contains and effectively eliminates the otherwise harmful effects of very low voter turnout in the African American community.

Although cheap seats are advantageous to African Americans from the standpoint of congressional representation, quite to the contrary of Guinier's assertions, they may also have other unanticipated consequences for the system. While African Americans may benefit in congressional representation and while African American congressional candidates may benefit from cheap seats, voter turnout of African Americans may suffer because of it and African American influence on political contests above the congressional level may be diminished. In low-turnout African American districts won safely by Democratic congressional candidates, there is little incentive for local Democrats to mobilize higher turnout. In fact, they have an incentive not to "rock the boat" and jeopardize their safe election. Who pays the price? Those below and those above. Potential voters are not mobilized and brought into the system, and Democratic candidates further up the ticket are denied these votes. From a self-interest standpoint, a Democratic congressional candidate is probably indifferent to winning an election with a high margin of few voters or a high margin of many voters.[37] Either way, he or she wins with a healthy vote percentage. But it makes a difference to voters and to candidates running for higher office. A Senate or presidential candidate would much rather win a high percentage in a heavy-turnout district than a higher percentage of a light-turnout district, because district boundaries are irrelevant to their election. They need votes, period.

Thus, although cheap seats benefit African Americans at the congressional level and accord African American voters a disproportionate amount of influence, they may effectively discourage other African Americans from turning out and diminish both their influence on contests for higher offices and the chances of Democrats winning these "top-of-the-ticket" races.

❑ The Equal Representation of Voters ❑

Ultimately, the existence and effects of cheap seats raise questions of political justice and equality. In the past chapters, we have been concerned with the just and equitable treatment of the political parties by the electoral system. The systematically different treatment of parties with the same number of votes raises serious concerns about the fairness of the political process. The organization of votes in such a way that Democrats win a greater number of seats than Republicans would have with an identical number of votes is from most perspectives inequitable.

The inequity of the electoral system in its treatment of the parties, while of great importance for public policy and the legitimacy of the system, is not the only inequity produced by cheap seats. The huge turnout differences among congressional districts raise questions regarding the equitable treatment of individual voters. In determining who shall be sent to Congress, is it fair and equitable that a voter in one district has twice the say of a voter in another district? Is it fair that a voter in one district has three or four or five times "the say" as a voter in another district? These are not hypothetical ratios. They are evident in every congressional election.[38]

The Supreme Court in its rulings over the last several decades has gone to great lengths to ensure that congressional districts drawn within states are of equal population. Even fairly minute differences are not tolerated (e.g., *Kirkpatrick v. Preisler*). States can no longer draw districts with slightly different populations out of respect for community or local governmental boundaries. For example, following the 1990 census and the reapportionment of districts to the states, California was allocated 52 House seats. By the 1992 election, the district boundaries were in place. The range of population size across these 52 districts (as measured by the 1990 U.S. Census) was from 573,684 to 570,874, a difference of only 2,810 residents. The largest district was less than a half of one percentage point larger than the smallest district in the state.

The rationale for requiring states to draw districts of as nearly equal population size as possible is the notion of political equality as embodied in the Fourteenth Amendment to the Constitution (*Wesberry v. Sanders*). Equal protection of the law requires that citizens have an equal opportunity to determine who represents them in Congress. This was the basis of the Court's principle of one person, one vote. If districts were of unequal size, a voter in an underpopulated district would have much more influence than a voter in an overpopulated district. This violated the equitable treatment of individuals before the government. As the Court put it, "as nearly as practicable, one man's vote in a congressional election is to be worth as much as another's" (Congressional Quarterly, 1985, 695). In their efforts to protect political equality in this regard, the Court has rejected redistricting plans that deviated by as little as "3.1 percent from perfectly equal population districts" (Congressional Quarterly, 1985, 695).

Although the Court's interpretation of the equal protection clause of the Constitution would prohibit malapportionment of districts, political equality is not the only constitutional provision that comes into play on the question of malapportionment. The Court is constrained by other explicit constitutional provisions. In Senate elections, for example, the explicit constitutional requirement of equal representation of the states in the Senate (and later the Seventeenth Amendment requiring the popular election of U.S. Senators) entails malapportionment. Voters in smaller states are accorded greater influence than voters in larger states. Similarly, the Electoral College provision for the election of the president, because it awards Electoral College votes to the states and does not do so in strict proportion to the state's population, allows for malapportionment.

There are two constitutional provisions that prevent the Court from entirely preventing malapportionment, the strict adherence to the principle of one person, one vote, in House elections. First, the Constitution assigns congressional representation to the separate states according to each state's population, with the additional provision that each state be allocated at least one member of the House. The total number of representatives to be divided to the states is set by law, and, although the 435 number set in 1911 is arbitrary, some limit is a practical requirement of a representative system. The constitutional provision assigning representatives to the states along with the statutory limitation on the number of representatives makes some malapportionment probable. Unless the population of the states divides perfectly evenly by the number of representatives, some states will be rounded up to an additional representative and other states will be rounded down.[39] Those rounded up will have a smaller ratio of seats to population than those rounded down. In the reapportionment of the 1990s, for instance, Montana had one member to represent a population of 799,065 and Idaho had two members to represent a population of 1,006,749, an average district population of 503,375 or almost 300,000 fewer than represented by the representative of Montana. Just because of the "lumpiness" inherent in representation (you cannot assign a fraction of a representative to a state), there is some malapportionment in the system. In the 1990s, following this example, this "lumpiness" provided greater representation to the resident of Idaho and less representation to the resident of Montana.

The second constitutional provision that allows malapportionment in congressional representation is the infrequency of reapportionment. The Constitution requires reapportionment of districts based on state population as measured by the decennial census. A decade between redistricting permits large population disparities to emerge, especially in a growing and mobile nation. Between the 1980 and 1990 Censuses, for instance, the nation's population grew by almost 10 percent (Duncan, 1991, 9). However, the population in some districts grew much more than this, while other districts actually lost population. At the extremes, through the 1980s, the Thirty-seventh District of California grew by 86 percent, while the Thirteenth District of Michigan declined by 23 percent. Although they started the decade with nearly the same population (about 520,000), by 1990 there were nearly a million residents of the Thirty-seventh District in California and only about 400,000 in the Thirteenth District of Michigan (Duncan, 1991, 8). Whether or not voters in these two districts were political equals at the beginning of the decade, by the end of the decade, they certainly were not. With population shifts between reapportionments, the districts became malapportioned.

Aside from the malapportionment that might result from representatives being awarded in a "lumpy" way to the states and population shifts that might occur over the course of a decade, the Court has expressed a zero-tolerance for malapportionment. It appears to be the Court's assumption that equally populated districts, at least within a state and at the time of the redistricting, provides political equality or the equal protection of the laws for the congressional voters of the state. This is an erroneous assumption.

Consider again the case of California's redistricting in the 1990s. From the standpoint of population equality, the districts are remarkably equal and, one might presume, as the Court apparently does, that this ensures the political equality of voters. It does so in only the most formalistic sense. In political reality, voters in California's congressional districts are very unequal. A California voter in one district may have almost six times the say in choosing a representative as a California voter in another district. In the Thirty-third District of California in 1992, a district in Los Angeles, a mere 50,779 voters elected a member to Congress. In that same election, 291,634 voters elected a member of the House from the Sixth District of California, in suburban San Francisco. Both seats were contested. This is a difference of over 240,000 voters. Despite the fact that the districts were equally populated, there were nearly six voters in the Sixth District for every one voter in the Thirty-third. In terms of political equality, to paraphrase the Court, what is politically important is whether one voter's vote is worth as much as another's, not how many bystanders are nearby. A voter in the Sixth District was one voice hidden among nearly three hundred thousand, while a voter in the Thirty-third District was one voice in a much smaller crowd, surrounded by a lot of nonvoting bystanders.

The contrast of the Sixth and Thirty-third Districts in California in 1992, though extreme, is not unique. District disparities are enormous even when looking at groups of districts. Turnout in each of the seven lowest-turnout districts in California in 1992 (each contested) was less than half the turnout of any of the seven highest-turnout districts in the state. A voter in the low-turnout district had more than twice the say of a voter in a high-turnout district. This is not political equality.

An examination of contested-district turnout disparities in other states yields similar results. Table 9.2 presents the 1992 turnout for the highest- and lowest-turnout districts and the ratio between them for each state. The turnout ratios are calculated for all states having at least two congressional districts. For example, the ratio of 1.42 in Alabama indicates that there were 1.42 voters in the state's high-turnout district for every one voter in its low-turnout district. Turnout in the 1992 election is examined because it is the first election following a redistricting and any malapportionment due to population shifts between reapportion-

Table 9.2

Effective Malapportionment in Congressional Districts in the States, 1992

State	Number of Contested Districts	Number of Voters in the Highest-Turnout District	Number of Voters in the Lowest-Turnout District	Ratio of Voters in Highest- to Lowest-Turnout Districts
Alabama	7	280,018	197,545	1.42:1
Alaska	1	239,116	—	—
Arizona	6	264,066	137,373	1.92:1
Arkansas	4	249,399	208,924	1.19:1
California	49	291,634	50,779	5.74:1
Colorado	6	271,361	227,531	1.19:1
Connecticut	6	247,520	219,606	1.13:1
Delaware	1	276,124	—	—
Florida	20	281,259	143,905	1.95:1
Georgia	11	274,957	150,382	1.83:1
Hawaii	2	180,955	177,476	1.02:1
Idaho	2	242,790	229,957	1.06:1
Illinois	20	274,088	116,606	2.35:1
Indiana	10	258,451	183,831	1.41:1
Iowa	4	267,863	257,175	1.04:1
Kansas	4	292,796	268,806	1.09:1
Kentucky	6	280,755	206,578	1.36:1
Louisiana	1	243,580	—	—
Maine	2	358,148	311,372	1.15:1
Maryland	8	280,419	178,993	1.57:1
Massachusetts	9	311,620	247,163	1.26:1
Michigan	15	293,078	184,957	1.58:1
Minnesota	8	314,010	264,282	1.19:1
Mississippi	5	204,616	174,609	1.17:1
Missouri	9	312,442	233,175	1.34:1
Montana	1	403,735	—	—
Nebraska	3	239,002	233,340	1.02:1
Nevada	2	270,461	221,488	1.22:1
New Hampshire	2	255,853	255,083	1.00:1
New Jersey	13	274,371	145,714	1.88:1
New Mexico	3	205,214	168,170	1.22:1
New York	30	265,278	73,067	3.63:1
North Carolina	12	265,060	163,101	1.63:1
North Dakota	1	291,554	—	—
Ohio	17	263,071	223,624	1.18:1
Oklahoma	6	230,816	198,802	1.16:1
Oregon	5	294,154	269,879	1.09:1
Pennsylvania	17	307,700	185,591	1.66:1

continued

Table 9.2 (*continued*)

Effective Malapportionment in Congressional Districts in the States, 1992

State	Number of Contested Districts	Number of Voters in the Highest-Turnout District	Number of Voters in the Lowest-Turnout District	Ratio of Voters in Highest- to Lowest-Turnout Districts
Rhode Island	2	204,413	194,089	1.05:1
South Carolina	5	198,347	183,086	1.08:1
South Dakota	1	332,902	—	—
Tennessee	8	216,530	154,504	1.40:1
Texas	25	264,653	98,673	2.68:1
Utah	3	252,969	229,061	1.10:1
Vermont	1	279,113	—	—
Virginia	11	298,642	168,473	1.77:1
Washington	9	283,950	209,584	1.35:1
West Virginia	2	203,090	186,291	1.09:1
Wisconsin	9	292,797	234,176	1.25:1
Wyoming	1	196,977	—	—
Nation	405	403,735	50,779	7.95:1

Note: The vote is the total vote cast for any congressional candidate running in 1992. Vermont is included here, even though it was won by an independent candidate and has been excluded from other portions of the analysis. In 1992, both major parties ran candidates in Vermont.

ments will be minimal.[40] The ratio of turnout in the highest to lowest districts is the maximum amount of *effective malapportionment* in the state—effective malapportionment meaning the unequal number of *voters* from one district to another rather than conventional or nominal malapportionment that refers to unequal numbers of *residents* in different districts, whether they vote or not or even whether they could legally vote or not.

Although nominal malapportionment within states may have been effectively outlawed by judicial rulings, table 9.2 indicates that effective malapportionment is rampant. The equal rights of residents may have been protected through one-person, one-vote rulings, but the equal rights of voters have not been. As we have already observed, within a state, the Court objects to interdistrict population differences of even a few percentage points. However, interdistrict turnout differences are commonly in excess of 25 percent and regularly in excess of 50 percent.

Put differently, within a single state and immediately following the adoption of a redistricting plan, it is common for a voter in one district to have one and a half times as much input into his or her representative as a voter from another part of the same state in the same election year.

Effective malapportionment is greatest where there is the most opportunity for it, in the large states. In the five largest states, California, New York, Texas, Illinois and Florida, turnout differences were consistently at or above the two-to-one ratio. That is, voters in at least one district of these states outnumbered voters in at least one other district of the same state by a margin of at least two to one. In California, depending on where you lived and on which side of a district line you were on, you could have been one voter in nearly 300,000 voters to elect a representative or one voter in about 50,000 voters. In New York, depending again on where precisely you lived in the state in relation to district boundaries, you could either have been one in over a quarter of a million voters to elect a House member or one in about 75,000 voters.

The empirical facts are clear. First, while congressional districts within the same state at the outset of a reapportionment are at least equal in population, they are often very unequal in the number of voters. Voters in some congressional districts are part of a relatively small number to decide who will represent their district in the House. Voters in other congressional districts are part of a much larger number to decide who will represent them. Second, the inequalities in the sizes of active electorates are not temporary matters. It would be one thing if turnout were low in one district in one election and high in the next. While this might be the basis of inequality in the treatment of voters in any particular election, there might be greater equity over time. This is not the case. Cheap seats in one election are very likely to be cheap seats in the next. As the analysis in chapter 5 and appendix C indicates, district turnout in one election is very strongly and positively correlated with turnout in the next election. District turnout was strongly correlated, for example, between the 1992 and 1994 elections ($r = .86$, for the adjusted vote in all districts, and $r = .88$, for districts contested in both years).

The normative implications of these facts are not so clear. What does the principle of political equality for citizens require of an electoral system? The Courts have determined that, baring constitutional provisions to the contrary, political equality requires congressional districts at least to be equally populated at the time of their formation. A district with many fewer potential voters than another district accords a greater opportunity for a citizen in the former district to determine which party's candidate is sent to Washington. The Courts recognized this malapportionment situation as inequitable. They are constitutionally restrained from attacking this same malapportionment problem across state lines, because the Constitution explicitly allocates representatives to the states, or through its development over time, because the Constitution explicitly calls for reapportionment every 10 years in accordance with the population count of the U.S. Census. However, they can and have vigorously attacked population malapportionment within states at the time of redistrictings. The question that the cheap-seats analysis raises is whether the Courts have gone far enough to protect real political equality in congressional elections.

The answer to this question, like many questions of equal rights, depends on what you regard as equal opportunity and what is required for it to be ensured. Some may find no inequality problem raised by turnout differences or may interpret the problem as inevitable and without remedy. From this perspective, the Court has ensured the equal opportunity of citizens to influence congressional elections by requiring equally populated districts. If some potential voters in these districts fail to avail themselves of the opportunity to participate in these elections, this is their problem. Equal opportunity was preserved. Anything more would move the Court toward ensuring equal influence, or equality of results, rather than equal opportunity. If the neighbors of these nonvoters have a greater say in congressional elections as a result of the nonvoting in the district, that is just an unintended consequence of the system. Following the disputed proxy voting interpretation of cheap seats, it could be further argued that this system appropriately compensates for nonvoting and is more representative of the nation as a result. Finally, since it is impossible to tell in advance exactly who will or will not vote in a particular election and since all citizens of voting age should be accorded the equal opportunity to vote, it can be argued that districts must be equally populated and that there is no feasible way of drawing district boundaries before the election to ensure that they have equal numbers of voters. In short, turnout equality in districts is neither necessary for the political equality of citizens nor feasible in a single-member-district electoral system.

From another standpoint, however, the inequality of a few voters in one congressional district having the same amount of representation as three or four times their number in another district is very troubling. Although equally populated districts provide for the equal political opportunity for citizens, the inequality of turnout in districts creates real political inequalities among voters. The one-person, one-vote principle demands more than paper equality. A greater equality in the number of voters in districts would not mean equal influence but would provide voters with the equal opportunity to influence the selection of their representative. Moreover, the continuity of turnout across election years, which causes the inequality problem for the individual voter to be more severe (he or she is consistently underrepresented or overrepresented), also makes a remedy more feasible. We know in advance where turnout can be expected to be high or low and can use this information in equalizing expected district turnouts. In short, from this view, large turnout differences across congressional districts means that all voters are not politically equal, and this violates basic constitutional rights.

❑ Reforming the House Electoral System ❑

The legitimacy of a representative democracy depends to a great extent on the fairness of its electoral system. If the system for obtaining public consent for the government is flawed, the popular basis for the government is called into question. Holding free, open, and competitive periodic elections is certainly a requirement of popular government, but it is also a requirement of representative government that the popular will expressed in these elections is fairly reflected in the results of elections. The preceding analysis calls into question the fairness of the electoral system for the House of Representatives, its fairness to the political parties, and its fairness to voters. In the aggregate, the system has been biased in favor of the Democrats. While generally insufficient to have determined which party controls the House (except perhaps in 1956), it has affected both the numbers of each party in the House and, ultimately, the public policies passed by the House. The fairness of the electoral system is also a concern for the political equality of individual voters. Under current arrangements, where you happen to live in a state, whether you live around others who vote or around those who do not, affects how much your vote counts toward the election of a representative.

Judgments about the fairness of the political system depend ultimately on values. On the basis of their values, the framers of the American constitutional system designed neither a purely democratic nor a more narrowly majoritarian system. They valued wisdom in the government and the consent from a broad spectrum of society as well as securing the consent of the majority. As such, they constructed a system that frustrated popular majorities in numerous ways. By modern democratic sensibilities, the Electoral College system for electing a president is undemocratic in that it allows the possibility that a president could be elected without a plurality of the popular vote. Critics of the Electoral College have for decades called for constitutional reform to make this undemocratic outcome an impossibility. Similarly, though the Seventeenth Amendment, instituting the popular election of Senators, democratized the Senate electoral system, the constitutional provision requiring equal representation of the states in the Senate is decidedly undemocratic. Regardless of how many live in or vote in a state, they receive the same two representatives to the U.S. Senate. The constitutional roots of the decidedly malapportioned presidential and Senate electoral systems do not exempt them from criticism as being undemocratic or, at least, antimajoritarian. However, while a democrat could well find fault with these electoral systems, regardless of their origin, they were nevertheless intentional and considered features of the political system and constitutional amendments would be required to reform them.

The effective malapportionment of the House electoral system has some similarities with the malapportionment of the presidential and Senate systems, but there are also some important differences. Like the presidential and Senate systems, the malapportionment in the House system has constitutional sources. As already noted, the allocation of House seats to the states and the requirement to reapportion following censuses induces some malapportionment.[41] However, unlike the presidential and Senate electoral systems, the effective malapportionment of the House electoral system was not explicitly intended by the Constitution and has significant extraconstitutional sources. The drawing of congressional district boundaries within the states by state governments allows turnout disparities among districts. First, the Constitution itself does not require single-member congressional districts within states. As noted in chapter 6, many states in the nineteenth century and some states up through midway through the twentieth century had at-large or multimember districts. Second, under the single-member-district system, the Constitution is silent with respect to how the states should draw congressional districts, except that they should be drawn in such a way that no person within a state is denied his or her "equal protection of the laws."

Without constitutional provisions requiring substantial turnout differences among congressional districts (at least those occurring within states), with constitutional provisions that might be interpreted as forbidding such large disparities (prohibited in the name of protecting political equality), and with the significant and consistently inequitable treatment of the parties that is produced by these turnout differences, there is good reason to consider electoral system reforms. Can the electoral system for "The People's House" be made to better reflect the will of the people? There are a number of possible reforms that would address the cheap-seats phenomenon. Potential reforms range from constitutional revisions to more modest and perhaps somewhat more viable proposals. Of course, the odds are against any reform of the electoral structure, but some reforms are less radical departures from present norms than others.[42]

There are four strategies that may be pursued to varying lengths in eliminating or reducing the impact of cheap seats in the electoral system. The strategies are based on the understanding that cheap seats are institutionally created by drawing district lines in such a way that there are significant turnout disparities among equally populated districts. In light of this, four strategies for reducing the impact of cheap seats seem possible:

1. by defining the relevant population for districts in a narrower way,
2. by drawing fewer district lines that allow for turnout disparities,
3. by drawing district lines in such a way as to reduce turnout differences among districts, or
4. by increasing turnout enough to reduce interdistrict variation in turnout.

The first strategy, the redefining of the relevant population study, is based on the fact that, in reapportionment and in redistricting, people are counted who not only do not vote but who cannot vote. The second strategy, the fewer districts strategy, is based on the understanding that greater turnout disparities among districts are possible with more districts. As the state-by-state analysis of district turnout differences in 1992 showed, larger differences in district turnout were evident in the larger states, where more districts allow more interdistrict turnout variation.[43] The third strategy, the turnout-sensitive redistricting strategy, is based on the notion that district lines are now drawn without concern for turnout differences and that the consideration of turnout in the redistricting process might reduce turnout variations across districts. The fourth strategy, the increased-turnout strategy, is based on the notion that bias is based on cheap seats, that cheap seats are based on turnout disparities among districts, and that increasing turnout nationally will reduce district turnout disparities. At the extreme, if turnout were 100 percent, there could be no turnout disparities among districts and no turnout-based cheap seats.

Redefining the Relevant Population

First, turnout disparities among districts might be reduced if the population counted for purposes of awarding and drawing districts bore a closer relationship to the electorate. As it stands, the national government counts all residents of a state for the purpose of allocating the 435 seats to the states and state governments count all residents of an area within a state for the purpose of drawing district boundaries within a state. Everyone is counted. They do not have to be registered to vote. They do not even have to be of voting age or eligible to vote. They do not have to be citizens. They do not even have to be in the country legally. The very broad definition of the relevant population is a source of malapportionment for voting-eligible citizens and for actual voters.

The definition of the relevant population for the electoral system could be tightened for either the awarding of seats to the states or in the drawing of districts within the states. In light of the fact that the Constitution, in both Article 1 and the Fourteenth Amendment, explicitly refers without qualification to representatives being apportioned to the states on the basis of the number of persons in the state, narrowing the definition of who is counted for reapportionment would seem to require a constitutional amendment. The Constitution was not explicit, however, in setting standards for determining districts within states. The equal population, one-person, one-vote rulings were based on judicial interpretations of the Fourteenth Amendment's clause guaranteeing equal protection of the laws. Since noneligibles (noncitizens and those not of voting age) by definition cannot vote, it may be argued that excluding them from the redistricting count does not infringe on their rights and that the current practice of counting them produces inequalities among those who can vote. Counting people who are not eligible to vote, including noncitizens and illegal immigrants, in the allocation of districts only serves to award arbitrary influence to their voting neighbors and to dilute the votes of those living and voting in other districts. Thus, although the definition of the relevant population for redistricting could certainly be narrowed by a constitutional amendment, this might also be accomplished by judicial interpretations refining the notion of one person, one vote. Either way, if districts were of more equal size in the number of *potential voters,* they would probably also be of more equal size in the number of *actual voters,* and this would reduce the effects of cheap seats.[44]

Fewer Districts

In pursuing the second strategy, there are a number of proposals that would reduce the number of districts and, therefore, the number of turnout discrepancies in the House electoral system. The most extreme reform along these lines would require national elections for the House. This would require both the repeal of the constitutional provisions designating House seats to the states and the establishment of some sort of proportional representation system of election.[45] Short of such a radical proposal, the system could reduce cheap seats by moving from single-member districts to multimember districts in states having more than a single seat. Multimember districts, with or without proportional representation, would make it more difficult to draw districts with such large turnout discrepancies. If the number of seats in a multimember district remained small, there would still be a possibility of multimember cheap seats (as in Queens in the 1980s), but the chances of this happening should decline with larger multimember districts. As noted in chapter 6, there is no constitutional prohibition against multimember or statewide at-large districts, and they were used in many states for many years.[46]

The creation of multimember districts is not the only way to reduce the number of district lines and thereby reduce turnout differences among districts. Interdistrict turnout differences might also be reduced by decreasing the number of representatives in the House. As with multimember district electoral systems, the electoral system of a smaller House would require fewer districts allowing fewer opportunities for building districts around pockets of nonvoters. Larger congressional districts, whether single-member in a smaller House or multimember in a House of the current size, are likely to be more socioeconomically diverse and therefore deviate less from normal turnout levels. In addition, larger districts, drawing on a deeper pool of available candidates and attracting greater media attention, are likely to be more hotly contested. If so, turnout might not only be more equal but equalized at a higher percentage of eligible voters. Finally, while from one perspective the reform to fewer and larger districts may mean that district representatives are less responsive to local constituency interests, the other side of the coin is that congressional representation might become less parochial because of the expanded size of districts.[47] In terms of implementation, like the multimember district reform, the reduced-House-size reform would not require a constitutional amendment. The Constitution is silent regarding the number of representatives in the House. The size of the House changed frequently throughout American history, until limited to 435 seats by statute in 1911.

Turnout-Sensitive Redistricting

The third strategy is less radical in that it addresses the cheap-seats phenomenon while maintaining the current number of single-member districts. The problem of large turnout differences among districts could be addressed in the normal course of redrawing district lines. Redistricting currently takes a whole host of considerations into account—equal population size within the state, the compactness of the district, the contiguity of the district, the effects of the district boundaries on the likely fortunes of the parties and the current incumbents, and the likelihood that the district would elect a candidate who is a member of a racial minority. Expected turnout could be added to the list of considerations for redistricting, either by state legislatures or by the Courts. While at some point tradeoffs among these districting goals are necessary, the electoral system could move toward equal-turnout districts without making tradeoffs in some other areas. Specifically, the system could move toward districts with more equal turnouts *without* creating further deviations from equal population districts. Although some cheap seats are surrounded by other low-turnout areas, others adjoin traditionally higher-turnout districts. Reaching out to include some voter-rich areas in currently cheap seats could help to equalize district turnouts. This reform is all the more plausible because of the high degree of stability in turnout.[48]

Districts in the Los Angeles area in the 1990s illustrate the possibilities of addressing cheap seats through redistricting. One of these districts was California's Thirty-first District, the district used as an example of a 1990s cheap seat in chapter 8. This East Los Angeles district ranked sixth from the bottom in turnout among contested districts in the 1994 election. Total congressional turnout in 1994 in the Thirty-first was just under 86,000 votes. The district was bordered by five other districts. Although two of the bordering districts were also low-turnout districts, the Thirteenth and Thirty-third on the eastern and southeastern sides of the district, the other three bordering districts had considerably higher turnout. Turnout in one district (the Thirty-fourth to the west) was 37 percent higher than turnout in the Thirty-first, and turnout in each of the other two adjoining districts was nearly twice as great. Turnout in the Twenty-seventh and Twenty-eighth Districts, on the north and east sides of the Thirty-first, were both over 162,000 voters. Certainly, exchanging some precincts between these adjoining high-turnout districts and the low-turnout Thirty-first would have made the Thirty-first less of a cheap seat.

California's Thirty-fifth and Thirty-sixth Districts also suggest the possibilities of turnout-sensitive redistricting. The districts are adjacent to one another, with the Thirty-sixth comprising coastal towns and the Thirty-fifth to its east comprising Watts and other parts of south-central Los Angeles. Turnout in the Thirty-fifth in 1994 was under 85,000 voters, fourth from the bottom of all contested districts. Next door, in the Thirty-sixth, turnout was almost two and a half times as great (195,808 voters). Turnout in the Thirty-fifth District, one of the cheap seats listed in table 8.6, probably could have been increased significantly by drawing the line between it and the Thirty-sixth a bit differently.

Increased Turnout

The fourth reform strategy involves attempts to change political behavior rather than the structure of the electoral system. The political behavior of interest is turnout. If turnout were less variable, particularly less variable from one geographic area to another, cheap seats would be less likely. One way to reduce turnout variation is to stimulate higher turnout rates.[49] At the extreme, as discussed above, there would be no turnout-related bias in the electoral system if turnout were complete (100 percent). If turnout rates rose significantly, turnout variation among districts would, at some point, decline. At present national rates of turnout, it is easy for turnout in some districts to be quite high while rates in other districts are very low. At high national turnout rates, turnout would have to increase particularly in now-low-turnout areas, the cheap seats.

Political reforms that might increase turnout have long been considered and many have been adopted. Most of these reforms have attracted interest because of the general culture supporting political inclusiveness and the potential political gains that some (particularly Democrats) think might come as a result of increased turnout. Diminishing the inequities of the House electoral system has not been a consideration in making these changes intended to stimulate turnout, but diminished cheap-seat effects might well be an unintended result. In recent decades, systemic reforms addressing low turnout have centered on making voter registration less of an obstacle to voting. Allowing eligible citizens to register close to or on election day and, more recently, the motor-voter provision allowing eligible citizens to register to vote while renewing their driver's licenses were the latest reforms intended to make registration less of an impediment to voting. More could be done, from expanding voting hours, to campaign reforms to stimulate turnout, to alternative mechanisms for casting ballots (e.g., greater use of mail-in ballots).

Most rules and practices of electoral systems do not change rapidly, nor should they. The electoral system is at the core of representative government. It should not be tampered with for "light or transient reasons." However, a system that is out of kilter, that systematically overrewards one party and underrewards another, that consistently and arbitrarily weighs the voices of some voters more heavily than those of others, that raises questions about the fundamental fairness of elections and the legitimacy of the representative process, is a system in which change should be seriously considered.

Appendix

A

□□

The Effects of Candidate
Advantages on
the Vote

This appendix presents in five tables the data and the calculations necessary for the simulation in chapter 3 of what the congressional vote might have been for Democrats and Republicans (1) if the parties had been equal with respect to the advantages of incumbency and (2) if all congressional seats had been contested. As discussed in chapter 3, the national vote count might not well reflect the intentions of voters if some candidates are systematically advantaged by the political system (incumbents) and if some voters cannot express a preference for a party because that option is not available on their ballot (uncontested seats). The analysis in the following tables attempts to determine what the vote for the parties would have been in elections from 1954 to 1992 if incumbency were not a consideration in the vote and if all congressional districts were contested by both parties.

Tables A.1 and A.2 estimate the number of votes that were attracted to each party because of incumbency and the number of votes that were forgone by each party by its failure to offer a candidate in every congressional district. Table A.1 offers these estimates in districts in which Democrats enjoyed these candidate advantages, and table A.2 offers the same for Republican districts. In estimating the vote value of both incumbency and uncontested seats, the same procedure was used. The number of votes cast in an average contested district won by a party (column 2) was multiplied by the percentage of votes that an advantage (either incumbency or an uncontested seat) was worth. The value of incumbency per district was obtained from Levitt and Wolfram (1994) and the value of an uncontested seat was set at 23 percent, based on Jacobson's analysis (1993) and an assumption that the number of votes that the candidate of

225

the advantaged party receives because of a lack of options approximately offsets the number of voters who "stayed home" because the candidate was not challenged. This product is the average number of votes attributable to the advantage in a district. This was then multiplied by the number of districts in which the party had the particular advantage to yield the total number of votes that were attributable to incumbency or uncontested seats in a particular year (columns 5 and 7).

Tables A.3 and A.4 use the above estimates of votes due to incumbency and uncontested seats to adjust the actual vote. Table A.3 makes the adjustments in the Democratic national vote, and table A.4 does the same for Republicans. In each case, the starting point is the actual total national votes cast for each party. These numbers were obtained from various volumes of the *U.S. Statistical Abstracts* and CQ's *Guide to U.S. Elections,* second edition. Tabulation of votes from the *Statistical Abstract* required some adjustments to take into account votes for cross-endorsed major party candidates, votes cast in multimember districts in several early years in the series, and several other problems noted in note 24 in chapter 3. Votes attributable to incumbency are subtracted from the party having the advantage and added to the opposing party's totals. For instance, in the case of the Democrats (table A.3), the additional votes attracted to the Democratic total because of Democratic incumbents are subtracted from the Democratic total and the additional votes in the Republican column because of Republican incumbents are added to the Democratic total. The votes that a party failed to receive because it failed to put forward a candidate to accept those votes are then added to that party's totals. Since the votes that a party would receive from contesting a formerly uncontested seat are supposed to come entirely from an increase in formerly depressed district turnout, rather than at the expense of the party holding the uncontested seat, these votes are added to the party that had left the seat uncontested but are not subtracted from the party with the advantage.[1] The candidate-adjusted vote totals for the parties are in the far-right columns of tables A.3 and A.4.

Table A.5 completes the calculations. The adjusted vote totals (the expected vote for a party after removing incumbency or uncontested seat effects) are taken from tables A.3 and A.4 and presented in the second and third columns of table A.5. The Democratic percentage of these adjusted votes is then calculated (column 4) and compared to the actual Democratic vote percentage (in column 5). The difference is then computed (column 6). This is the basis for table 3.5.

Table A.1

Votes Attributable to Democratic Incumbency and Uncontested Seat Advantages, 1954–1992

Year	Mean Total Vote in Democratic Districts	Percentage Value of Incumbency	Running Democratic Incumbents	Votes Due to Incumbency	Uncontested Democratic Seats	Votes Republicans Would Have Received if Seats Were Contested
1954	104,202	3.4	119	421,601	84	2,013,183
1956	135,028	3.4	153	702,416	69	2,142,894
1958	118,494	3.4	127	511,657	96	2,616,348
1960	149,653	4.0	194	1,161,307	76	2,615,934
1962	121,146	4.0	180	872,251	50	1,393,179
1964	154,469	4.0	191	1,180,143	41	1,456,643
1966	123,445	4.0	224	1,106,067	53	1,504,795
1968	151,023	4.0	192	1,159,857	41	1,424,147
1970	125,260	6.8	166	1,413,935	58	1,670,968
1972	165,538	6.8	179	2,014,929	46	1,751,392
1974	125,235	6.8	161	1,371,073	58	1,670,635
1976	171,894	6.8	210	2,454,646	46	1,818,639
1978	128,752	6.8	205	1,794,803	51	1,510,261
1980	176,936	8.0	212	3,000,835	41	1,668,506
1982	150,775	8.0	170	2,050,540	47	1,629,878
1984	198,266	8.0	201	3,188,117	54	2,462,464
1986	142,685	8.0	178	2,031,834	56	1,837,783
1988	194,655	8.0	185	2,880,894	61	2,731,010
1990	145,615	8.0	199	2,318,191	48	1,607,590
1992	218,743	8.0	196	3,429,890	18	905,596

Note: The value of incumbency is from Levitt and Wolfram (1996). The number of votes due to incumbency is the product of the columns 2, 3, and 4, the mean number of votes in Democratic districts multiplied by the value of incumbency (.034, .04, etc.) (to yield the number of incumbency related votes per district) multiplied by the number of running Democratic incumbents. The number of votes Republicans would have expected to receive had they contested the uncontested seats is the product of the mean number of votes in Democratic districts multiplied by the value of uncontested seats (.23) and the number of uncontested Democratic seats.

227

Table A.2

Votes Attributable to Republican Incumbency and Uncontested Seat Advantages, 1954–1992

Year	Mean Total Vote in Republican Districts	Percentage Value of Incumbency	Running Republican Incumbents	Votes Due to Incumbency	Uncontested Republican Seats	Votes Democrats Would Have Received if Seats Were Contested
1954	120,885	3.4	202	830,238	2	55,607
1956	165,462	3.4	183	1,029,505	3	114,169
1958	134,290	3.4	167	762,499	1	30,887
1960	183,327	4.0	130	953,300	3	126,496
1962	144,173	4.0	150	865,038	1	33,160
1964	175,778	4.0	159	1,117,948	1	40,429
1966	139,339	4.0	126	702,269	4	128,192
1968	170,570	4.0	167	1,139,408	7	274,618
1970	145,842	6.8	165	1,636,347	5	167,718
1972	182,669	6.8	146	1,813,538	8	336,111
1974	138,162	6.8	162	1,521,993	2	63,555
1976	190,875	6.8	122	1,583,499	6	263,408
1978	148,042	6.8	109	1,097,287	19	646,944
1980	204,441	8.0	128	2,093,476	15	705,322
1982	161,517	8.0	158	2,041,575	11	408,639
1984	213,574	8.0	140	2,392,029	14	687,708
1986	154,134	8.0	142	1,750,962	18	638,115
1988	217,706	8.0	144	2,507,973	20	1,001,448
1990	168,151	8.0	122	1,641,154	36	1,392,290
1992	238,081	8.0	125	2,380,810	13	711,862

Note: See the note to table A.1 for the calculation of the number of votes due to incumbency and the number of Democratic votes that would have been expected if challenges were mounted for uncontested Republican seats.

Table A.3

Expected Democratic Vote without Incumbency Advantage and Uncontested Seats, 1954–1992

Year	Actual Democratic Vote	Votes Due to Incumbency		Votes That Democrats Would Have Received if They Had Run in Uncontested Republican Districts	Expected Democratic Vote without Incumbency Advantages and with All Districts Contested
		Democratic	Republican		
1954	22,355,921	421,601	830,238	55,607	22,820,165
1956	29,996,724	702,416	1,029,505	114,169	30,437,982
1958	26,100,713	511,657	762,499	30,887	26,382,441
1960	35,322,673	1,161,307	953,300	126,496	35,241,162
1962	27,010,143	872,251	865,038	33,160	27,036,090
1964	38,218,751	1,180,143	1,117,948	40,429	38,196,985
1966	27,017,727	1,106,067	702,269	128,192	26,742,120
1968	33,304,867	1,159,857	1,139,408	274,618	33,559,036
1970	29,524,283	1,413,935	1,636,347	167,718	29,914,414
1972	37,772,308	2,014,929	1,813,538	336,111	37,907,028
1974	30,898,055	1,371,073	1,521,993	63,555	31,112,529
1976	42,389,976	2,454,646	1,583,499	263,408	41,782,236
1978	30,537,710	1,794,803	1,097,287	646,944	30,487,138
1980	40,768,550	3,000,835	2,093,476	705,321	40,566,513
1982	36,110,782	2,050,540	2,041,575	408,638	36,510,455
1984	44,435,193	3,188,117	2,392,029	687,708	44,326,813
1986	33,025,287	2,031,834	1,750,962	638,115	33,382,530
1988	44,892,268	2,880,894	2,507,973	1,001,448	45,520,795
1990	32,837,751	2,318,191	1,641,154	1,392,290	33,553,004
1992	48,685,900	3,429,890	2,380,810	711,862	48,348,682

Note: The total national vote was calculated from various volumes of the *Statistical Abstract of the United States* and from Congressional Quarterly's *Guide to U.S. Elections*, 2d ed. The incumbency and uncontested-seat estimated figures are from tables A.1 and A.2. The expected vote is calculated by subtracting the Democratic votes due to incumbency from the total Democratic vote and adding to that vote the votes due to Republican incumbents and Republican uncontested seats. For example in 1954: 22,355,921 − 421,601 + 830,238 + 55,607 = 22,820,165. Numbers have been rounded to the nearest whole integer.

Table A.4

Expected Republican Vote without Incumbency Advantage and Uncontested Seats, 1954–1992

Year	Actual Republican Vote	Votes Due to Incumbency		Votes That Republicans Would Have Received if They Had Run in Uncontested Democratic Districts	Expected Republican Vote without Incumbency Advantages and with All Districts Contested
		Democratic	Republican		
1954	20,006,706	421,601	830,238	2,013,183	21,611,252
1956	28,552,310	702,416	1,029,505	2,142,894	30,368,115
1958	19,898,734	511,657	762,499	2,616,348	22,264,240
1960	28,754,240	1,161,307	953,300	2,615,934	31,578,181
1962	24,093,008	872,251	865,038	1,393,179	25,493,400
1964	27,930,000	1,180,143	1,117,948	1,456,643	29,448,838
1966	25,517,488	1,106,067	702,269	1,504,795	27,426,081
1968	32,041,139	1,159,857	1,139,408	1,424,147	33,485,735
1970	24,415,000	1,413,935	1,636,347	1,670,968	25,863,556
1972	33,276,320	2,014,929	1,813,538	1,751,392	35,229,103
1974	21,272,000	1,371,073	1,521,993	1,670,635	22,791,715
1976	31,403,615	2,454,646	1,583,499	1,818,639	34,093,401
1978	25,184,360	1,794,803	1,097,287	1,510,261	27,392,137
1980	38,407,925	3,000,835	2,093,476	1,668,506	40,983,790
1982	27,908,458	2,050,540	2,041,575	1,629,878	29,547,301
1984	40,137,812	3,188,117	2,392,029	2,462,464	43,396,364
1986	27,065,058	2,031,834	1,750,962	1,837,783	29,183,713
1988	37,914,616	2,880,894	2,507,973	2,731,010	41,018,547
1990	28,718,172	2,318,191	1,641,154	1,607,590	31,002,799
1992	43,008,500	3,429,890	2,380,810	905,596	44,963,176

Note: See table A.3 for sources and steps in calculations.

Table A.5

Democratic Congressional Vote Adjusted for Incumbency and Uncontested Seat Advantages, 1954–1992

Year	Expected Partisan Votes without Incumbency or Uncontested Seat Advantages			Actual Democratic Percentage of Two-Party Vote	Expected versus Actual Vote Difference
	Democrats	Republicans	Democratic Percentage of Two-Party Vote		
1954	22,820,165	21,611,252	51.36	52.77	-1.41
1956	30,437,982	30,368,115	50.06	51.23	-1.18
1958	26,382,441	22,264,240	54.23	56.74	-2.51
1960	35,241,162	31,578,181	52.74	55.13	-2.38
1962	27,036,090	25,493,400	51.47	52.85	-1.39
1964	38,196,985	29,448,838	56.47	57.78	-1.31
1966	26,742,120	27,426,081	49.37	51.43	-2.06
1968	33,559,036	33,485,735	50.05	50.97	-.91
1970	29,914,414	25,863,556	53.63	54.74	-1.10
1972	37,907,028	35,229,103	51.83	53.16	-1.33
1974	31,112,529	22,791,715	57.72	59.23	-1.51
1976	41,782,236	34,093,401	55.07	57.44	-2.38
1978	30,487,138	27,392,137	52.67	54.80	-2.13
1980	40,566,513	40,983,790	49.74	51.49	-1.75
1982	36,510,455	29,547,301	55.27	56.41	-1.14
1984	44,326,813	43,396,364	50.53	52.54	-2.01
1986	33,382,530	29,183,713	53.36	54.96	-1.60
1988	45,520,795	41,018,547	52.60	54.21	-1.61
1990	33,553,004	31,002,799	51.98	53.35	-1.37
1992	48,348,682	44,963,176	51.81	53.10	-1.28

Note: The expected votes without candidate advantages were calculated in tables A.3 and A.4. The actual vote percentages were computed from the actual votes in tables A.3 and A.4.

231

Appendix
B

The Unwasted-Vote Measure, Wasted Votes, and Alternative Estimates of Bias

The single-member-district, plurality-rule electoral system is a responsive system. That is, in converting votes into seats it magnifies the impact of the plurality vote. The party with the most votes receives an even larger share of seats. This occurs because the party with the minority vote wastes a larger portion of its votes on losing candidates. As discussed in chapter 4 (see table 4.10), the majority party can avoid wasting votes in some districts where it is less popular than average, while the minority party wastes votes even in some districts where it exceeds its national vote. However, an electoral system can also be structured (biased) so that a party wastes more of its votes than its opponent even if the party wins the majority of votes. It is possible that bias is based on wasted, as well as unwasted, votes.

In this appendix we (1) formally deduce the basis for the unwasted-vote measure of bias, (2) determine whether a minority-vote party, as assumed, wastes a larger portion of its vote than the majority-vote party, (3) determine whether any bias could be traced to differences in wasted votes, rather than the unwasted votes examined in the main analysis, (4) offer two alternative estimates of bias based on a modified uniform district vote-swing analysis and a fixed-swing-ratio analysis, and (5) compare these alternative estimates to the unwasted-vote estimate of bias.

The Formal Basis of the Unwasted-Vote Measure of Bias

The basis of the unwasted-vote measure of electoral system bias and its assumption of an even division of unwasted votes at an even division of the national vote can be demonstrated formally. As already defined, bias is present if

$$S_{wd} \neq S_{wr} \text{ when } V_{td} = V_{tr}, \tag{1}$$

where S stands for the proportion of seats and V for the proportion of votes. The subscript w indicates seats won by d, Democrats, or r, Republicans. The subscript t indicates the total for all districts.

A party's total vote is the sum of votes cast in the districts it won and the districts it lost:

$$V_{tp} = V_{wp} + V_{lp}, \tag{2}$$

where V is votes, t is the total for all districts, p designates the party, w is districts won by the party, and l is districts lost by the particular party.

How are these votes converted into seats? By definition, only the votes cast in districts won by the party are directly converted into seats. They are the party's unwasted votes.[1] Votes cast in districts lost by the party, the party's wasted votes, indirectly affect seat winnings, since a party wasting a smaller portion of its votes has more unwasted votes achieving representation. We turn first to unwasted votes (V_{wp}) and then to the issue of wasted votes (V_{lp}).

The number of seats that a party wins depends on two factors: the price it pays in votes for a seat and the number of votes it pays for these seats. Like any commodity, a party will win more seats if it pays a low price and spends a great deal. The price paid for a seat, the number of votes expended to obtain a seat, in turn, depends on the district vote percentage of the winning party and the total district turnout. A party barely winning a seat expends its votes efficiently. A party winning low-turnout districts also gets a bargain. The relationship of the three factors translating a party's vote into seats is stated formally in equation 3:

$$S_{wp} = (1/(\Sigma(P_{wp} \times T_{wp})/S_{wp})) \times V_{wp}, \tag{3}$$

where S_{wp} is the number of seats won by party p, P_{wp} is the percentage of the district vote received by the party in each district that it won, T_{wp} is the total district turnout in each district it won, and V_{wp} (as above) is the total vote for the party in districts that it won (its unwasted votes). The mean of the product of a party's vote percentage in districts that it won and turnout in those districts is the mean number of votes per victory (the mean number of unwasted votes). Thus, the first right-hand-side term indicates that a party won one seat for every ($\Sigma(P_{wp} \times T_{wp})/S_{wp}$) un-wasted votes.[2] The same votes-to-seats formula could be applied to votes cast for a party in districts that it lost, except the numerator of the first term would be zero instead of one, since the party received no seats for its votes in these districts, and the seats variable would, thus, also equal zero.[3]

This formalization allows us to locate the reason that the electoral system works to one party's advantage over its opponents. With both parties having an equal number of votes, bias would be indicated by one party winning a greater than equal number of seats ($S_{wd} \neq S_{wr}$). According to equation 3, bias (a larger S_{wp}) is the result of some mix of the following three factors: (1) a party having more unwasted votes than its opposition (higher values of V_{wp}), (2) a party winning districts by smaller vote percentages (lower values of P_{wp}), or (3) a party winning lower-turnout districts (lower values of T_{wp}).

If the parties have an equal number of votes ($V_{td} = V_{tr}$) and waste a common proportion ($(V_{ld}/V_{td}) = (V_{lr}/V_{tr})$), then they have an equal number of votes to expend in districts that they win ($V_{wd} = V_{wr}$).[4] If this is so, based on equation 3, the only way that the parties can win an unequal proportion of seats at this equal proportion of votes is for the price of a seat to be different for the two parties ($[1/(P_{wd} \times T_{wd})] \neq [1/(P_{wr} \times T_{wr})]$). This is the foundation of the unwasted vote measure.

Wasted Votes

Tables B.1 and B.2 provide information regarding the total vote and wasted votes for the parties in contested seats from 1954 to 1992. We should expect that the party winning the larger share of the popular vote would waste a smaller portion of that vote in losing causes. Generally this means that the Democrats should have wasted a smaller portion of their vote, but we should also note that in 6 of the 20 election years Republicans won a majority of the vote in contested districts. In these six elections, we should expect Republicans to have wasted a smaller portion of their vote.

Table B.2 presents the percentage of their votes that each party wasted. The parties wasted anywhere from a quarter to one half of their votes. The majority party typically wasted a third of its votes, while about 41 percent of the minority party's votes were cast for losing candidates. In most elections, the expected difference between the wasted votes for the majority and minority parties leading to system responsiveness were found. The majority party wasted a smaller portion of its votes in 15 of the 20 elections. The exceptions were in 1960, 1962, 1970, 1972, and

Table B.1
Votes in Contested Districts by Political Party, 1954–1992

Year	Votes in Contested Districts			Democratic Percentage	
	Democratic	Republican	Total	Votes	Seats
1954	19,581,300	19,642,800	39,221,400	49.92	42.77
1956	25,985,900	27,907,100	53,893,000	48.22	45.22
1958	22,316,200	19,597,500	41,913,700	53.24	54.79
1960	29,906,300	28,140,400	58,046,700	51.52	51.85
1962	24,386,500	23,813,300	48,199,800	50.59	52.46
1964	34,727,800	27,674,900	52,402,700	55.65	63.99
1966	23,759,800	24,970,500	48,730,400	48.76	51.07
1968	29,937,800	31,043,900	60,981,600	49.09	51.95
1970	25,649,200	23,977,800	49,627,000	51.68	52.96
1972	33,073,600	32,250,700	65,324,300	50.63	51.58
1974	26,672,400	21,128,200	47,800,600	55.80	62.03
1976	36,975,600	30,519,600	67,495,200	54.78	64.23
1978	26,083,400	23,132,500	49,215,900	53.00	61.92
1980	35,024,600	35,534,400	70,559,000	49.64	53.32
1982	31,033,400	26,758,700	57,792,100	53.70	59.04
1984	37,008,900	37,510,600	74,519,600	49.66	53.95
1986	27,899,700	25,014,500	52,914,200	52.73	55.83
1988	36,860,500	34,858,800	71,719,400	51.40	56.21
1990	28,410,800	24,690,600	53,101,400	53.50	62.46
1992	47,093,800	41,662,900	88,756,700	53.06	60.00

Note: Votes are rounded to the nearest hundred.

1984. In these five elections, contrary to expectations, the minority party wasted a smaller share of its votes. In two of the five cases (1970 and 1972), the differences were quite small (2.4 percentage points) and the vote majorities themselves were small (50.6 percent and 51.7 percent of the vote). Of the remaining three aberrant cases (also involving narrow vote majorities), two involved Democratic majorities, and one involved a Republican vote majority (1984). The minority party in these cases wasted more than four percentage points less of their votes than did the majority party. Despite these exceptions, in most elections, the majority party, as expected, wasted fewer of its votes in losing causes, thereby producing responsiveness in the electoral system.

The assumption that the wasted portion of a party's vote increases when the party fares poorly at the polls is tested more rigorously in the

Table B.2
Wasted Votes by Political Party, 1954–1992

Year	Wasted Votes in Contested Seats				Party Winning a Majority of the Vote in Contested Seats	Difference in Percentages	Did the Majority Party Waste a Smaller Percentage of Its Votes?
	Wasted Votes		Percentage of the Party's Votes That Were Wasted				
	Democrats	Republicans	Democrats	Republicans			
1954	9,939,700	5,699,000	50.8	29.0	Republicans	21.8	Yes
1956	12,771,200	8,450,000	49.2	30.3	Republicans	18.9	Yes
1958	8,667,300	7,977,500	38.8	40.7	Democrats	1.9	Yes
1960	12,883,900	10,136,800	43.1	36.0	Democrats	−7.1	No
1962	9,963,400	8,742,100	40.9	36.7	Democrats	−4.2	No
1964	10,338,000	13,623,000	29.8	49.2	Democrats	19.5	Yes
1966	9,206,200	8,827,000	38.8	35.4	Republicans	3.4	Yes
1968	11,256,100	10,997,700	37.6	35.4	Republicans	2.2	Yes
1970	9,481,700	8,280,700	37.0	34.5	Democrats	−2.4	No
1972	12,172,200	11,111,500	36.8	34.5	Democrats	−2.4	No
1974	7,855,300	9,694,000	29.5	45.9	Democrats	16.4	Yes
1976	9,579,900	14,186,300	25.9	46.5	Democrats	20.6	Yes
1978	7,339,700	10,098,400	28.1	43.7	Democrats	15.5	Yes
1980	12,254,600	12,304,000	35.0	34.6	Republicans	.4	Yes
1982	9,349,200	11,426,800	30.1	42.7	Democrats	12.6	Yes
1984	11,932,900	13,803,400	32.2	36.8	Republicans	−4.6	No
1986	8,397,600	9,060,700	30.1	36.2	Democrats	6.1	Yes
1988	10,874,600	12,443,500	29.5	35.7	Democrats	6.2	Yes
1990	8,167,800	11,157,600	28.8	45.2	Democrats	16.4	Yes
1992	14,215,300	18,542,500	30.2	44.5	Democrats	14.3	Yes

Note: Votes are rounded to the nearest hundred. The percentage of a party's vote that was wasted on losing candidates is computed by dividing the number of wasted votes for a party in contested seats by the total number of votes for that party in contested seats (from table B.1).

Table B.3

The Effect of the National Vote on the Percentage of the Vote Wasted
on Losing Candidates in Contested Districts, 1954–1992

Independent Variable	Dependent Variables: Percentage of a Party's Vote That Was Wasted			
	Wasted Democratic Vote		Wasted Republican Vote	
	OLS	GLS	OLS	GLS
Democratic Percentage of	−2.10	−1.34	2.21	1.94
the Two-Party Vote	(.53)	(.19)	(.28)	(.23)
Constant	144.11	102.55	−75.74	−61.18
N	20	19	20	19
R^2	.47	.74	.78	.81
Adjusted R^2	.44	.72	.76	.80
Standard Error	5.25	2.27	2.76	2.40
Durbin-Watson	.50	1.85	1.40	1.83

Note: Standard errors are in parentheses. The pseudo-Generalized Least Squares estimates (GLS) address the autocorrelation problem apparent in the Ordinary Least Squares (OLS) regression results. The data were partial differenced using weights of .6 in the Democratic vote equation and .35 in the Republican vote equation. The constants in the GLS equations were converted to their comparable OLS equivalents ($a = a'/[1 - p]$).

regressions reported in table B.3. The dependent variables are the percentage of each party's votes that were wasted in an election year, indicated in the third and fourth columns of table B.2. The independent variable is the percentage of the two-party vote in contested districts for Democrats, indicated in the third column of table B.1. We expect that Democrats will waste a smaller portion of their vote as they fare better at the polls (a negative coefficient) and that Republicans will waste a greater portion of their vote as Democrats generally receive more votes (a positive coefficient). Because of positive autocorrelation in the initial regression estimates, the regression for each party has also been estimated using partial differences (the GLS estimate). The results are entirely in accord with expectations. The coefficients are in the expected directions, statistically significant ($p < .01$), and of similar magnitudes for both parties. Most importantly, we can use these regressions to estimate the expected proportion of votes that each party would waste if the national vote were equally divided. With 50 percent of the two-party vote, Democrats would expect to waste 35.6 percent of their votes ((50×-1.34) + 102.55). Republicans with half the national vote would expect to waste 35.8 percent of their votes ((50 x 1.94) − 64.18). This is impressively close to the equality assumption of the unwasted vote measure of bias and permits us to expect that the parties would have an equal number of wasted votes if they evenly divided the national vote.

Although the assumptions regarding wasted votes being associated with vote percentage of a party and electoral system responsiveness seems generally supported by this analysis (leaving electoral system bias to be a matter of unwasted votes), the several exceptions to the expectation that the plurality party wastes a smaller portion of its votes (table B.2) and the autocorrelation in vote-wasted vote regressions (table B.3) suggest that wasted votes may on occasion affect bias. The 1954 election is a good example. In 1954, though on the short end counting all districts, Republicans narrowly won a majority of the vote in contested districts. As expected, they wasted a smaller share of their votes than did Democrats. However, as table B.2 indicates, the difference in proportion of wasted votes between the two parties was much greater than one would expect because of the narrow Republican plurality. Although the parties received nearly an equal share of the vote in contested districts, Democrats wasted more than half of their votes in lost districts, while Republicans wasted less than a third of their votes.

Alternative Bias Estimates

Table B.4 presents two alternatives to the unwasted-vote measure of bias. The first is a modified version of the hypothetical uniform-district-vote-swing measure. The hypothetical uniform-vote-swing method was discussed in chapter 4. The uniform-vote-swing method simulates vote and seat distributions by assuming uniform incremental vote percentage changes across all districts. There are two principal problems with this technique as conventionally used: the assumption of uniform change for all districts is unrealistic, and the technique estimates bias when the mean district vote (rather than the national vote percentage) reaches 50 percent. The modification to the technique used here (and also in chapter 8 for the 1994 election) addresses the second problem. District vote percentages for the two parties are adjusted uniformly across all contested districts. These adjusted vote percentages are then converted into new district vote totals for the two parties (assuming no change in total turnout) and aggregated nationally. Vote percentages are adjusted incrementally until the aggregate national vote from the simulation is evenly divided. The would-be winners, given the nationally divided vote,

Table B.4

Three Estimates of Partisan Bias in Contested Seats, 1954–1992

Year	Uniform-District-Vote-Swing Measure of Bias		Fixed Swing-Ratio Bias Estimate	Unwasted Vote Measure of Bias
	Adjustment to the Democratic Vote	Uniform-Swing Bias Estimate		
1954	+.0784	+7.2 Republican	+7.1 Republican	+2.3 Democratic
1956	+1.7823	+.8 Republican	+1.2 Republican	+5.9 Democratic
1958	−3.2949	+5.4 Republican	+1.7 Republican	+.6 Democratic
1960	−1.5282	+2.1 Republican	+1.2 Republican	+3.3 Democratic
1962	−.5797	+1.1 Democratic	+1.3 Democratic	+3.6 Democratic
1964	−5.8149	+2.8 Republican	+2.7 Democratic	+.4 Democratic
1966	+1.2609	+3.2 Democratic	+3.6 Democratic	+3.9 Democratic
1968	+.9315	+2.7 Democratic	+3.8 Democratic	+3.7 Democratic
1970	−1.6804	+.8 Democratic	+.4 Republican	+2.2 Democratic
1972	−.6115	+1.1 Democratic	+.3 Democratic	+1.9 Democratic
1974	−5.7905	+.8 Republican	+.4 Democratic	+.1 Republican
1976	−4.7864	+3.3 Democratic	+4.7 Democratic	+1.3 Democratic
1978	−2.8972	+5.3 Democratic	+5.9 Democratic	+2.5 Democratic
1980	+.3530	+4.1 Democratic	+4.0 Democratic	+3.8 Democratic
1982	−3.7254	+2.1 Democratic	+1.6 Democratic	+.4 Democratic
1984	+.3279	+5.0 Democratic	+4.6 Democratic	+2.5 Democratic
1986	−2.7263	+3.3 Democratic	+.4 Democratic	+.7 Democratic
1988	−1.3955	+4.4 Democratic	+3.4 Democratic	+2.1 Democratic
1990	−3.5029	+7.3 Democratic	+5.5 Democratic	+2.0 Democratic
1992	−2.9395	+3.2 Democratic	+3.9 Democratic	+1.1 Democratic

Note: The adjustment to the Democratic vote is the percentage point swing in the district votes necessary to achieve convergence of the national party votes. The numbers for the three bias estimates indicate bias in percent of seats.

are then determined. Any deviation from an even division of seats indicates bias.

The second alternative measure of bias is based on an assumption of a fixed swing ratio equal to two. A swing ratio of two comports with Jacobson's pre-1966 estimate (1990) and the estimate in equation 3 of table 6.4. With this assumption, an expected seat division for an unbiased system can be computed and compared to the actual seat division. With a known vote share, an assumed swing ratio, and a known seat share, we can deduce the extent of bias. For instance, consider a party winning 56 percent of the seats with 51 percent of the vote (approximately the numbers for 1968). An unbiased system with a swing ratio of two would have awarded the party 52 percent of the seats ($2 = (52 - 50)/(51-50)$). The difference of 4 percent of the seats must result from bias, since the vote-to-seat conversion only involves the two processes, and we have already accounted for the magnifying effects of the swing ratio.

The amount of adjustment or uniform-district-vote swing necessary to converge on an even vote division and the estimates of bias (in contested seats) are presented in table B.4, along with the unwasted vote measure of bias (from table 5.9). The table indicates that, for instance, in the 1992 election, if each contested district cast 2.935 percentage points less for the Democratic congressional candidate and 2.935 percentage points more for the Republican congressional candidate, the national vote would have been evenly divided. At this even vote division, Democrats would have won 53.2 percent of the contested seats (215 of the 404 contested that year), or 3.2 percent more than they would have won in an unbiased system. The fixed-swing-ratio estimate for 1992 starts with the assumption that a party receiving 53.06 percent of the vote, as the Democrats did, should receive 56.12 percent of the seats in an unbiased system (assuming a swing ratio of two). Since the Democrats actually won 60 percent of the seats, the difference indicates a pro-Democratic bias of 3.88 percent of contested seats.

Comparison of the two alternative measures of bias in table B.4 to the unwasted vote measure finds that both the modified uniform-vote-swing measure of bias and the fixed-swing-ratio measure less consistently indicate a pro-Democratic electoral system bias than the unwasted-vote measure. The major differences are in the 1950s. Contrary to the unwasted-vote measure, the swing measure of bias and the fixed-swing-ratio measure indicate that the system favored Republicans from 1954 to 1960. From 1962 to 1992, however, the three measures are in fundamental agreement in finding the electoral system to be biased in favor of the Democrats. In the 16 elections from 1962 to 1992, the three measures of bias are consistent in finding pro-Democratic bias in 13 elections. In two of the remaining three elections (1964 and 1970), one of the alternative measures agreed with the unwasted-vote measure that the system favored the Democrats. The remaining post-1960 election was 1974, in which all three measures indicate a nearly neutral system.

Over the last several decades, the greatest difference between the three measures is that the uniform-vote-swing measure and the fixed-swing-ratio measure have consistently indicated a stronger pro-Democratic slant to the electoral system than the unwasted vote measure. In elections since 1976, the alternative measures typically indicated a pro-Democratic bias of more than two percentage points greater than the unwasted-vote measure. In short, while the modified uniform-vote-swing analysis and the fixed-swing-ratio analysis of bias raise questions about the presence of a pro-Democratic tilt to the electoral system in the first few elections of the Democratic majority, they reinforce the finding that electoral system bias helped to preserve the Democratic House majority through its last three decades. In essence, only 2 of the 32 alternative estimates of bias from 1962 to 1992 (two measures for each of 16 elections) differ materially from the unwasted-vote measure. In a comparison of the unwasted-vote measure to the two alternatives, we see that the unwasted-vote measure tended to indicate a slightly stronger pro-Democratic tilt over the whole series, but that each of the other measures indicated a greater Democratic bias in the 16 elections since 1960. However, in all cases the mean differences were less than a single percentage point. In contrast, each of the three measures in table B.4 found a much more Democratically tilted system than did King and Gelman (1991). For the 16 elections from 1954 to 1984, the King and Gelman estimates of bias differed from the uniform-swing measure by a mean of 1.9 percentage points, from the fixed-swing-ratio measure by 2.6 percentage points, and from the unwasted-vote measure by 3.7 percentage points. Differences with the King and Gelman "incumbency controlled" estimates were, of course, even greater.

Appendix
C

□□

The Carryover Effect of Partisan
Bias through Incumbency

As discussed in chapter 5, the effects of the electoral system's bias may not be confined to a single election. Bias in one election may have repercussions for the results of later elections. The effects of bias in an earlier election are carried forward into later elections via incumbency. Since bias in the system, by definition, causes one party to win seats that it would otherwise not have won, that party has more incumbents who can run for reelection in later years and since incumbency is worth votes, bias in the previous election inflates a party's votes in subsequent elections. In this appendix, this carryover effect of incumbency is examined.

Several calculations and assumptions are necessary to estimate the additional votes and seats affected by partisan bias in a previous election. Take 1970 as an example. In the prior election of 1968, 14 Democrats were elected as a consequence of partisan bias in that election. That cast 14 additional Democrats as incumbents going into the 1970 election who held that status by virtue of previous partisan bias. Because some incumbents retire, run for other offices, or are defeated in the primary, not all 14 bonus incumbents can be expected to run in the 1970 general election. The 14 must be discounted by the rate of incumbents not on the next election's general election ballot. In 1970, about 9 percent of incumbents did not make it to the general election.[1] By this rate, about 13 of the 14 bonus incumbents from 1968 should have run in 1970. If incumbency was worth about 7.1 percent of the district vote in the 1970s (Levitt and Wolfram, 1996) and the mean district turnout was about 135,000 votes in 1970, then the vote value of each additional incumbent was just less than 10,000 votes.[2] The vote value of 13 additional incumbents would have shifted about 134,000 votes from the Republican to the Democratic column in the 1970 election. The removal of the bias in 1968 would, thus, have meant 13 fewer Democratic incumbents running in 1970 and 13 more Republican incumbents. With this shift of incumbency would also go the 134,000 votes in 1970 that it attracted. What difference would this make in terms of seats? Not all of these votes would be cast in Republican winning causes or would have been drawn from what had been Democratic victories. We assume that roughly half the votes had been wasted by Democrats and half would be wasted by Republicans.[3] We further assume that the 67,000 new unwasted votes for Republicans would be added to the formerly wasted votes of Republicans, since they come from districts in which Democrats had won. In 1970, these votes are added to the Republican column in districts in which the mean number of Republican wasted votes had been approximately 43,000. Since the mean number of votes for a victory was approximately 86,000 votes and Republicans, on average, started with a base of 43,000 votes, we could expect that the shift of 67,000 unwasted votes from Democrats to Republicans in 1970 would have shifted one or two more seats to the Republicans.[4] This would have raised the estimated partisan bias of 1970 from 8 to 9 or 10 seats (table 5.10).

Although the carryover of bias from one election to the next is not large, it is worth noting. Moreover, partisan bias in earlier elections may also carry over beyond the next election. For example, incumbents elected because of partisan bias in elections prior to 1968 may also have affected the 1970 vote. This is a real possibility because of the high rate of incumbent reelections. If Democrats elected another 14 incumbents because of partisan bias in 1966, some of these incumbents would have survived to run in 1970. Like the bonus incumbents of 1968, the presence of these 1966 bonus incumbents in the 1970 campaign would boost the Democratic vote and this boost would be traceable to partisan bias in the electoral system.

There is a complication to estimating the carryover effects of partisan bias from earlier elections that has not yet been considered. The issue is one of double counting. Does partisan bias in earlier elections affect the same districts or different districts? The matter can be illustrated by the 1970 example. In 1970, Democrats benefited from the candidacies of 13 incumbents who were incumbents because of partisan bias in the 1968 election. In 1970, there were also 11 Democratic incumbents running who had been elected because of the pro-Democratic bias in the 1966 election. To what extent are these incumbents likely to be the same? To the extent that these are different incumbents, incumbency has a greater multiplier effect. If they are completely different, 24 incumbents would have entered the 1970 campaign by virtue of partisan bias in the previous two elections. This would mean that previous partisan bias has a more substantial effect on the current election. On the other hand, if the 1966 bonus incumbents were returned in 1968 because of partisan bias in that election, we would not want to count them as independently contributing more to the inflated Democratic vote in 1970.

How independent are the effects of partisan bias from one election to the next? Since partisan bias is a quality of the entire electoral system and cannot be isolated to specific incumbents, the best evidence of the independence of bias from one election to the next is the correlations between the number of unwasted votes in individual districts across elections. If there are strong negative correlations in the number of unwasted votes in adjacent election years, this suggests minimal overlap of partisan bias effects. A zero correlation suggests that partisan bias in the two years can be treated as independent events.[5] Strong positive correlations would indicate considerable overlap in the location of partisan bias effects from one election to the next. This would mean that the effects of partisan bias from prior elections would be primarily limited to those incumbents owing their election to partisan bias in the most recent elections. The incumbents benefiting from partisan bias in the current election tend to be the same as those benefiting from bias in earlier elections. This would suggest that the residual or multiplier effects of earlier partisan bias are minimal.

To examine the extent to which partisan bias effects overlapped from one election to the next, the correlations of the number of unwasted votes in districts won by Democrats in adjacent election years were examined for four sets of elections: 1954–56, 1964–66, 1974–76, and 1984–86. In all four sets, the number of unwasted votes in a district in one election year were positively correlated with the number of unwasted votes in that district in the next election year. The correlation between the number of unwasted votes in the same district in adjacent elections was .84 in 1954–56, .63 in 1964–66, .65 in 1974–76, and .69 in 1984–86.[6] These correlations suggest that there was considerable overlap in the location of the partisan bias favoring Democrats from one election to the next. In the 1970 example, of the 11 incumbents owing their 1966 election to partisan bias and surviving to run in 1970, probably only 3 were not helped into office because of electoral bias in 1968. Thus, beyond those not already counted based on the 1968 election, 1966 adds only three incumbents who owe their election to bias.[7] This overlap, in turn, suggests that incumbency effects from earlier elections do not transmit much of the partisan bias found in those earlier elections beyond that evidenced in more recent elections. Moreover, for elections further removed from the present election to carry over the earlier election's partisan bias, the incumbents added by the early election must not only survive to the present but must not have been the product of partisan bias in the intervening elections.[8]

Incumbency exerts a sort of multiplier effect for partisan bias in future elections. However, the extent of its effects are constrained by the stability of partisan bias. The bottom line in most elections is that incumbency boosts the number of seats attributable to partisan bias by about two or three seats beyond that estimated at the particular election.

Notes

□□

Chapter 1

1. Khrushchev was Communist party leader in 1954 but was vying with Georgy Malenkov, the Soviet premier, for full political power. Other time markers were that hydrogen-bomb tests had just been made public, Gamel Abdel Nasser was wresting control of political power in Egypt, Juan Peron still ruled in Argentina, Edmund Muskie had just been elected to his first term as governor of Maine, Johnny Carson was host of the CBS game show *Earn Your Vacation*, polio was still a common disease in the United States, and *Sports Illustrated* was in its first year of publication.

2. In 1992, only 3 of the 258 Democrats elected to the House had been members when their party was last in the minority. The three Democrats who had served under a Republican majority were Jamie Whitten (MS, 1941), Jack Brooks (TX, 1953), and William Natcher (KY, 1953). Natcher passed away in early 1994. Sidney Yates (IL) also served prior to 1954 but did not serve continuously throughout this period. None of the 176 Republicans elected in 1992 served when their party was last in the majority. As of the 1992 election, the longest serving Republican was then-minority leader Bob Michel (IL). He began his congressional career in the 1956 election, two years after the Republicans last controlled the House. He retired from the House in 1994.

3. The U.S. Bureau of the Census report of *Voting and Registration in the Election of November 1992* indicates that the median age of voters in that election was 44 years of age, indicating that the median-aged voter in that election had been born in 1948. In 1994, if one assumes the same age distribution of voters (and midterm electorates are usually several years older than presidential electorates on average [Campbell, 1993, 49]), a median-aged voter of 44 years of age would have been born in

1950. In 1954, this median-aged 1994 voter would have been only four years old. In 1992, over 35 percent of those reporting having voted in that election were born after 1954.

4. Because of the diversity of views within the parties, it is possible for a coalition crossing party lines to control the policy-making process. The conservative coalition of predominantly southern conservative Democrats and most Republicans has from time to time emerged as an important factor shaping the congressional policy-making process. However, in most cases, the party rules; and even when a majority coalition forms, the majority party continues to have substantial institutional powers.

5. The origin of the savings-and-loan crisis might be traced to the deregulation of that industry begun in the late 1970s and the raising of the insurance cap to $100,000. This occurred under unified Democratic control of the government. However, the crisis did not materialize immediately but eventually grew to gigantic proportions under divided government in the 1980s.

6. The infrequency of close elections or marginal districts, especially in contests involving incumbents, has been well documented in the congressional elections literature. Moreover, although districts won with a higher vote margin in recent years may be just as marginal as those won previously with smaller margins because of the vote volatility of a less partisan electorate, there has been a decline in recent years in the number of marginal or vulnerable seats. See Mayhew (1974), Jacobson (1990, 1992, and 1993), Bauer and Hibbing (1989), and Garand et al. (1993).

7. Of the 382 incumbents running in the 1994 general election, 347 (90.8 percent) won reelection. All 35 defeated incumbents were Democrats. In regard to term limits, 7 of 8 states considering term-limit initiatives approved them, bringing to 22 the number of states approving some form of term limits on members of the House. The only state defeating a term-limit initiative in 1994 was Utah. However, this was not a real setback to the term-limits movement, since Utah had previously adopted term limits and was voting on a more restrictive measure.

8. The idea of what constitutes good representation continues to be a matter of controversy. Viewpoints of appropriate representational ideals range from the delegate to trustee perspectives. There are many unsettled normative questions regarding how representatives should do their jobs—whether they should do what they think is right or only what their constituents want, whether they should respond to all of their constituents or those who care most about issues, whether they should try to represent the immediate concerns of their constituents or anticipate the constituency's more permanent concerns, whether they should confine

their concerns for the limited geographic constituency or the nation as a whole. The present discussion does not require a position on these questions, rather only an understanding that elections are an inducement to good representation however defined.

9. It is true that surveys indicate that citizens have only a hazy idea of which party is in the congressional majority. From one perspective, this may raise doubts about whether the Democratic dynasty caused voter frustration. From a different perspective, however, citizens may have "tuned out" congressional politics in light of the lack of real competition. Additionally, the argument is not that the perceived permanence of the Democratic majority frustrated everyone, or even most people, only that it frustrated a significant number of citizens (perhaps a large subset of the politically knowledgeable public).

10. The range of realistic combined presidential-congressional choices also appear restricted. Rather than having options spanning the spectrum from unified Democratic government to divided government to unified Republican government, the electorate actually confronts a situation in which the practical choice is between a unified Democratic government and divided government.

11. David Rohde (1991) found that party unity in congressional roll-call voting increased through the 1980s. However, this increase appears to have occurred despite the permanence of the Democratic dynasty. Rohde traces the increase to congressional leadership, reforms that provided resources for leadership, and an increasing homogenization of the Democratic Party. A generation of older southern Democrats once much more conservative than their nonsouthern colleagues were being replaced over the years by southern Democrats who were more ideologically similar to nonsouthern Democrats. Many of the more conservative seats in the South were being won by Republicans. An additional reason for increasing party unity was President Reagan's conservative program. It is quite possible, however, that party unity would have been even greater in the 1980s if the Democratic majority was seriously imperiled.

12. Rep. Jim Leach labeled the Democratic dominance of the House as a problem of "padlock" at a conference entitled "Government in Gridlock: What Happens Now?" cosponsored by the Committee on the Constitutional System and the Brookings Institution at the National Press Club, 24 February 1993. Sundquist (1993) provides a report of this conference.

13. For example, the Democratic dynasty may directly weaken political parties, but it may also indirectly weaken them by increasing the likelihood of divided government, exacerbating institutional conflicts, weakening public support for the political system, and dampening

political competition. Similarly, fixed Democratic control of the House may also directly weaken public support for the system but may also weaken it by reducing political competition, increasing the likelihood of "gridlock," and weakening the political parties. The causal model omits a variety of factors external to the model that might be taken into account. It also omits, for the sake of clarity, several possible interaction effects, including the likely interaction effects of both party competition and party strength with divided government on interbranch conflict. That is, divided government may have weaker effects on interbranch conflict when parties are weaker and also when they are less competitive.

14. While Republicans undoubtedly are also concerned about obtaining a share of federal largesse for their districts, more Democrats may tackle the assignment without compunction, if not with relish, while more Republicans may be less enthusiastic about obtaining local benefits for their districts that they might consider unwise or inappropriate pork-barrel legislation. This ideological difference may also be reflected in the candidates nominated by the parties. Because of their progovernment inclinations, Democrats may have an easier time finding qualified candidates willing to make the sacrifices necessary to run for office.

15. A related explanation is that congressional Democrats have not yet felt the full effects of the partisan realignment that has reshaped presidential politics over the last two decades. Southern congressional Democrats have been able to keep their national party at arm's length and have not been pressed by Republicans, since the Republican organizational and activist base in the South was extremely weak. As a result, southern congressional Democrats, who might have been defeated if there had been an established competitive party system in the region, survived. Some have termed this the development of a two-tier party system, a realigned presidential system and patched-together New Deal system for other offices.

16. A third Democratic candidate advantage is in the quality of their candidates, quality being defined by the objective characteristics that are usually associated with a successful candidacy. For a variety of reasons, compared to their Republican counterparts, Democratic challengers more often have greater prior political experience and are thus more formidable campaigners. Republican incumbents are more likely to face tougher opponents than are Democratic incumbents. While this is a candidate effect, it also may be intrinsic to differences between the parties. Ehrenhalt (1991) argues that the Democratic ideology and progovernment orientation naturally provides the party with a richer pool of candidates. Thus, this particular candidate advantage may provide voters with good partisan reasons to vote for Democrats and thus may be as

much an intentional reason for the Democratic majority as a contextual reason.

17. Votes are termed "unwasted" or "wasted" on the basis of whether they obtain representation in the legislature. Unwasted votes obtain representation in the election of a candidate (and party) for which the vote is cast. Wasted votes, those cast for losing candidates, do not receive this representation. One might claim that unwasted votes in excess of those necessary to win a seat are wasted. However, these voters do obtain representation. The unwasted votes (beyond the minimum necessary to win the seat) may better be thought of as an inefficient expenditure of votes rather than a waste of votes.

18. In this part of the analysis, votes will be counted as either wasted or unwasted according to whether they were cast for the candidate winning the seat, unwasted votes being those cast for the winner. Both types of votes enter into the overrepresentation of voters. The responsiveness of the electoral system, as for instance reflected in the "cube law" of single-member-district plurality-vote systems, is a result of a larger share of the minority party's vote being wasted in losing causes. Bias, in contrast, shows up in one party generally using more unwasted votes in each of its victories.

19. The difference in the example of 20,000 votes may not sound like a big difference. In fact, it would make little difference if we were only talking about two districts. However, the mean votes for each party are based on many districts, and therefore the discrepancy can shift a substantial number of seats from one party to the other. If each party in the example held 217 seats in the House, Republican winners would have totalled almost 4.5 million more votes than Democratic winners (23.9 million to 19.5 million).

20. The Fourteenth Amendment, ratified in 1868, among other things amended the original apportionment criteria of Article 1, Section 2. As originally ratified, the Constitution apportioned seats to the states according to "the whole Number of free Persons, including those bound to Service for a Term of Years, and excluding Indians not taxed, three fifths of all other Persons." This was the infamous three-fifths compromise regarding the counting of slaves. The second section of the Fourteenth Amendment indicates that "Representatives shall be apportioned among the several States according to their respective numbers, counting the whole number of persons in each State, excluding Indians not taxed." It is important to note that both the original and the amended apportionment provisions based the allocation of representatives to the states on the number of people in the state, not the number of actual citizens, the number of voting-age citizens, the number of eligible voters, the number

of registered voters, or the number of actual voters. While these distinctions may not have made much difference in the early years of the republic, the population criterion now has important implications. Among other reasons, it is important because of illegal immigration and the extension of the population criteria to the apportionment of districts within states (through one-person, one-vote apportionment standards mandated by judicial rulings). This establishes the seemingly odd arrangement by which many people are counted for the purposes of apportioning districts but who are then not allowed to participate in the selection of the district's representative.

21. Some states maintained at-large elections on a regular basis and some used them on a temporary basis until district boundaries could be redrawn after reapportionments. For instance, as late as 1962, eight states (Alabama, Connecticut, Hawaii, Maryland, Michigan, New Mexico, Ohio, and Texas) having more than a single seat held at-large elections for at least one of their representatives.

Chapter 2

1. A comparison to other national offices is also instructive. Democrats sustained a 26-year majority in the Senate, from the 1954 to the 1980 election. Earlier Senate majorities had been maintained over 18 years (Republicans from 1860 to 1876 and 1894 to 1910). Since 1854, the longest continuous single-party control of the presidency was the Republicans' 24-year rule beginning in Lincoln's 1860 election and ending with Cleveland's election in 1884. Democrats held the presidency for 20 continuous years from 1932 to 1952, with Franklin Roosevelt's four terms followed by Truman's 1948 victory. Even considering aberrant elections in each of these series (breaking up perfect continuity), the recent Democratic dynasty in the House is impressive by comparison. It is all the more impressive in light of the shorter terms for the House, putting consistent party control more often at risk.

2. Keith et al. (1992) and Miller (1991) find that the decline of partisanship has been exaggerated. The analysis by Keith et al. indicates that measurement error contributed to the perception that partisanship declined more than it really did. By counting independents leaning toward a party as independents rather than as partisans, the correct classification according to their analysis, political observers had overestimated the percentage of independents in the electorate.

3. In actuality, only one of these presidential elections, Cleveland's first election in 1876, produced divided results between the president and the House of Representatives. The other case (1884) was a case of a division between the party controlling the presidency and the party

controlling the Senate. While it might be said that the 1916 election yielded divided results, since Democrat Woodrow Wilson won the White House while Republicans outnumbered Democrats in the House, the Democrats with the help of third-party members organized the House.

4. There actually appear to be three eras of divided government. Fiorina (1992b) rightly observes that divided government was not so rare an event in the later half of the nineteenth century, although it usually occurred as a result of presidential party losses in midterm elections and not in presidential election years. Thus, in its first era (before 1900), divided government occurred in midterm elections. In the second era (from 1900 to 1952), divided government was quite uncommon. In the third era (from 1954 to the present), divided government has been common.

5. As an indication of how close the Democrats came to the perfect consistency of dominance of lower chambers in state legislatures, they would have equalled or exceeded the number of lower chambers controlled by Republicans in 1968 if they had won: two more seats in California (out of 80), or three more seats in Nevada (out of 70), or one more seat in Tennessee (out of 99), or three more seats in Wisconsin (out of 100).

6. The presidency has characteristics of both a national office and an office elected by state electoral systems, since nearly all Electoral College votes are determined by winner-take-all systems at the state level. On the other hand, unlike statewide races for governor or senator, presidential campaigns are national in scope, are covered by the media as national events and involve the same set of candidates. If it is classified as a statewide office, given the Electoral College electoral system, the lower success rates of Democratic presidential candidates than those for other "statewide" offices may be attributable to (1) the greater volatility of the higher-profile presidential contest, in which voters might rely less on either incumbency or partisanship, and (2) the more heterogenous nature of the Democratic coalition, which is more difficult to hold together for a single presidential candidate than a number of Senate or gubernatorial candidates tailored to each state's particular mix of the Democratic coalition.

7. This pattern is all the more notable since presidential coattails are stronger for these offices and the coattails of successful presidential candidates have as often as not belonged to a Republican. That is, Republican success in presidential contests should made a Democratic dynasty in the House (and in state legislatures) less likely than in the Senate or governorships. Presidential coattails in House elections are roughly twice as long as those in Senate elections (Campbell, 1993, 185). Some of this difference, however, may be offset by the fact that coattails in the House

are more often wasted because of uncontested seats. This has been particularly true for several recent Republican presidential candidates who had strong drawing power in the southern states, where the Republican Party locally remains weak and has often left Democratic incumbents unchallenged (Campbell, 1993, 194). Nevertheless, one would expect that Republican presidential coattails would have done greater damage to House Democrats than to Senate or gubernatorial Democrats.

8. One possibility is that fewer and smaller districts more accurately reflect the preferences of the national vote and that, as the majority party, this should have been beneficial to Democrats. However, this explanation would not anticipate the large variance in the effective size of districts (the numbers of voters) that we will see shortly. Fiorina (1992, 66–85) also suggests several alternative explanations for why Democrats have a stronger record in legislative elections. He suggests that voters upset with government practices and policies have reason to vote for executives of the opposing party while maintaining the dominant party in their legislative districts. The maintenance of the dominant party in the district reflects the aggregate advantages of party incumbency or majority status (with the powers to reward their incumbents and their districts with pork-barrel projects). He also suggests that some moderate voters who view Republicans as closer to their issue positions and the executive branch as more responsible for determining policy would vote for a Republican executive and Democratic legislative split ticket to get a policy blend closer to their preferred position. However, neither version of the Republican executive and Democratic legislative distinction accounts for the difference between Democratic success in the House versus the Senate. The cheap-seats distinction between large and small electoral districts, on the other hand, is consistent with the different records of Democratic success in House and Senate elections.

9. The statement refers only to the direct effects of turnout. Turnout may, indirectly, affect the electoral fortunes of candidates. The vote divisions in many elections are affected one way or the other by district turnout—whether supporters or opponents are mobilized.

10. Put differently, because of unequal turnout among districts, it is mathematically possible for a party to win a majority of the vote in a majority of a state's congressional districts and still not win a majority of the vote statewide. Note also the different reasonable preferences of House versus statewide candidates in the following situation. A candidate for a district office would rather receive 80 percent of the district vote than 60 percent, regardless of turnout. However, a rational, vote-maximizing statewide candidate would rather get 60 percent of the vote from a district casting 400,000 votes than 80 percent of the vote in a district casting 150,000 votes. The high-turnout district adds 80,000 votes

to the candidate's margin (240,000 for and 160,000 against), while the low-turnout district adds on 60,000 votes to the candidate's margin (120,000 for and 80,000 against).

11. There are two exceptions to the election of House members by the single-member-district, plurality-rule system. First, multimember districts or at-large seats have been used in the past (though infrequently since the 1940s and usually only if redistricting had not been completed in time for the election). New Mexico and North Dakota, for instance, held at-large elections for its seats into the early 1960s. Texas had an at-large seat until the mid-1960s. Second, some states use a majority-rule runoff system rather than a plurality-rule system.

12. The electoral system characteristics of "responsiveness" and "partisan bias" often raise questions of the fairness of representation under an electoral system. Since partisan bias is asymmetric, benefiting one party regardless of circumstances, a biased electoral system is generally regarded as unfair to some voters and parties. The "overrepresentation" of the majority because of system responsiveness is generally not considered unfair representation, since it is an advantage to any party that obtains a majority. Some views of fairness, however, would indict any system that deviates from proportional representation for any reason, including system responsiveness and the wasting of votes by minority parties. While this is an extreme view of electoral system fairness, Lani Guinier (1994) proposes an even more extreme view based on her "principle of taking turns." By this standard, proportional representation of a majority could be considered unfairly prohibiting a minority from exercising its turn at governance. In examining the effect of the electoral system on racial politics in chapter 9, we will return to Guinier's analysis.

13. The association between party coalition characteristics and turnout only makes a difference to the representation of the parties because of the equal population (rather than equal number of voters) basis on which congressional districts are drawn. Congressional districts are initially constructed so that they are as nearly equal in population (rather than actual voters) as state boundaries, census accuracy and the division of a fixed number of seats will allow rather than constructed so that they are as nearly equal in their number of actual voters. If boundaries took different turnout rates into account, potential bias would be attenuated.

14. It is ironic that the equal-population, single-member-district rules grew out of legislative statute and that Supreme Court rulings meant to ensure fairness are required elements in the creation of partisan bias in the electoral system. It is a further irony that this system has not only created inequity in the treatment of parties but also in the treatment of voters. This may be yet another case of the unintended consequences of electoral reforms.

15. While the thesis does not require gerrymandering to produce partisan bias in favor of the Democrats, it does not exclude the possibility either. Pro-Democratic partisan bias, reflected in their winning cheap seats, may be caused by a variety of factors, including the gerrymandering of district boundaries to create safe Democratic districts without expending many Democratic votes.

16. The proposition linking the sociodemographic characteristics to partisan bias in single-member-district systems depends on the size of the district and the extent of turnout. Obviously, in the extreme case, where there is a district for every citizen, there can be no bias (if one assumes that a vote is required to obtain representation from the one-person district). Also, there can be no bias from this arrangement if all eligible voters actually vote. The proposition depends on a quasi-proxy voting arrangement in the district, representation being accorded to citizens (whether voting or not) and representation being decided by a subset of citizens actually voting.

17. This would also apply to the districting schemes that attempt to reflect the turnout-related sociodemographic characteristics more directly, paying less heed to geographic concentrations. As an example, districting systems designed to concentrate racial minorities into common districts, regardless of geographic concentrations, may produce partisan bias if those minorities vote at lower-than-average rates and associate with one party significantly more than the other.

18. The cheap-seats thesis in its most general form may apply to a wide range of electoral systems. It may even apply to multimember district, proportional representation systems, although the links of geographic units to socioeconomic backgrounds, turnout, and partisanship may be substantially weakened by both district magnitude (the number of representatives) and the proportional representation rule. In addition, high levels of turnout in many nations, which suggest reduced variance among their districts in turnout (to obtain a high overall turnout rate, most districts must have high turnout which compresses the distribution), indicates a smaller potential for cheap-seat effects.

19. Bias might still be created by different winning vote margins for the parties. If one party, on average, won with higher district vote percentages than the opposition, it would expend more unwasted votes per victory than the opposition (indicating bias), even though it did not do disproportionately well in low-turnout districts.

Chapter 3

1. Connelly and Pitney's (1994) *Congress' Permanent Minority?* provides an excellent review of what Republicans believed to be the basis

of their inability to end the Democratic dynasty. Republicans named the usual systemic suspects for their minority status—gerrymandering, incumbency advantages, and generally buying votes, albeit indirectly, through big-government pork-barrel programs. Connelly and Pitney (12) cite the 1992 Republican platform that claims the Democratic control of the House is based on a "swindle by law." However, they also observed a good deal of self-criticism among Republicans. Specifically, according to Connelly and Pitney (12–14), Republicans thought that their party had often failed to mount sufficiently aggressive challenges to the Democrats because of the complacency by entrenched Republican incumbents, the nomination of weak and politically unattractive challengers, the failure to articulate clearly and consistently a palatable and coherent national message to the public, and the incompetence of the national party campaign organizations and advisors.

2. In contrast to professional politicians, political scientists have showed only marginal interest in exploring the reasons for the Democratic success in the House. The Democratic dominance in the House has been examined directly by Ornstein (1990) and Connelly and Pitney (1994). It has also been examined indirectly in the course of explaining the increased frequency of divided government by Jacobson (1991) and Brady (1993) and indirectly in addressing charges of congressional stagnation by Mann (1987). However, with these notable exceptions, the subject has not received the scholarly attention that it deserves. David Broder, dean of Washington pundits and columnist for the *Washington Post,* noted in a pre–1994 election column the general inattention to the consequences of the longevity of the Democratic control of the House (1994). Broder quoted former Representative Lynn Martin's (R-IL) comments from 10 years before: "If the presidency had been in control of one party for almost thirty years that fact—and its implications for our political and governmental system—would be the topic of half the newspaper columns and Ph.D. theses in political science. The Democrats have been in control of the House of Representatives that long—and no one seems to notice."

3. This categorization of causes is similar to the categories identified by Jacobson (1990) in his exploration of the causes of divided government.

4. These figures are based on National Election Study (NES) respondents who claim to have voted in the election. The elections are from 1952 to 1990, omitting 1954 because of the lack of a comparable NES study that year. The figures were calculated from data reported in Keith et al. (1992, tables 1.1, 3.4, and 3.5). The summary percentages of partisans count independents leaning toward one party as partisans of that party, as the research by Keith et al. strongly indicates, is the appropriate

assignment. Pure independents typically amounted to about 9 percent (varying from 6 to 12 percent) of self-reported voters. The few apolitical voters in the surveys were excluded in calculating the percentages. The typical number of self-reported voters in partisan categories are the medians of the 19 NES studies.

5. This may be a function of the Democratic Party's majority status (Riker, 1962). Making the same point as Will Rogers, former Democratic congressman Morris Udall decades later said, "When the Democratic Party forms a firing squad we form a circle" (Henning, 1992, 67). Also, recall in figure 1.2 that the nature of the parties' coalitions was specified as having a positive interaction effect on the impact of partisanship on the congressional vote.

6. This is actually a contextual explanation of the Democratic dynasty rather than purely an intentional explanation. The nature of the Democratic and Republican Party coalitions only helps Democrats obtain a majority of congressional votes because of the congressional electoral system. The system of single-member districts and the provision of voting for individual candidates rather than party slates often segregates conflicting portions of the Democratic coalition in different districts. These institutional arrangements allow the separate and contentious elements of the Democratic coalition to win representation without doing so at the expense of other parts of the coalition.

7. It should be emphasized that all of the claims regarding why voters might be more inclined to favor Democrats for Congress than for other offices concern a small minority of voters. Although ticket splitting (House and presidential votes) rose from roughly 15 percent of ballots cast from 1952 to 1968 to about 26 percent after 1972, about three of four voters do not split their tickets for these offices. Additionally, roughly a quarter (between 17 percent and 36 percent, since 1972) of split tickets in recent years have voted for Republican congressional candidates and Democrats at the presidential level. Moreover, of the roughly 20 percent of the electorate that casts Democratic-congressional and Republican-presidential split tickets, many undoubtedly are not casting them as any sort of combination vote. That is, the choice of a Democrat at the congressional level and a Republican at the presidential level may be independent decisions affected by any number of factors, from candidate character to incumbency to visibility to particular issue stands. Thus, it is likely that the votes of 10 percent or less of the electorate are motivated by an attempt to balance partisan influence in government.

8. The notion that a significant number of voters intentionally favors divided representation is generally stated at the district level (a Democratic member of the House and a Republican president). However, it is sometimes raised to the institutional level that voters want divided gov-

ernment. At this level the thesis becomes less plausible, because of evidence of voter ignorance. Bennett and Bennett (1993), in examining NES data from 1960 to 1984, found low levels of public knowledge about which party controls the House of Representatives, despite the fact that there was no change in decades. They examined an index of "Knowledge of Party Control of the House of Representatives," an index based on the number of correct responses to two questions, which party had a majority in the House before and then after the election (individuals could score 0, 1, or 2). Mean scores ranged from about .9 (1980) to about 1.4 (1964). The public was least clear about who held a majority in the House when the government was divided. For instance, the 1980 NES postelection survey indicated that nearly half of the respondents thought that the election had installed a Republican majority in the House, another third indicated that they did not know which party now held the House, and only about one in six respondents correctly identified the Democrats as being in the majority! Correcting for guessing would suggest even greater public ignorance. Moreover, Bennett and Bennett (1992) found that split-ticket voting was least frequent among those who knew which party controlled the House. These findings pose a serious challenge any thesis suggesting that voters intentionally seek divided government.

9. Jacobson (1990, 65) also argues that Republicans have suffered because many of their candidates are inexperienced. The puzzle of weak Republican candidates may, however, be rooted in the party's conservative ideology, which more highly prizes the private sector over public service, as Ehrenhalt suggests (1991). It may also be the case that the same partisan bias in House elections is present in state legislative election. As noted in chapter 2, Democrats have also done especially well in state legislative races, for offices that, like the House, are elected at the district level and therefore allow the cheap-seats phenomena. If so, then the natural pool of potential experienced Republican House candidates, Republican state legislators, may also be sparse for the same structural reasons that work against the election of Republican House candidates.

10. Independents leaning toward a party are counted as partisans. Democratic identification dropped below 50 percent in 1984 (48.5 percent) and 1988 (47.5 percent).

11. Assuming no bias in the system, the swing ratio can be applied by the following equation: $(V - 50) \times R = (S - 50)$, where V is the party's vote percentage, R is the swing ratio, and S is the party's seat percentage. Thus, using a swing ratio of 2 yields an expected seat percentage of $S = [(V - 50) \times 2] + 50$. For example, a vote of 55 percent should yield 60 percent of the seats. Alternatively, with known seat and vote percentages (assuming again no bias) a swing ratio can be computed as $R = (S - 50)/(V - 50)$.

12. The data in table 3.1 indicate that the Democratic majorities in seats in each of these elections would have been sizable even if they fell short of a majority of votes. Assuming that Democrats had won exactly 50 percent of the vote in these elections, they would have maintained a majority of seats in each case (54.4 percent of seats in 1962, 55 percent of seats in 1966, 54.5 percent in 1968, 54.1 percent in 1980, and 54.3 percent in 1984). These figures, of course, assume that Jacobson's swing-ratio estimate is accurate. Other estimates differ relatively little from Jacobson's. Tufte (1978, 546) estimated a swing ratio of 2.2 from 1900 through 1970. Ansolabehere et al. (1992, 31) estimate a swing ratio for all districts of 2.9 from 1946 to 1964 and 1.3 from 1966 to 1990. If the swing ratio is actually greater than 2 before 1964 and 1.5 thereafter, the size of Democratic seat majorities won with less than a majority of votes could be expected to be smaller. However, as the last column in table 3.1 indicates, it is unlikely that the true swing ratio has been large enough that Democrats would have lost their seat majorities in these elections if their vote totals had fallen short of a majority. The "necessary" swing ratio is based on the slope between two points in each year—the observed vote and seat percentages for the Democrats and the 50 percent vote and 50 percent seat point from the assumption of an unbiased electoral system.

13. A third candidate advantage has received a great deal of attention in recent years, the quality or experience of candidates, especially challengers. According to Jacobson (1990, 62–65), Democratic challengers have generally had greater political experience and have been higher-quality candidates than Republican challengers. This candidate advantage is not considered a contextual factor that helped preserve the Democratic dynasty since it may more appropriately be categorized as an intentional reason for voting for Democrats. The fact that Democratic candidates have been more experienced may be an advantage intrinsic to the party or part of being a Democrat. Ehrenhalt (1991) argues that Democrats have had more experienced, stronger candidates because Democrats are progovernment and many want to make politics a career. Republicans, on the other hand, may be innately at a disadvantage since they are often antigovernment and are less enthusiastic about making politics a career. To the extent that the Democrats' candidate quality advantage reflects a systemic advantage rather than something intrinsic to the parties and their philosophies, the analysis will have underestimated contextual effects.

14. This is not to claim that incumbency provides automatic votes. It should be seen as a set of opportunities for candidates, opportunities that are readily exploited by most incumbent candidates.

15. The Democratic incumbency and uncontested-seat advantages

must be considered together to avoid double counting, since incumbents hold the overwhelming number of uncontested seats.

16. It should be noted that incumbency produces votes through a variety of mechanisms, and the effects of some of these mechanisms are in dispute (e.g., the value of casework). Among other things, these mechanisms include the incumbents' campaign-fund-raising and name-recognition and familiarity advantages over challengers. While incumbency itself offers *opportunities* to exploit in order to enjoy these benefits and therefore varies from incumbent to incumbent rather than being a constant or across-the-board sort of vote boost, there is little evidence to suggest that it varies by party. That is, incumbency generally seems to be as beneficial for Republican incumbents as it is for Democratic incumbents. The calculations that follow in the chapter assume this general equivalence.

17. Gilmour and Rothstein (1993) observed that the retirement rate of Republican incumbents has been greater than the retirement rate of Democratic incumbents in every congressional election from 1954 to 1990. While this contributes to the Democratic incumbency advantage and, therefore, the Democratic dominance of the House, this contribution is rather modest. The effect of this consistent difference is limited since the retirement rate differences are themselves often small (e.g., a 0.3 percent difference in 1982, a 0.5 percent difference in 1968, and a 0.6 percent difference in 1980), since typically more than 90 percent of incumbents of both parties seek reelection, and since, as Jacobson (1990, 36) and Fiorina (1992a, 23) observe, the parties typically hold better than 70 percent of the seats left by their retiring incumbents.

18. The principal challenge to this notion is that Democrats do about as well in open seats as in incumbent seats (Gaddie, 1995). Citing the partisan standoff in open seats, Jacobson argues that "it is clear from this evidence that incumbency cannot, by itself, explain why Republicans have not done better in House elections" (1990, 37). Fiorina (1992a, 21–23, 1992c, 395–96) also challenges the incumbency basis for Democratic seat majorities, noting from Jacobson that Democrats have retained 80 percent of their open seats while Republicans have held 72 percent of their seats. This retention rate conflicts with a pure incumbency explanation of Democratic dominance. According to Fiorina, "If the Republicans had achieved parity except for incumbency, they would have narrowed the gap in the House. *That they have not indicates that some other pro-Democratic force(s) is at work*" (1992c, 396). However, the continuity of a party holding seats despite the loss of incumbent candidates is quite understandable in light of both the importance of partisanship and the cheap-seats thesis. Because of partisanship, Democratic districts tend to

remain Democratic, though at lower margins. Similarly, Republican districts stay Republican, though also at lower margins. There tend to be more Democratic than Republican districts partly because Democratic voters are scattered across many cheap seats while Republicans are concentrated in fewer high-turnout districts.

19. As Jacobson noted "since 1954, no election year has produced more than 2 uncontested open seats" (1990, 46).

20. The drop-off in presidential election years between the total presidential vote and the total congressional vote cast in uncontested districts, compared to contested districts, indicates that congressional turnout would increase if the seat were contested. In addition, it is apparent that the unchallenged candidate receives some votes that would have gone to the opposing party had that alternative been available on the ballot.

21. The 23 points represent a 20 percent discount of the 29 percentage point change observed by Jacobson (1993, 50).

22. The uncontested advantage may be best understood with a hypothetical district. We start with a base of 100 votes in a contested district. On the basis of the adjusted estimate of the uncontested advantage, the vote would divide 77 percent to 23 percent. If the district were uncontested, on the basis of the net drop-off of 23 percent, there would be 77 votes (of course, all cast to the dominant party). Perhaps 3 to 5 of these 77 would have voted for the opposition party if that option were available. On the other hand, perhaps 3 to 5 would-be supporters of the dominant party stayed home because there was no challenge. The net expected result of the opposition party mounting a challenge would result in 23 votes out of 100 for the opposition party with the dominant party holding its base of 77 votes (though not necessarily the same 77 votes that it held in the uncontested situation).

23. The decade estimates of the incumbency advantage (in the vote percentage expected due to incumbency) are from Levitt and Wolfram (1996, figure 1). Decade, rather than yearly, estimates are used since the decade estimates are more likely to tap the structural effects of incumbency rather than the cumulative successes or failures of candidates who also happen to be incumbents. The reported standard errors of these estimates range from .2 to .4.

24. The total national vote for each party was estimated from various volumes of the *U.S. Statistical Abstract* and Congressional Quarterly's *Guide to U.S. Elections*. The starting point was the total vote for each party reported in the *Statistical Abstracts*. These were a number of adjustments required to these figures. Included in the adjustments were the exclusion of votes cast in the District of Columbia; a recalculation of votes cast in New York prior to 1960 so that votes cast for a major party candidate

cross-endorsed on a minor party line would be counted for the major party; a recalculation of votes cast in multiseat, at-large elections in New Mexico, North Dakota, and Hawaii in the 1950s and 1960s; and estimates of votes cast in uncontested seats in states that do not report the vote in uncontested elections (Arkansas, Oklahoma, and Florida). The estimates of votes in uncontested seats in these states was made by adjusting the reported presidential vote in these districts by the mean drop-off rate between the presidential and congressional votes in uncontested districts for states that report the vote in uncontested districts. To estimate these votes in midterm elections, reported or estimated votes in adjacent years were used and further adjusted by the rate of the national turnout decline from the on-year to the midterm election.

25. Recall that even with candidate advantages, the Democratic vote fell short of 52 percent in four cases—1956, 1966, 1968, and 1980. Without the candidate advantages, we can add the 1954, 1962, 1972, 1984, 1990, and 1992 elections to those in which Democrats had narrow vote majorities of 52 percent or less of the two-party vote.

Chapter 4

1. The basic questions addressed here are essentially measurement questions rather than explanatory questions. We seek to determine whether and to what extent partisan bias exists. While the alternative measure of partisan bias will, in a sense, also reveal why partisan bias exists (because Democrats are winning cheap or low-turnout seats), it will be explained (or treated as a dependent variable) in chapter 6. Chapter 9 will offer some speculations regarding the effects of partisan bias (partisan bias as an independent variable).

2. Grofman (1983) examined eight different measures of partisan bias. These included two measures that would not distinguish between bias and responsiveness as sources of over- or underrepresentation or the deviation from proportional representation. Several of the other measures attempt to summarize the extent of bias across the entire range of the vote rather than at a single point (i.e., the 50 percent of the vote mark), though they require the hypothetical approach to the estimation of bias. While it is conceptually satisfying to have a measure of bias that summarizes bias across the full vote range (bias when both parties receive 50 percent of the vote, 51 percent of the vote, etc.), there is no reason to believe that the conventional 50 percent of the vote bias estimate would not be highly correlated with the summary measure. Moreover, the conventional measure is more directly interpretable, and, in a two-party system, the majority vote or seat threshold is of particularly great theoretical and practical significance.

3. A nonlinear estimation technique is technically the most appropriate, since both vote and seat proportions are bounded at 0 and 100 and since the relationship between seats and votes in every electoral system is anchored, awarding a party no seats if it gets no votes and all the seats if it receives all the votes. Nonetheless, since the distribution of seats and votes in the congressional electoral system is exclusively in the middle of the range of both seats and votes, estimation by linear regression is quite acceptable from a practical standpoint (see Tufte, 1973).

4. For instance, a Democratic Party vote-seats regression with a slope equal to 2 and a constant of negative 50 would yield an expected Democratic seat percentage of 50 $((2 \times 50) - 50 = 50)$ when the vote percentage is 50. This indicates a neutral electoral system. If the constant had been a negative 45, however, the expected seat percentage would have been 55 $((2 \times 50) - 45 = 55)$, indicating a pro-Democratic bias of 5 percentage points.

5. The violation of the uniform-district vote swing is especially problematic if, as in the example in the text, the true vote swing is associated with the district's vote. In this example, the hypothetical data approach would underestimate electoral system responsiveness.

6. Other equally meritorious studies estimating partisan bias have also reached divergent findings. Among these are Dahl (1956), March (1957), Campagna and Grofman (1990), and Ansolabehere et al. (1992).

7. Prior to Tufte's analysis, Dahl (1956, 148) examined the electoral system using national election results from 1928 to 1954. His analysis indicates a 5 percent pro-Democratic bias. This estimate is calculated from Dahl's seats-votes regression of Democratic seat percentage = (2.5 × Democratic vote percent) − .7. At 50 percent of the vote, this yields Democrats 55 percent of the seats. March (1957, 527) reestimated the 1928-to-1954 series only with contested seats. This yielded a pro-Democratic partisan bias of 2.25 percent. In a later analysis of elections from 1946 to 1976, Patterson (1979, 139–41) found a 1.75 percent pro-Democratic electoral system bias.

8. A further update to include the election triplet of 1990, 1992, and 1994 will be examined in detail in chapter 8. It also finds a pro-Democratic bias, a bias of 4.2 percent of all seats.

9. The very high estimate of Democratic bias in the most recent elections (1984 to 1988) is probably a result of the small variance in this triplet (see Niemi and Fett, 1986). In the three elections there was only a range of seven seats and less than 2.5 percent of the national congressional vote.

10. Ansolabehere et al. (1992, 31) essentially concur with Jacobson's findings in his mean district-vote analysis. Jacobson's estimates are for all

congressional districts, contested and uncontested. They were calculated from equation 3 of table 5. 5. Jacobson also estimated partisan bias with the mean district congressional measure on only contested seats, rather than on all districts. This analysis also indicated a Republican bias in the period from 1946 to 1964, but the bias was much smaller than that estimated over all districts (7.2 percent pro-Republican rather than 14.6 percent pro-Republican). The contested-seat-only analysis also produced a slight difference in more recent elections, though like the analysis of all-districts partisan bias, by these estimates bias was nearly negligible in recent years (.6 percent pro-Democratic rather than .5 percent pro-Republican).

11. Campagna and Grofman (1990, 1253), in their analysis of redistricting in the 1980s, concur that there is no partisan bias in the electoral system (see also, Cain and Butler, 1991, 37).

12. The conclusions King draws from his separate analyses (using different methods and data) initially appear at odds with one another. King and Browning (1987, 1261) conclude that "the average (bias) of the states is not too biased toward one party more than the other." In a cross-national study, King (1990, 172) concludes that the "U.S. system is moderately biased in favor of the Democratic and against the Republican party." King and Gelman (1991, 129) find "an electoral system that has remained severely biased toward the Republican party for all elections in the last four decades." In addition to the choice of a congressional vote measure, King's estimates of partisan bias depends on whether or not controls for incumbency are included. Before controlling for incumbency, King and Gelman find that "overall bias moves from favoring Republicans to favoring Democrats by about 6 percentage points. The current electoral system in the House favors the Democrats overall" (King, 1991). A strong pro-Republican bias is found after controlling for incumbency, This finding has been relied upon by both Jacobson (1990, 93–94) and Fiorina (1992a, 18–21) to dismiss partisan electoral bias as a cause of divided government. The rationale for controlling for incumbency is not so clear. First, incumbency might cause partisan bias since incumbents influence the drawing of district boundaries. As such, it would seem that incumbency might *explain* the extent of bias, since incumbents seek to safeguard their seats, but is irrelevant to estimating the actual extent of bias. Moreover, if one wants to explain partisan bias, all effects should be considered, not just one. By examining the extent of bias after controlling for incumbency, King is estimating bias over and above that associated with incumbency itself rather than the full extent of bias. Second, the relationship between incumbency and partisan bias would seem to be nonrecursive. There is an apparent endogeneity problem. Incumbents

may affect (through redistricting and otherwise) partisan bias, but partisan bias affects incumbency by affecting which party is elected. While incumbents have reason to increase partisan bias in favor of their party, by its very nature partisan bias should also increase the number of incumbents for a party.

13. Gelman and King's more recent analysis, limited to congressional elections in *nonsouthern states* in this century reaches a similar conclusion. According to this analysis, "the evidence demonstrates unambiguous bias in favor of the Republican party from the 1930s until the mid-1960s. After that, the trend toward Democratic bias is consistent and sustained" (1994, 539). Their estimates (in their figure 1) indicate that the electoral system typically favored Republicans by more than 5 percent of seats in the 1950s, was nearly neutral in the 1960s and 1970s, and typically tilted in favor of Democrats by 2 to almost 4 percent of seats in the 1980s and early 1990s.

14. Simon Jackman has generously (in a personal communication) reestimated the national vote and seat relationship, also drawing the data from table 2.8, using logit analysis. His point estimate of bias is a 3.1 percent Democratic advantage. He further examined the confidence interval around this point estimate. Based on uncertainty regarding parameter estimates and the extrapolation required to estimate seat shares at an even division of the vote (since the 50 percent mark is outside the range of votes in this series and well removed from the series mean vote value), the 95 percent confidence bounds are from 48.1 percent of seats to 58.0 percent of seats for the Democrats, a possible bias range of 1.9 percent pro-Republican to 8.0 percent pro-Democratic. The chance of a pro-Democratic bias, given these results, however, is quite remote. Jackman estimates that the probability of a pro-Democratic bias is .89. The consideration of uncertainty in the estimates highlights the importance of the 1994 analysis in chapter 8. Because the vote crossed the 50 percent threshold for the first time since 1954, we can interpolate rather than extrapolate and gain greater certainty in our bias estimates.

15. Other differences in the regressions also deserve note. Estimates of electoral system responsiveness or the swing ratio are greater when the national vote, rather than the mean district vote, is used. Also, the national vote division more successfully accounts for variance in partisan seats than does the mean district vote. We will reexamine the swing ratio (or responsiveness) in chapter 6. In addition, the difference between the two measures is even more pronounced in examining elections from 1938 to 1992. The seats-vote regression using the national vote measure indicated a pro-Democratic bias of 2.6 percent of seats while that using the mean district vote measure indicated a pro-Republican bias of nearly 5 percent, more than a 7.5 percent difference.

16. Jacobson's equations in his table 5.5 support the claim that the decision to use the mean district vote rather than the national vote substantially affects estimates of partisan bias. His equations 1 and 3 in the table are identical in specification and cases and differ only in the measurement of the congressional vote. For both the 1948–64 and the 1966–88 periods, the equation using the national vote variable indicated a stronger pro-Democratic bias than that using the mean district vote. The two equations produced wildly divergent results for the 1946 to 1964 period. The national vote equation indicated a 2.1 percent Democratic bias (1990, 93) while the mean district-vote equation indicated 14.6 percent Republican advantage. From 1966 to 1988 the national vote equation indicated a 3.9 percent Democratic advantage while the mean district-vote equation suggests a 0.5 percent Republican advantage. These estimates are based on all districts, rather than only contested seats.

17. In their analysis of the "electoral abuse" of malapportionment (broadly construed to mean districts with "different numbers of voters" [336] rather than different population sizes), Taylor and Johnson (1979, 342) compared the national vote and the average constituency vote. They used the difference of these votes as a measure of malapportionment. In a case in which the national vote was 50 percent and the average constituency vote was 56 percent, they concluded that the malapportionment of the electoral system *benefited* this party by 6 percent. The true strength of the party was indicated by the national vote. The electoral system designation of constituencies created the average constituency vote, and the difference indicated the effect or bias of the electoral system. They note that the average constituency vote is the vote that "matters" in that it (like the percentage of seats won) reflects the actual outcome of the system, bias and all. Gudgin and Taylor (1979, 56) refer to electoral system bias as "the distribution problem," which occurs when "one party tends to win smaller constituencies than its rival."

18. Erikson (1972) found Republicans to be overrepresented in elections from 1952 to 1970 because of a 5.4 percent partisan bias, although the bias was virtually eliminated by the late 1960s. Erikson's pro-Republican findings are quite likely due to restricting the analysis to nonsouthern and nonborder states. The northern states were more likely to be Republican, especially early in the series, and more likely to bias district lines against Democrats. Unlike the national party division, Democrats achieved a majority of the two-party northern congressional vote in only 4 of the 10 elections Erikson examined.

19. Some may argue that the district vote totals should be examined rather than the national vote, since voters cast their ballots at the district level and the national vote is an artifact of combining votes cast

across districts. There are two problems with this argument. First, district boundaries are in fact artifacts, in that they are chosen and may divide the vote in an extraordinary number of ways. The particular choice of boundaries may be the principal way bias can creep into the electoral system. Second, the question of partisan bias is itself a question of national politics: which party, if either, is advantaged nationally by the method in which votes are translated into seats?

20. There is a conceptual flaw, as well, in the mean district-vote measure. Since our purpose is to examine the impact of the electoral system on the translation of votes into seats, our measures should not themselves be direct functions of the electoral system they are to gauge. The mean district vote is almost entirely an artifact of the electoral system. It reflects how votes have been organized by the electoral system into districts. It is therefore a contaminated measure unsuitable for estimating partisan bias. Put differently, the national vote percentages will be the same for a nation regardless of how districts are drawn. This is not true of the mean district vote. Each redrawing of district lines can produce a different mean district vote—without the voters ever changing a single vote.

21. The difference between the mean district vote and the national vote percentage was also consistent in the nine elections from 1936 to 1952. In each case the mean district vote was substantially more Democratic than the national vote percentage. Differences ranged between 6.2 and 11.6 percentage points.

22. The improper equal weighting of districts has plagued hypothetical analyses, even those that have gone to great lengths to simulate district vote swings (e.g., King and Gelman, 1991). Jackman (1994) offers a solution to this in his fix for formal malapportionment in the Australian electoral system. Jackman weights district vote percentages by the size of the district. The same method could be applied to the House electoral system, weighting by the number of voters in each district rather than the district's population and thus correcting for effective malapportionment rather than just formal malapportionment. However, in chapter 8, we make a further improvement on the hypothetical vote analysis both by interpolating vote swings rather than modeling them and by summing hypothetical district votes to a national vote (which is equivalent to Jackman's conducting an analysis of weighted district votes).

23. The problem with using district percentages is entirely an aggregation problem and not an intrinsic problem with the hypothetical vote (percentage)-swing analysis of the district vote. The problem of the previous hypothetical vote-swing studies is that they estimate bias as the seat share (deviation from 50 percent) when the mean district vote is 50 percent rather than when the national vote total is 50 percent. Jackman

(1994) offers a corrective to this method, and a similar corrective is made in chapter 8's analysis of bias in the 1994 election and in appendix B for elections from 1954 to 1992.

24. We could add to the differences among studies the specification of linear or nonlinear (e.g., logistic) relationship between votes and seats.

25. One reader of this analysis suggested that differential turnout rates related to party should not be considered an aspect of the electoral system—that it might be stretching things to include the political sociology of turnout and partisanship in the mix of factors thought of as an electoral system. However, an important distinction needs to be made between the presence of different turnout rate and partisan voting patterns and how those behaviors are organized to affect election results. Their organization is very much a matter of the electoral system (see Tufte, 1973). No electoral system has any effect whatsoever, apart from how it organizes the behaviors of voters. For instance, given the right distribution of votes, a majority-rule system could produce proportional results. Thus, the particular House electoral system being studied is very much responsible for *the effects* of differential turnout rates. If districts were drawn differently or not drawn at all (at-large elections), as might happen under different electoral systems, different turnout rates would have different consequences for election results.

26. The mean number of unwasted votes is based on the four districts, three of type A, in which the winning party received 80,000 votes, and one of type B, in which the winning party received 240,000 votes (i.e., $[(3 \times 80,000) + 240,000]/4 = 120,000$).

27. For example, if a party wins a 55 percent majority of the vote nationally (a margin of 5 percent), in any district it could receive exactly 55 percent (situation 1), between 55 percent and 60 percent (situation 2), more than 60 percent (situation 3), between 50 percent and 55 percent (situation 4), or less than 50 percent of the district vote (situation 5).

28. It is also logically possible for a system to be biased because of wasted votes. Consider a system of six districts in which Party A wins 100 to 90 votes in five of the districts and Party B wins 100 to 50 votes in the sixth district. In this system, parties evenly divided the total vote (550 to 550) and each party has a mean unwasted vote per victory rate of 100 votes, yet Party A has won five of the six seats (83 percent) with 50 percent of the vote. The system is clearly biased in favor of Party A, yet the unwasted vote rates do not indicate this. The system is biased because Party B wastes a disproportionate percentage of its votes (82 percent vs. 9 percent for Party A). The reason bias is possible in this situation is that, despite the even division of the total vote, there is an uneven division of unwasted votes (500 to 100). If the total number of unwasted votes had

270 NOTES TO CHAPTER 4

been evenly divided (as it was with the total vote), the rate of unwasted votes per victory would accurately reflect the extent of bias. The unwasted-vote measure of bias assumes an even split of unwasted votes at an even split of the total vote. This assumption is examined in detail, along with the effects of the distribution of wasted votes, in appendix B. Appendix B also examines a corrected hypothetical vote estimate of bias (estimating bias at the 50 percent mark of the national vote rather than the mean district vote) and a fixed swing-ratio estimate of bias (assuming a swing ratio equal to 2 and attributing further discrepancies of the actual seat division to bias) and compares them to the unwasted-vote measure. With the exception primarily of the elections in the 1950s, each of the three measures indicates a consistent pro-Democratic bias throughout the 1960s, 1970s (except for 1974), 1980s, and into the 1990s.

29. Gerrymandering by packing opposition partisans into fewer districts contributes to partisan bias by raising the winning vote percentage in a district for that party. Controlling for the total votes cast in a district, a party winning with a high percentage of the votes will pay a higher price in unwasted votes for its victories than the opposition, and the system will be biased against the party paying the higher price. If all districts had the same number of votes cast, the electoral system would be biased in favor of the party winning districts with a lower percentage in districts' votes. Thus, Fiorina's point that the system works against Democrats because they run up large vote percentages in uncompetitive, urban districts would be valid if low turnout in these districts did no more than offset the high winning-vote margins (Fiorina, 1992a, 18).

30. The two principal interactive paths in the partisan bias model analytically must take a value of 1. The number of potential voters in a district multiplied by the turnout rate (percentage of potential voters actually voting) equals the total number of actual voters in a district. The number of actual voters in a district multiplied by the percentage of votes cast for the winning candidate equals the number of unwasted votes in a district.

31. The fact that the parties had already been assumed to have evenly divided the vote means that some of these calculations are the same as the values already hypothesized in this case. However, the method handles all nondegenerative cases (cases in which each party wins a nontrivial number of seats on which to base the mean number of unwasted votes). An alternative calculation was also made and produced very similar results. Rather than determining the share of seats that the Democrats would win with half of all unwasted votes expended at their mean number of votes per victory, we can determine how many seats the Democrats would win with their number of unwasted votes expended at the overall mean number of votes per victory.

Chapter 5

1. See Congressional Quarterly's *Guide to U.S. Elections* (1985, 683–97) and Butler and Cain (1992) for excellent reviews of the development of standards for reapportionment and redistricting.

2. The highest-turnout district in 1992 was actually the single-district state of Montana. Over 400,000 Montana voters cast ballots in the state's congressional contest. The disparity between Montana's total vote for one representative and the low-turnout contested district in 1992 (California's Thirty-third) was nearly eight to one.

3. The descriptions of these four districts draw from various editions of Barone and Ujifusa's *The Almanac of American Politics* and Congressional Quarterly's *Politics in America*.

4. Alton Waldon, also a Democrat, won a special election to complete Addabbo's unexpired term. Waldon was later defeated by Flake for the 1986 Democratic congressional nomination.

5. The *1985 Republican Almanac: State Political Profiles* (474) indicated that 65.3 percent of registered voters in Queens voted in 1984, compared to 75.3 percent statewide. The *1987 Republican Almanac* (764) indicated that 44.9 percent of registered voters in Queens voted in 1986, compared to 53.2 percent statewide.

6. The exact population per district figures are 621,400 for Kansas and 526,267 for Oklahoma. I thank Jack Pitney for suggesting this comparison.

7. In 1992, a total of 1,382,175 votes were cast in California's five highest-turnout districts (districts 4, 6, 10, 15, and 29). More than a quarter million votes were cast in each of these districts. In comparison, less than half a million votes (466,392) were cast in the five lowest-turnout districts combined (districts 20, 30, 31, 33, and 46). The total votes cast in the 5 highest-turnout districts in California exceeded (by over 70,000 votes) the total votes cast in its 11 lowest-turnout districts. All seats examined had major-party competition.

8. Districts, contested by congressional candidates of both major parties, are grouped by turnout, measured as the total votes cast for congressional candidates and not as a rate of the eligible electorate.

9. Because logit fits an S-shaped curve to the relationship, there is no single slope for the entire range of the independent variable. The derivatives presented in table 5.3 indicate the slope of the curve in the middle of the independent-variable distribution.

10. While many might suppose that these low-turnout Democratic districts are predominantly southern, this is not the case. Many light-turnout districts are northern. In 1990, for instance, four of the five lowest-turnout districts were in New York City, and the fifth was in New

Jersey. If there is any typical Democratic low-turnout district in recent years, it would appear to be an urban and minority-populated district rather than a rural southern district.

11. Other cities on this low-turnout district list are Memphis, Baltimore, Detroit, and Newark.

12. There is a fairly close correspondence between a district's turnout level and the number of unwasted votes cast in the district. The mean correlation between the total number of voters in a district and the number of unwasted votes in elections over this period was .85. The correlations ranged from about .7 to .9. Probably because of the reapportionment rulings of the mid-1960s, the association between turnout and unwasted vote tended to be a bit smaller in recent years (although in 1990 it was .88).

13. The difference of 9 or 10 additional Republicans is computed by dividing the total vote difference between the 67 low-turnout Democratic districts and the 67 low-turnout Republican districts (1,356,602) by the mean vote for a winning Republican candidate in 1992 (142,719).

14. We assume that in an unbiased electoral system a party that wins half of the total vote should also be expected to receive half of the unwasted vote. With both parties receiving the same number of total votes, this appears to be a safe assumption. Only bias in the system would cause either party to receive more or less than half of the unwasted vote in this situation. For an analysis of wasted votes, see appendix B.

15. The two alternative estimates of bias presented in appendix B, one based on a modified uniform-vote-swing analysis and the second on an assumed fixed swing ratio (equal to 2), concur with the unwasted-vote measure that Republicans would have won a majority of contested seats in an unbiased electoral system in the 1966, 1968, and 1980 elections, in addition to the contested-seat majorities that they actually won in 1954 and 1956. They differ from the unwasted-vote measure regarding the 1960, 1962, and 1972 elections, which indicates that Democrats would have maintained their majorities even in an unbiased system. On the other hand, whereas the unwasted-vote measure of bias suggests that Democrats would have held their majority in 1984 without bias, the other measures indicate that bias made the difference that year and that without it Democrats would not have maintained their majority. At the bottom line, an unbiased electoral system would have elected Republican majorities in contested seats between 1954 and 1992 in 8 of 20 elections, according to the unwasted-vote measure of bias, and in 6 of 20 elections, according to the alternative bias measures.

16. Two alternative estimates of bias reported in appendix B dispute the unwasted-vote estimate of bias for 1956. They suggest that the

removal of electoral system bias from the 1956 election would have helped rather than hurt Democrats.

17. The relationship between incumbency and partisan bias is not a simple one. It is most probably nonrecursive and positive in both directions, partisan bias increasing the incumbency advantage of a party and the incumbency advantage of a party increasing partisan bias. The analysis recognizes both links. By its very nature, an electoral system with partisan bias will seat more representatives for the advantaged party, and some large proportion of these bonus seats will seek reelection as incumbents. Conversely, once in office, incumbents attempt to have district boundaries drawn to their advantage. While this is often also to the party's advantage and certainly to the advantage of any successor partisan candidate in the district, the interests of the incumbent and his or her party are not always in accord. Incumbents are primarily interested in increasing the security of their district. Although parties are also interested in securing districts for their incumbents, they might be willing to trade some incumbent security for a greater chance of winning additional districts.

18. The lower turnout in the average Democratic district probably partially mitigates the multiplier effect of incumbency on partisan bias. A 10 percent incumbency advantage translates into fewer votes in a low-turnout district than in a high-turnout one. Also, the increased incumbency advantage in recent elections suggests that the extent of pro-Democratic bias is also more underestimated in recent years.

19. Note that it is not necessary for this bias to have increased over the last four decades to help explain the increased occurrence of divided government. With partisan dealignment, as well as the realignment, favoring Republicans, Republican presidential candidates have met with greater success. It is enough that partisan bias in the election of the House was, at least up to 1994, an obstacle to a similar Republican shift in the House.

20. As Achen insightfully pointed out some time ago (1977), correlations, as standardized measures of association, do not tell us many things about a relationship. The fact that there are strong district-level unwasted-vote correlations between election years only indicates that the location of bias tends to be the same from one year to the next. They do not say anything about the extent of bias from one year to the next. A constant could be added or a scaler multiplied to unwasted votes in districts in one election year, changing the extent of partisan bias in that year drastically without disturbing the correlation over time. Thus, the stability of the location of partisan bias should not be mistaken to suggest stability in the extent of partisan bias.

Chapter 6

1. The standard deviation of bias from 1954 to 1992 was 1.5 percent of the seats, or nearly 7 seats.

2. The assumption of a constant partisan bias is implicit in all existing estimates of partisan bias examining the relationship of votes to seats with longitudinal data. This includes Tufte (1973) and would also include Jacobson (1990, table 5.5), although the analysis in both cases allows for some change in partisan bias over time.

3. In *Wesberry v. Sanders* the Court extended to congressional apportionment its one-person, one-vote ruling that it had set for state elections in *Baker v. Carr* and *Gray v. Sanders*. In the rulings following the Wesberry case (*Kirkpatrick v. Priesler* and *Karcher v. Daggett*), the Court insisted that district population sizes within a state vary by as little as practically possible. Even with the judicial mandate for minimum population differences among districts within a state, district sizes unavoidably still vary a good deal from one state to the next. For an excellent summary of apportionment issues see Congressional Quarterly's *Guide to U.S. Elections* (1985, 683–97) and Butler and Cain (1992).

4. The post-1960s redistricting population figures for the states are from *U.S. Statistical Abstract* (1980, table no. 835). The figures were originally drawn from the U.S. Bureau of the Census *Congressional District Data Book*. The data are 1960 census figures for districts of the Eighty-eighth Congress. Jacobson (1992, 11) also offers several examples of pronounced malapportionment.

5. The figures are from the *U.S. Statistical Abstract* (1974, table no. 688). The original source is the U.S. Bureau of the Census, *Congressional District Data Book, Districts of the 93rd Congress*. The population figures are from the 1970 census for congressional districts of the Ninety-fourth Congress. Also, Cox (1981, 15–23) presents a very detailed and illuminating examination of the variance in district populations from 1900 to 1974.

6. The decline in white turnout appears traceable to a decline in political efficacy and a decline in partisanship. Some portion of the decline may also be related to disaffection from both parties, indifference to the candidate choice, and cross-pressures.

7. This racial history of turnout in national elections over the last four decades has been described in a number of studies. For instance, Rosenstone and Hansen summarized the trends simply: "White Americans turn out less now than they did forty years ago. Black Americans—especially in the South—turn out more" (1993, 60). See, also, Asher (1992, 49–50).

8. To assess the stability of the trend estimate, the regression was

run with and without the 1952 election. Including the 1952 election, the regression indicated a .12 percentage point decline in partisan bias with each passing election ($p = .03$, one-tailed). With the series beginning in 1954, the regression indicated a .09 decline in bias with each succeeding election ($p = .09$, one-tailed).

9. The stability of these estimates was also examined by reestimating the regression with and without the 1952 election. With 1952 included, expected bias dropped from 3.1 to 1.7 percent, or 55 percent of its prior level ($p = .03$, one-tailed). With 1952 included, expected bias dropped from 2.9 to 1.7 percent or 60 percent of its prior level ($p = .05$, one-tailed).

10. Recognition of voter volatility itself acts to moderate the gerrymandering impulse. It can be dangerous for a party to draw district boundaries too finely to their advantage. A party cannot be satisfied with a very tenuous majority and, because of the uncertainty, must build some excess votes into their districts as insurance against unfavorable political climates that the future might hold. See Jacobson (1992, 12) and Cain (1985).

11. This is in accord with most prior findings that gerrymandering has had an inconsequential net impact nationally. See Fiorina (1992a, 16), Mann (1987), and Jacobson (1990, 94–96). Born (1985), in a thorough time-series analysis of 79 redistricting plans from 1952 to 1982, found that "redistricting does seem to benefit the controlling party, but not impressively" (309) and that partisan effects were even weaker following the 1964 ruling requiring districts in a state to be nearly equal in population.

12. It is also possible that Democrats might have benefited from the passage of time since the last redistricting, thereby offsetting the deterioration of any benefits from gerrymandering. Suburbanization may have depleted the population in many Democratic urban strongholds over the course of a decade, producing increasing malapportionment in favor of the Democrats until corrected at the next reapportionment. Thus, while the political forces of redistricting may have most strongly favored Democrats early in a decade, sociodemographic forces may have most strongly favored Democrats late in a decade. The case of California in the 1970s and 1980s illustrates this masking effect.

13. One piece of evidence suggesting the extent of pre-1982 malapportionment is a comparison of the diversity of district turnout (in raw votes) throughout the state. In 1980, one standard deviation in district turnout equalled 54,355 voters. After redistricting, this variance was considerably reduced to 32,488 voters.

14. A similar analysis for 1978 also indicates pro-Democratic bias in California prior to the Burton plan. Democrats won 60.5 percent of seats

with 51.8 percent of the vote. If there were no bias in the system, this would suggest a swing ratio of nearly six. The unwasted vote analysis, with Democrats having a mean unwasted vote of about 87,000 and Republicans of about 110,000, indicates a pro-Democratic bias of about 5.1 percent of California's seats. Analysis of California elections in 1990 and 1992 indicate that the system remained biased in favor of the Democrats in 1990 (4.9 percent of seats), but was essentially neutral following the 1992 redistricting (with Democrats having a mean unwasted vote of 121,206 and Republicans of 120,450). Cain (1985) found that the 1982 Burton plan redistricting worked well enough to "swing five seats to the Democrats" (331). The unwasted-vote analysis, like Cain's, found substantial pro-Democratic bias, although his figures include pro-Democratic boosts due to system responsiveness as well as partisan bias. Also, his figures appear high when simply contrasting the 1982 system to the already pro-Democratic 1980 system. Keefe (1988, 47) presents a very brief analysis of the California redistricting that also finds pro-Democratic effects of the gerrymander.

15. Some nonvoters cannot be counted on as likely Democratic votes also because cross-pressures and indecision regarding their prospective vote caused them to abstain (Campbell, 1993). It might also be noted that while conventional wisdom now holds that nonvoters are likely Democratic votes, many believed in the 1960s that nonvoters were likely Republican voters (see Clausen et al., 1965, 322).

16. Wolfinger and Rosenstone (1980, 109) find that voters were 3.7 percentage points more likely than nonvoters to be Republican in their party identification, although even this small difference was not reflected in consistent policy differences. They did not examine likely vote preference differences, and their 1972 election data might have been affected by a depressed turnout of cross-pressured Democrats faced with their very unpopular presidential nominee George McGovern. However, Verba and Nie's (1972, 224–48) earlier study also found evidence of what they termed "Hyperactive Republicans," higher-than-expected participation of Republican partisans. Comparisons of reported votes of voters with the reported presidential preferences of nonvoters in NES surveys in 1980, 1984, and 1988 indicate no strong systematic pro-Democratic leanings among nonvoters. Nonvoters in 1980 were 7.4 percentage points more likely than voters to prefer Democratic candidate Carter to Republican Reagan. However, nonvoters in 1984 and 1988 were slightly more likely than voters to indicate a Republican presidential preference (3.1 percent and 2.1 percent, respectively). While several studies have found no pro-Democratic bias, Radcliff (1994, 1995) claims a strong and robust relationship between turnout and the presidential vote, suggesting that nonvoters, if activated, would add to the Democratic vote. Radcliff

examines state votes from 1928 to 1980. He finds, both in states grouped by prior Democratic support and in a pooled analysis of all states across time, that the Democratic vote increases with turnout. However, the findings may be challenged on several grounds. First, while turnout is statistically significant in his analysis, it usually accounts for very little variance in the vote. Second, and more importantly, Radcliff finds that turnout was *not* associated with the presidential vote *before 1960* but was strongly related after 1960. This is precisely the opposite of what one would expect, given the somewhat more partisan character of the earlier period and the strong socioeconomic basis of that earlier partisanship. This suggests that the relationship may be coincidental. There were two unrelated trends in voting behavior, a decline in Democratic voting and a decline in turnout, that are correlated in a time-series (pooled or otherwise) simply because they occurred through the same period. There is little to suggest that the post-1960 rise in Republicanism was based on the post-1960 decline in turnout.

17. To assess the likely partisan consequences of potential voters not voting in congressional elections, the congressional preferences of nonvoters were compared to the reported vote of voters in several recent NES surveys (1978, 1980, 1984, 1986, 1988, and 1990). While the reported preferences of nonvoters after an election are subject to rationalization and imperfectly reflect how the nonvoters might have voted had they actually bothered to vote, they are the best available evidence. The analysis of these responses suggests that nonvoters often tilt in favor of Democratic congressional candidates, but differences are both slight and inconsistent (aspects in accord with the model of the peripheral voter). Nonvoters reporting a congressional preference were more likely than voters to report a preference for the Democratic candidate in six of the seven election surveys examined. However, the difference between voters and nonvoters was less than 4 percentage points in two of the six cases (and the difference was never as great as 10 percentage points), a majority of nonvoters in most years stated that they had no preference whatsoever, and a large percentage of those nonvoters who indicated a preference stated that their preference was "not strong."

18. The regression included the Democratic congressional two-party vote as the dependent variable and the percentage of voting-age population turning out to vote in the congressional election as the independent variable. The unstandardized regression coefficient for turnout was .013, not statistically significant ($p < .1$, one-tailed). Turnout also did not have a statistically significant effect in a regression including a dummy variable for presidential election years.

19. A bivariate regression of turnout on bias for elections from 1954 to 1992 indicated that pro-Democratic bias could be expected to increase

by .08 ($p < .1$, two-tailed) for every 1 percent increase in turnout. The regression had an adjusted R^2 of .12 ($r = +.41$). A further regression, with a midterm-election dummy variable interaction term, produced substantively similar results. However, we know that time (as a surrogate for sociodemographic and legal changes) is negatively associated with bias, and it is well known that turnout decreased over this period. Therefore, turnout would have a spurious positive effect if the trend in the data series were not taken into account.

20. The greater responsiveness of high-turnout districts is consistent with Caldeira et al.'s (1985) finding that congressional turnout is greater in more competitive districts.

21. The coefficients are not statistically significant in the three lowest categories of unwasted votes ($p > .05$, one-tailed) but are positive and statistically significant ($p < .01$, one-tailed) in the regressions on the two highest categories of unwasted votes in table 6.2.

22. I considered the possibility that the inverse association of the Democratic congressional vote and partisan bias might be affected by the number of uncontested Democratic seats. It is a plausible hypothesis that in good Democratic years (a higher Democratic congressional vote) more Democratic seats would be left uncontested by Republicans hesitant to fight an uphill battle. Conversely, in bad Democratic years it is plausible that more seats often left uncontested would be contested by Republicans. If these usually uncontested Democratic and low-turnout seats enter calculations of partisan bias among contested seats, it might depress the mean number of unwasted votes for Democrats and thereby inflate partisan bias. In causal model terms, the negative relationship between the Democratic congressional vote and partisan bias may really be the product of a positive effect of the congressional vote on the number of uncontested Democratic seats and a negative effect of the number of uncontested seats on partisan bias (because of the low turnout in these districts and the estimation of partisan bias in only contested districts). The analysis, however, indicated that the Democratic congressional vote did not have the expected significant positive effect on the number of uncontested Democratic seats. Therefore, we can conclude that the effects of the Democratic vote on partisan bias is not the result of the Democratic vote pushing different districts into the contested category from which partisan bias was calculated.

23. Converting bias estimates for contested seats to all seats reduces the rate by a factor of about .88 (382/435). Also, there is the extrapolation danger to estimating what bias might be at the even division of the vote, since the election series from 1954 to 1992 contains no cases in which Republicans won a majority or evenly split the vote. Moreover, although we have seen that the pro-Democratic bias increases as the Democratic

vote decreases, this must logically reverse at some point, since there can be no bias when either party receives 100 percent of the votes. That is, if the Republican vote increased greatly, they would eventually crack the Democratic hold on the cheap seats. Thus we should be cautious about extrapolating bias from this series. The analysis in chapter 8 of the 1994 election in which Republicans finally crossed the 50 percent threshold provides us with better information about bias at the even vote split.

24. These estimates correspond closely to Jacobson's (1990, 86) own. Jacobson's first equation in his table 5.5 indicates a responsiveness coefficient of 2.01 from 1946 to 1964 and 1.50 from 1966 to 1988.

25. The fact that the electoral system was and is more responsive than previously estimated has limited implications. The higher level of responsiveness is, after all, offset by partisan bias varying inversely with the congressional vote. Thus, a shift of one percentage point of the congressional vote toward the Democrats still translates into a shift of only about 1.4 percent of seats to the Democrats in the post-1964 period. However, the modest shift can now be understood to be a result of two processes. With a stronger Democratic vote, Democrats waste fewer votes in losing causes (responsiveness) and thus gain more than an equivalent percentage of seats. However, these gains are restrained because many of these additional votes are cast in districts that they would have won anyway, only with a smaller number of votes—a reduction in partisan bias.

26. In tracing the existence of districts with large and consistent turnout differences to the Constitution it is sometimes implied that the constitutional source of these differences eliminates them as a basis for partisan bias. That is, if the system is working as the framers intended, this cannot be the foundation for bias. However, while the tracing of cheap seats to the Constitution may speak to the intentionality of partisan bias, it does not speak to its presence. To say that Democrats pay a lower price per victory because of constitutional arrangements serves only to *explain* bias and does not mean that bias does not *exist*. Factors producing partisan bias may be unintentionally or intentionally built into a constitutional system. The evaluation of the electoral system examines only the translation of actual *votes* into seats—not people into seats, not citizens into seats, and not adults over the age of 18 years into seats. A constitution may have representational goals other than the representation of voters (the representation of the entire population, the representation of whites and three-fifths of slaves, the representation of property holders, the representation of members of a particular religion, the representation of left-handed people, or whatever) and this may impinge on the representation of voters, but analysts should not alter their evaluation criteria as a consequence. The electoral system should not be able to define success in its own terms. In other words, we wish to make first-order assessments of

the electoral system—the system represents voters well or not so well, and *not*, for a system that is attempting to represent population (citizens, left-handers, etc.), the system represents voters well or not so well.

27. In the elections of 1824 and 1825, 10 states with more than one House seat held purely single-member-district elections. Three (Maryland, New York, and Pennsylvania) elected most of their members from single-member districts but also had several multimember districts. Five states (Connecticut, Georgia, New Hampshire, New Jersey, and Rhode Island) held at-large elections. Ohio's arrangements are unknown. See Congressional Quarterly's *Guide to U.S. Elections*, 2d ed. (1985).

28. The single-member-district system became established through both state adoption and federal statutes. Congressional Quarterly's *Guide to U.S. Elections* (1985, 678) notes that multimember districts were prohibited by statute in 1842. Davidson and Oleszek (1981, 61) note that at-large elections in states with more than a single member were prohibited by statute in 1967. As previously noted, a series of federal judicial rulings established the requirement of equally populated districts.

29. In 1954, of the 68 districts in the lowest-turnout quintile, 32 (47 percent) were in the 11 southern states. This is despite the fact that only 36 of the 346 contested districts (10 percent) were in the South.

30. The inner-city, minority nature of a number of cheap seats in recent years was noted in chapter 5 (table 5.5). Other cities with multiple cheap seats in 1990 were Chicago with four (districts 1, 2, 5, and 7), Miami with two (districts 17 and 18), Baltimore with two (districts 3 and 7), and Detroit with two (districts 1 and 13).

31. Oppenheimer (1989) similarly observed that "if the House were apportioned on the basis of voters instead of population, it is likely that the Republicans might have won a majority of seats in the early 1980s" (665–66).

32. Where geographic contiguity and compactness have been ignored in recent years to create majority-minority districts, which sometimes produces oddly shaped and far-flung districts, the effect is to emphasize the socioeconomic homogeneity of the district and thereby create greater turnout disparities among districts.

Chapter 7

1. It would also be logically possible that some systematic countervailing pro-Republican advantage offset the pro-Democratic electoral system advantage in this earlier period. Such a factor could explain why Democrats lost their House majorities in the 1946 and 1952 elections. However, it appears that short-term issues may have broken the Democratic majority in 1946 and that a combination of issues, reapportionment

and presidential coattails may account for Republican success in the 1952 elections.

2. Despite Democratic strength in the electorate, they were not quite as strong in state governments. State constitutional arrangements reflecting geographic areas of states in state senates, regardless of population, often led to state legislative electoral systems biased in favor of Republicans. Republicans often won cheap seats in rural areas. This partially offset Democratic electoral strength. In 1950, for example, Democrats controlled 27 lower chambers of state legislatures while Republicans controlled 18 (2 were tied and 2 were nonpartisan). However, Democrats controlled both houses of the state legislature in only 19 states, and Republicans controlled both houses in 16 states. Control was split in 11 states and 2 states were nonpartisan (The Council of State Governments, 1950–51, 112).

3. The correlations and logit coefficients in table 7.1 tell about the same story, although not quite as clearly, since they are not especially sensitive to the differences at the low end of the turnout and unwasted votes. In statistical terms, the grouped data suggests a pattern of heteroskedasticity and perhaps nonlinearity. Low-turnout districts are strongly associated with Democratic victories. Beyond the lowest quintile, however, things are not quite as dependable. In some years, there was a linear relationship. Democrats did best in the cheap seats, not quite as well in districts with moderate turnout, and worst in high-turnout areas. In other years (e.g., 1936, 1940, and 1944), Democrats did better in high-turnout districts than in districts with middling turnout. This attenuates the correlation and logit measures of the relationship.

4. The equivalent information for the 1952–90 series of elections was presented in tables 5.7, 5.8, and 5.9.

5. The mean two-party voter turnout in contested seats in 1942 was over 79,300 voters. The 20 contested districts with the lowest turnout had total votes of less than 28,000. Four of these very cheap seats were in Tennessee, another four in Virginia, two in North Carolina, and one each in Florida, Kentucky, Maryland, Oklahoma, and Texas. The number of cheap seats in the South in this period is especially noteworthy because of the many southern and border state districts that were uncontested.

6. While the 1950 election demonstrates the effects of partisan bias quite well, the subsequent election, in 1952, might be viewed as a counterexample. In the 1952 election, Democrats received 49.9 percent of the vote (or perhaps slightly more if the Liberal Party cross-endorsement votes in New York are counted as Democratic votes [50.3 percent]) and only 213 seats (49.2 percent). With nearly the same national vote as in 1950, why did Democrats lose 21 seats, and does this mean that the electoral system was not biased in their favor? One reason for the difference

is that Democrats had a diminished uncontested-seat advantage in 1952 than in 1950. In 1950, 92 Democrats and only 7 Republicans went unchallenged, giving Democrats an 85-seat advantage. In 1952, only 80 Democrats and 11 Republicans ran unopposed. This 69-seat Democratic advantage in 1952 was sizable but was still 16 seats smaller than their 1950 margin. In addition, the 1952 election followed reapportionment and Republicans picked up six of the seven new districts allocated to California. Finally, although Democrats received about half of the total congressional vote, they received only 46.6 percent of the vote in contested districts. The responsiveness of the electoral system worked strongly against them. Democrats wasted a large portion of their votes in losing causes.

7. Regressions of total district turnout and total unwasted votes on the party winning the seat indicated that the likelihood of a Democratic winner decreased by three percentage points with every additional 10,000 votes cast in the district. For every additional 10,000 unwasted votes in a district the likelihood of the winning candidate being a Democrat decreased by five percentage points.

8. In 1950, the average winning candidate, regardless of party, received 65,300 votes and the Democrats received 8,220,600 unwasted votes. At a rate of 65,300 unwasted votes per victory rather than the actual Democratic rate of 58,300 unwasted votes, Democrats would have won 126 contested seats rather than their 141, a difference of 15 seats.

9. The number of unwasted votes in the Ohio Republican district was more than 16 times that in the Democratic Texas district. The number of total votes cast in the Ohio district was over 21 times the number in the Texas district. Also, there were five nominally contested districts in 1950 with lower turnouts than Twelfth District in Texas. I considered the Texas district as the low end of seriously contested districts since the Republican challenger received about 20 percent of the vote.

10. Despite the assistance of substantial bias in their favor, their minority vote (45.7 percent) cost Democrats their seat majority in 1946. However, a combination of electoral system bias and a substantial uncontested-seat advantage provided Democrats in 1942 with a sufficient boost to hold their seat majorities despite attracting less than a majority of the vote (48.2 percent).

11. A regression on these nine elections with the extent of pro-Democratic bias as the dependent variable and the Democratic share of the national two-party congressional vote as the independent variable indicated a strong and significant negative effect. The regression produced a slope of -1.14 ($t = 4.26$) with a constant of 62.89. The equation accounted for about three-quarters of the variance in bias (adjusted $R^2 = .71$; SEE $= 2.8$). With 50 percent of the vote, the expected partisan bias was 5.9 percent of the contested seats.

12. The pre-1954 elections were also examined by Democratic victory rates in quintiles of turnout and unwasted votes (see tables 5.3 and 5.6). In 1946, Democrats won 74 percent of districts in the lowest quintile of turnout and an average of 20 percent in the three highest-turnout quintiles. In 1936, they won 94 percent in the highest turnout category and an average of 73 percent (as opposed to 1946's 20 percent) in the three highest-turnout groupings.

13. States were categorized by using the Inter-university Consortium for Political and Social Research (ICPSR) categories. Virginia, Alabama, Arkansas, Florida, Georgia, Louisiana, Mississippi, North Carolina, South Carolina, and Texas were counted as Southern states. Kentucky, Maryland, Oklahoma, Tennessee, and West Virginia were counted as border states. Of the 135 districts in these states, only a third (45) were contested in 1942. Of these contested districts, 55 percent (34) were in the lowest-turnout quintile and 53 percent (33) were in the lowest unwasted-vote quintile.

14. The mean number of unwasted votes in the 268 contested nonsouthern districts in 1942 was 51,692 votes. By contrast, the mean number of unwasted votes among the 45 contested southern districts was only 24,761 votes, 48 percent of the mean in nonsouthern districts.

15. Many southern cheap seats failed to make the list because they were uncontested at some point. Even so, 12 of these 17 "hard-core" cheap seats are from southern and border states.

16. In the reapportionment of the 1940s, the Ninth District was composed of Bland, Buchanan, Dickinson, Giles, Lee, Pulaski, Russell, Scott, Smyth, Tazewell, Washington, and Wise Counties. Redistrictings since then have expanded the district eastward into adjacent counties as far as Roanoke. However, in the 1940s the district did not even extend as far east as Blacksburg (Cox, 1981, 1122–32). Barone et al. (1972, 853) indicate that as of the 1970s, the district was 72 percent blue-collar in terms of employment. In racial and ethnic composition, the district was only 2 percent black and less than 1 percent of "foreign stock." Undoubtedly, the district as constituted in the 1940s was even more working-class and poor white in composition than it was in the 1970s.

17. There was no Ninth District in the 1932 election. Failing after the 1930 census to redistrict in time for the 1932 election, Virginia's nine House members were elected at-large (Congressional Quarterly, 1985, 931).

18. Although the 16,655 votes cast for the winner, John Flannagan, were few by national standards, they were the most cast for any winner in Virginia in 1942. However, only one other Virginia district was contested.

19. Nine of the 12 cheaper seats in 1942 were in the southern or border states (4 in Tennessee alone), and the remaining 3 were in New York. The 2 cheapest seats were the Fourth and the Ninth Districts of

Tennessee, both won by Democrats with fewer than 8,000 votes. The Fourth reelected Albert Gore, later elected to the Senate and Vice President Gore's father.

20. Harry Truman, who had succeeded Franklin Roosevelt to the Presidency in 1945, was able to win in his own right in 1948 and was admired by both politicians and historians in hindsight, but he was not especially popular with voters in 1946. Postwar dislocations, shortages, and inflation caused his job approval standings to plummet into the low 30s prior to the 1946 election. This was the lowest midterm rating of any president from 1946 to 1990. The average rating is in the 50-to-55 percent range. For an examination of Eisenhower's coattails see Campbell (1993, 130–31).

Chapter 8

1. Democrats actually lost 57 of the seats that they had won in 1992. They also lost two additional seats won in 1992 in the special elections during the intervening two years. Republicans lost five seats from their 1992 victories, all open seats. The difference is the net Democratic Party loss of 52 seats.

2. With adjustments made for the smaller size of the House in the earlier years in the century and for third-party seats (to make congresses comparable), net partisan shifts in excess of 60 seats occurred in 7 of the 25 elections between 1902 and 1950 (1910, 1914, 1920, 1922, 1932, 1938, and 1948). Three of these elections (1922, 1938, and 1948) shifted 75 or more seats between the parties. In addition, there were another two elections from the first half of the century in which a party lost more than 50 seats. The Republicans lost 51 seats in the 1930 midterm, and the Democrats lost 56 seats in the 1946 midterm.

3. The post-1950 elections that transferred a substantial number of seats between the parties are most notably the 1958 election (a 49-seat shift to the Democrats), the 1966 election (a 48-seat shift to the Republicans), and the post-Watergate 1974 election (a 49-seat shift to the Democrats). Although these elections produced substantial partisan seat changes, they fell short of the 52-seat shift of the 1994 election.

4. The single exception to this law of midterm presidential losses was 1934, when Franklin Roosevelt's Democrats gained nine seats in the first midterm of the Democratic realignment.

5. The median seat loss in the 1970 to 1990 period was even smaller, only 13.5 seats. The one midterm eruption of recent years was the 1974 midterm, in which Republicans lost 48 seats in the wake of the Watergate scandal. There was little reason to think that Democrats in 1994 carried anything like the baggage that Republicans carried in 1974.

6. For an extensive review of the different explanations of midterm losses for the president's party and evidence that they are inversely proportional to the size of the prior presidential victory, see Campbell (1993). It is not necessary for the president's party to have gained seats in a presidential election for it to have had coattails, although gains are the most obvious coattails. The winning presidential party may have coattails and actually lose seats if the losses are less than they otherwise would have been. This is the case for Democrats in 1992. They lost 10 seats but would have lost many more had Clinton lost the presidential election. The 1992 case is also complicated by the large vote, nearly 20 percent, for independent presidential candidate Ross Perot. As a proportion of the two-party vote, winning Democratic candidate Bill Clinton received 53.4 percent of the vote, a modest rejection of then incumbent George Bush portending modest midterm congressional losses for the party in the White House. However, if Perot votes are counted as anti-incumbent votes, then 62.5 percent of presidential ballots cast in 1992 were anti-incumbent votes. This suggests that short-term forces were significantly more anti-Republican in 1994 than the two-party vote indicated. On the basis of this estimate of the 1992 political climate, large Democratic losses should have been expected in 1994, though even then not as great as actually witnessed.

7. Tufte (1975) and Lewis-Beck and Rice (1992) and others also look to the state of the economy as part of the conditions surrounding the midterm referendum. The economic growth rates in the 1994 election year were about average, suggesting nearly average in-party losses. The most prominent forecasting models of midterm elections offered predictions ranging from very minor Democratic losses (Lewis-Beck's model predicted a four-seat loss) to modest Democratic losses (Campbell [1994] and Abramowitz [1994] each predicted losses in the range of 20 to 25 seats). "On the ground" or district-by-district estimates of Democratic losses were on the same order. *Congressional Quarterly Weekly Report*'s preelection evaluation of individual races categorized seats as having front-runners or being toss-ups (Kaplan, 1994). If the parties held districts in which their candidates were front-runners and evenly split the toss-up districts, Democrats would have been expected to lose 24 seats. A similar preelection analysis based on district evaluations by *U.S. News and World Report* (Roberts et al., 1994, 34–35) suggested Democratic losses of about 27 seats. Even most pundits making calls just a couple of days before the election expected smaller Democratic losses. David Broder reported the election-eve forecasts of 14 pundits. Only 3 of the 14 predicted a Republican majority, and none predicted Republicans to gain more than 50 seats.

8. Of the more than 104.4 million votes cast in the 1992 presidential election, Democratic candidate Bill Clinton received about 44.9

million. The large difference between Clinton's share of the vote and the total vote cast for candidates other than then-President Bush is mostly attributable to the large vote for the third presidential candidate in the field, Texas billionaire, populist Ross Perot. Perot received the largest presidential vote share of any nonmajor party candidate since Teddy Roosevelt ran on the Bull Moose ticket in 1912. Perot received about 19 percent of the total vote.

9. Before the election, Republicans held majorities in 29 state legislative chambers, and Democrats controlled 66. After the election, Republicans controlled 47 and Democrats 48, a shift of 18 chambers in the Republican direction (Ladd, 1995, 1). In terms of the control of both state legislative chambers in a state, Republicans after the 1994 midterm controlled 19 state legislatures, Democrats controlled 18, and 12 were divided. The election placed more state legislatures under unified Republican control than at any time since the 1968 election, when Democrats and Republicans each controlled 20 states.

10. The concept of a partisan realignment refers to fundamental or long-term partisan change as opposed to transitory or short-term change. The subject of this change, however, varies in different uses. Some refer to partisan realignment as a long-term shift in the partisan allegiances of different social, economic, or demographic groups. A more frequent use, and the one employed here, refers to a long-term shift in the balance of electoral support between the parties—in other terms, a change in the parties' "normal vote" (Converse, 1966). While group change usually accompanies partisan change, it is not required for it and is not synonymous with it.

11. The New Deal realignment toward the Democratic Party began in 1928 and was for the most part in place by the 1936 election, though as both Ladd (1995) and Sundquist (1983) point out, related changes and adjustments continued for some time. The evidence indicates an unusual amount of mobilization occurred over this period. Of the 1936 electorate, nearly half had not voted before 1928. A majority of these new voters were Democrats. Of the nearly 16 percentage point shift in the normal partisan vote, about two-thirds can be traced to mobilization and about a third to the conversion of former Republicans to the Democrats (Campbell, 1985, 373). Much as one would expect, the mobilization component of this realignment occurred more rapidly than the conversion component, which requires the rejection of a previous attachment as well as the adoption of a new attachment.

12. Several researchers have well documented the rise of Republicanism in the South. See Petrocik (1987), Bullock (1988), Stanley (1988), Carmines and Stimson (1989), Wattenberg (1991), and Black and Black (1992), among others. This focus on the South does not mean that the

realignment took place only in this region or that the realignment did not affect the politics of other regions. The greatest regional shift was in the South and particularly in the "deep South." However, the realignment was evident in other areas as well, with some regions moving in the Republican direction, while others became more Democratic. My examination of presidential voting and Bullock's analysis of several offices indicates that Republicans also made significant gains in the Rocky Mountain states in the late 1970s, while Democrats had made up for some of these losses with earlier gains of their own in New England and the north central states (see Bullock, 1988).

13. Texas, North Carolina, Virginia, and Florida were also nearly perfect in the Democratic loyalty over this period. They voted 16 of 17 times for the Democratic presidential candidate. Each deviated in 1928 to vote for Hoover in his landslide over Democrat Al Smith, the first Catholic to head a major-party ticket. Tennessee deviated only twice, voting 15 of 17 times for the Democrat. In addition, from the first election in which it cast electoral votes in 1908 until 1944, Oklahoma deviated only twice from the solid Democratic line, voting for the Democratic standard-bearer 8 of 10 times.

14. The 12 southern states were Alabama, Arkansas, Florida, Georgia, Louisiana, Mississippi, North Carolina, Oklahoma, South Carolina, Tennessee, Texas, and Virginia. Forty-seven electoral votes were cast for nonmajor party candidates, and 46 of these were for George Wallace in the 1968 election. The only recent election in which a Democratic presidential candidate received as much as a third of the region's Electoral College votes was 1976, when Jimmy Carter carried 10 of the 12 states. The southern Democratic ticket of 1992 carried only 4 of the 12 states, indicating how the region has been slipping further away from the Democratic Party.

15. In the 1960s, the 12 southern states had 136 of the 538 electoral votes (25 percent). In the 1990s, these states have 155 electoral votes (about 29 percent of the Electoral College).

16. Of the 136 districts in the twelve southern states in 1968, Democrats won 86 seats, and Republicans won 26. Democrats were uncontested in 35 districts that year.

17. Some went even further. Because of the twists, turns, delays, dealignment, and the general confusion in the development of the Republican realignment, along the way a number of prominent analysts suggested that the value of the very concept of realignment or its applicability to modern American politics was in doubt (Shafer, 1991).

18. Subsequent analysis of partisan dealignment indicates that earlier conclusions exaggerated its extent. Keith et al. (1992) found that independents leaning toward one of the parties in their identifications were

much more like partisans than independents and had often been misclassified as independents. The correct classification indicates a much smaller drop in partisanship than previously estimated. In addition, Miller (1991) found no decline in the correlation of partisanship and the presidential vote choice.

19. The only southern state legislatures to have more than 12 percent of seats held by Republicans following the 1964 election, a good year for Republicans in the South though a Democratic landslide year elsewhere, were in Tennessee (24 percent Republican) and Oklahoma (21 percent). Oklahoma is often not counted in the South, although it appeared as loyally Democratic as many border states in the era of the solid Democratic south.

20. Following the 1974 election, Republicans held less than 5 percent of the seats in the lower houses of Alabama (no Republicans), Arkansas (2 percent), Louisiana (4 percent), and Mississippi (2 percent). They also held fewer than 15 percent of the seats in the state legislatures of Georgia (13 percent), North Carolina (8 percent), South Carolina (14 percent), and Texas (11 percent).

21. Republicans after the 1984 election had a significant presence in the state legislatures of Florida (35 percent), North Carolina (32 percent), Oklahoma (32 percent), Tennessee (37 percent), Texas (35 percent), and Virginia (34 percent). They were still a small minority in the legislatures of Alabama (12 percent), Arkansas (9 percent), Georgia (14 percent), Louisiana (13 percent), and Mississippi (5 percent).

22. Republicans held more than 30 percent of state legislative seats following the 1992 election (or 1991, in odd-year states) in Florida (41 percent), North Carolina (35 percent), Oklahoma (32 percent), South Carolina (41 percent), Tennessee (36 percent), Texas (39 percent), and Virginia (41 percent). They held more than 20 percent of seats in Alabama (22 percent), Georgia (29 percent), and Mississippi (23 percent). The least-Republican state legislatures in 1992 were Arkansas (10 percent Republican) and Louisiana (15 percent).

23. In the 12 states of the formerly solid Democratic South (including Oklahoma in the count), Republicans won 69 seats in 1994 and Democrats won 62.

24. There were 22 Democrats and 2 Republicans elected to the House in the 1976 election.

25. Several polls of this era (including the 1940s) place the racial gap at about 25 percentage points. The Gallup Poll finds a 36-point gap in 1952, a 20-point gap in 1956, and a 19-point gap in 1960. Abramson et al.'s (1994, 146) examination of National Opinion Research Center (NORC) data indicates an average racial gap of 25.4 percentage points in the five presidential elections from 1944 to 1960. The mean racial gap in

the eight presidential elections from 1964 to 1992 was 49.9 percentage points.

26. Because of sampling error and measurement errors in the surveys and exit polls examined, there is some uncertainty around the size of the gender gap, the dividing line for when it portends Republican victory or failure, and the election in which the gender gap began to be related to election outcomes (1972, 1976, or 1980?). Other polls in 1984, for instance, had the gap at seven or eight percentage points (NES and ABC News Poll). Mitofsky International exit polls in 1994 (Wilcox, 1995, 18) indicated an 8-point gender gap in 1994—less than the 11-point gap reported by Ladd (1995) but still above the apparent 6 percent threshold. Additionally, we should expect the gap to shrink a bit in landslide Republican elections when large numbers, regardless of gender, are attracted to the Republican candidate. The smallest gender gap with a successful Republican candidate in recent years, for instance, was for Reagan in his 1984 landslide election.

27. As further evidence that incumbency remained potent, nearly half (16 of 34) of the defeated Democratic incumbents were freshman. Thus the reelection rate of freshman Democratic incumbents was 75.8 percent (50 of 66 running) while the reelection rate of nonfreshman Democratic incumbents was 88.7 percent (141 of 159 running).

28. There were 209 contested Democratic incumbents and 122 contested Republican incumbents. There were 16 uncontested Democratic incumbents and 35 uncontested Republican incumbents. The mean total two-party vote was 154,658 votes in Democratic districts and 173,200 in Republican districts. The analysis used the 1992 estimated vote value of incumbency of 8 percent and a vote value of uncontested seats of 23 percent. The total votes were adjusted by subtracting from a party votes that it won because of its incumbents, adding to its total votes that were won because of the other party's incumbents, and adding to its total votes that it would have won in the districts that it had left uncontested. The initial base vote for the parties included adjustments for uncontested districts with unreported votes. This was the adjusted vote in table 8.3. On the basis of the adjustments for uncontested seats and incumbency, the Democratic vote would have increased in numbers from about 32,306,000 votes (46.2 percent) to about 32,804,000 votes (45.7 percent), and the Republican vote would have increased from about 37,563,000 votes (53.8 percent) to about 39,028,000 votes (54.3 percent).

29. The even division of the national vote is the split of the aggregated national vote totals rather than a mean district vote percentage of 50 percent. The split of the aggregated national vote takes into account the very real differences in the effective size of district votes. Calculating bias on the basis of a mean district vote of 50 percent erroneously counts

each district equally and ignores the large differences among district vote totals.

30. None of these estimates include the multiplier effect of the Democrats' incumbency advantage. That is, the votes in 1994 have been taken as exogenous. In fact, however, we know that past pro-Democratic partisan bias increased the number of Democratic incumbents and that increased their 1994 vote. Including this multiplier effect would have increased estimates of the pro-Democratic bias by several seats.

31. There are alternative vote simulations for districts that do not report the vote. In the district-level analysis that follows, the vote is simulated using the presidential vote totals in the district and the average drop-off rate in uncontested districts that did report the House vote. A further refinement was made in this second simulation, simulating the vote that the uncontesting party would have been expected to have received had it mounted opposition in the district. The national vote division using this second simulation does not vary much from the more simple simulation using the vote in reporting uncontested districts. There is no difference between the simulations in the 1992 national vote division: both estimated Democratic votes of about 52.7 percent. In 1994, the second simulation indicated a Republican vote of 53 percent, whereas the first simulation indicated a Republican vote of 53.8 percent.

32. This is not what a neutral electoral system would have produced. It is the expected outcome of a hypothetical system as biased in favor of Republicans as the actual system is biased in favor of Democrats. The expectation of 61 to 62 percent of seats is based on a comparison of the adjusted votes for Democrats in 1990 to the Republican vote in 1994. A majority vote of 53.8 percent (the size of the 1994 Republican majority) is one-tenth of a percent point more than the 1994 Democratic vote majority. In that election, Democrats won more than 61 percent of House seats.

33. In addition to unreported votes in states that do not report the vote in uncontested districts, there were no votes for the seven districts in Louisiana. Louisiana's runoff open-primary system does not require a general election if a candidate receives a majority vote in the initial voting. All seven district races were settled in the first round of voting.

34. The mean turnout drop-off from presidential to House voting in uncontested districts that reported the vote in 1992 was 15.2 percent. Therefore, in uncontested districts not reporting the 1992 House vote, a district's House vote was initially simulated as 84.8 percent of its presidential vote. As a point of reference, the rate in contested seats for 1992 was 94.2 percent. The mean turnout drop-off from the 1992 presidential vote to the 1994 midterm vote in uncontested districts reporting the district vote was 41.4 percent, reflecting in large part the regular turnout

decline from the on-year to the midterm election. The 1994 House vote in uncontested districts in which the vote is not reported is initially simulated as 58.6 percent of the district's prior presidential vote total (1 − 0.414). Again, as a point of reference, the equivalent mean rate in districts contested in 1994 was 70.5 percent of the district's 1992 total presidential vote. These simulated votes in unreporting uncontested seats, along with the votes in uncontested seats in which the vote was reported, were adjusted further to take into account the vote that would have gone to the party not contesting the seat and then the mean drop-off in contested districts.

35. The simulated vote in uncontested seats was calculated as 29.8 percent of the winning party's vote in the district. This amounts to a district vote division of 77 percent (100/129.8) to 23 percent. This procedure assumes that the votes for the uncontesting party were entirely produced by higher turnout. However, some of these votes may have been at the expense of the winning party. To take this into account, votes for both parties (in the uncontested districts) were discounted so that the district's drop-off rate equalled that in contested districts in the election. The discount rate was 14 percent in 1992 and 7 percent in 1994.

36. Note that the unwasted-vote measure of system bias indicated a smaller bias in 1992. It indicated a 1.1 percent pro-Democratic bias. However, this measure examined only contested elections. Additionally, as noted in chapter 4, some bias may also be caused by an asymmetrical difference in wasted votes. That is, if the electoral system causes one party to waste more of its votes when the parties evenly divide the vote, the system is biased in favor of the other party. See appendix B.

37. There was no change between 1992 and 1994 in 17 districts. In districts with Democratic gains, the mean gain was about 5 percent of the vote.

38. One could conceivably use district characteristics to model the proportionate swing, just as the vote swing itself has been simulated by King and Gelman (1991) and Jackman (1994). That is, if an even national vote division would have been achieved after about half of the swing from 1992 to 1994, it is not necessarily the case that all districts would have equally experienced half of their vote swing. Some might have more easily swung in the Republican direction and others might have held back. However, given that the 1992 and 1994 elections were each only about three percentage points off center, and given the likely difficulty of modeling proportions of district vote swings, the simple iterative application of constant proportions would seem adequate to estimate bias and an improvement over hypothetical methods that do not examine pairs of elections and actual district level vote swings.

39. The vote swing was calculated from the 1992 vote percentage

base in each district. The adjusted swing was multiplied by the average total vote in the district for the 1992 and 1994 elections. This provided a hypothetical vote for both parties in each district. These were then aggregated to determine whether the national vote was equally divided. If not, further proportions of the vote swing were examined until the national party votes converged.

40. Combining the district level analysis with the unwasted vote analysis clarifies the basis for the pro-Democratic bias. The average hypothetical vote for Democratic winners was about 114,400 votes. The average hypothetical vote for Republican winners, on the other hand, was about 128,300 votes. Democrats paid almost 14,000 votes less than Republicans did for a victory.

41. Looking at turnout, rather than votes for the winning candidate, produces the same conclusion. Democrats won 36 (90 percent) of the 40 lowest-turnout districts (all contested) in 1994. Each of these districts had a total turnout of fewer than 120,000 voters compared to the average district's 170,000.

42. The over-140 club is, if anything, even more diverse than the cheapest seats. The 30 most-vote-expensive seats represent 19 different states. There seems a slight, but only slight, tilt toward northern, eastern, and midwestern states rather than southern and western states.

43. The high showing of Democrats since 1962 was in 1974 and 1976, when Democratic candidate Danielson won 74 percent of the vote. Of the 17 elections since 1962, the Democrat won with less than 60 percent of the vote 8 times. The district numbers changed over several redistrictings over the years. It was the Twenty-ninth District in the 1960s and the Thirtieth in 1970s.

44. An even division would have been 217 of the 434 seats examined, Vermont's single seat excluded because it was won by a third-party candidate. The aggregate analysis indicates that Democrats would have won 235 seats. The 1992 uniform district swing to the Republicans indicated that Democrats would have won 233 seats. The 1994 uniform district swing to the Democrats indicated that Democrats would have won 229 seats. The 1992-to-1994 proportionate-swing analysis indicated that Democrats would have won 235 seats. The unwasted-vote analysis for all districts indicated the Democrats would have won 236 seats.

45. The two alternative estimates of bias in appendix B, the modified uniform-vote-swing measure and the fixed-swing-ratio measure, also generally support these findings of the direction and magnitude of electoral system bias. Although the alternative measures differ in the assessment of bias in the 1950s and though they do not suggest a strong relationship with the congressional vote, for elections after 1960, they indicate a median pro-Democratic bias in contested seats of 3.5 percent

in the case of the fixed-swing-ratio measure and 3.2 percent in the case of the modified uniform-vote-swing measure. By converting this for all districts and on the basis of the average election of 376 contested districts (from 1962 to 1992), this amounts to a bias of 3 percent of all districts for the fixed-swing-ratio measure and 2.8 percent for the modified uniform-vote-swing measure. Both are within the 2.8-to-4.4 percent range of estimates generated in the 1994 election analysis.

Chapter 9

1. The 1954-to-1992 analysis indicated a 15.5-to-17.7 seat bias (table 6.3). The five estimates of bias in 1994 placed it at between 13 and 19 seats, with a mean of 16 seats. None of these estimates includes the carryover effect of prior bias through incumbency. The analysis in chapter 4 and appendix C indicates that the carryover effect of bias amounted to two or three additional seats. The analysis of two alternative bias estimates in appendix B, although differing from the unwasted-vote measure for elections in the 1950s, also finds a pro-Democratic electoral system bias for elections in the 1960s, 1970s (except 1974), 1980s, and into the 1990s. In recent decades, these estimates have indicated an even greater pro-Democratic bias than the unwasted-vote measure.

2. Bias, along with the Democratic advantages in incumbency and uncontested seats, may also have preserved the Democratic seat majority in 1968. First, without candidate advantages in 1968, the analysis in chapter 3 indicates that the parties would have evenly divided the national vote (see table 3.5)—in which case the pro-Democratic bias of the electoral system would have kept the House under Democratic Party control.

3. These are conservative estimates. Including the incumbency carryover effect would increase the estimated impact to between 10 and 12 seats. In addition, bias estimates in particular elections are lower than the bias of 15 to 18 seats for the system because bias was found to increase inversely with the Democratic vote, and the average Democratic congressional vote from 1936 to 1992 was 53.2 percent, 3.2 percentage points beyond the 50 percent vote mark. Thus, bias in particular elections in which the Democratic vote exceeds 50 percent, which includes all elections from 1954 to 1992, will generally be smaller than bias when the vote was 50 percent.

4. Observers have long suspected that electoral systems using the states as political districts are biased in favor of the Republicans. In light of the great population differences among the states, an electoral system based on the equal representation of the states, like the Senate electoral system, is likely to be biased in favor of the party with greater voting strengths in the small states. Since Republicans have been generally more

popular with those living in rural areas and in the less populated western states, the Senate system is mostly likely biased in favor of the Republicans. Oppenheimer and Sandstrum (1995), using an indirect approach to estimating bias, found that the Senate system has been consistently biased in favor of Republicans from 1958 to 1994. Bias occasionally was as great as eight seats, but typically was about five seats. In 1994, bias was only a single seat. The presidential electoral system, although also based on the states, is more complicated, since states have unequal numbers of electoral votes based largely, though not exclusively, on their population. Most observers regard the Electoral College system as also favoring Republicans, though Garand and Parent (1991), in a uniform-vote-swing analysis similar to King and Gelman's analysis of the House system, claim that the conventional wisdom is incorrect and that the system has favored Democratic presidential candidates in recent decades. Garand and Parent's analysis indicated that the Electoral College system favored Democrats in 10 of the 12 presidential elections between 1944 and 1988. The results, however, are suspect since they are derived by using the mean district vote rather than the national vote percentage (1019 n. 4).

5. The impact of partisanship on roll-call voting is well documented. Bond and Fleisher (1990) found that the interaction of the representative's partisanship and ideology were the most important variables affecting the passage of bills endorsed by a president.

6. The slope coefficient is based on an assumption of linearity. The quintile analysis, however, suggests that the greatest differences are at the low end of the spectrum and that there are not consistent differences at the upper end.

7. There are numerous examples of very partisan, very close votes in the House on important bills. Bond and Fleisher (1990) recount one example involving the 1987 budget reconciliation bill. After losing the vote on the rule to the Republicans helped by some defecting conservative Democrats, Speaker Jim Wright made a few changes in the bill and brought it back up for a vote immediately: "The vote on final passage appeared to be a loss for the Speaker. When the fifteen minutes normally allowed for voting had expired, the vote was 205–206. Wright delayed announcing the outcome until Jim Chapman, a second-term Democrat from Wright's home state, rushed back to the floor and changed his vote and the outcome" (129). This is another bill that might well have gone against the Democrats if their numbers had not been augmented by electoral system bias.

8. These estimates begin with the recorded vote of 221 in favor and 210 opposed. This vote includes the nine Democrats in the House by virtue of electoral system bias. If the votes of these nine Democrats on this legislation had divided like those of other Democrats, they would

have voted seven or eight votes in favor and one or two votes against. If these nine Democrats had not voted, the vote would have been 213 or 214 in favor and 208 or 209 opposed. If these nine Democrats had been replaced by nine Republicans, who voted like other Republicans (virtually unanimous in opposition), the final vote would have been 213 or 214 in favor and 217 or 218 against.

9. A very controversial aspect of the income-tax-rate hike was that it would be imposed retroactively. The proposed tax-rate increase also violated the movement toward tax simplification (at least with respect to the number of tax brackets or rates) that was hammered out in the mid-1980s. The tax provision also included an additional 10 percent surtax for those with incomes (excluding capital gains) over $250,000.

10. These revenue losers included an expansion of the "earned-income tax credit," a tax break for lower-income taxpayers, and the creation of tax-preferred federal "empowerment zones," both of which reduced federal revenues. Rules regarding the tax treatment of intangible assets, passive losses, and business investments also were changed. The luxury tax on certain items (airplanes, yachts, etc.) was repealed or indexed to inflation rates. Finally, long-held investments would have been subjected to a reduced capital gains tax.

11. The reconciliation process requires various committees to produce savings in programs under their jurisdiction. Congressional Quarterly indicated that the bill froze many discretionary programs "at or below fiscal 1993 levels through fiscal 1998 (29 May 1993, 1386). A more detailed discussion of these proposed savings can be found in *Congressional Quarterly Weekly Report* (7 August 1993, 2138–42). In reviewing these reconciliation changes, it is clear that some were not spending reductions but spending increases (for example, $2.5 billion more for the food stamp program over five years) and others were more specific revenue increases rather than spending cuts (for example, extending the tax on diesel fuel to recreational boaters and extending the period of the tonnage fees on foreign cargo ships entering U.S. ports).

12. *Congressional Quarterly Weekly Report* (7 August 1993, 2134) offered an excellent summary of how the bill changed at various stages from Clinton's initial proposal to the House to the Senate and eventually through the conference committee.

13. One seat was vacant, the Third District in Michigan. The seat had been held by Paul Henry, a moderate Republican, until his death.

14. There cannot be perfect certainty about whether bias made the difference on these votes. There is some chance that the Democrats in the House because of bias might have voted more like Republicans on these particular bills, and thus replacing them with Republicans (through an unbiased electoral system) would not have made as much of

a difference. For instance, in the example of the 1992 vote on H.R. 4210, if the nine Democrats in the House because of bias had voted 5 to 4 for the bill (instead of 7.5 to 1.5), the bill might have passed narrowly even without the votes that Democrats had because of system bias. In addition, Democratic leaders might have been able to persuade additional Democrats to the party's side on these issues. Some members might have voted their constituency position, since their votes were not needed for the Democratic position to prevail. In an unbiased House in which their votes would have mattered to the outcome, they might have been pulled back to the party line. Through various deals, compromises, promises, or threats, Democratic leaders might also have been able to pull in a few additional votes if needed. Of course, the same uncertainties are present on the Republican side, although on these votes Republicans (the most likely source of additional votes on the Republican side of the issue) were nearly unanimous at the outset, so there were fewer prime opportunities to attract additional support for the party's position. In addition, the minority party has fewer resources or levers to use as inducements to their position. Nevertheless, it is possible both that some issues that appeared to have been decided because of electoral system bias might not have been and that some issues that appeared not to have been decided because of bias in fact were.

15. It might be noted that Margolis-Mezvinsky was not elected from a low-turnout district. This is true. However, without the extra Democratic votes of those who did sit in the cheap seats, Margolis-Mezvinsky's vote would not have decided the outcome of this bill.

16. Abramson (1983) documents a general decline from 1952 to 1980 among white respondents to surveys in several civic attitudes. He observes a decline in "external" political efficacy as measured by responses to the statements "People like me don't have any say" and "Public officials don't care what people think" and also a decline in political trust, measured by an index of four or five survey questions including "How much of the time do you think you can trust the government in Washington to do what is right—just about always, most of the time, or only some of the time?" Abramson found no consistent bivariate relationship between Republican Party identification and political trust (198). However, he noted that the association between education and trust was weaker than expected (232). He also noted that political trust reflects evaluations of incumbents as well as more system-based evaluations. In light of these findings, it seems plausible that trust among Republicans suffered under the 40-year reign of Democrats in the House, that this may have masked the expected more positive effects of education (education being positively associated with income, which is positively associated with Republican identification), and that the higher educational attainment of

Republicans may have offset the depressing effect of being in a seemingly permanent minority. In terms of external political efficacy, Abramson also notes that respondents were sensitive to whether their party was in government. He notes that the efficacy of Democrats rose when a Democrat was in the White House and that the efficacy of Republicans rose with a Republican administration. Given this, it seems plausible that efficacy would be affected by partisan control of Congress and that there may be a cumulative effect of the years, at least among those who were aware of who held control of the House.

17. Republican Representatives Armey, Dunn, and Shays and their staffs (Koopman et al., 1994) documented declines in public approval of and confidence in Congress and the more generalized trust in government. They attribute these declines to the long tenure of Democratic control of the House and what they regard as the related scandals.

18. Patterson and Caldeira (1990) draw their aggregate national poll results mostly from Harris Polls, but also from the NORC and NBC surveys. They indicate that the mean rating for the confidence question was "41.5 percent in the 1960s, 17.1 percent in the 1970s, and 15.5 percent in the 1980s" (30). The mean positive congressional evaluation percentages by decade were "43.9 percent in the 1960s, 26.9 percent in the 1970s, and 33.3 percent in the 1980s" (30). Since they were drawing on data only through 1985, I updated the mean with four additional Harris surveys done in the late 1980s (Keene and Ladd, 1992, 87). The updated mean for the 1980s was 37.5 percent, still well below evaluations in the 1960s.

19. The congressional approval ratings series are from Gallup Poll surveys reported by Keene and Ladd (1992). The 18 percent approval rating was from a March 1992 Gallup Poll. It was the lowest rating in the series dating back to April 1974.

20. Partisan bias may also help to explain the conundrum of why voters seem to like their congressman individually while they are disdainful of Congress as a whole (Fenno, 1975). It is, in part, an aggregation problem. Congress in the aggregate is skewed toward those few voters in low-turnout districts. Just as the national vote percentage is less Democratic than the mean district-vote percentage, the median voter nationally is not represented well by the median representative.

21. If bias had the suspected effects on efficacy, they were probably not uniformly felt throughout the public. The political efficacy of consistently Democratic voters probably did not suffer (and might have been enhanced). However, those who occasionally voted Republican might have judged the system to be unresponsive or beyond their ability to influence.

22. Hibbing and Theiss-Morse (1995, 119) draw a distinction

between public regard for the members of Congress and public support for the institution of Congress itself. While they find that Republicans held members of Congress in significantly less esteem than did Democrats, they found no direct effect of partisanship on approval of Congress as an institution. However, partisanship may have affected approval of Congress as an institution indirectly by affecting levels of efficacy. Additionally, very little of the variance in approval of Congress as an institution was explained by the 11 independent variables (adjusted R^2 = .08), raising the possibility of a large amount of random error in the measurement of the dependent variable. This combined with potential multicollinearity concerns (partisanship's multiple correlation with the other independent variables, particularly socioeconomics, demographics, ideology, and views regarding representation) suggests caution before dismissing possible direct and indirect partisan effects.

23. As an aside, the what-if question (what if everyone voted?) is the most commonly asked question regarding the cheap-seats thesis by my fellow political scientists. Implicit in the what-if perspective are two highly questionable notions, that nonvoters are would-be Democrats and that a system of proxy voting through weighting some votes more and diluting the impact of others is a just form of representative democracy (if everyone voted, nothing would change, so nothing is wrong with the present system). This despite the fact that neither electoral system analysis nor democratic theory would allow for the counting in any way of votes that were never cast. The commonness of this what-if question also stands in sharp contrast to the inattention to the more obvious what-if questions regarding the impact of incumbency and uncontested seats on the aggregate vote. Examinations of the Democratic Party's big incumbency advantage over the decades was limited to examining which party won seats after incumbents left them. The focus on the what-if question regarding system bias minimizes the reality of Republican votes being given short shrift by the system.

24. A third option for simulating the vote of nonvoters can be drawn from rational-choice theory, the thesis that nondecisions are actually implicit decisions, and empirical research indicating that many nonvoters are likely to feel cross-pressured by (Campbell, 1993), indifferent to, or alienated from (Zipp, 1985) the candidates. From these perspectives the nonvote is an expression of a near-equal preference (or dislike) of both candidates and amounts to half a vote for each. Since a split vote is not an available option and a nonvote has the same effect without some of the costs of voting, these would-be voters express their will by not voting. If they were to vote as a group, we would expect them to divide their votes evenly. In terms of the aggregate impact of this scenario, the national vote would be moved toward an even-vote division, with the cur-

rent majority-vote party maintaining its majority status. For the period of 1954 to 1992, this would have meant reducing Democratic vote majorities. There would be no change in district seat winners, but the winning candidates would win by smaller margins. With complete turnout, there would be no interdistrict turnout differences (except those resulting from malapportionment from the lumpiness of assigning a limited number of districts and respecting state boundaries in the allocation of districts) and no system bias resulting from such differences.

25. The arithmetic can be illustrated by returning to the two hypothetical districts of chapter 4 (table 4.7). Recall that the low-turnout district, won by the Democrat, had a turnout of 100,000 voters and the high-turnout district, won by the Republican, had a turnout of 300,000 voters. The vote percentage margin in each case was 80 percent for the winning candidate and 20 percent for the losing candidate. The national vote percentage was 65 percent for Republicans and 35 percent for the Democrats. We now also assume that there are half a million possible voters in each district (400,000 nonvoters in the low-turnout district and 200,000 in the high-turnout district). Under the assumption that nonvoters are like those who voted in the district (splitting their votes in the same partisan ratio), if everyone who could have voted did, the vote division in the districts would have remained the same and the Democratic portion of the national vote would have risen from 35 to 50 percent (each party would have received half a million votes). Under the alternative assumption that nonvoters are like those who voted nationally (splitting their votes at the national partisan ratio), the national vote division would have remained the same, now with 650,000 Republican voters and 350,000 Democratic voters. There are big differences within the districts. In the first district, the formerly Democratic cheap seat is now neither cheap nor Democratic. With perfect turnout and assuming that new voters split identically to the national vote division, Republicans would have received 280,000 votes (56 percent, 260,000 added to the initial 20,000) and Democrats would have received 220,000 votes (44 percent, 140,000 added to the initial 80,000). Republicans would still have won the formerly higher-turnout district, now with 370,000 votes (74 percent, 130,000 added to the initial 240,000) and 130,000 votes for the Democrats (26 percent, 70,000 added to the initial 60,000).

26. A difference of three percentage points or so may not seem especially great, but it is substantial from one perspective. The typical (median) congressional vote change from one election to the next was only 2.3 percentage points in elections from 1954 to 1992. Of course, from another perspective, the difference is not so consequential. If nonvoters were voting as their voting neighbors had, the Democratic vote would have increased by three or four or more percentage points, but no seats

would change hands. The district-vote percentages, now based on many more votes cast and no longer cheap in the once-low-turnout areas, would (by our assumption regarding the new voters) remain unchanged.

27. There is some research suggesting that voters nationally do not reflect the views of nonvoters. Radcliff (1994, 1995) found Democrats to benefit from higher turnout, but flaws in this research were addressed by Erikson (1995) and also in chapter 6. The critique suggests that a decline in turnout accompanied a decline in Democratic voting through the 1970s and 1980s and that this coincident trend was mistakenly interpreted as a causal one. As further evidence of this, the relationship between the Democratic vote and turnout should been even stronger in earlier years when the socioeconomic basis of partisanship was even stronger but, tellingly, was not. Others (Rosenstone and Hansen, 1993; Verba et al., 1993) have also tried to make the case that voters do not well reflect the views of nonvoters, but they have not been able to point to systematic differences in preferences or opinions (other than some possible differences in issue emphases between the two groups).

28. Assume that the V_e is the Democratic district-vote percentage among existing voters and that V_n is Democratic district-vote division among newly added voters, the previous nonvoters in the district. The combined or total vote (V_t) when both groups voted would be a weighted average of the two percentages, $V_t = (b_1 \times V_e) + (b_2 \times V_n)$, where b_1 and b_2 are the weights ($1 \geq b_1 \geq 0$, $1 \geq b_2 \geq 0$, and $b_1 + b_2 = 1$). In cheap-seat districts, b_2 is much greater than b_1. However, as long as the original vote (V_e) is over 50 percent Democratic and the vote of new voters (V_n) is over 50 percent Democratic (as it would have been if the former nonvoters voted like existing voters had in elections from 1954 to 1992, although not in 1994), then the new total vote (V_t) would be over 50 percent Democratic, regardless of the relative magnitudes of b_1 and b_2. If because of the volatility of new voters, V_n drops below 50 percent in some districts, it would be possible for V_t to drop below 50 percent and the likelihood increases with higher values of b_2, the cheap seats.

29. The simulation was done on the 32 districts won with less than 70,000 votes in 1994. These are listed in table 8.6. Democrats won 30 of the 32 districts. The simulation involved four steps. First, the voting-age population for districts was estimated from national census information. On the basis of a voting-age population of approximately 186 million and 435 districts, the voting-age population of each district was initially estimated at approximately 428,000. Because of uneven apportionment among states, various rates of state growth in the interim, presence of noncitizens in the count, and other factors that might add some error to this estimate, a more conservative estimate of 400,000 potential voters was used. The second step involved estimating the number of nonvoters

in the 32 districts. This was done by subtracting the number of actual voters from the 400,000 possible voters. The third step simulated the number of votes each party would receive from these nonvoters if they had voted and had cast their ballots in the same partisan proportions as voters had. Republican votes in the district would have increased by 53.8 percent of the number of previous nonvoters. Democratic votes in the district would have increased by 46.2 percent of the number of previous nonvoters. The fourth step added these new votes for each party to their previous vote totals (among actual voters) and calculated the new district vote percentages for each party. According to these new vote percentages, Republicans would have won 20 of the 32 districts (adding 18 to the 2 they had won), and Democrats would have kept 12 of the seats, although 7 of these by less than a 51 to 49 percent margin. When considering the impact of uncertainty on possible Republican gains in these cheap seats, we might also expect Democrats not to hold some of these marginal districts as well as expect Republicans not to reap all 18 of their possible seat gains.

30. Guinier is careful to draw a distinction between permanent and temporary minorities. Each election will place someone in the minority. Although her principle of "taking turns" suggests that she is troubled by anyone being a political loser, Guinier is more concerned about groups being permanent losers.

31. Lani Guinier, then a professor at the University of Pennsylvania's Law School, was nominated by President Clinton in April of 1993 to serve as the Assistant Attorney General of Civil Rights. Her nomination was quite controversial. Conservatives found Professor Guinier's views on civil rights and democratic processes to be radical, unacceptable, and out of the mainstream. They dubbed her "the Quota Queen." Senator Minority Leader Bob Dole saw Guinier as being "consistently hostile to the principle of one person, one vote; consistently hostile to the majority rule; and a consistent supporter, not only of quotas, but of vote-rigging schemes that make quotas look mild" (Guinier, 1994, ix). Liberals defended her views, arguing that her writings had been misinterpreted and misunderstood and that she was well within the democratic mainstream. On further reflection and a determination that the nomination was in trouble, President Clinton withdrew Guinier's nomination before the Senate had even begun holding hearings. In *The Tyranny of the Majority,* Guinier offers a collection of her essays and law review articles on race and representation to clarify the record and, presumably, refute the charges against her.

32. The list of impediments to majority rule is lengthy. Among the many impediments are staggered elections of fixed and long durations, separation of powers, the presidential veto, bicameralism, federalism,

filibusters in the Senate, the two-term limit for the president, the Electoral College, the congressional committee system, the Bill of Rights and other constitutional safeguards of minority rights, and judicial review. A system that requires successive majorities elected for different terms and under different procedures essentially requires an extraordinary majority to act. This provides minorities with an effective veto over the will of the majority.

33. Although much of Guinier's research concerns the effects of the institutional structures and decision rules (plurality rule) on racial representation, her essays are bereft of serious empirical analysis. In view of the fact that the subject matter involves attributes, opinions, votes, boundaries, election outcomes, and the behavior of representation, all very quantifiable matters, the lack of rigorous analysis is all the more startling. It leaves the nonlegalistic portions of Guinier's arguments unsupported by direct and systematic evidence.

34. In *Shaw v. Reno,* the Court in 1993 struck down "bizarrely shaped" districts drawn to maximize the chances of electing an racial minority representative. The court took further steps away from affirmative action redistrictings two years later. In the case of *Miller v. Johnson,* the Court in 1995 invalidated a prominority racially gerrymandered Georgia district on the grounds that the equal protection clause of the Fourteenth Amendment "does not permit the state to separate citizens into districts on the basis of race without compelling justification" (Greenhouse, 1995, 4E). The majority opinion found that race could not be "the predominant factor" for drawing a congressional district, but left open the extent to which race could affect redistricting decisions (Idelson, 1995, 1944–46). The Eleventh District in Georgia was one of several districts nationally that were drawn with little regard for geographic compactness or communities. The district stretched 250 miles from Atlanta's southern suburbs across to the South Carolina border and south to Savannah in order to create a district with a majority of minority voters. As structured, the district's population was 64 percent black and 60 percent of its registered voters were black. In 1994, the district elected Cynthia McKinney, a Democrat of African American heritage (Mauro and Watson, 1995, 8A).

35. Of the 76 lowest-turnout districts in 1994, 17 were majority-minority districts and 59 were not. Of the 32 majority-minority districts, 5 were uncontested. Of the 27 contested majority-minority districts, 17 were in the lowest-turnout quintile, 8 were in the next-to-lowest, and 2 were in the middle quintile. There were no majority-minority districts in the two high-turnout quintiles. The relationship between race and turnout was similarly strong and negative in 1992.

36. There were 37 districts in 1994 with African American populations, which constituted between 20 and 50 percent of the district. Of

these 37, 7 were uncontested in 1994. Of the 30 remaining contested districts, 11 were in the lowest quintile, and another 11 were in the next-to-lowest quintile.

37. Alternatively, these congressional candidates may actually prefer winning with fewer voters, if this corresponds with smaller campaigns and reduced fund-raising efforts.

38. The notion of equal political influence in voting is not a matter of just equal numbers of citizens in each district nor even an equal number of voters. Even with the numbers of voters equalized, voters in districts with close contests may have greater influence than voters in districts with landslides. Alternatively, however, one could argue that districts should be drawn not to equalize or maximize voter influence but to maximize voter satisfaction with his or her representation. That principle might group voters to produce landslide rather than competitive results. Fewer voters would find themselves on the losing end of the election (although they might not be satisfied in an absolute sense if many thought that they were voting for the lesser of two evils). Yet further, one could argue that districts should be drawn to maximize choice so that, with both candidates nearly equally appealing, as many voters as possible would be indifferent to who won. These competing virtues of close and lopsided elections complicate the question of whether redistrictings ought to take competitiveness into account to equalize voter influence. These competing virtues, however, have nothing to do with the inequities related to the different effective sizes of districts.

39. There have been a number of methods for allocating seats. Congressional Quarterly's *Guide to U.S. Elections*, 2d ed., summarizes the various methods that have been used over the years (1985, 685–90). Congress initially assigned seats according to a quota of inhabitants in the state. For instance, at 40,000 inhabitants per seat (the rate adopted in the 1820s), a state with 80,000 inhabitants would receive two seats. However, a state with 119,000 inhabitants would also receive just two seats and a state with 79,000 inhabitants (just 1,000 less than a two-seat state) would receive only one seat, since there was no rounding up. Congress later adopted the Vinton Method, which uses major fractions to assign seats to states. After determining the number of inhabitants per district nationally, the state population was divided by this quota and additional seats were assigned sequentially to states with the largest fractions until the total number for the House was allocated. Seats are now allocated through the "method of equal proportions," which minimizes the proportional difference between the average size of districts in different states.

40. Table 9.2 also presents the greatest national turnout disparity between districts. The greatest difference was between the number of

voters in Montana's at-large district and the Thirty-third District of California, a ratio of nearly eight voters in Montana to every one voter in California's Thirty-third. The effective malapportionment between these two districts is due to three factors: turnout differences, the "lumpiness" of representation, and the constitutional requirement that representatives be allocated to the states. Because of this last factor, the Court might not attempt a remedy of this particular malapportionment, even if they recognized the effective malapportionment resulting from turnout differences.

41. These constitutional provisions for the House system are less compelling to malapportionment than those in the presidential and Senate systems. The designation of representatives to the states (Article 1, Section 2, and Amendment 14, Section 2) would produce less malapportionment if the size of the House were adjusted to more evenly divide into state population counts. The number of seats in the House is set by statute rather than designated by a constitutional provision. In general, a larger number of seats would leave states with smaller remainders. A larger number of seats, for instance, would have remedied the severe malapportionment of Montana in the 1990s. Montana fell just short of being awarded two seats. Its one at-large district is the most heavily populated district in the country. Also, the constitutional provision that districts be reapportioned following every census (Article 1, Section 2) would not appear to prevent more frequent redistricting as severe malapportionment develops throughout a decade.

42. The five conditions believed to provide the basis for cheap seats were discussed in chapter 2. Beyond the existence of the single-member-district system, these conditions included (1) the correlation of partisanship and socioeconomic status, (2) the correlation of turnout and socioeconomic status, (3) the spatial concentration of those with common socioeconomic backgrounds, and (4) the reflection of this spatial concentration in congressional districts. Since cheap seats depend on the conjunction of these conditions, any development that would weaken any one condition would reduce cheap seats. For instance, all other things being equal, cheap-seat bias would be diminished if the parties changed so that they were more socioeconomically similar. If socioeconomics were less strongly associated with turnout, cheap seats would be less consequential. Also, if housing patterns became more socioeconomically heterogeneous, cheap seats would make less of a difference. In considering reforms that might reduce cheap-seat effects, these conditions are regarded as being beyond conceivable manipulation or, in statistical terms, exogenous.

43. All things being equal, turnout disparities would appear to be curvilinearly related to the number of districts. Turnout disparities are

impossible when there are no districts (one at-large election) and also when there are as many districts as there are voters. While this suggests that turnout disparities might be reduced by either increasing or decreasing the number of districts, it seems plausible that turnout disparities would increase with the number of districts until the number of residents in the district became quite small.

44. Malapportionment could also be addressed by more frequent reapportionments and redistrictings. As noted earlier, over a 10-year period districts (both within and among states) can grow very unequal in population. While practically unlikely, one remedy would be more frequent censuses or using other intercensal population estimates to address gross population shifts that occur between censuses.

45. In actuality, an at-large, plurality-rule system would also eliminate cheap seats, although it is extremely unlikely that anyone would prefer at this level of aggregation a winner-take-all House to some form of proportional representation.

46. A significant side benefit of multimember districts would be that each representative from these districts would be elected from a somewhat broader and probably more diverse constituency. This might help to counteract the parochialism often found in House members, who often represent narrow interests at the expense of broader public interests.

47. If the number of districts were reduced by reducing the number of representatives, it would also affect the legislative functioning of the House of Representatives. Representatives in a smaller House might be less specialized, and the House might be less formal in its proceedings, taking on some characteristics of smaller legislative bodies like the U.S. Senate.

48. This analysis has observed substantial stability in turnout from one election to the next. One cannot necessarily infer from this that there is a similar degree of turnout stability at smaller units that would be used to compose new, more equal turnout districts. However, some significant stability is probably present and allows turnout to be seriously considered in assembling a district.

49. As noted in the analysis presented in chapter 6, bias has not varied significantly with variation in national turnout. However, congressional turnout has varied over this period within a restricted range, from the low 30s to about 60 percent. Logically, bias generated by turnout differentials, a major but not the only possible source of electoral system bias, is eliminated if turnout is equal among districts. Apart from differences caused by the numbers of noneligibles in districts (noncitizens, felons, and those under age) or interstate differences in apportionment, equally populated districts should have equal numbers of voters when turnout is complete.

Appendix A

1. While the effects of contesting a seat appear much larger than the incumbency advantage (.23 vs. from .034 to .08), the difference is less than one might first suppose. Votes affected by incumbency are at the expense of the opposing party, while votes affected by uncontesting a seat are not. The effects of not contesting a seat are felt primarily through depressed turnout.

Appendix B

1. Unwasted votes are defined as those cast for a winning candidate. Wasted votes are those cast for losing candidates. Votes are deemed unwasted if they are awarded representation. A party may expend an inordinate number of votes in a winning cause and, in one sense, waste votes. However, we preserve the distinction and suggest that these are inefficiently spent unwasted votes. Their impact on seats shows up in the higher winning vote percentage for the party (high levels of P_{wp}) and, therefore, higher numbers of unwasted votes per victory (the denominator $(P_{wp} \times T_{wp})$).

2. The turnout variable could be further broken down into its components, beginning with the district's population and discounted by the proportion of the population that are citizens, the district's population of citizens discounted by the proportion who are of voting age, and further by the proportions registered and actually turning out to vote. This would allow us to locate with even greater precision the reason for low priced districts.

3. The more general equation, tracing all votes for a party to seats that it won, would be: $S_{wp} = ((1/(\Sigma(P_{wp} \times T_{wp})/S_{wp}) \times V_{wp}) + ((0/(\Sigma(P_{lp} \times T_{lp})/S_{lp}) \times V_{lp}))$. This simplifies to equation 3, since the numerator of the second term, indicating that a party wins no seats for votes cast in districts that it loses (subscript l), is zero.

4. The fact that bias may also be traced to the parties having an unequal number of unwasted votes even with an equal number of total votes may also be traced to the different unwasted-vote prices per seat that the parties pay. For instance in 1994, based on the proportional swing analysis of Chapter 8, Democrats had about 1.35 million more unwasted votes (votes cast for winning candidates) than Republicans at an even division of the national vote. Or, from the other perspective, Republicans wasted about 1.35 million more votes in losing candidacies than did Democrats. Why did Republicans waste more votes than Democrats even though both parties had an equal number of votes? Republicans wasted more votes than Democrats not because they were losing the

closer races (the parties' average losing-vote percentages were about equal) and not because they were losing in higher-turnout districts (they were actually losing more often in lower-turnout districts than were Democrats) but because they lost more seats than Democrats, and they lost more seats because of the turnout district differential between the parties. That is, the lower price that Democrats paid for victories saved them from wasting votes and caused Republicans to waste more of their votes. Thus, the Democratic electoral system advantage was based both directly and indirectly on the distribution of the parties' votes and Democratic strength in low turnout districts.

Appendix C

1. The figures are extracted from Ornstein et al. (1992, 58). To obtain the drop-out rate for incumbents, the number of retirements and number of those defeated in primaries are divided by the total number representatives. In 1970, there were 29 retirements and 10 primary defeats, for a total of 39 not making it to the general election. This amounted to 9 percent of the 435 members.

2. I use the mean turnout of all contested districts rather than Democratic districts since the incumbency-advantage percentage is based on an analysis of all contested districts.

3. The assumption that half the votes are wasted and half are unwasted is probably not entirely correct, but this should not alter the estimated number of seats being shifted. The Democrats as the majority party will probably lose more than half of their votes in the unwasted-vote category, and the Republicans will probably expend more than half of the shifted votes in the wasted-vote category. The former would mean that the assumption of the analysis would underestimate seat changes from eliminating prior bias, and the latter would mean that the assumption would overestimate this change.

4. The number of seats added from prior bias can be calculated as the number of unwasted votes shifted divided by the number of additional votes needed for a victory. The number of additional votes needed for a victory can be calculated as the mean number of unwasted votes (regardless of party) less the mean number of wasted votes for the party benefiting from the shift of votes. In the case of 1970, Republicans needed about 43,000 votes to add to their mean of 43,000 wasted votes to obtain the mean of about 86,000 votes for a victory. Since 67,000 unwasted votes were shifted, Republicans could be expected to gain 1.6 seats (67,000/43,000 = 1.6 seats).

5. There would be an overlap of incumbents due to partisan bias

in this case. It would be equal to the product of the proportion of these incumbents to all Democratic incumbents in each election.

6. The correlations of unwasted votes for all contested districts were similar to those of districts which were won by Democrats. Lagged correlations with the total numbers of voters in districts (both for all contested districts as well as just those won by Democrats) also indicated a good deal of stability. The correlations of the total vote for all contested districts were .91 in 1954–56, .70 in 1964–66, .79 in 1974–76, and .72 in 1984–86. The correlations of the total vote in districts won by Democrats in both election years were .91 in 1954–56, .68 in 1964–66, .78 in 1974–76, and .82 in 1984–86.

7. The estimate that only 3 of the 11 bias-incumbents of 1966 being new is based on the lagged correlation of unwasted votes and a simulation. The unwasted vote or bias correlations were on the order of .7. A simulation was conducted on adjacent elections with 100 districts with varying degrees of overlap among seven incumbent seats that were won by virtue of partisan bias. The extreme case is the perfect replication of the first election, producing a correlation of 1. With six of the seven seats overlapping (86 percent), the correlation was .85. With five of the seven overlapping (71 percent), the correlation was .69. With four of the seven (57 percent), the correlation was .54. With three of the seven (43 percent), the correlation was .39. It would appear that the simulation of an overlap of five of seven districts most closely fits the observed correlation of bias using the unwasted-vote measure. This would mean that about 30 percent of incumbents traceable to partisan bias in an election at time t are not counted among such incumbents produced by the election at time $t + 1$. Of course, this simulation assumes an equal proportion of these incumbents in the two elections. If there are fewer in the time $t + 1$ election, more from the election at time t will not have been already counted. Conversely, if there are more in the time $t + 1$ election, fewer from the election at time t will not have been already counted.

8. There is an additional reason why partisan bias in earlier elections might have a reduced impact on later elections. The carryover effect of partisan bias is based on the installation of incumbents (because of system bias) who would not otherwise have been elected continuing to win election because of their partisan bias based incumbency. However, it is quite possible that a Democrat elected because of partisan bias in an election at time $t - 2$ would have been elected in the next election ($t - 1$) without the benefit of the bias based on incumbency obtained at $t - 2$. If so, then the effects of partisan bias at $t - 2$ would not be carried through by incumbency to the election at time t.

Bibliography

□□

ABC News. 1989. *The '88 Vote*. New York: Capitol Cities/ABC.

Abramowitz, Alan I. 1983. "Partisan Redistricting and the 1982 Congressional Elections." *Journal of Politics* 45: 767–70.

———. 1994. Comments at a "Roundtable on the 1994 Elections." Southern Political Science Association, Atlanta.

Abramson, Paul R. 1983. *Political Attitudes in America: Formation and Change*. San Francisco: W. H. Freeman.

Abramson, Paul R., John H. Aldrich, and David W. Rohde. 1991. *Change and Continuity in the 1988 Elections*, rev. ed. Washington, D.C.: CQ Press.

———. 1994. *Change and Continuity in the 1992 Elections*. Washington, D.C.: CQ Press.

Achen, Christopher H. 1977. "Measuring Representation: Perils of the Correlation Coefficient." *American Journal of Political Science* 21: 805–15.

Alesina, Alberto, and Howard Rosenthal. 1989. "Partisan Cycles in Congressional Elections and the Microeconomy." *American Political Science Review* 83: 373–98.

———. 1995. *Partisan Politics, Divided Government, and the Economy*. Cambridge: Cambridge University Press.

Alford, John R., and David W. Brady. 1993. "Personal and Partisan Advantage in U.S. Congressional Elections, 1846–1990." In Lawrence

C. Dodd and Bruce I. Oppenheimer, eds., *Congress Reconsidered,* 5th ed., 141–57. Washington, D.C.: CQ Press.

Alford, John R., and John R. Hibbing. 1981. "Increased Incumbency Advantage in the House." *Journal of Politics* 43: 1042–61.

Ansolabehere, Stephen, David Brody, and Morris Fiorina. 1992. "The Vanishing Marginals and Electoral Responsiveness." *British Journal of Political Science* 22: 21–38.

Asher, Herbert B. 1992. *Presidential Elections and American Politics.* Chicago: Dorsey.

Axelrod, Robert. 1972. "Where the Votes Come From: An Analysis of Electoral Coalitions." *American Political Science Review* 66: 11–20.

———. 1986. "Presidential Election Coalitions in 1984." *American Political Science Review* 80: 281–84.

Ball, Howard, Dale Krane, and Thomas P. Lauth. 1984. *Compromised Compliance: Implementation of the 1965 Voting Rights Act.* Westport, Conn.: Greenwood.

Barone, Michael, and Grant Ujifusa. 1987. *Almanac of American Politics, 1988.* New York: E. P. Dutton.

Bauer, Monica, and John R. Hibbing. 1989. "Which Incumbents Lose in House Elections: A Response to Jacobson's 'The Marginals Never Vanished.'" *American Journal of Political Science* 33: 262–71.

Bendyna, Mary E., and Celinda C. Lake. 1995. "Gender and Voting in the 1992 Presidential Election." In Karen O'Connor, ed., *American Government: Readings and Cases,* 372–82. Boston: Allyn and Bacon.

Bennett, Stephen Earl, and Linda L. M. Bennett. 1992. "I Voted for Old What's His Name: The Impact of Information on the Electoral Bases of Divided Government." Paper presented at the Annual Meeting of the Midwest Political Science Association, Chicago, April 9–11.

———. 1993. "Out of Sight, Out of Mind: Americans' Knowledge of Party Control of the House of Representatives, 1960–1984." *Political Research Quarterly* 46: 67–80.

Black, Earl, and Merle Black. 1987. *Politics and Society in the South.* Cambridge: Harvard University Press.

Bond, Jon R., and Richard Fleisher. 1990. *The President in the Legislative Arena.* Chicago: University of Chicago Press.

Born, Richard. 1979. "Generational Replacement and the Growth of Incumbent Reelection Margins in the U.S. House." *American Political Science Review* 73: 811–17.

———. 1985. "Partisan Intentions and Election Day Realities in the Congressional Redistricting Process." *American Political Science Review* 79: 305–19.

Bowman, Karlyn H. 1995. "The Gender Factor." In Everett Carll Ladd, ed., *America at the Polls, 1994*, 52–57. Storrs, Conn.: Roper Center for Public Opinion Research.

Brady, David W. 1993. "The Causes and Consequences of Divided Government: Toward a New Theory of American Politics?" *American Political Science Review* 87: 189–94.

Brady, David W., and Bernard Grofman. 1991. "Sectional Differences in Partisan Bias and Electoral Responsiveness in U.S. House Elections, 1850–1980." *British Journal of Political Science* 21: 247–56.

Broder, David. 1994. "One Party's 40-Year House Rule a Concern." *Portland (Maine) Press Herald,* 10 August, p. 9A.

Bullock, Charles S., III. 1988. "Regional Realignment from an Officeholding Perspective." *Journal of Politics* 50: 553–74.

Burns, James MacGregor. 1967. *The Deadlock of Democracy.* Englewood Cliffs, N.J.: Prentice-Hall.

Butler, David. 1951. "Appendix." In H. G. Nicholas, ed., *The British General Election of 1950*, 306–33. London: MacMillan.

Butler, David, and Bruce Cain. 1992. *Congressional Redistricting.* New York: Macmillan.

Cain, Bruce E. 1985. "Assessing the Partisan Effects of Redistricting." *American Political Science Review* 79: 320–33.

Cain, Bruce E., and David Butler. 1991. "Redrawing District Lines: What's Going On and What's at Stake." *The American Enterprise* 2 (July/August): 29–39.

Caldeira, Gregory A., Samuel C. Patterson, and Gregory A. Markko. 1985. "The Mobilization of Voters in Congressional Elections." *Journal of Politics* 47: 490–509.

Calvert, Jerry W., and Jack Gilchrist. 1993. "Suppose They Held an Election and Almost Everybody Came!" *PS* 26: 695–99.

Campagna, Janet, and Bernard Grofman. 1990. "Party Control and

Partisan Bias in 1980s Congressional Redistricting." *Journal of Politics* 52: 1242–57.

Campbell, Angus. 1960. "Surge and Decline: A Study of Electoral Change." *Public Opinion Quarterly* 24: 397–418.

Campbell, James E. 1985. "Sources of the New Deal Realignment: The Contributions of Conversion and Mobilization to Partisan Change." *Western Political Quarterly* 38: 357–76.

———. 1986. "Predicting Seat Gains from Presidential Coattails." *American Journal of Political Science* 30: 165–83.

———. 1991. "The Presidential Surge and Its Midterm Decline in Congressional Elections, 1868–1988." *Journal of Politics* 53: 477–87.

———. 1992. "The Presidential Pulse of Congressional Elections, 1868–1988." In Allen D. Hertzke and Ronald M. Peters Jr., eds., *The Atomistic Congress: An Interpretation of Congressional Change*, 49–72. Armonk, N.Y.: M. E. Sharpe.

———. 1993. *The Presidential Pulse of Congressional Elections*. Lexington: University Press of Kentucky.

———. 1994. Comments at a "Roundtable on the 1994 Elections." Southern Political Science Association, Atlanta.

Carmines, Edward G., and James A. Stimson. 1989. *Issue Evolution: Race and the Transformation of American Politics*. Princeton, N.J.: Princeton University Press.

Cassel, Carol A. 1982. "Predicting Party Identification, 1956–80: Who Are the Republicans and Who Are the Democrats?" *Political Behavior* 4: 265–82.

Clausen, Aage R., Philip E. Converse, and Warren E. Miller. 1965. "Electoral Myth and Reality: The 1964 Election." *American Political Science Review* 59: 321–32.

Collie, Melissa P. 1981. "Incumbency, Electoral Safety, and Turnover in the House of Representatives, 1952–76." *American Political Science Review* 75: 119–31.

Congressional Quarterly. 1985. *Guide to U.S. Elections*, 2d ed. Washington, D.C.: Congressional Quarterly.

———. 1993. *The CQ 1992 Almanac*. Washington, D.C.: Congressional Quarterly.

Connelly, William F., Jr., and John J. Pitney Jr. 1994. *Congress' Permanent*

Minority? Republicans in the U.S. House. Lanham, Md.: Rowman and Littlefield.

Converse, Philip E. 1966. "The Concept of the 'Normal Vote.'" In Angus Campbell, Philip E. Converse, Warren E. Miller, and Donald E. Stokes, eds., *Elections and the Political Order,* 9–39. New York: Wiley.

Council of State Governments. Vols. 1950–1992. *The Book of the States.* Lexington, Ky.: Council of State Governments.

Cover, Albert D. 1977. "One Good Term Deserves Another: The Advantage of Incumbency in Congressional Elections." *American Journal of Political Science* 21: 523–41.

Cover, Albert D., and David R. Mayhew. 1981. "Congressional Dynamics and the Decline of Competitive Elections." In Lawrence C. Dodd and Bruce I. Oppenheimer, eds., *Congress Reconsidered,* 2d ed., 62–82. Washington, D.C.: CQ Press.

Cox, Edward Franklin. 1981. *The Representative Vote in the Twentieth Century.* Bloomington: Institute of Public Administration, Indiana University.

Cox, Gary W., and Samuel Kernell. 1991. *The Politics of Divided Government.* Boulder, Colo.: Westview.

Cutler, Lloyd N. 1986. "Political Parties and a Workable Government." In Burke Marshall, ed., *A Workable Government,* 49–58. New York: W. W. Norton.

———. 1987. "To Form a Government." In Robert A. Goldwin and Art Kaufman, eds., *Separation of Powers—Does It Still Work?* 1–17. Washington, D.C.: American Enterprise Institute.

Dahl, Robert A. 1956. *A Preface to Democratic Theory.* Chicago: University of Chicago Press.

Davidson, Roger H., and Walter J. Oleszek. 1981. *Congress and Its Members.* Washington, D.C.: CQ Press.

DeNardo, James. 1980. "Turnout and the Vote: The Joke's on the Democrats." *American Political Science Review* 74: 406–20.

———. 1986. "Does Heavy Turnout Help Democrats in Presidential Elections?" *American Political Science Review* 80: 1298–304.

Dodd, Lawrence C., and Bruce I. Oppenheimer. 1985. *Congress Reconsidered,* 3d ed. Washington, D.C.: CQ Press.

Duncan, Phil, ed. 1991. *Politics in America 1992*. Washington, D.C.: CQ Press.

———. 1993. *Politics in America 1994*. Washington, D.C.: CQ Press.

Ehrenhalt, Alan. 1991. *The United States of Ambition*. New York: Times Books.

Erikson, Robert S. 1971. "The Advantage of Incumbency in Congressional Elections." *Polity* 3: 395–405.

———. 1972. "Malapportionment, Gerrymandering and Party Fortunes in Congressional Elections." *American Political Science Review* 66: 1234–45.

———. 1995. "State Turnout and Presidential Voting: A Closer Look." *American Politics Quarterly* 23: 387–96.

Erikson, Robert S., Thomas D. Lancaster, and David W. Romero. 1989. "Group Components of the Presidential Vote, 1952–1984." *Journal of Politics* 51: 337–46.

Fenno, Richard F. 1975. "If, as Ralph Nader Says, Congress Is 'The Broken Branch,' How Come We Love Our Congressmen So Much?" In Norman J. Ornstein, ed., *Congress in Change*, 277–87. New York: Praeger.

Fiorina, Morris P. 1991. "Divided Government in the States." *PS* 24: 646–50.

———. 1992a. *Divided Government*. New York: MacMillan.

———. 1992b. "An Era of Divided Government." In Gillian Peele, Christopher J. Bailey, and Bruce Cain, eds., *Developments in American Politics*, 324–54. New York: St. Martin's Press.

———. 1992c. "An Era of Divided Government." *Political Science Quarterly* 107: 387–410.

———. 1994. "Divided Government in the American States: A Byproduct of Legislative Professionalism?" *American Political Science Review* 88: 304–16.

Gaddie, Ronald Keith. 1995. "Is There an Inherent Democratic Advantage in U.S. House Elections? Evidence from the Open Seats." *Social Science Quarterly* 76: 203–12.

Garand, James C., and Donald A. Gross. 1984. "Changes in the Vote Margins for Congressional Candidates: A Specification of Historical Trends." *American Political Science Review* 78: 17–30.

Garand, James C., and T. Wayne Parent. 1991. "Representation, Swing, and Bias in U.S. Presidential Elections, 1872–1988." *American Journal of Political Science* 35: 1009–31.

Garand, James C., Kenneth Wink, and Bryan Vincent. 1993. "Changing Meanings of Electoral Marginality in U.S. House Elections, 1824–1978." *Political Research Quarterly* 46: 27–48.

Gelman, Andrew, and Gary King. 1990. "Estimating Incumbency Advantage without Bias." *American Journal of Political Science* 34: 1142–64.

———. 1994. "A Unified Method of Evaluating Electoral Systems and Redistricting Plans." *American Journal of Political Science* 38: 514–54.

Gilmour, John B., and Paul Rothstein. 1993. "Early Republican Retirement: A Cause of Democratic Dominance in the House of Representatives." *Legislative Studies Quarterly* 18: 345–61.

Greenhouse, Linda. 1995. "Farewell to the Old Order of the Court." *New York Times,* 2 July, sec. 4, pp. 1–5.

Grofman, Bernard. 1983. "Measures of Bias and Proportionality in Seats-Votes Relationships." *Political Methodology* 9: 295–327.

Grofman, Bernard, Lisa Handley, and Richard G. Niemi. 1992. *Minority Representation and the Quest for Voting Equality.* Cambridge: Cambridge University Press.

Gudgin, Graham, and Peter J. Taylor. 1979. *Seats, Votes, and the Spatial Organisation of Elections.* London: Pion.

Guinier, Lani. 1994. *The Tyranny of the Majority.* New York: Free Press.

Hager, George, and David S. Cloud. 1993. "Democrats Tie Their Fate to Clinton's Budget Bill." *Congressional Quarterly Weekly Report* 51 (7 August): 2122–42.

Henning, Chuck. 1992. *The Wit and Wisdom of Politics,* expanded ed. Golden, Colo.: Fulcrum.

Hibbing, John R., and Elizabeth Theiss-Morse. 1995. *Congress as Public Enemy.* Cambridge: Cambridge University Press.

Idelson, Holly. 1995. "Court Takes a Harder Line on Minority Voting Blocs." *Congressional Quarterly Weekly Report* 53 (1 July): 1944–46.

Ingberman, Daniel, and John Villani. 1993. "An Institutional Theory of Divided Government and Party Polarization." *American Journal of Political Science* 37: 429–71.

Jackman, Simon. 1994. "Measuring Electoral Bias: Australia, 1949–93." *British Journal of Political Science* 24: 319–57.

Jacobson, Gary C. 1987. "The Marginals Never Vanished: Incumbency and Competition in Elections to the U.S. House of Representatives, 1952–82." *American Journal of Political Science* 31: 126–41.

———. 1990. *The Electoral Origins of Divided Government: Competition in U.S. House Elections, 1946–1988.* Boulder, Colo.: Westview Press.

———. 1992. *The Politics of Congressional Elections,* 3d ed. New York: HarperCollins.

———. 1993. "Getting the Details Right: A Comment on 'Changing Meanings' of Electoral Marginality in U.S. House Elections, 1824–1978." *Political Research Quarterly* 46: 49–54.

———. 1995. "The 1994 House Elections in Perspective." Paper delivered at the Midwest Political Science Association Meeting, Chicago.

Kaplan, Dave. 1994. "This Year, Republicans Gamble That All Politics Is National." *Congressional Quarterly Weekly Report* 52 (22 October) 3005–10.

Keefe, William J. 1988. *Congress and the American People,* 3d ed. Englewood Cliffs, N.J.: Prentice-Hall.

Keene, Karlyn H., and Everett Carll Ladd. 1992. "Congress's Ratings at an All-time Low." *The Public Perspective* 4 (November/December): 86–87.

———. 1991. "Preview 1992: Party Images." *The American Enterprise* 2 (May/June): 85–95.

Keith, Bruce E., David B. Magleby, Candice J. Nelson, Elizabeth Orr, Mark C. Westlye, and Raymond E. Wolfinger. 1992. *The Myth of the Independent Voter.* Berkeley and Los Angeles: University of California Press.

King, Gary. 1990. "Electoral Responsiveness and Partisan Bias in Multiparty Democracies." *Legislative Studies Quarterly* 15: 159–82.

King, Gary, and Robert X. Browning. 1987. "Democratic Representation and Partisan Bias in Congressional Elections." *American Political Science Review* 81: 1251–73.

King, Gary, and Andrew Gelman. 1991. "Systematic Consequences of Incumbency Advantage in U.S. House Elections." *American Journal of Political Science* 35: 110–38.

Koopman, Douglas L., Martha Johnston, Robert Ludke, and Nancy Speights. 1994. "It's Long Enough: The Decline of Popular Government under Forty Years of Single Party Control of the U.S. House of Representatives." A White Paper for Representatives Richard Armey, Jennifer Dunn, and Christopher Shays of the Joint Economic Committee, U.S. Congress.

Krashinsky, Michael, and William J. Milne. 1993. "The Effects of Incumbency in U.S. Congressional Elections, 1950–1988." *Legislative Studies Quarterly* 18: 321–44.

Ladd, Everett Carll. 1989. "The 1988 Elections: Continuation of the Post–New Deal System." *Political Science Quarterly* 104: 1–18.

————, ed. 1995. *America at the Polls 1994*. Storrs, Conn.: Roper Center for Public Opinion Research.

Lazarsfeld, Paul, Bernard Berelson, and Hazel Gaudet. 1944. *The People's Choice*. New York: Duell, Sloan, and Pearce.

Leighley, Jan E., and Jonathan Nagler. 1992. "Individual and Systemic Influences on Turnout: Who Votes?" *Journal of Politics* 54: 718–40.

Levitt, Steven, and Catherine Wolfram. 1996. "Decomposing the Sources of Incumbency Advantage in the U.S. House." *Legislative Studies Quarterly* forthcoming.

Lewis-Beck, Michael S., and Tom W. Rice. 1992. *Forecasting Elections*. Washington, D.C.: CQ Press.

Mann, Thomas E. 1987. "Is the House Unresponsive to Political Change?" In A. James Reichley, ed., *Elections American Style*. Washington, D.C.: Brookings.

March, James G. 1957. "Party Legislative Representation as a Function of Election Results." *Public Opinion Quarterly* 21: 521–42.

Mauro, Tony, and Tom Watson. 1995. "Court Grows Critical When Race, Law Intersect." *USA Today*, 30 June 1995, p. 8A.

Mayhew, David R. 1974. "Congressional Elections: The Case of the Vanishing Marginals." *Polity* 6: 295–317.

————. 1991. *Divided We Govern: Party Control, Lawmaking, and Investigations, 1946–1990*. New Haven, Conn.: Yale University Press.

Mezey, Michael L. 1989. *Congress, the President, and Public Policy*. Boulder, Colo.: Westview.

Miller, Warren E. 1991. "Party Identification, Realignment, and Party Voting: Back to the Basics." *American Political Science Review* 85: 557–68.

Miller, Warren E., and Santa Traugott. 1989. *American National Election Studies Data Sourcebook, 1952–1986.* Cambridge: Harvard University Press.

Niemi, Richard G., and John Deegan Jr. 1978. "A Theory of Political Districting." *American Political Science Review* 72: 1304–23.

Niemi, Richard G., and Patrick Fett. 1986. "The Swing Ratio: An Explanation and an Assessment." *Legislative Studies Quarterly* 11: 75–90.

Oppenheimer, Bruce I. 1989. "Split Party Control of Congress, 1981–1986: Exploring Electoral and Apportionment Explanations." *American Journal of Political Science* 33: 653–69.

Oppenheimer, Bruce I., and Frances Sandstrum. 1995. "The Effects of State Population on Senate Elections: Competitiveness and Partisan Bias." Paper presented at the Annual Meeting of the Midwest Political Science Association, Chicago.

Ornstein, Norman J. 1990. "The Permanent Democratic Congress." *Public Interest* 100: 24–44.

Ornstein, Norman J., Thomas E. Mann, and Michael J. Malbin. 1990. *Vital Statistics on Congress, 1989–1990.* Washington, D.C.: CQ Press.

———. 1992. *Vital Statistics on Congress, 1991–1992.* Washington, D.C.: CQ Press.

Ostrom, Charles, Jr. 1978. *Time Series Analysis: Regression Techniques.* Beverly Hills: Sage Publications.

Patterson, Kelly D., and David B. Magleby. 1992. "The Polls-Poll Trends: Public Support for Congress." *Public Opinion Quarterly* 56: 539–51.

Patterson, Samuel C. 1979. "The Semi-Sovereign Congress." In Anthony King, ed., *The New American Political System,* 125–77. Washington, D.C.: AEI.

Patterson, Samuel C., and Gregory A. Caldeira. 1990. "Standing Up for Congress: Variations in Public Esteem since the 1960s." *Legislative Studies Quarterly* 15: 25–47.

Patterson, Samuel C., Randall B. Ripley, and Stephen V. Quinlan. 1992. "Citizens' Orientations toward Legislatures: Congress and the State Legislature." *The Western Political Quarterly* 45: 315–38.

Payne, James L. 1980. "The Personal Electoral Advantage of House Incumbents, 1936–1976." *American Politics Quarterly* 8: 465–82.

Petrocik, John R. 1981. "Voter Turnout and Electoral Oscillation." *American Politics Quarterly* 9: 161–80.

————. 1987. "Realignment: New Party Coalitions and the Nationalization of the South." *Journal of Politics* 49: 347–75.

————. 1991. "Divided Government: Is It All in the Campaigns?" In Gary W. Cox and Samuel Kernell, eds., *The Politics of Divided Government*, 13–38. Boulder, Colo.: Westview.

Radcliff, Benjamin. 1994. "Turnout and the Democratic Vote." *American Politics Quarterly* 22: 259–76.

————. 1995. "Turnout and the Vote Revisited: A Reply to Erikson." *American Politics Quarterly* 23: 397–403.

Rae, Douglas W. 1971. *The Political Consequences of Electoral Laws,* rev. ed. New Haven, Conn.: Yale University Press.

Republican National Committee. *1985 Republican Almanac: State Political Profiles.* Washington, D.C.: Republican National Committee.

Republican National Committee. *1987 Republican Almanac: State Political Profiles.* Washington, D.C.: Republican National Committee.

Riker, William. 1962. *The Theory of Political Coalitions.* New Haven, Conn.: Yale University Press.

Roberts, Steven V., with Katia Hetter, Jim Impoco, and Scott Minerbrook. 1994. "Why Are We So Angry?" *U.S. News and World Report,* 7 November 1994, 30–36.

Rohde, David W. 1991. *Parties and Leaders in the Postreform House.* Chicago: University of Chicago Press.

————. 1992. "Agenda Change and Partisan Resurgence in the House of Representatives." In Allen D. Hertzke and Ronald M. Peters Jr., eds., *The Atomistic Congress: An Interpretation of Congressional Change,* 231–58. Armonk, N.Y.: M. E. Sharpe.

Rosenstone, Steven J. 1985. "Explaining the 1984 Presidential Election." *Brookings Review* 3 (Winter): 25–32.

Rosenstone, Steven J., and John Mark Hansen. 1993. *Mobilization, Participation, and Democracy in America.* New York: MacMillan.

Schattschneider, E. E. (1942) 1977. *Party Government*. Westport, Conn.: Greenwood.

Shafer, Byron. 1991. *The End of Realignment? Interpreting American Electoral Eras*. Madison: University of Wisconsin Press.

Stanley, Harold W. 1988. "Southern Partisan Changes: Dealignment, Realignment or Both?" *Journal of Politics* 50: 64–88.

Stanley, Harold W., William T. Bianco, and Richard Niemi. 1986. "Partisanship and Group Support over Time: A Multivariate Analysis." *American Political Science Review* 80: 969–76.

Sundquist, James L. 1983. *The Dynamics of the Party System*, rev. ed. Washington, D.C.: Brookings.

———. 1987. *Constitutional Reform and Effective Government*. Washington, D.C.: Brookings.

———. 1988. "Needed: A Political Theory of the New Era of Coalition Government." *Political Science Quarterly* 103: 613–35.

———, ed. 1993. *Beyond Gridlock?* Washington, D.C.: Brookings.

Taagepera, Rein, and Matthew Soberg Shugart. 1989. *Seats and Votes*. New Haven, Conn.: Yale University Press.

Taylor, P. J., and R. J. Johnson. 1979. *Geography of Elections*. New York: Holmes and Meier.

Teixeira, Ruy A. 1992a. *The Disappearing American Voter*. Washington, D.C.: Brookings.

———. 1992b. "Voter Turnout in America: Ten Myths." *The Brookings Review* 10 (Fall): 28–31.

Thurber, James A., ed. 1991. *Divided Democracy*. Washington, D.C.: CQ Press.

Tucker, Harvey J., and Arnold Vedlitz. 1986. "Does Heavy Turnout Help Democrats in Presidential Elections?" *American Political Science Review* 80: 1291–98.

Tufte, Edward R. 1973. "The Relationship between Seats and Votes in Two-Party Systems." *American Political Science Review* 67: 540–54.

———. 1975. "Determinants of the Outcomes of Midterm Congressional Elections." *American Political Science Review* 69: 812–26.

———. 1978. *Political Control of the Economy*. Princeton, N.J.: Princeton University Press.

U.S. Bureau of the Census. Vols. 1944–92. *Statistical Abstract of the United States*. Washington, D.C.: U.S. Government Printing Office.

———. 1993. Current Population Reports, P20–466, *Voting and Registration in the Election of November 1992*. Washington, D.C.: U.S. Government Printing Office.

Verba, Sidney, and Norman H. Nie. 1972. *Participation in America*. New York: Harper and Row.

Verba, Sidney, Kay Lehman Schlozman, Henry Brady, and Norman H. Nie. 1993. "Citizen Activity: Who Participates? What Do They Say?" *American Political Science Review* 87: 303–18.

Wattenberg, Martin. 1990a. "From a Partisan to a Candidate-Centered Electorate." In Anthony King, ed., *The New American Political System*, 2d ed., 139–74. Washington, D.C.: AEI Press.

———. 1990b. *The Decline of American Political Parties: 1952–1988*. Cambridge: Harvard University Press.

———. 1991. *The Rise of Candidate-Centered Politics: Presidential Elections in the 1980s*. Cambridge: Harvard University Press.

Will, George F. 1988. *The New Season: A Spectators Guide to the 1988 Election*. New York: Simon and Schuster.

Wolfinger, Raymond, and Steven J. Rosenstone. 1980. *Who Votes?* New Haven, Conn.: Yale University Press.

Zagarri, Rosemarie. 1987. *The Politics of Size: Representation in the United States, 1776–1850*. Ithaca, N.Y.: Cornell University Press.

Index

Abortion policies, as factor in congressional elections, 23

Abramson, Paul R., 124, 288 n. 25, 296 n. 16

Achen, Christopher H., 273 n. 20

Ackerman, Gary (rep., N.Y.), 99

ACU (American Conservative Union), congressional ratings, 184, 192–93

ADA (Americans for Democratic Action), liberalism index ratings, 99, 184, 192–93

Addabbo, Joseph (rep., N.Y.), 99, 271 n. 4

AFL-CIO, congressional ratings, 99, 184

African Americans: effect of 1965 Voting Rights Act, 124; as factor in congressional elections, 24, 163, 166, 183; racial politics and representation, 205–9, 301 nn. 30–32, 302 nn. 33–36; voter turnout in urban areas, 99, 105–6

Age, median, in November 1992 election, 2, 247 n. 3

Alabama, turnout rates, 212

Alesina, Alberto, 50

Aliens, illegal, inclusion in population counts, 124–25, 220

American Conservative Union (ACU), congressional ratings, 184, 192–93

Americans for Democratic Action (ADA), liberalism index ratings, 99, 184, 192–93

Ansolabehere, Stephen, 264 n. 10

Apportionment, district: effects on partisan bias, 122–23; Fourteenth Amendment on, 17–18, 141, 210, 251 n. 20. See also Malapportionment; Reapportionment

Approval ratings: congressional, surveys on, 198, 297 nn. 18, 19; presidential, and effect on midterm House elections, 159–60

Archie Bunker district, in New York City, 100

Armey, Dick (rep., Tex.), 6–7

Asian Americans, as factor in congressional elections, 24, 183

At-large elections, for House seats, 18, 40, 142, 218, 252 n. 21, 255 n. 11, 280 n. 28, 305 n. 45

Australian electoral system, 268 n. 22

Baker v. Carr, 274 n. 3

Baltimore, Md., cheap-seat districts, 280 n. 30

Barone, Michael, 50, 100, 153–54
Bennett, Linda L. M., 258 n. 8
Bennett, Stephen Earl, 258 n. 8
Bias. *See* Partisan bias
Blacks. *See* African Americans
Bond, Jon R., 294 nn. 5, 7
Border states, cheap seats during
  1940s, 152, 283 n. 13
Brady, David W., 77, 257 n. 2
Broder, David, 257 n. 2, 285 n. 7
Brown, George (rep., Calif.), 183–84
Browning, Robert X., 77
Budget deficits, of the 1980s, 4
Budget Reconciliation Bill, 1993
  (H.R. 2264), as example of
  partisan roll calls, 195–97, 295
  nn. 9–14, 296 n. 15
Bullock, Charles S., III, 287 n. 12
Burton, Phil (rep., Calif.), 129
Burton plan, 129–30, 275 n. 14
Bush, George, 27, 161, 195, 285 nn.
  6, 8
Butler, David, 95, 127, 129;
  hypothetical approach to
  analyzing bias, 73, 77

Cain, Bruce E., 95, 127, 129
Caldeira, Gregory A., 198, 199, 297
  n. 18
California: district turnouts and
  votes cast, 101, 215, 271 n. 7;
  as gerrymandered state,
  129–30, 141, 275 nn. 12–14;
  Los Angeles districts, 143,
  222–23; redistricting and
  population sizes, 210, 212;
  Sixth District voter turnout,
  212; Thirty-first District
  as example of cheap seat,
  183–84, 190, 222–23, 292 n.
  43; Thirty-third District as
  turnout example, 96, 212,
  271 n. 2, 303 n. 40; Thirty-
  seventh District growth in
  the 1980s, 211
Campagna, Janet, 265 n. 11
Campaigns, congressional: fund-
raising, 261 n. 16; increase
  in media use, 24
Campbell, Angus, 131
Candidates: advantages of
  Democrats, 58–66, 225–31,
  306 n. 1; caliber of as factor, 8,
  33, 55, 250 nn. 14–16, 259 n.
  9, 260 n. 13. *See also*
  Incumbency
Carryover effects: of incumbency
  partisan bias, 242–45, 307 nn.
  1–5, 308 nn. 6–8; in very-low-
  turnout districts, 118–19
Carter, Jimmy, 26–27, 163, 164, 287
  n. 14
Catholics, as religious majority in
  New York's Ninth District, 100
Census, U.S., House representation
  determined by, 18, 211, 216,
  305 n. 44
Chapman, Jim (rep., Tex.), 294 n. 7
Cheap seats: basis of, 140–43; before
  1954, 146–51; in the 1940s,
  152–54, 283 nn. 13–19; in
  1994 election, 180–83; thesis,
  39–43
Chicago, Ill., cheap-seat districts, 280
  n. 30
Civic attitudes, as affected by
  partisan bias, 197–200
Civil rights movement, as factor in
  congressional elections,
  23–24, 163
Cleveland, Grover, 252 n. 3
Clinton, Bill, 27, 159, 161, 163, 285
  nn. 6, 8
Coalition politics, 248 n. 4; based on
  socioeconomic groups, 41;
  compositions of party blocs,
  49, 258 nn. 5, 6; effect on
  congressional seats, 13
Coattails, presidential, 24, 155, 253
  n. 7, 285 n. 6
Cochrane-Orcutt pseudo-GLS
  technique, 80–81
Colorado, disparity in district
  populations, 123

Competition, political: effect of permanent party majority, 4–6, 248 nn. 6–8, 249 n. 10; for the presidency, 25–28

Congressional approval ratings, surveys on, 198, 297 nn. 18, 19

Congressional districts. *See* Districts, electoral

Congressional Quarterly Weekly Report, 285 n. 7

Congressional vote, national. *See* National vote

Connelly, William F., Jr., 256 n. 1, 257 n. 2

Constituents: district representation of, 200–205. *See also* Nonvoters

Constitution, U.S., on House electoral system, 17–18, 141, 216, 218, 279 n. 26

Contested seats, 136, 278 n. 22; drop-off rates during on-year elections, 62–63; percentiles in, 96–98; Republican majorities in, 51. *See also* Uncontested seats

Cover, Albert D., 63

Cox, Edward Franklin, 274 n. 5

Cube law, the, 36–39

Dahl, Robert A., 264 n. 7

Danielson, George (rep., Calif.), 183, 292 n. 43

Davidson, Roger H., 280 n. 28

Dealignment, party: effect on Democrats, 23, 24–25. *See also* Realignment

Democratic Party
candidates, caliber and experience of, 33, 55, 250 nn. 14–16, 260 n. 13
control of state legislatures, 30–32, 162, 259 n. 9, 281 n. 2, 286 n. 9
as House majority during

Republican presidential terms, 24
low-turnout district elections, 102–6
manipulation of House rules, 7
middle- and high-turnout district gains in good years, 134–36, 275 n. 22
New Deal alignment, 162, 165, 286 n. 11
1992 losses in perspective, 158–62, 284–86 nn. 1–9
nonvoters viewed as supporters, 130–31, 200–205, 276 n. 15, 298 nn. 23, 24
and partisan dealignment, 23, 24–25
percentages of identifiers, 48–49, 257 n. 4
southern conservatives: lack of Republicans to contest seats, 250 n. 15; replacement by mainline Democrats, 249 n. 11; and Republican coalitions in the House, 248 n. 4; wooing of by Republican party (*see* South, the)
successes in statewide elections, 28–30, 43–44
theories on successes in House elections, 45–47, 141, 256 n. 1, 257 n. 2
See also Districts, electoral; Turnouts, election; Unwasted votes; Wasted votes

Demographic changes, effects on voter turnout, 124–25

DeNardo, James, 131

Department of Justice, U.S., max-black policy, 207

Detroit, Mich., cheap-seat districts, 280 n. 30

Districts, electoral, 95; as compared to statewide elections, 28–30, 43–44; constituents, 49, 200–205; percentiles in contested elections, 96–98;

Districts, electoral (*continued*)
population sizes of, 209–11;
reduction of, 219, 221–22,
305 nn. 45–47; results and
partisan bias, 174–78. *See also*
Constitution, U.S.; Mean
district vote; Populations,
state; Turnouts, election
Divided governments, 3–4; as
desired by voters, 50, 258 n.
8; frequency of, 27–28, 191,
252 n. 3, 253 n. 4; southern
influence in 1978, 164, 287
nn. 15, 16
Dixiecrats, 163
Dodd, Lawrence C., 96
Drop-off rates, in seats during on-
year elections, 62–63

Economy, state of: as factor in
congressional elections, 23;
and midterm House elections,
285 n. 7
Education, and likelihood of voting,
189
Ehrenhalt, Alan, 250 n. 16, 259 n. 9,
260 n. 13
Eisenhower, Dwight D., 1, 2, 26, 35,
155, 190
Elections, for Senate seats and
governorships, 28–30, 32,
210, 218
Electoral College: Democratic vote
percentages, 34–39; possibility
of losing candidate having
majority vote, 188, 218;
states' votes and populations,
210; viewed as favoring
Republicans, 293 n. 4; as
winner-take-all system, 253
n. 6
Electoral system: Constitutional basis
for House, 17–18, 141, 279 n.
26; and national Democratic
congressional vote, 133–34;
in the 1990s, 170–87;
reforming the House system
of representation, 217–24. *See*

also Single-member-district
electoral systems
Erikson, Robert S., 267 n. 18, 300
n. 27
Ethnic groups, as factor in
congressional elections, 24,
99–100, 183. *See also*
Minorities

"Fat cats," view of Republicans as, 45
Federalist, The (56th paper), on
districted elections, 141
Ferraro, Geraldine (rep., N.Y.), 99
Fett, Patrick, 72, 73
Fiorina, Morris P., 32, 48, 252 n. 4,
254 n. 8, 261 n. 17; on
partisan bias, 85, 270 n. 29
Flake, Floyd (rep., N.Y.), 99, 271 n. 4
Flannagan, John W., Jr. (rep., Va.),
154, 283 n. 18
Fleisher, Richard, 294 nn. 5, 7
Florida: gerrymandered Third
District in 1994 election, 183;
1994 Republican House
victories, 165, 170
Foley, Tom (rep., Wash.), 157
Ford, Gerald, 26
Foreign policy issues, as factor in
congressional elections, 23
Fourteenth Amendment, U.S.
Constitution: effect on House
electoral system, 17–18, 141,
210, 251 n. 20; possible
amendment to redefine
eligible electorates, 220
Fugate, Thomas B. (rep., Va.), 154
Fund-raising, and advantages of
incumbency, 261 n. 16

Gallup Poll, 288 n. 25, 297 n. 19
Garand, James C., 293 n. 4
Gelman, Andrew: on advantages of
incumbency, 241; on partisan
bias, 77–79, 85, 265 n. 12, 266
n. 13, 291 n. 38
Gelman-King estimate of
incumbency advantage, 169
Gender gap, and Republican

realignment, xix, 165–68, 289 n. 26

Geographic location, as basis for legislative districts, 142–43, 145, 280 n. 32

Gerrymandering: effect on partisan bias, 122, 126–27, 144, 275 nn. 10–12, 14; to obtain partisan results, 15, 41, 89, 183, 206, 256 n. 15, 270 n. 29; as possible explanation of Democrats' successes, 45, 46, 141, 256 n. 1

Gingrich, Newt (rep., Ga.), 187, 206

GLS (pseudo-Generalized Least Squares), computations for wasted votes, 237–38

Goldwater, Barry, 26

Gore, Al, Jr., 164, 197

"Government in Gridlock: What Happens Now?" (1993 conference), 249 n. 12

Governments, divided, 3–4; as desired by voters, 50, 258 n. 8; frequency of, 27–28, 191, 252 n. 3, 253 n. 4; southern influence in 1978, 164, 287 nn. 15, 16

Governorships: Democratic victories, 28, 30; importance of votes cast in high-turnout districts, 34, 254 n. 10

Gray v. Sanders, 274 n. 3

Great Depression, and Democratic realignment, 162, 286 n. 11

Gridlock, imposition by House majority party, 3–4, 9, 50, 191, 249 nn. 11, 12

Grofman, Bernard, 77, 263 n. 2, 265 n. 11

Gubernatorial elections. *See* Governorships

Gudgin, Graham, 81, 267 n. 17

Guinier, Lani, 205–9, 255 n. 12, 301 nn. 30–32, 302 n. 33

Hansen, John Mark, 274 n. 7

Harris Polls, 297 n. 18

Henry, Paul (rep., Mich.), 295 n. 13

Hibbing, John R., 297 n. 22

High-growth areas, as high-turnout districts, 105

High-turnout districts. *See* Turnouts, election

Hispanic Americans: as factor in congressional elections, 24, 183, 190; voting turnout of, 106, 125

Historical (multiyear) approach, of assessing electoral systems characteristics, 72, 74

Hoover, Herbert, 287 n. 13

House of Representatives, U.S., xix, 2–3, 7, 248 n. 4, 249 n. 11; alternative calculation to determine unbiased chamber, 114–17; at-large elections, 18, 40, 252 n. 21, 255 n. 11; effect of split-ticket voting, 12–13, 39, 49–50, 254 n. 8, 258 n. 7; electoral system, 17–19, 251 n. 20; possible imposition of divided government, 3–4, 9, 249 nn. 11, 12; theories on Democrats' successes in elections, 45–46, 256 n. 1, 257 n. 2

Housing patterns (neighborhoods), 41, 145, 304 n. 42

Hypothetical (single-year) approach: to the assessment of electoral system characteristics, 72, 73–74, 77, 238; for 1992 and 1994 elections, 171, 175, 185, 289 n. 29

Idaho, population and House representation, 211

Identification, party, 48–49, 52, 257 n. 4, 259 n. 10

Ideology, and consequences of cheap seats, 192–200

Illinois: Chicago cheap-seat districts, 280 n. 30; disparity in district populations, 123

Immigrants, illegal, inclusion in population counts, 124–25, 220

Income, and likelihood to vote, 41

Incumbency, 261 n. 16, 265 n. 12, 307 n. 1; as asset in the 1994 elections, 160–61, 168–70, 289 nn. 27, 28; carryover effect of partisan bias, 242–45, 307 nn. 1–5, 308 nn. 6–8; effect on partisan bias, 139–40; estimates of vote value, 63, 262 n. 23; and partisan bias analysis, 117–19, 273 n. 17; reelection victories, 4–5, 13, 248 nn. 6–8; as possible explanation of Democrats' successes, 45, 51, 55, 56–57, 256 n. 1, 262 nn. 16–18; worth of in vote percentages, 65, 262 n. 24, 263 n. 25

Independent voters, and split-ticket voting, 164, 287 n. 18

Inter-university Consortium for Political and Social Research (ICPSR), 283 nn. 13

Jackman, Simon, 266 n. 14, 268 nn. 22, 23, 291 n. 38

Jacobson, Gary C., 50, 225, 257 n. 2, 259 n. 9, 260 n. 13, 261 n. 17; analysis of partisan bias, 76–77, 80, 264 n. 10, 267 n. 16, 274 n. 2; on mean votes for incumbents in uncontested elections, 62; on swing ratio in expected seat percentages, 53–54, 239

Jews, as ethnic majority in New York City, 100

Johnson, Lyndon B., 26

Johnson, R. J., 81, 267 n. 17

Justice Department, max-black policy, 207

Kansas, population per district, 271 n. 6

Karcher v. Daggett (1985), 41, 274 n. 3

Keene, Karlyn H., 297 n. 19

Keith, Bruce E., et al., 252 n. 2, 257 n. 4

Kennedy, Ted (sen., Mass.), 206

King, Gary: on incumbency advantages, 241; on partisan bias in the electoral system, 74, 77–79, 85, 265 n. 12, 266 n. 13, 291 n. 38

Kirkpatrick v. Priesler, 209, 274 n. 3

Ladd, Everett Carll, 286 n. 11, 289 n. 26, 297 n. 19

Leach, Jim (rep., Iowa), 9, 249 n. 12

Leadership, political, and absence of competition, 6–7

Legislatures, state, control of, 30–32, 162, 165, 259 n. 9, 281 n. 2, 286 n. 9, 288 nn. 21, 22; as influencing redistricting, 126

Levitt, Steven, 225

Lewis-Beck, Michael S., 285 n. 7

Liberalism, of Democratic representatives, 192–94

Liberal Party, in 1950 election, 281 n. 6

Local interests, in House elections, 12–13, 23, 50, 250 n. 14

Logit analysis: of turnouts and victories, 102–4, 179–80, 271 n. 9; of unwasted votes, 106–8

Los Angeles, Calif., cheap-seat districts, 143, 222–23

Louisiana, open-primary system, 290 n. 33

Lower houses, state legislatures, Democratic control of, 32, 253 n. 5

McGovern, George (sen., S.Dak.), 24, 276 n. 16

Madison, James, 141, 205

Maine, turnouts contrasted with New York, 96, 98–99

Majorities: and current Electoral College and Senate provisions, 217–18; durability of Democratic longevity, 22–25; popular votes compared to seats won, 52–53, 161–62; sustained by the major parties, 20–22; tyranny of, 205, 301 n. 32

Malapportionment, 305 n. 44; and electoral abuse, 90, 216, 218, 267 n. 17, 268 n. 22, 304 n. 40; Supreme Court on, 40–41, 210–15, 255 n. 14

Males, and election gender gap, xix, 166–67

Mann, Thomas E., 257 n. 2

Manton, Thomas (rep., N.Y.), 99

Margolies-Mezvinsky, Marjorie (rep., Pa.), 196–97, 296 n. 15

Martin, Lynn (rep., Ill.), 257 n. 2

Martinez, Matthew (rep., Calif.), 183

Max-black policy, of the Justice Department, 207

Mayhew, David R., 5, 63

Mean district vote: and aggregated national vote, 76–77, 80–85, 89, 171, 201–2, 233, 264 n. 10, 266 n. 15, 267 n. 16, 268 n. 20, 289 n. 29; and extent of partisan bias, 109–14

Media, use in congressional campaigns, 24

Miami, Fla., cheap-seat districts, 280 n. 30

Michigan: Detroit cheap-seat districts, 280 n. 30; disparity in district populations, 123; Thirteenth District population loss, 211

Midterm elections, presidential party losses in House, 1, 2, 155, 159–60, 252 n. 4, 284 n. 20, 284 nn. 2–5, 286 nn. 6–7

Miller, Warren E., 252 n. 2

Miller v. Johnson (1995), 206, 302 n. 34

Minnesota, Third District as turnout example, 96

Minorities: effects on voting turnout, 24, 143, 145, 150, 183, 280

nn. 29, 30, 32; and state redistricting policies, 19, 127; tailoring district appeals to, 49; and voter turnout, 105–6, 124, 274 n. 7. *See also* African Americans; Hispanic Americans

Mitofsky International exit polls, gender gap findings, 289 n. 26

Mondale, Walter, 24, 99

Montana: congressional turnout, 271 n. 2; population size and House representation, 101, 211, 303 n. 40, 304 n. 41

Mosely-Braun, Carol (sen., Ill.), 206

Motor-voter registration, 224

Multi-member districts, past use of, 40, 142, 218, 255 n. 11, 280 nn. 27, 28, 305 n. 46

National Election Study (NES), 257 n. 4, 258 n. 8, 276 n. 16, 277 n. 17

National Opinion Research Center (NORC), 288 n. 25, 297 n. 18

National vote: and mean district vote, 76–77, 80–85, 89, 171, 201–2, 266 nn. 14, 15, 267 n. 19, 289 n. 29; and partisan bias, 70–71, 111–12, 132–38, 172–73

NBC opinion surveys, 297 n. 18

Neighborhoods (housing patterns), 41, 145, 304 n. 42

NES. *See* National Election Study (NES)

New Deal alignment, in the Democratic Party, 162, 165, 286 n. 11

New England states, Democratic gains, 287 n. 12

New Jersey, turnout, 271 n. 10

New Mexico, at-large House elections, 255 n. 11

New York State, 96; turnouts and representation, 215; turnouts in contrast with Maine, 98–99

New York City, 143, 271 n. 10;
  Queens district turnouts,
  99–101
Nie, Norman H., 276 n. 16
Niemi, Richard G., 72, 73
Nixon, Richard M., xix, 24, 159
Noncitizens, inclusion in district
  populations, 124–25, 220
Nonlinear estimation technique,
  for estimating bias, 71–72,
  264 n. 3
Nonsouthern states, partisan bias in,
  77, 266 n. 13
Nonurban areas, as high-turnout
  districts, 105
Nonvoters, 144, 226; party
  affiliations of, 130–31, 276 nn.
  15–19; unknown views of,
  200–205, 298 nn. 23, 24, 300
  nn. 27–29
NORC (National Opinion Research
  Center), 288 n. 25, 297 n. 18
North, the, representation of
  Republicans in, 267 n. 18
North Carolina: cheap seats in 1942,
  281 n. 5; 1994 Republican
  House victories, 165; Twelfth
  District in 1994 election, 183
North Dakota, at-large House
  elections, 255 n. 11

Offices, district, Democratic election
  effectiveness, 33–34, 254 n. 8
Offices, statewide, Democratic
  strength, 28–30, 43–44
Ohio, Twenty-second District, 151,
  282 n. 96
Oklahoma: Democratic majorities in,
  287 n. 13, 288 n. 19; 1994
  Republican House victories,
  165; population per district,
  271 n. 6
Oleszek, Walter J., 280 n. 28
One-party rule, results of, 6–7, 9,
  249 n. 12
One-person, one-vote principle,

xviii, 122, 139; Supreme
  Court rulings on, 41, 210,
  214
On-year elections, turnouts for
  contested and uncontested
  seats, 62–63
Opinion, public, as affected by
  partisan bias, 197–200
Oppenheimer, Bruce I., 96, 280 n.
  30, 294 n. 4
Opposition, lack of, as benefiting
  majority party, 10–11
Ornstein, Norman, xvii, 20–21, 96,
  257 n. 2
Over-140 club, 183, 292 n. 42

"Padlock" concept, of one-party rule,
  9, 249 n. 12
Parent, T. Wayne, 293 n. 4
Parties, political: district turnouts
  and overall victories, 101–6;
  identification with (*see*
  Identification, party);
  weakening of unity under
  one-party rule, 7, 249 n. 11.
  See also Democratic Party;
  Republican Party; Victories,
  party
Partisan bias: alternative calculation
  to determine an unbiased
  House, 114–17; alternative
  measure of, 85–91, 238–41;
  analysis of and incumbency,
  117–19, 273 n. 17; analysis
  of low-turnout districts, 95;
  as asymmetrical, 38, 255 n.
  12; calculation of extent of,
  109–11; carryover effect
  through incumbency, 242–
  45, 307 nn. 1–5, 308 nn. 6–8;
  and causes of responsiveness,
  87–91; concept and
  measurement of, 14, 70–74;
  consequences of, 190–92,
  293 nn. 2–4; as a constant,
  121–22, 274 n. 2; district
  election results, 174–78;

estimates of, 74–85; influence
on, 122–38; and national
congressional vote, 132–38,
278 nn. 20, 22; and national
election results, 172–73;
through redistricting, 126–30;
sociolegal changes as causes
of, 122–26; unwasted vote
measurements, 92, 232–34,
306 n. 1; variations in and the
swing ratio, 138–40
Partisanship: in House elections, 3;
and party strength, 23, 252
n. 2
Patterson, Samuel C., 198, 199, 264
n. 7, 297 n. 18
People's Choice, The (Lazarsfeld et al.),
131
Perot, Ross, 27, 285 n. 6
Pitney, John J., Jr., 256 n. 1, 257 n. 2
Plurality-vote system, in
congressional elections, 18
Political competition: effect of
permanent party majority,
4–6, 248 nn. 6–8, 249 n. 10;
for the presidency, 25–28
Popular-vote majorities, 52–53,
161–62
Populations, state: as basis for
electoral districts, 18, 40–42,
141, 255 nn. 13, 14; disparity
in district numbers, 123–24,
274 n. 3; and district turnout
differences, 18, 123–24;
inclusion of illegal aliens,
124–25, 220; redefining to
obtain relevant electoral
districts, 219, 220–21, 305 n.
44; Supreme Court rulings
on district size, 209–11
Power: of political parties in the
House, 2–3; of states in
determining House
representation, 18, 141–42,
252 n. 21
Presidency, the, xvii; candidates and
high-turnout districts, 209;

Democratic Party control, 32,
253 n. 6; Democratic survival
of Republican victories, 24;
lengths of party control,
252 n. 1; party competition
for, 25–28; prerogatives of
and House majority, 3–4;
Republican House gains
during elections, 163–64.
See also Midterm elections
Proportional representation, 140;
relationship between votes
received and seats, 36, 37, 255
n. 12
Proportional swings, in national
votes, 171–72
Public opinion, as affected by
partisan bias, 197–200, 296 n.
16, 297 nn. 17–19
Public policy, and consequences of
cheap seats, 192–200

Queens borough (New York City)
districts, comparison of
turnouts and representation,
99–101, 190, 271 nn. 4, 5

Racial considerations: effect on
House elections, xix, 165–66,
288 n. 25; politics and
representation, 205–9, 301
nn. 30–32, 302 nn. 33–36
Radcliff, Benjamin, 276 n. 16, 300 n.
27
Reagan, Ronald, 24, 26, 289 n. 26
Reagan administration, policies
affecting House elections, xix,
249 n. 11
Realignment: Democrats during
New Deal era, 162, 165, 286
n. 11; Republican efforts
in the South, xix, 160–61,
162–68, 170, 286 n. 12, 287
nn. 13–16
Reapportionment: of congressional
seats, 18, 123–24, 211, 215;

Reapportionment (*continued*)
and redefining relevant
populations, 220–21, 305 n.
44
Redistricting: influence on partisan
bias, 126–30; within a state,
18–19
Representation: of constituents in a
district, 200–205; Constitution
on, 17–18, 141, 216, 218, 279
n. 26; equitable treatment of
voters, 209–17; influence of
cheap seats on policy and
public opinion, 192–200; as
possible overrepresentation in
low-turnout districts, 191–92;
and racial politics, 205–9, 301
nn. 30–32, 302 nn. 33–36;
and reduction of number of
districts, 305 n. 47; under
uncompetitive systems, 5, 248
n. 8
*Republican Almanac: State Political
Profiles* (1985 and 1987 issues),
271 n. 5
Republican Party, 293 n. 4
control of the presidency, 252 n. 1
House gains during presidential
election years, 163–64
low-turnout district elections,
102–6
presidential victories and
Democratic Houses, 24
in the South, 249 n. 11; coalitions
with conservative Democrats,
248 n. 4; realignment efforts,
xix, 160–61, 162–68, 170, 286
n. 12, 287 nn. 13–16
See also Unwasted votes; Wasted
votes
Responsiveness, causes of and
partisan bias, 87–91, 140, 279
nn. 24, 25
Retirement rates, as affecting
incumbency advantages, 63,
261 n. 17, 307 n. 1
Rice, Tom W., 285 n. 7

Rocky Mountain states, Republican
realignment gains, 287 n. 12
Rogers, Will, 49, 258 n. 5
Rohde, David, 249 n. 11
Roll calls, partisan bias of, 194–97,
294 n. 5
Roosevelt, Franklin D., 252 n. 1, 284
n. 4
Rosenstone, Steven J., 274 n. 7, 276
n. 16
Rosenthal, Benjamin (rep., N.Y.), 99
Rosenthal, Howard, 50
Rostenkowski, Dan (rep., Ill.), 195
Run-off systems, use in House
elections, 19
Rural areas, Republican cheap seats
in, 281 n. 2, 293 n. 4

Sandstrum, Frances, 293 n. 4
Savings and loan crisis, and divided
government, 4, 248 n. 5
Scandals: congressional, 199–200;
under one-party rule, 7
Schattschneider, E. E., 3
Scheuer, James (rep., N.Y.), 99
Seats, House: contested races and
Republican victories, 51;
drop-off rates during
presidential election years,
62–63; proportions of and
partisan bias, 70–71;
uncontested races, 4, 10–11,
13, 51, 58, 59, 253 n. 7
Seats and votes relationship: cube
law description, 36–39;
majorities of popular votes
compared to seats won,
52–53, 161–62; in
proportional representation
systems, 36, 37, 255 n. 12
Senate, U.S., 252 n. 1; as in favor of
Republicans, 293 n. 4;
Democratic successes in
elections, 28–30; importance
of votes cast in high-turnout
districts, 34, 209, 254 n. 10;

Seventeenth Amendment on election by states, 210, 218

Seventeenth Amendment, U.S. Constitution, on election of senators, 210, 218

Shaw v. Reno (1993), 206, 302 n. 34

Simpson, O. J., trial, 205

Single-member-district electoral systems, xviii, 10, 17, 18, 200, 232; Constitution's silence on, 18, 218; the cube law description between seats and votes, 36–39, 255 n. 11; exaggeration of majorities under, 52–53; geographic compactness, 142–43; lower socioeconomic group biases, 41–43, 256 n. 16; votes wasted in losing causes, 87–91

Single-year (hypothetical) approach, to the assessment of electoral systems, 72, 73–74

Smith, Al, 287 n. 13

Social issues, as factors in congressional elections, 23

Socioeconomic groups: changes in and voter turnout, 124–25; Democratic successes among lower classes, 33–34, 40, 130, 143; and single-member-district electoral systems, 41–43, 122, 256 nn. 16, 17

Sociolegal changes, and partisan bias, 122–26

South, the: Democratic electoral advantage in, 77; lower socioeconomic groups, 41; 1965 Voting Rights Act, 124; Republican realignment strategy, xix, 160, 162, 163–65, 170, 286 n. 12, 287 nn. 13–16; as solidly Democratic in the 1930s–40s, 147, 152–54, 281 n. 5, 283 nn. 13–19; turnout in, 104–5, 143, 271 n. 10, 280 n. 29

Split-ticket voting, effect on

executive and House victories, 12–13, 39, 49–50, 164, 254 n. 8, 258 n. 7

States: determining powers in House representation, 18, 141–42, 252 n. 21; as political districts and partisan bias, 293 n. 4; populations and seat malapportionment, 211, 303 n. 39; regional partisan bias, 77, 266 n. 13, 267 n. 18. *See also states by name*

Statewide offices, Democratic successes, 28–30, 43–44

Stevenson, Adlai E., 26

Suburbs, white flight to, 125, 275 n. 12

Sundquist, James L., 286 n. 11

Supreme Court, U.S., 206, 302 n. 34; on malapportionment, 40–41, 255 n. 14; reapportionment rulings, 123, 274 n. 3; rulings on equal population districts, 209–11, 214

Surveys, of public opinion on congressional ratings, 198, 297 nn. 18, 19

Swing ratios, 189; analysis of 1992 and 1994 elections, 175, 176, 177–79, 290 nn. 38, 39, 292 n. 44; in expected seat percentages, 53–54, 72, 259 n. 11, 260 n. 12, 266 n. 15, 267 n. 16; fixed assumptions, 239–41, 272 n. 15, 292 n. 45; modified uniform vote swing, 272 n. 15; uniform vote method, 238–41; when partisan bias varies, 138–40

Switchers, party, and loss of Democratic seats, 187

Tax bill, 1992 (H.R. 4210), as example of partisan roll calls, 294 n. 8

Taylor, Peter J., 81, 267 n. 17

Tennessee, Democratic majorities in, 281 n. 5, 287 n. 13, 288 n. 19
Term-limit proposals, 160, 248 n. 7
Texas: at-large House seat, 255 n. 11; cheap seats in 1994 election, 183; 1950 election in Twelfth District, 151, 282 n. 96; 1994 Republican House victories, 165, 170
Theiss-Morse, Elizabeth, 297 n. 22
Thurmond, Strom (sen., S.C.), 163
Triplets analysis, of sets of consecutive elections, 74–76, 173, 186, 264 nn. 7, 8
Truman, Harry, 155, 284 n. 20
Trust, by public in politicians, 197–200, 296 n. 16
Tufte, Edward R.: analysis of election triplets, 74–76, 173, 186; on conditions surrounding midterm referendums, 285 n. 7; on partisan bias in the electoral system, 80, 85–86, 90, 274 n. 2
Turnouts, election: analysis of party victories, 101–6; carryover effect in very low turnouts, 118–19; comparison of low and high districts, 42, 82, 84–85, 101–6; in congressional districts, xviii, 14, 15, 19; Democratic gains in middle- and high-turnout districts in good years, 134–36, 140, 278 n. 2; efforts to increase, 223–24; mean drop-off from presidential to house voting, 175, 290 n. 34; New York contrasted with Maine, 98–99; 1965 Voting Rights Act effect on black participation, 124; and partisan bias, 130–31, 276 nn. 15–19; percentiles for disputed seats, 96–98; in Queens borough districts, 99–101; redistricting to

equalize, 219, 222–23; for seats during on-year elections, 62–63; in the South, 104–5, 143, 271 n. 10, 280 n. 29; for uncontested seats, 60–61, 262 n. 20; victories in low-voting districts, 10, 33–34, 39–40, 254 nn. 9, 10; and voter representation, 215
Two-tiered realignment, 164–65
Tyranny of the Majority, The (Guinier), 205, 301 n. 31

Udall, Morris (rep., Ariz.), 258 n. 5
Ujifusa, Grant, 50, 100
Uncontested seats: advantages for majority party, 4, 10–11, 13, 51, 58, 59, 253 n. 7; as affecting preference voting, 55–56; in the 1994 election, 168, 169–70, 289 n. 28; in Queens borough districts, 100; reported elections results of, 173
Under-70 club, 180–81, 183
Uniform partisan seat analysis, of 1992 and 1994 elections, 171, 176–77
Uniform-vote-swing method, 238–41
Unwasted votes, 14, 251 nn. 17, 18; compared to price of victory, 106–9, 272 nn. 12–14; as measure of partisan bias, 86–87, 110–11, 171, 269 nn. 26–28, 272 n. 15; and measurement of partisan bias, 232–34, 306 n. 1; from 1936 to 1952, 147–50, 282 nn. 7–9; and partisan bias in the 1994 election, 184–87, 292 nn. 44, 45; reduction through reapportionment of the 1970s, 123–24. *See also* Wasted votes
Upper houses, state legislatures, 32, 162, 281 n. 2, 286 n. 9
Urban areas, 280 n. 30; African

American voter turnout, 105–6; Los Angeles districts, 143, 222–23; Queens borough districts, 99–101, 190, 271 nn. 4, 5
U.S. News and World Report, 285 n. 7
Utah, term-limit initiative, 248 n. 7

Verba, Sidney, 276 n. 16
Vermont, third-party winner, 292 n. 44
Veto-proof majorities, 21
Victories, party, 24; contested seats and Republican wins, 51; Democratic survival of Republican presidencies, 24; of Democrats in the Senate, 28–30, 252 n. 1; and district turnouts, 101–6; gover-norships, 28, 30; logit analysis of turnouts, 102–4, 271 n. 9; in low-voting districts, 10, 33–34, 39–40, 254 nn. 9, 10; reelection of incumbents, 4–5, 13, 248 nn. 6–8; split-ticket voting effects, 12–13, 39, 49–50, 254 n. 8, 258 n. 7; unwasted votes compared to price, 106–9. *See also* Legislatures, state, control of
Vietnam War, as factor in congressional elections, 23
Vinton Method, of allocating House seats by population, 303 n. 39
Virginia: cheap seats in 1942, 281 n. 5; Ninth District in the 1930s–40s, 153–54, 155, 189, 283 nn. 16–18
Vote, national. *See* National vote
Voter registration: effect of 1965 Voting Rights Act, 124; simplified methods, 223–24
Voters: and Democrats' successes, 45, 46–47, 54–55; and parties, 47–54
Votes: margins of reelected incumbents, 5, 248 n. 6;

percentages in low-turnout districts, 34, 254 n. 10; percentages of Democrats in presidential elections, 34–39; reporting of for House elections by individual states, 173, 290 nn. 31, 33; share of compared to House seats, 34–39; split-ticket effect on executive and House victories, 12–13; values of each additional incumbent, 242–43, 307 n. 3. *See also* Unwasted votes; Wasted Votes
Votes and seats relationship. *See* Seats and votes relationship
Voting and Registration in the Election of November 1992 (U.S. Bureau of the Census Report), 247 n. 3
Voting Rights Act (1965), 122, 124, 163, 207

Wallace, George, 287 n. 14
Wasted votes: by Democrats in 1950 election, 281 n. 6; in excess Democratic majorities, 85; and partisan bias, 86–87, 87–91, 92, 95, 269 nn. 26–28, 270 n. 29; position of minority party, 37–38; tabular data, 234–38. *See also* Unwasted votes
Watergate, effect on 1970s elections, 158, 160, 164, 284 n. 4
Wesberry v. Sanders (1964), 41, 123, 210, 274 n. 3
Western states, Republican bias in, 293 n. 4
White House. *See* Presidency, the
Whites: declining turnout of, 124, 274 n. 6; flight to suburbs, 125. *See also* Racial considerations
Wilson, Woodrow, 252 n. 3

Winner-take-all systems, Electoral
College as example, 253 n. 6
Wolfinger, Raymond, 276 n. 16
Wolfram, Catherine, 225
Women, and election gender gap,
166

Working-class majority, in Queens
borough districts, 100
Wright, Jim (rep., Tex.), 294 n. 7
Wyoming, population size and
representation, 101